AN INTRODUCTION TO THE PHILOSOPHY OF SPINOZA

Aimed at those new to studying Spinoza, this book provides a comprehensive introduction to his thought, placing it in its historical and philosophical contexts, and assessing its critical reception. In addition to providing an analysis of Spinoza's metaphysical, epistemological, psychological, and ethical views in the *Ethics*, Henry Allison also explores his political theory and revolutionary views on the Bible, as well as his account of Judaism, which led to the excommunication of the young Spinoza from the Jewish community in Amsterdam. Although the book's main focus is on the analysis of Spinoza's views, including a close reading of the central arguments of the *Ethics*, it also considers many of the standard objections to these arguments as well as possible responses to them. This completely revised and updated new edition of Allison's classic book, with two new chapters, will help a new generation of students to understand and value Spinoza's work.

Henry E. Allison is Professor Emeritus of Philosophy at the University of California, San Diego and Boston University. He has published fourteen books, most recently *Kant's Conception of Freedom: A Developmental and Critical Analysis* (Cambridge, 2020). He is a former President of the Pacific Division of the American Philosophical Association, winner of the International Kant Prize (2005), and De Gruyter Kant Prize Lecturer (2014).

T0382155

AN INTRODUCTION TO THE PHILOSOPHY OF SPINOZA

HENRY E. ALLISON

University of California San Diego and Boston University

CAMBRIDGE
UNIVERSITY PRESS

CAMBRIDGE
UNIVERSITY PRESS

University Printing House, Cambridge CB2 8BS, United Kingdom

One Liberty Plaza, 20th Floor, New York, NY 10006, USA

477 Williamstown Road, Port Melbourne, VIC 3207, Australia

314–321, 3rd Floor, Plot 3, Splendor Forum, Jasola District Centre, New Delhi – 110025, India

103 Penang Road, #05–06/07, Visioncrest Commercial, Singapore 238467

Cambridge University Press is part of the University of Cambridge.

It furthers the University's mission by disseminating knowledge in the pursuit of education, learning, and research at the highest international levels of excellence.

www.cambridge.org
Information on this title: www.cambridge.org/9781009098199
DOI: 10.1017/9781009099066

First published 2022

A catalogue record for this publication is available from the British Library.

ISBN 978-1-009-09819-9 Hardback
ISBN 978-1-009-09686-7 Paperback

Contents

Preface   *page* vii
Acknowledgments   x
Note on the Text   xi
List of Abbreviations   xii

1   The Life of Spinoza   1
    1.1   The Jewish Community in Amsterdam and Spinoza's Life Within It   1
    1.2   The Years at Rijnsburg, 1660–1663   8
    1.3   The Years at Voorburg, 1663–1670   12
    1.4   The Years at The Hague, 1670–1677   16

2   Spinoza's Philosophy in Its Historical Context   22
    2.1   The Roots of Spinoza's Philosophy in the New Science
          and Its Conception of Nature, and the Relevance of Descartes   22
    2.2   Some Central Themes in Spinoza's Philosophy   31
    2.3   The Geometrical Method   36

3   God   42
    3.1   God as Substance   43
    3.2   Divine Causality and the Modal System   66
    3.3   Some Theological Implications   78

4   The Human Mind   83
    4.1   The Mind and Its Relation to the Body   83
    4.2   Human Cognition   100
    4.3   The Will   116

5   The Human Emotions   120
    5.1   Descartes and Spinoza on the Actions and Passions of the Mind   121
    5.2   The Conatus Principle   126
    5.3   Spinoza's Catalog of the Passions   135
    5.4   The Active Emotions   146

6   Spinoza's Virtue Ethic   149
    6.1   The Metaethical Foundation: A Model of Human Nature   150
    6.2   Human Bondage   155
    6.3   The Prescriptions of Reason   158
    6.4   Spinoza's Evaluation of the Affects   168
    6.5   The Free Person   175

7   Freedom and Blessedness   182
    7.1   The Way to Autocracy   183
    7.2   The Way to Blessedness   188

8   The Individual and the State   203
    8.1   Natural Law and the Social Contract: Hobbes versus Grotius   205
    8.2   Spinoza's Critique of Hobbes   209
    8.3   The Proper Uses and Limits of Political Power   214
    8.4   Forms of Governance   223

9   The Theology of the *Theological-Political Treatise*   233
    9.1   The Critique of Revelation   235
    9.2   The Critique of Jewish Exceptionalism   242
    9.3   The Interpretation of Scripture   246
    9.4   Faith and Superstition   251

Bibliography   256
Index   264

Preface

This is the third version of my introduction to the thought of Spinoza. The first, titled simply *Benedict de Spinoza*, was published by Twayne in 1975. The second, titled *Benedict de Spinoza: An Introduction*, was significantly revised in light of the intervening literature and was published by Yale University Press in 1987. In addition to the change of title, the present version has yet again been significantly revised and expanded in an endeavor to deal with the veritable explosion in the literature on Spinoza in the past thirty-odd years. While there has continued to be important work on Spinoza produced in the more historically oriented European or, as it is commonly called, "continental" philosophical community, particularly in France and the Netherlands, the place of Spinoza's birth, there has also been a dramatic increase in such work in the Anglophone or "analytic" community. There are, I believe, two reasons for this. One is a renewed focus on the history of philosophy in this community, which marks a decisive break with the decidedly antihistorical views of logical positivism and ordinary language philosophy, which were the dominant trends in analytic philosophy for much of the twentieth century. This has also led to a *rapprochement* with much of continental thought, which, because of its Hegelian heritage, has retained its historical orientation. The other, which marks an even sharper break with its earlier concerns, is a renewed interest in metaphysics. And Spinoza's thought, particularly as it is contained in the first two parts of the *Ethics*, with its focus on the nature and existence of God, the laws of nature, and the mind–body problem, became a natural subject of interest for metaphysically inclined philosophers working in the analytic tradition. The renewed interest in Spinoza is not limited, however, to his treatment of these core metaphysical topics, but extends to his psychological, ethical, and political theories, as well as his views on religion, his relation to the views of his predecessors, and his subsequent influence; in short, it encompasses the whole range of Spinoza's thought.[1]

This spate of new literature has provided me with an impetus to rethink my views on Spinoza. Although I cannot claim to have mastered all of the literature on the various aspects of his thought that has appeared since the previous version of this study, I have worked through a considerable portion of it. In some instances I have changed my views on essential points in interpretation and evaluation; in others I have attempted to defend my earlier views against some of the objections that have been raised in this literature; while in still others I have focused my attention on issues that I had either glossed over or treated only in a passing or superficial manner. There are, however, two changes to which I wish to call attention because they connect directly with my study of Kant, which has long been the central focus of my work. The first concerns my discussion of Spinoza's recast version of the classical ontological argument for the existence of God, which he identifies with nature. In light of recent work, which has refocused attention on the similarities between this argument and Kant's argument for the existence of God as the *ens realissimum*, which he defended in his earlier work, but criticized in the *Critique of Pure Reason* and later writings,[2] I have amended my earlier treatment of this argument to incorporate the Kantian critique and to illustrate its applicability to Spinoza's. The second and most substantive change concerns my discussion of Spinoza's naturalistic moral theory. This theory is grounded in the proposition that the fundamental endeavor of everything in nature, including human beings, is self-preservation (Spinoza's conatus doctrine), and my treatment of it has two aspects. On the one hand, in contrast to commentators who tend to see this theory as providing a proto-Nietzschean deconstruction of traditional morality,[3] I regard it as an attempt to reestablish much of traditional morality – more particularly, a version of the so-called Golden Rule, namely: "Do unto others as you would have others do unto you," on this egoistic basis; while, on the other, wearing my Kantian hat, I question the viability of this project and

---

[1] This breadth of interest is reflected in the recent publications of Cambridge University Press, including, in addition to numerous monographs on Spinoza, *The Cambridge Companion to Spinoza* (1996), *The Cambridge Companion to Spinoza's Ethics* (2009), and *Critical Guides* to Spinoza's *Theological-Political Treatise* (2010) and *Political Treatise* (2018), as well as *Spinoza and German Idealism* (2012) and *Spinoza and Medieval Jewish Philosophy* (2012).

[2] See Omri Boehm, *Kant's Critique of Spinoza*.

[3] See Gilles Deleuze, *Spinoza: Practical Philosophy*.

challenge a recent attempt to defend Spinoza's position by way of a comparison with Kant's views.[4]

These changes have necessitated a partial change in the format of the work. While its content has been significantly revised and expanded, the organization of the first four chapters, which dealt respectively with Spinoza's biography, a sketch of the historical context and central themes of his thought, and the first and second parts of the *Ethics*, which are concerned respectively with God and the human mind, has been retained. The previous fifth chapter, however, which dealt with the final three parts of the *Ethics* and was concerned with Spinoza's account of the emotions, his moral theory, and his highly heterodox views on immortality, has been expanded into separate chapters. Although likewise rewritten and expanded in order to take account of the recent literature, Chapters 6 and 7 of the previous version, which dealt respectively with Spinoza's political philosophy and his views on the Bible, and more generally revealed religion, have become Chapters 8 and 9 in the present version.

Like the earlier versions, as an introduction to Spinoza's philosophy, this work is intended primarily for the general reader or student with some background in philosophy, though I hope that it will also be of interest to the more advanced student and perhaps even the specialist. As before, my aim is to provide a balanced and comprehensive account of Spinoza's thought that offers the reader a sense of its breadth, as well as its depth and historical importance. To this end, I have tried not only to provide an accurate account of Spinoza's doctrines and their historical context, but also to explain as clearly and concisely as possible the main arguments he provides in support of them. But while my main focus is on the exposition and explanation of Spinoza's views, I have also attempted to indicate the difficulties in and possible objections to many of these arguments and to present and evaluate to the best of my ability the major responses to them found in the literature.

---

[4] See Matthew Kisner, *Spinoza on Human Freedom*.

Acknowledgments

I wish to thank Hilary Gaskin for her support of this project, the two anonymous readers for Cambridge University Press for their constructive criticisms of the portions of the earlier versions of this work that they commented upon, Thomas Kiefer for preparation of the index, and Princeton University Press for permission to cite from their two-volume edition of Edwin Curley's translation of *The Collected Works of Spinoza*. Throughout the book I have cited the pagination in Curley's translation as well as the pagination in the Gebhardt edition of *Spinoza Opera* for the benefit of those who wish to consult the Latin and Dutch texts.

Note on the Text

References to Spinoza's works are to *Spinoza Opera*, edited by Carl Gebhardt, 4 vols. (Heidelberg: Carl Winter, 1925) (referred to as G) and the following translations: *The Collected Works of Spinoza*, vol. 1, edited and translated by Edwin Curley (Princeton, NJ: Princeton University Press, 1985) (referred to as C1) and *The Collected Works of Spinoza*, vol. 2, edited and translated by Edwin Curley (Princeton, NJ: Princeton University Press, 2016) (referred to as C2).

Abbreviations

a	axiom
app	appendix
C1	*The Collected Works of Spinoza*, vol. 1
C2	*The Collected Works of Spinoza*, vol. 2
c	corollary
d	definition [when not after proposition number]
d	demonstration [when after a proposition number]
da	definition of affects at the end of the third part of the *Ethics*
G	*Spinoza Opera*
L	correspondence
l	lemma
p	proposition
po	postulate
pr	preface
s	scholium
CM	*Metaphysical Thoughts*
DPP	*Descartes' Principles of Philosophy*
KV	*Short Treatise on God, Man, and His Well-Being*
TdIE	*Treatise on the Emendation of the Intellect*
TP	*Political Treatise*
TTP	*Theological-Political Treatise*

CHAPTER I

The Life of Spinoza

1.1 The Jewish Community in Amsterdam and Spinoza's Life Within It

Baruch (also called Bento) de Spinoza was born in the city of Amsterdam on November 24, 1632.[1] His parents (Michael and Hanna) were members of the community of Jewish immigrants from Portugal, who had been living in the Netherlands since 1593. This community was composed largely of descendants of the Marranos, also called "New Christians" or "crypto-Jews," which were the names given to the originally Spanish Jews who had been forcibly converted to Christianity by the Inquisition in the late fifteenth century. After their "conversion," which was usually, but not always, merely nominal, many of these Jews had risen to positions of great prominence in the intellectual, economic, political, and even ecclesiastical life of Spain. But precisely because of their success they were again persecuted by the Inquisition and expelled from the country. The first stop in this new diaspora was nearby Portugal, where, even from the beginning, life was far from pleasant. Moreover, when the Inquisition officially arrived in that country in the late sixteenth century, the Marranos were once again subjected to wholesale persecution and were forced to flee.

The logical place to seek refuge was the Republic of the Netherlands, which had recently declared its independence from Spain and was engaged in war with that country. Not only did it share with the Marranos a hatred of Spain and the Inquisition; it was also the most enlightened country in

---

[1] My earlier versions of this sketch of Spinoza's life were based largely on the contemporary account *The Life of the Late Mr. de Spinoza*, generally attributed to J. M. Lucas, translated and edited by A. Wolf as *The Oldest Biography of Spinoza*; John Colerus, *The Life of Benedict de Spinoza*, reprinted as an appendix to Sir Frederick Pollock, *Spinoza: His Life and Philosophy*; Pollock's own account in the above-mentioned work; J. Freudenthal, *Spinoza Leben und Lehre*; A. Wolf, "The Life of Spinoza," in the introduction to his edition and translation of *Spinoza's Short Treatise*; and Lewis Samuel Feuer, *Spinoza and the Rise of Liberalism*. For the present version I have consulted the masterful biography by Steven Nadler, *Spinoza: A Life*, and W. N. A. Klever's "Spinoza's Life and Works."

Europe at the time and allowed some measure of religious toleration. Furthermore, this was the time of the formation of the East India and West India Companies and the emergence of the Republic as a great commercial power. For this reason, both the capital and the commercial abilities of the Marranos were welcome, and because of these they were allowed to settle in Amsterdam, which, with their help, soon became the commercial center of Europe. It should be noted, however, that even in the Republic, religious toleration was far from complete. The political strength of the Calvinist clergy was far too great to allow that. Thus, although the first of the Marrano settlers arrived in Amsterdam in 1593, it was not until 1619 that they received official permission to hold public worship, and not until 1657 that they were granted citizenship.[2]

As a direct result of this experience, many of the leaders of the community were highly cultivated men, though their culture was more Iberian and broadly European than Jewish. Their native languages were Spanish and Portuguese, and they had been educated in Spanish universities. Moreover, their commercial adventures had brought them into contact with a wide variety of people, which further tended to inculcate a cosmopolitan rather than ghetto outlook. And while their knowledge of the Hebrew language and traditional Jewish law was evidently quite limited,[3] the commitment of most members of the community to Judaism was sincere; perhaps reinforced, as we shall see Spinoza himself claimed in his *Theological-Political Treatise* (henceforth TTP), by their persecution. In addition to this religious factor, economic interests also served as a powerful unifying force in the community and as a source of shared values. In fact, it has been claimed that the Amsterdam Jewish community was not only a religious group, but also "a virtually autonomous socio-economic entity, which negotiated with other nations, cities and Jewish communities."[4] Although this may be something of an overstatement, the fact remains that the community was a tightly knit economic unit; that, as a result of the capital and expertise of some of its members, the community as a whole was fairly prosperous; and that commercial success was a focal point of community concern.

Not surprisingly, these factors led to a basically conservative political stance. Externally, the Jewish community was a strong supporter of the

---

[2] This material is based on the account in Graetz, *Popular History of the Jews*, 48–75, and Freudenthal, *Spinoza Leben und Lehre*, 3–16.
[3] For an interesting analysis of both the broad culture and the Jewish commitment of these men, see Popkin, "The Historical Significance of Sephardic Judaism in 17th Century Amsterdam."
[4] Feuer, *Spinoza and the Rise of Liberalism*, 5.

reigning House of Orange, the Stadtholders or chief magistrates of which
had served as its protectors. Power within the community was concen-
trated in the hands of the wealthy commercial leaders. The synagogue was
the real seat of this power, however, and its ruling council functioned as
a virtual dictatorship, exercising almost absolute control over all aspects of
communal life. Dissent was prohibited and the publication of allegedly
libelous writings or the expression of disrespect for the presiding authority
was punished by excommunication.[5] Such control was rendered necessary
not only by the desire of the commercial oligarchy to remain in power, but
also by the precarious position of the community within the Republic.
Having only recently escaped from the clutches of the Inquisition and
keenly aware of the far-from-liberal attitude of the Reformed clergy, the
community was understandably anxious to keep its own house in order.
Moreover, the danger to the community was exacerbated by the activities
of notorious heretics such as Uriel da Costa, who was excommunicated in
1640. In many ways a precursor of Spinoza, da Costa not only aroused the
wrath of the leaders of the community by ridiculing their religious practices
and materialistic values, but he also openly denied personal immortality,
an act that was guaranteed to arouse the attention of the Reformed clergy.[6]

Both Spinoza's fraternal grandfather, Abraham Espinoza, and his father,
Michael Espinoza, were among the leaders of the community. The latter in
particular was a prosperous, though not wealthy, merchant and held
several honorary positions in this community. Thus, Spinoza was by
birth part of the commercial establishment and was undoubtedly instilled
with its values as a child. Apart from the fact that the Espinoza family
suffered a number of domestic sorrows, with Michael outliving all three of
his wives and all but two of his six children (Baruch and Rebecca, an older
half-sister), not much is known about the philosopher's early home life.
Nevertheless, we do have considerable information concerning his early
education. This was essentially religious in nature, and it took place at the
Jewish boys' school, Talmud Torah, in Amsterdam, of which Spinoza's
father was a warden, and which all the boys in the community attended as
a matter of course. This school consisted of seven grades with a precisely
prescribed curriculum. In the early grades, the students began to learn
prayers in Hebrew and were introduced to the study and translation of the
Hebrew Bible. In the higher grades, they studied Hebrew grammar and

---

[5] Ibid., 8–9.
[6] For a discussion of the views and life of da Costa and their bearing on the young Spinoza, see Nadler,
Spinoza: A Life, 66–74.

selections from the Talmud and the later codes. At the final stage, they were
introduced to some of the great medieval Jewish philosophers, such as
Maimonides and Gersonides.[7] It was, therefore, within this purely religious context (secular subjects being taught at home) that Spinoza received
his first introduction to philosophical thought. Although he soon repudiated much of what he learned, we shall see that some of it exerted
a considerable influence on his intellectual development and became
integrated into his final philosophical position.

Not even the briefest account of Spinoza's Jewish education would be
complete, however, without some mention of his teachers. Foremost
among them were the rabbis Saul Levi Mortera and Menasseh ben Israel,
two classical representatives of Marrano culture. At the time, Mortera was
the senior rabbi in Amsterdam.[8] Born in Venice around 1596, he had
studied medicine under Elias Rodriguez Montalto, the Marrano court
physician of Marie de Medici. Upon Montalto's sudden death in 1616 he
had gone to Amsterdam in search of a Jewish cemetery for his teacher.
While there, he had accepted a call to the rabbinate of the older of the two
synagogues in existence at that time. A third synagogue was established two
years later, and when all three were amalgamated in 1638, Mortera was
appointed senior rabbi, a post in which he served until his death in 1660.
Although his orientation was basically medieval and orthodox, he had had
some training in philosophy, and as a result of his experience at the Medici
court, he obviously knew something of the world. It is reported that when
Spinoza was only fifteen years old, the rabbi had marveled at the boy's
intelligence and predicted a great future for him. It must, therefore, have
been with a heavy heart that he presided over the court of rabbis that
excommunicated Spinoza in 1656.

Menasseh ben Israel, a major figure in seventeenth-century Judaism, was
a far more positive influence on Spinoza.[9] Born in Lisbon in 1604, he had
been brought as an infant to Amsterdam, where he lived almost all his life.
He became rabbi of the second Amsterdam synagogue in 1622, started
a Hebrew printing house in 1627, and in 1640, when about to emigrate to
Brazil, received an appointment to the senior department of the
Amsterdam Jewish school. It was in that capacity that he taught the
young Spinoza. In 1655 he went to England on a special mission to

---

[7] For an account of the educational program at Talmud Torah and the level of Spinoza's participation
in it, see Nadler, *Spinoza: A Life*, 61–79 and 89–93.
[8] For an account of Rabbi Mortera and his relation to Spinoza, see Nadler, *Spinoza: A Life*, 90–93.
[9] For an account of Rabbi Menasseh ben Israel and his relation to Spinoza, see Nadler, *Spinoza: A Life*,
93–100.

Oliver Cromwell for the purpose of securing the readmission of the Jews to England. He remained there for two years and was thus absent from Amsterdam at the time of Spinoza's excommunication. He died soon after his return in 1657.

Evidently well educated in secular subjects, Menasseh ben Israel was the author of numerous, albeit not particularly original, philosophical and theological writings. These are replete with references not only to traditional Jewish writers but also to figures such as Euripides, Virgil, Plato, Aristotle, Duns Scotus, and Albertus Magnus. He also had many Gentile friends, corresponded with people of the stature of Queen Christina of Sweden and Hugo Grotius, and even sat for a portrait by Rembrandt. His great legacy to Spinoza was to introduce him to this rich secular culture. It was in all probability Menasseh ben Israel who first induced him to undertake the study of Latin, non-Jewish philosophy, modern languages, mathematics, and physics.

Contrary to Menasseh ben Israel's intentions, however, Spinoza's study of these secular subjects led him to abandon completely all Jewish beliefs and practices. Spinoza's secular studies were begun under the tutelage of Francis Van Den Enden. An ex-Jesuit, bookseller, diplomat, and classicist, Van Den Enden had opened a school in Amsterdam in 1652 to instruct the sons of the merchants of the city in Latin and the sciences. As his background suggests, he was a highly unorthodox figure and acquired considerable notoriety as a freethinker, atheist, and political radical. As a result of this notoriety, he was eventually forced to close his school in 1671. After moving to France, he was involved in a revolutionary project to found a republic in which all men would be equal. The project backfired, and its leaders, including Van Den Enden, were imprisoned and later executed.

Under Van Den Enden's tutelage, Spinoza not only studied Latin and the sciences but was also introduced to the philosophy of Descartes, as well as to the underground world of free thought and radical politics. More than that, he and Van Den Enden became intimate friends, and after the death of Spinoza's father in 1654, Van Den Enden took him into his own house, asking in return only that Spinoza help with the instruction of his pupils in the rudiments of the Hebrew language. Spinoza is reported to have said years later that he had wished to marry Van Den Enden's daughter, Clara. He apparently lost out to a wealthier suitor, however, and so the only reported romantic episode in Spinoza's life ended in disappointment.[10]

---

[10] For an account of the life and views of Francis Van Den Enden and his relationship with Spinoza, see Nadler, *Spinoza: A Life*, 103–115. The story of Spinoza's affection for Van Den Enden's daughter, which stems from Colerus, is noted by Nadler, *Spinoza: A Life*, 108–109.

Although he continued to appear occasionally at the synagogue, by living at the home of Van Den Enden, Spinoza had, in effect, already removed himself from the Jewish community. This removal reflected his growing alienation from Jewish beliefs and practices, as well as from the materialistic, commercial values of the community. For Spinoza the philosopher, this alienation was both a spiritual and an intellectual affair, which was grounded in his recognition of the inadequacy of the rational foundations of biblical religion and the rabbinic tradition, and the emptiness of a life devoted to the pursuit of wealth. Moreover, his alienation was accelerated by his contact with Van Den Enden and his circle, as well as by his study of philosophers such as Descartes and possibly Giordano Bruno; but its roots undoubtedly lie in his childhood experience and his first encounter with Jewish thought.

Spinoza's official break with Judaism was forced upon him, however, by the actions of the leaders of the Jewish community. Both the motives of the rabbis and the actual course of events are the subject of some dispute. Strict doctrinal orthodoxy had never been a central concern in Judaism, and it certainly would not have been in the Amsterdam community. Likewise, as men of the world, the rabbis would not have been upset by the mere fact of Spinoza's association with Gentiles. But because of all they had suffered for the right to practice their faith, they would have been deeply offended by any aspersions cast on the uniqueness and significance of the Jewish people and their way of life. In addition, they would have been concerned by any reports that Spinoza was adversely influencing the youth of the community, or that his heretical views, which were fairly close to those of Da Costa, might become public knowledge. It has also been suggested that the rabbis' concern might have been aroused not by Spinoza's theological beliefs but by his alleged revolutionary activities and associations.[11]

In any event, an investigation was launched. This led first to the charge that Spinoza had been contemptuous of the Mosaic Law, and sometime in June 1656 he was called before the council of rabbis to answer this charge. He promptly denied it, only to find new charges brought forth concerning his views on the authority of the Bible and the doctrine that the Jews were the chosen people. This time Spinoza could not deny the charges, and instead he submitted a written defense of his beliefs. Unfortunately, this document has been lost, but it is generally believed that many of its arguments reappear in the TTP, which Spinoza published some fourteen years later. Needless to say, this defense did not satisfy the rabbis, and he

11 Feuer, *Spinoza and the Rise of Liberalism*, 4–9, 24–37.

was initially excommunicated for a period of thirty days. This action was probably taken in the hope that he might still repent. He declined to do so, however, and on July 27, 1656 the final and permanent ban or *cherem*, which was apparently exceedingly harsh compared with others issued at the time, was pronounced against him publicly in the synagogue.[12] In response to this news, Spinoza is reported to have remarked:

> All the better; they do not force me to do anything that I would not have done of my own accord if I did not dread scandal; but, since they want it that way, I gladly enter on that path that is opened to me, with the consolation that my departure will be more innocent than was the exodus of the early Hebrews from Egypt. Although my subsistence is no better secured than was theirs, I take away nothing from anybody, and whatever injustice may be done to me, I can boast that people have nothing to reproach me with.[13]

This led to Spinoza's permanent isolation from the Jewish community, which included members of his own family. One of his first acts was to replace his Hebrew name, Baruch, with its Latin equivalent, Benedict (both of which mean "blessed"). He also left Amsterdam for a time to stay with friends at Ouwerkerk, a small village just south of the city. He soon returned, however, and seems to have spent much of the next four years in Amsterdam. As the above quote suggests, Spinoza was very much concerned at the time with the question of earning a living. With his father deceased and the estate willed to his half-sister, Rebecca, he was totally without financial resources. Moreover, with a commercial career now out of the question, he was forced to learn a trade. The trade he chose for himself was the highly skilled one of making and polishing lenses for spectacles, microscopes, and telescopes. Spinoza was engaged in this activity for the rest of his life, and it was his reputation in this field that first attracted the attention of leading figures such as Christian Huygens, the mathematician and physicist, and the young Leibniz.[14] Unfortunately, the unhealthy nature of the work, which made the inhalation of glass dust unavoidable, greatly weakened his already frail constitution and probably contributed significantly to his early death by consumption.

During this period Spinoza acquired for the first time a circle of admirers, which consisted largely of followers of the Cartesian philosophy

---

[12] On the nature and circumstances of Spinoza's *cherem*, see Nadler, *Spinoza: A Life*, 116–154.

[13] Lucas, *Oldest Biography*, 52.

[14] The significance of Spinoza's scientific work, both in terms of its recognition by contemporaries and his own philosophical views, is emphasized by Klever, "Spinoza's Life and Works."

and members of the Collegiant community. In contrast to the rigid orthodoxy of the Reformed church, the Collegiants, who were disaffected members of various Reformed sects, affirmed an ethically oriented, non-dogmatic form of Christianity, which emphasized the role of reason and the necessity for toleration in religious affairs. Although Spinoza obviously did not share in their Christian commitment, he must certainly have found much in common with them. It is believed that he joined in study clubs with members of this community, in which they discussed Spinoza's own emerging philosophy, as well as the dominant Cartesian system. Moreover, it was to these men that he initially communicated his own revolutionary philosophical doctrines, which he did not dare to make public.

Within this group were some who figured prominently in Spinoza's subsequent career and what we have of his philosophical correspondence. They include Peter Balling, a merchant who translated Spinoza's *Descartes' Principles of Philosophy* (henceforth DPP) into Dutch in 1664; Jarig Jelles, another merchant, who abandoned his business career and wrote a book showing that Cartesianism was compatible with Christianity; Lodewijk Meyer, a physician, scientist, and humanistic scholar, who wrote the preface to the above-mentioned work of Spinoza;[15] Simon Joosten De Vries, still another Amsterdam merchant, who became a disciple of Spinoza and who, just before his own premature death, tried to make the philosopher his heir; and Jan Rieuwertsz, a bookseller in Amsterdam, who published the writings of Spinoza, as well as of many other heterodox authors.

1.2   The Years at Rijnsburg, 1660–1663

Sometime early in 1660, Spinoza left Amsterdam for the village of Rijnsburg, which is located about six miles northwest of Leiden. The move was probably made at the suggestion of his Collegiant friends, since the village contained the main headquarters of the group. Its purpose was no doubt to give Spinoza time and repose to pursue his philosophical reflections, something he was not always able to do in the bustling city with its many distractions. This change of environment proved to be highly beneficial, for it was during this period that Spinoza not only produced his

---

[15] For a discussion of the importance of Meyer, see Nadler, *Spinoza: A Life*, 171–173. In addition to being a friend and supporter of Spinoza, who not only urged him to publish and then contributed a preface to DPP, in which he notes important differences between Spinoza's views and those of Descartes (see later), Meyer was a significant figure in his own right, who, prior to Spinoza, developed a radically rationalistic theory of biblical interpretation.

first philosophical writings but actually worked out the main lines of his mature system.

Among these early writings was the *Short Treatise on God, Man, and His Well-Being* (henceforth KV). Although written originally in Latin, like all of Spinoza's works, only a Dutch translation has survived, and it was not published or generally known until its discovery in the nineteenth century. This rather strange fate for the work of such a major figure as Spinoza is no doubt due to the caution of the philosopher, the loyalty of his friends, and the mistaken assumption of the editors of his posthumous works that it was merely an early, discarded draft of the *Ethics*. Spinoza composed it for the circle of friends with whom he had been discussing philosophical issues rather than for general publication, and his caution is clearly reflected in the note on which it ends:

> To bring all this to an end, it only remains for me to say to the friends to whom I write this: do not be surprised at these novelties, for you know very well that it is no obstacle to the truth of a thing that it is not accepted by many.
>
> And as you are also aware of the character of the age in which we live, I would ask you earnestly to be very careful about communicating these things to others. I do not mean that you should keep them altogether to yourselves, but only that if you ever begin to communicate them to anyone, you should have no other aim or motive than the salvation of your fellow man, and make as sure as possible that you will not work in vain.
>
> Finally, if in reading this through you encounter any difficulty regarding what I maintain as certain, I ask you not to hasten, on that account, immediately to refute it before you have given enough time and reflection to mediating upon it. If you do this, I feel you will attain the enjoyments of the fruits you promise yourselves from this tree. (G1 112–113; C1 149–150)

This note of caution was well justified, for among the "novelties" contained in the work are the identification of God with nature, and hence the repudiation of the Judeo-Christian doctrine of the creation of the world; the affirmation of the necessity of God's activity, and thus the denial of any purpose in nature or of any divine providence; and the denial of the freedom of the will. On all these points, which remained central to his mature system, Spinoza had already clearly broken with the more conservative Cartesian position, which attempted to combine an under-standing of nature based on the new mathematical physics with a basically theistic worldview. Since Spinoza's friends were Cartesians, as well as Christians, this certainly underlies his admonitions to them not to reject his doctrines without careful consideration.

Although Spinoza had arrived at many of the fundamental tenets of his philosophy, he had not yet determined the manner in which they could best be presented and demonstrated. This led him directly to a consideration of the problem of method, which was a central issue in seventeenth-century thought. Modern thinkers – that is, those who took as their point of departure the new, mathematical science of nature – were united in their repudiation of the essentially syllogistic method of scholastic philosophy and science. They differed profoundly among themselves, however, concerning what was to be put in its place. Since the issues involved are complex and go to the very heart of the intellectual life of the period, it is impossible to do justice to them here, though some of the key questions will be discussed in the next chapter. For present purposes, it suffices to note that the broad line of division was between a basically inductive-empirical approach, advocated by Francis Bacon and his followers, and a more deductive-mathematical approach, which was most forcefully advocated by the Cartesian school. The actual text of the KV shows us a philosopher torn between these two poles, casting about for an appropriate form in which to present his thought. For example, a priori and a posteriori proofs of the existence of God are juxtaposed, and straightforward narrative is combined with dialogue forms. Moreover, it is only in an appendix, evidently written somewhat later than the main text, that we find a crude anticipation of the geometrical form of the *Ethics*.

The decision to side with the Cartesians in the advocacy of a deductive-geometrical method is reflected in the important, but unfortunately unfinished, essay, *Treatise on the Emendation of the Intellect* (henceforth TdIE). This work, which probably dates from 1661, was initially intended as a systematic treatise in which the discussion of method was to serve as an introduction to Spinoza's metaphysics. The discussion is preceded, however, by a quasi-autobiographical prologue, which has often been compared with the opening of Descartes' *Discourse on Method*. In it, Spinoza relates the concerns that led him to philosophy in a way that not only brings to mind many classical religious and even mystical writings but also seems to reflect the spiritual or, perhaps better, intellectual crisis he must have undergone after his excommunication. The basic theme is the quest for a true and lasting good. The ordinary objects of desire such as wealth, honor, and sensual enjoyment are dismissed as transient and empty, and the true good is said to lie in "the knowledge of the union that the mind has with the whole of Nature" (G2 8; C1 11). The location of the true good in knowledge leads Spinoza to a consideration of the best method for attaining this knowledge. But the essay breaks off in the middle of the discussion of method and, therefore, never gets to the metaphysical issues. Nevertheless, the completed portion delineates a conception of knowledge as a deductive system, which naturally suggests the geometrical method as the most suitable means for ordering and demonstrating such knowledge.

Meanwhile, in 1662, Spinoza was visited by one Johannes Casearius, a student of theology at the University of Leiden. He came to Spinoza for instruction in the newest philosophy, but while Spinoza apparently liked the young man and was willing to help him, he was quite understandably hesitant about initiating him into his own thought. He decided instead to teach him the essentials of scholastic metaphysics, as it was then being taught at most of the universities, and to introduce him to the basic principles of Cartesian philosophy. Toward this latter end and in line with his recent methodological reflections, he put into geometrical form the arguments of the second and a portion of the third part of DPP. During a visit to Amsterdam, Spinoza evidently showed this work to his friends, who persuaded him to do the same thing with the first part of Descartes' work and to publish the entire text. Spinoza agreed to do so on the condition that Meyer edit the work and add a preface explaining that the author was not in complete agreement with Cartesian philosophy. Meyer readily agreed, and it was published in 1663 by Rieuwertsz as *Descartes' Principles of Philosophy*, together with an appendix titled *Metaphysical Thoughts* (henceforth CM). Moreover, these were the only works of Spinoza to appear in his lifetime under his own name.

By then, Spinoza was already hard at work on the *Ethics*, and he continued to work on it intermittently from 1662 until sometime in 1675.[13] As the correspondence with Simon Joosten De Vries clearly shows, his Amsterdam friends were in possession of a substantial portion, if not the whole, of the first part by February 1663 and they discussed it in their philosophical club.[14] Their discussion led to some questions, which De Vries, in his role as spokesman for the group, raised concerning the nature of definitions and their role in Spinoza's demonstrations. These questions were answered by Spinoza in two letters of March 1663, which not only show the stage of his thought at the time but are also important documents for the interpretation of his philosophy.[16]

Shortly thereafter, Spinoza decided to leave Rijnsburg, probably for much the same reason that had brought him there in the first place, namely the desire for peace and quiet. This move was necessitated by the constant stream of visitors from Leiden. The most significant of these was Henry

---

[16] These are letters 9 and 10 G4 42–47; C1 193–196.

Oldenburg, whose interest in Spinoza is a good indication not only of the force of Spinoza's personality but also of the reputation he had already achieved at that early date. A native German, who was some twelve years older than Spinoza, Oldenburg was one of the more interesting figures in European intellectual circles of the time. Although not himself either a creative philosopher or scientist, he was nevertheless in constant touch with those who were. He specialized in the dissemination of information concerning the research activities of others and thus functioned as a vital link between scientists working in various parts of Europe.

While on a diplomatic mission to London in 1660, Oldenburg helped to found the Royal Society and served as its first secretary. During a visit to Leiden in 1661, he was evidently told about the young philosopher and lens-maker, and, eager to make the acquaintance of anybody who was in any way remarkable, he decided to visit Spinoza. This visit had a profound effect on Oldenburg and led to an important correspondence between the two men, which deals with both scientific and philosophical subjects. In the scientific realm, Oldenburg told Spinoza about the latest developments at the Royal Society, asked for news in return, and served as an intermediary between Spinoza and the famous chemist Robert Boyle, founder of the "Corpuscular Philosophy." This led to a series of letters in which Oldenburg reported the results of Boyle's experiments on nitre (potassium nitrate) and other matters, while Spinoza responded with his own criticisms and reflections regarding Boyle's work. Oldenburg forwarded Spinoza's remarks to Boyle, but the exchange seems to have had little effect on either thinker. Boyle stuck to his empirical-inductive method, while Spinoza continued to advocate a more deductive model of scientific explanation. Moreover, the philosophical side of the correspondence was even less fruitful. In spite of his expressions of interest and constant requests for further explanation, which Spinoza readily provided, Oldenburg was never able to grasp the radical implications of Spinoza's thought. Consequently, when the real nature of Spinoza's unorthodox religious views became clear to him after the publication of the TTP, Oldenburg's interest cooled considerably and he ceased encouraging him to publish the *Ethics*.

1.3   The Years at Voorburg, 1663–1670

Spinoza's next place of residence was Voorburg, a small village about 2 miles from The Hague. Its size provided him with the desired peace and quiet, while its proximity to The Hague, then the seat of the States-General and the capital of the United Provinces, placed him near powerful protectors, who made it possible for him to pursue and publish his philosophy without fear of harassment. Such protectors were to be found in the De Witt brothers, especially the younger and more powerful John De Witt, with whom Spinoza shared both a deep concern for the republican form of government and a strong interest in mathematics and physical science.

John De Witt was not only the leader of the republican cause against the royalist-federalist supporters of the House of Orange, but also, as the Grand Pensionary of Holland, since 1653 he had been the effective ruler of the United Provinces. Moreover, at the time when Spinoza first settled at Voorburg, De Witt was at the height of his power. Having successfully extricated his country from a disastrous war with England that had begun before his ascendancy, he was not yet involved in the second English war, which started in 1665. In addition, by promising to withhold support from the Stuarts in England, he had gained, to some extent at least, the support of the House of Orange. Beyond that, he had managed to put the financial affairs of the country in order and to secure religious toleration and freedom of the press. But despite this, he had never achieved great popularity. The masses had always been supporters of the House of Orange and the monarchist cause; and De Witt's defense of religious toleration and of the supremacy of the civil power had earned him the bitter enmity of the Reformed clergy, who had desired to establish a state church.

Although an ardent supporter of De Witt and the republican cause, Spinoza's central concern was philosophy rather than politics. After all, he had moved to Voorburg so as to be better able to continue his work on the *Ethics*; and from a letter to a friend, John Bouwmeester, dated June 1665, we learn that the work had advanced as far as what in the final version became the fourth part.[17] In September of the same year, however, we find Oldenburg chiding Spinoza: "I see that you are not so much *philosophizing* as, if one may say so, *theologizing*, since your thoughts are turning to angels, prophecy and miracles" (L G4 165; C2 11). This suggests that in the interim Spinoza had informed Oldenburg that he had set aside the *Ethics* and was already hard at work on what was to become the TTP. Moreover, Spinoza confirms this in his response, in which he admits that he is currently writing a treatise on the interpretation of Scripture and lists the following reasons:

(1)   The prejudices of the theologians; for I know that they are the greatest obstacle to men's being able to apply their mind's to philosophy; so

---

[17]   L28 G4 163; C1 396. Spinoza writes that he will send his friend (Johannes Bouwmeester) the text up to the eightieth proposition of the third part. Since the third part of the *Ethics* in the final version does not have that many propositions, it is assumed that Spinoza initially intended the work to be divided into three parts and that the proposition referred to falls into what became the fourth part.

I am busy exposing them and removing them from the mind's of the more prudent;

(2) the opinion the common people have of me; they never stop accusing me of atheism, and I am forced to rebut this accusation as well as I can; and

(3) the freedom of philosophizing and saying what we think, which I want to defend in every way; here the preachers suppress it as much as they can with their excessive authority and aggressiveness (L30 G4 166; C2 14–15).

Underlying the reasons given to Oldenburg was a sense of urgency created by the political situation. In 1665 the Republic was in a state of crisis. The immediate cause of the crisis was the renewal of the war with England and Sweden, as a result of which the Dutch forces were so hard pressed that they had to employ French troops, an action that served only to increase the popular discontent. In addition, the situation was greatly exacerbated by the actions of the Reformed clergy. Still bent on Calvinizing everyone and resenting the liberalism of De Witt's party, with its strong advocacy of religious liberty, the clergy used the military situation as an occasion for mobilizing public opinion behind the young Prince of Orange and against De Witt. They did this by citing the progress of the war as evidence of divine judgment on the country because of the godlessness of its rulers. Furthermore, the transfer of power to the House of Orange was claimed to be necessary not only for the military, but also for the spiritual well-being of the country.

Similar outcries had been raised earlier against that great champion of liberalism and republicanism John Van Oldenbarnevelt, who, at the instigation of the clergy, had been executed for treason in 1619. Thus, De Witt and his supporters were well aware of the potential danger of the situation, as well as of the urgent need for people willing to speak out on the issue and to argue for the principles of republican government and religious liberty. Spinoza likewise saw this need; and it is perhaps the strongest proof of the fact that he was not an "ivory tower" thinker divorced from the cares of the world that he set aside his lifework in order to do something about it. As a philosopher, however, his concern was not simply to produce another pamphlet in favor of freedom of thought. Rather, he endeavored to get to the very heart of the matter and expose the foundations of the prejudices of the theologians that stand in the way of such freedom. The basis for the clerical position was the Bible, especially the belief that it was a divinely inspired, infallible book that, as such, functions as the supreme authority on all matters with which it deals. Since it was through an appeal to the Bible, thus construed, that the clergy justified their repressive stance, Spinoza thought that it was only by exposing the illegitimacy of this appeal that their position could be undermined and freedom of thought defended.[18]

With this in mind, Spinoza returned to the study of the Bible and to the arguments against its alleged infallibility, which he had raised some years earlier in defense of his beliefs before the rabbinic tribunal. The result is what is generally regarded as the first modern work on interpreting the Bible – the initial attempt at "higher criticism." Confining himself mainly to the Old Testament, with which he was obviously most familiar, Spinoza treats it in a thoroughly naturalistic and historical fashion, demonstrating that the various books date from different times and reflect widely different conditions and points of view. He combines this with a thoroughgoing critique of prophecy and miracles, which shows that the authors of the biblical books were not men of extraordinary intellectual gifts. And, on the basis of this analysis, Spinoza concludes that, aside from the inculcation of true virtue, which he considered its only divine aspect, the Bible contains no consistent message or set of doctrines. Moreover, he reasons, if it sets forth no uniform teaching or any special speculative insights, it can hardly serve as an authority in these matters. Having thereby undermined the authority of the Bible, Spinoza proceeds in the final chapters of the TTP to offer his positive arguments for freedom of thought and expression, as well as his negative arguments opposing any interference by a church in the affairs of the state.

The seriousness with which Spinoza approached this task is reflected in the five years it took him to complete his work on the TTP, most of which was devoted to research into the text of the Bible, Jewish history, and the Hebrew language. Unfortunately, when the book finally appeared in 1670, the political situation had deteriorated to such an extent that there was little hope of it achieving its main purpose of providing an effective support for the policies of the De Witts and absolutely no hope of it achieving its subsidiary purpose of defending Spinoza against charges of atheism. Keenly aware of the dangers involved and having given up any hopes of justifying himself in the eyes of the public, Spinoza decided to

---

[18] An affair that evidently played a large role in radicalizing Spinoza's views at the time concerned his friend Adrian Koerbagh, who published vehemently antireligious works, which espoused Spinozistic themes, for which he was sentenced in July 1699 to ten years in prison, followed by ten years in exile, plus a large fine; but he died of an illness after just over one year of imprisonment. For an account of the Koerbagh affair and its effect on Spinoza see Nadler, *Spinoza: A Life*, 265–270.

publish the book anonymously and under a false imprint (the place of publication being listed as Hamburg rather than Amsterdam). This stratagem proved to be completely ineffective, however, since his authorship was soon common knowledge, and both he and the book became the object of frequent and violent attack. Typical of these attacks is a description of the TTP as a wicked instrument "forged in hell by a renegade Jew and the devil, and issued with the knowledge of Mr. De Witt."[19] The attacks were further intensified as a result of the rapid spread of the work. By the end of 1670, there had already been four reprints of the first edition in Germany and the United Provinces, with many others under false titles. This naturally led to efforts to suppress it, all of which were frustrated by De Witt. Thus, the project that began as an effort to defend De Witt and his cause ended up requiring defense in its own right. Spinoza was clearly disillusioned by the whole affair and came to the realization that he could never publish the *Ethics* during his lifetime.

1.4   The Years at The Hague, 1670–1677

In 1670 Spinoza moved again, this time to The Hague, where he remained until his death in 1677. Once again, he was probably motivated by the desire for peace, and once again this desire was frustrated; for these years proved to be the most eventful of his life, especially in terms of his involvement in the affairs of the country.

Upon settling in The Hague, Spinoza returned to work on the *Ethics*. The long period of neglect had brought with it the need for substantial revisions, and he worked on these until 1675, when the book attained its final form. In the meantime, he was either actually engaged in or contemplating a number of other projects. These included a Dutch translation of the Hebrew Bible, a scientific treatise on the Hebrew language, a treatise on political science, a work on natural science to supplement the very sketchy discussion in the *Ethics*, and a new exposition of the principles of algebra. Of these projects, the only visible fruits found at his death were the unfinished texts of the *Hebrew Grammar* and the *Political Treatise* (henceforth TP), and two essays, "On the Rainbow" and "On the Calculation of Chances." The first two works were published together with the similarly unfinished TdIE, the complete text of the *Ethics*, and a selection from Spinoza's correspondence in the *Opera Posthuma*, which was edited by a number of his friends and appeared in the very year of his death. As an

[19] Wolf, "The Life of Spinoza," lxxxii.

indication of how Spinoza was generally viewed at the time, it is note-worthy that it was felt necessary to remove all names and other means of identification from the correspondence and to omit the names of the editors and publisher, as well as the place of publication. Not even the full name of the author was mentioned, and only Spinoza's initials (B. D. S.) appeared on the title page.

Many of these projects were not completed simply because of Spinoza's ill health and early death. But political developments during the last years of Spinoza's life must certainly have been a contributing factor, especially in the case of the TP. The first and most shattering of these developments was the brutal murder of the De Witt brothers by a frenzied mob. This act was the culmination of a long series of events and of continued rabble-rousing by the clergy, but its immediate cause was the joint declaration of war against the Republic by England and France in 1672. The resulting military crisis led to a popular outcry for the Prince of Orange to take over the country and save it from its enemies, as his father had done previously. Moreover, this was combined with a demand for vengeance against De Witt, who was treated as a scapegoat in the whole affair. This demand was satisfied on August 20, 1672, when a mob broke into the prison at The Hague, where John, who had resigned his post as Grand Pensionary of Holland on August 4, was visiting his brother Cornelius, who had been arrested on a charge of conspiring against the prince. Finding the brothers together, the mob murdered both of them, practically tearing them to pieces in the process and then hanging their mangled remains from a post.

When he heard of what had happened, Spinoza reportedly lost all his philosophical calm. He is said to have burst into tears and then written a placard on which he expressed his utter abhorrence of "the very lowest of barbarians" who had committed this heinous crime. His intent was to place this placard near the scene of the crime, but fortunately his landlord, Van Der Spyck, realized the danger of the situation and locked Spinoza in the house.[20] Otherwise, it seems quite probable that Spinoza would have suffered a fate similar to that of the De Witts.

The next major episode in Spinoza's life took place the following year and was likewise occasioned by the war with France. The French army, at the time under the leadership of Prince Condé, was occupying Utrecht. Condé was a man of liberal views, with an interest in science and philoso-phy. One of his officers, a Colonel Stoupe, who was a former Calvinist

---

[20]　Ibid., lxxxvi.

minister serving a Catholic king in the invasion of a Calvinist country, and who later wrote a pamphlet attacking Spinoza, informed the prince that the philosopher lived nearby and suggested that he might invite him to visit. Condé agreed and, through Stoupe, sent an invitation to Spinoza to visit him at Utrecht.

Spinoza seems to have regarded this invitation as a possible opening for peace negotiations and, being anxious to do what he could for the cause of peace, he decided, after getting permission from the Dutch authorities, to accept. Thus, armed with the necessary safe-conducts, Spinoza traveled across enemy lines to Utrecht in May 1673. In the meantime, however, his host had been unexpectedly called away. Spinoza was invited to remain and await his return, which he did, and during this period he was treated well. Moreover, while waiting, he was offered a pension on the condition that he dedicate a book to Louis XIV, which Spinoza respectfully declined; and when, after several weeks of pleasant conversation, the word came that Condé could not return, he decided to leave.

Upon learning of Spinoza's visit to the enemy, the people of The Hague immediately concluded that he must be a spy or a traitor. Reportedly, they threatened to break into his house and murder him, just as they had previously murdered the De Witts. Spinoza came out of his house, however, and, confronting the mob directly, proclaimed his innocence and concern for the Republic. Such frank and fearless conduct in this moment of danger must have allayed the suspicions of the mob, for they apparently dispersed and left him alone.

That same year Spinoza received another and even greater honor than the offer of a pension from Louis XIV, which he likewise rejected. In February 1673, the Elector Palatine, Karl Ludwig, brother of the Princess Elizabeth, who had befriended and corresponded with Descartes, offered him the professorship of philosophy at the University of Heidelberg. Karl Ludwig had spent many years in Holland and was a strong advocate of the republican philosophy of religious and economic freedom. The existence of a distinguished faculty, which included Samuel Pufendorf, the great authority on international law, as well as a Jewish rector, bears ample witness to the fact that these principles were in force at the University of Heidelberg, which Karl Ludwig had founded in 1652. Moreover, the offer included a promise of absolute freedom of thought and expression, as long as he did not disturb the public religion. But though the opportunity to abandon his trade and devote more time to philosophy must have seemed attractive (he took six weeks before responding), it is clear that Spinoza could not accept this offer.[21] His reasons for this decision, as expressed in a polite letter of refusal to Professor Johann Ludwig Fabritius, the Heidelberg philosopher who had tendered the offer on behalf of Karl Ludwig, were a hesitancy to embark on a teaching career at that stage of his life and a characteristic refusal to compromise in any way the independence for which he had paid so dearly. Spinoza's affirmation of this latter point is worth quoting in full:

> I think that I don't know within what the limits of that freedom of philosophizing might have to be, for me not to seem to want to disturb the publicly established religion. In fact, schisms arise not so much from ardent zeal for Religion as from men's varying affects, or their eagerness to contradict one another. This results in their habit of distorting and condemning everything, even things rightly said. I have experienced these things already, while leading a solitary life. How much more would I have to fear them after I rose to an office of this rank. (L48 G4 234–235)

Although Spinoza decided to remain in the mode of life to which he had grown accustomed, he did increase his circle of acquaintances. Indeed, the last years of Spinoza's life are among the most significant in this regard, for it was during this period that he first met and began a correspondence with the promising young scientist Ehrenfried Walter von Tschirnhaus, and through him became acquainted with the great philosopher Gottfried Wilhelm von Leibniz, who at the time was in the process of developing his own philosophical system.

Tschirnhaus was a German count who had studied at the University of Leiden from 1668 to 1675, while also serving part of this time as a volunteer with the Dutch army in the war with France. In 1674, he made the acquaintance of Spinoza's physician, Georg Hermann Schuller, who told him about Spinoza. Having already studied the works of Descartes, Tschirnhaus became immediately interested in Spinoza, which led him to begin a correspondence and to visit him that same year. Moreover, this correspondence is of considerable philosophical importance, since Tschirnhaus succeeded in pointing out many of the basic difficulties in Spinoza's system and elicited in return some significant responses from Spinoza. The following year Tschirnhaus visited London, where he met Oldenburg and Boyle, and the contact with Oldenburg apparently led directly to the resumption of the latter's long-interrupted correspondence with Spinoza. After leaving London, Tschirnhaus went to Paris, where he

---

[21] For a discussion of the offer and the reasons for Spinoza's rejection of it, see Klever, "Spinoza's Life and Works," 41–42 and Nadler, *Spinoza: A Life*, 311–314.

met Leibniz and told him of Spinoza's work, specifically about some of the doctrines in the *Ethics* that he had read in a manuscript copy. For his own part, Tschirnhaus later proved to be a man of some accomplishments in the sciences. He is credited with having discovered the tangential movement of circles and with the invention of porcelain. His main philosophical work, *Medicina Mentis* of 1683, was essentially a development of some of the views expressed by Spinoza in the TdIE.

In the meantime, hearing Tschirnhaus' reports, Leibniz became immensely interested in Spinoza's work. He had already read the DPP and in 1671 had sent Spinoza a copy of his "Notice on the Progress of Optics." In return, Spinoza had sent him a copy of the TTP. Leibniz had also already read this work and had, in fact, described it as "an unbearably free-thinking book." Apparently, however, he had not known that Spinoza was its author. Now, after hearing about the *Ethics*, he desired to read it for himself and requested Tschirnhaus' assistance in procuring a copy for him. Tschirnhaus wished to oblige, but could not show Leibniz his own copy without Spinoza's permission. When he wrote to Schuller in order to obtain this permission from Spinoza, however, it was denied. Spinoza, who as a result of his experiences had become increasingly cautious, simply did not trust Leibniz, and suspected (quite correctly) that Leibniz, a German, was in Paris on a mission for the reunion of Protestants and Catholics, an effort that, if successful, would inevitably lead to the suppression of all liberal tendencies. Nevertheless, Leibniz did not give up. He came to The Hague in the fall of 1676 and managed to gain Spinoza's confidence. While there, he not only acquired a firsthand knowledge of the *Ethics*, but also engaged in conversations with the dying philosopher. Because of the importance of Leibniz's own philosophy and its kinship in many ways with the thought of Spinoza, the interchange between these two men must be ranked as one of the major intellectual events of the seventeenth century.[22]

Although Spinoza's health was by then declining rapidly, he continued to be active and to go about his business until the end. This came suddenly and peacefully at three o'clock on February 21, 1677 in the presence of Schuller. Numerous reports of deathbed confessions, frantic recantations, and requests for divine forgiveness began circulating immediately after the death was announced, and some seem to

---

[22] For an interesting discussion of this encounter and its historical implications see Stewart, *The Courtier and the Heretic: Leibniz, Spinoza, and the Fate of God in the Modern World*.

have gained considerable credence. It is clear from all the evidence, however, that Spinoza died as he had lived; that is, in accordance with his own description of a free man as one who "thinks of nothing less than of death, and whose wisdom is a meditation on life, not on death" (E4p67).

CHAPTER 2

Spinoza's Philosophy in Its Historical Context

Spinoza's *Ethica Ordine Geometrico Demonstrata* (*Ethics Demonstrated in a Geometrical Manner*) is a notoriously difficult and forbidding book. Both its unfamiliar scholastic terminology and the geometrical manner in which its argument is presented provide formidable barriers to even the philosophically trained reader, and undoubtedly help to explain the great diversity of ways in which it has been interpreted. Thus, rather than plunging immediately into the argument of the work, I shall attempt to sketch the historical context in which Spinoza wrote and, in light of this, to introduce the central themes of his philosophy, or at least those dealt with in the *Ethics*. This will be the task of the present chapter, which is intended to provide the context for the more systematic and detailed analysis contained in the following five chapters.

2.1 The Roots of Spinoza's Philosophy in the New Science and Its Conception of Nature, and the Relevance of Descartes

We have seen that as a youth Spinoza studied and was profoundly influenced by medieval Jewish philosophy, most notably Maimonides and Gersonides, who were major figures in that tradition. It is also generally assumed that, in the course of his secular studies, largely under the direction of Francis Van Den Enden, he came under the influence of anti-Aristotelian Renaissance philosophers of nature such as Giordano Bruno and Bernardino Telesio. A full-scale intellectual biography of Spinoza would thus have to deal with these and a wide variety of other influences, including Kabbalistic texts, to which a Jewish intellectual living in seventeenth-century Holland would inevitably be exposed. Nevertheless, for understanding the distinctive features of his thought the decisive factor is the development of the mathematical science of nature, which was occurring at a rapid rate during Spinoza's lifetime, and the single most important influence was René Descartes. Unlike Descartes, Spinoza was not himself a creative scientist; but, as his relationships with men like Huygens, Boyle, and Oldenburg indicate, he was a keen student of contemporary developments in a number of sciences, especially optics and chemistry, as well as fundamental problems of scientific methodology. This new science inspired Spinoza's naturalistic approach to ethical questions, as it did for Thomas Hobbes, whose thought we shall see was also an important influence on Spinoza in a variety of areas. More importantly, it provided Spinoza with the basis for the conception of nature as an infinite, law-governed whole, which he identified with God, and for the knowledge of the unity of the human mind with which he placed the highest good for human beings.

The modern scientific conception of nature on the basis of which Spinoza modeled his metaphysics can best be understood by contrasting it with what it replaced. Broadly speaking, this is the medieval worldview in its Islamic, Jewish, and Christian expressions, which was itself based on a synthesis of Aristotelian physics and the biblical conceptions of God, humankind, and creation. According to this view, the natural world is a cosmos in the original sense of the term; that is, a finite, ordered whole in which everything has its determinate place and function. This cosmos was created by God, largely for the benefit of human beings, while the earth stands at its center and the incorruptible heavenly bodies, including the sun, revolve around it. The doctrine of a creation out of nothing (*ex nihilo*), which is central to this worldview, runs counter to the Aristotelian account, which considered the cosmos to be eternal, and this gave rise to some of the most difficult problems for thinkers like Maimonides and Aquinas, who endeavored to synthesize Aristotle and Scripture. But, apart from the doctrine of creation, the medieval conception of the cosmos as a well-ordered whole, composed of distinct types of substances, falling into fixed genera and species or "natural kinds," each kind obeying its own set of laws, was basically Aristotelian.

Beyond the cosmological dimension of this conception, which was undermined by Copernicus, Kepler, Galileo, and others, two aspects of the medieval – or, perhaps better, premodern – worldview are particularly germane, since they were the main targets of the critique of this conception launched by the early modern – i.e., seventeenth-century – philosophers, namely hylemorphism and the appeal to final causes in the explanation of natural phenomena. Hylemorphism is the term used to describe the Aristotelian conception of substance. Simply put, it is the view that every substance consists of a combination of prime matter (*hyle*) and substantial form. In sharp contrast to the matter (or material substance) of modern natural science, which is endowed with determinate physical properties such as size, shape, and mobility, the prime matter of Aristotle and his medieval followers (most notably Aquinas) was regarded as a propertyless or completely indeterminate stuff, with all of the properties attributed to a substance being due to its form. Accordingly, matter, so conceived, was considered to be purely passive, while the form of a substance is its active – or, better, actualizing – principle, though the picture is further complicated by the distinction between substantial and accidental form. The former determines the nature or kind of thing that a particular substance is, e.g., a human being, a horse, or a tree, whereas the latter pertains to its qualities that are not necessary conditions of its membership in the species to which it belongs, e.g., wisdom as predicated of Socrates.[1] It was, however, the conception of substantial form, particularly as it was understood by scholastic thinkers of the late sixteenth and early seventeenth century, that became the prime target of the early modern thinkers. Their basic objection to the scholastic view, which was raised by virtually all the important early modern thinkers save Leibniz, is that the appeal to substantial form is explanatorily vacuous. For example, its substantial form was used to explain why water is cold, why gold is heavy, and why horses have four legs and human beings only two, which effectively means that a thing's substantial form was understood as a kind of efficient cause. Moreover, this was deemed vacuous because the principle provided in the *explanans* itself stands in need of an explanation. The vacuity of the appeal to the conception of substantial form received its classical literary expression by Molière, when a character in his play *Le Malade imaginaire* attempts to explain why opium puts one to sleep by claiming that it is because it contains a dormitive virtue.[2]

For Aristotle, a final cause is one of the four causes or explanatory factors that are appealed to in the explanation of natural phenomena (the others being the efficient, material, and formal causes). It refers to the end or purpose that a natural process or entity is thought to serve and in terms of which its nature can be understood, e.g., the eye is thought to be structured in a way that makes vision possible. And since the structure of the eye for Aristotle is also its form or formal cause, as distinct from the material of which it is composed (its material cause), the formal and final causes coincide, though they differ conceptually in that they address different questions about the nature of the eye (its essence or what makes it the kind

[1] See Ariew and Gabbey, "The Scholastic Background."
[2] See Nadler, "Doctrines of Explanation in Late Scholasticism and in the Mechanical Philosophy," 518.

of thing it is and its function). But whereas Aristotle's conception of teleology or final causation was immanent in the sense that it eschewed any reference to conscious design and was concerned merely with the function that the entity or process in question serves in making a putative end possible, many of the medieval accounts, most famously that of Aquinas, conceived this teleology in theological terms as involving an appeal to God's purposes or design, which, in turn, underlies the teleological argument for the existence of God.[3] Moreover, it is this medieval conception of teleology, more so than the actual teachings of Aristotle, that was the main target of most early modern thinkers (including Spinoza, though again with the notable exception of Leibniz), who dismissed the conception of final causes as a product of the imagination – which, like the closely related conception of substantial form, was deemed to be without any explanatory value.

The objections raised by the early modern thinkers to conceptions like substantial forms and final causes stem from a conception of nature as broadly mechanistic in the sense that it considers all bodies, at least all inanimate bodies, as governed by a set of universal laws, which are expressible in terms such as size, mass, speed, and direction. And since these laws are all formulated in quantitative terms, mathematics (together, of course, with observation) was seen as the essential tool for investigating nature. In the famous and oft-quoted words of Galileo:

> Philosophy is written in that great book which ever lies before our eyes – I mean the universe – but we cannot understand it if we do not first learn the language and grasp the symbols, in which it is written. This book is written in the mathematical language, and the symbols are triangles, circles, and other geometrical figures, without whose help it is impossible to comprehend a single word of it; without which one wanders in vain through a dark labyrinth.[3]

As this passage suggests, the universe of Galileo and the new science is fundamentally geometrical in character. Rather than being hylemorphic substances with their natural places, functions, and purposes, the phenomena with which this science is concerned are completely describable in mechanistic terms, and as such are subject to a mathematical treatment. Moreover, it was the assumption that all the salient relations between phenomena could be expressed in such terms that underlay the quest for universal laws of nature. It is also important, however, to realize that,

---

[3] Among those arguing for the immanent nature of Aristotelian teleology are Ross, *Aristotle: A Complete Exposition of His Works and Thought*, 125, and Randall, *Aristotle*, 229.

though they sometimes presented it as such in order to avoid attacks by the Inquisition, for Galileo, Descartes, and other founders of modern physical science, the mechanistic structure of nature was not merely a convenient hypothesis that proved useful for scientific description and prediction.[4] Rather, it was viewed as the truth about the nature of things. The "real world," or at least the physical world, was in their view quite simply the geometrical, quantitative world of the mathematical physicist. It consisted solely of bodies moving in space and interacting with each other according to mathematically expressible laws, and as such it had no room for the final causes, substantial forms, or occult powers, which were all essential ingredients in the medieval-scholastic conception of nature.

As a direct result of this changed perspective, the world of ordinary human experience, with its colors, sounds, and odors, was assigned a merely secondary status; a view that found its classical expression in the widely held distinction between primary and secondary qualities. The primary qualities of a body, on this view, are properties such as shape, size, mass or weight, and mobility, all of which can be measured and dealt with quantitatively. It was these qualities of which bodies were thought to be really composed, while secondary qualities, including the above-mentioned colors, sounds, and odors, were regarded as subjective, or in the mind. Galileo himself characterized these secondary qualities as "mere names" having no place in nature. Accordingly, for him, as for many others, perceptual experience of these qualities was understood to be the result of an interaction between the real physical object, composed solely of primary qualities, and sentient beings.[4]

This changed conception of nature brought with it a host of philosophical problems, which set the agenda for post-scholastic or what we have come to call "early modern" philosophy. Paramount among these were the relationship between this conception of nature and the scriptural view of God and his relation to nature, as well as the place of human beings in nature so conceived. At issue are the questions of whether human beings are completely subject to nature's mechanistic laws; and, if so, what becomes of the freedom of the will, by virtue of which one supposedly earns either salvation or damnation? Finally, there is the problem of knowledge, which arises in a distinctively modern form: namely, how can the human mind acquire knowledge of the nonsensible yet supposedly

---

[4] It is also the case, however, that Descartes' scientific methodology was explicitly hypothetical, since it was based on the construction of mechanistic models to explain phenomena such as light from which conclusions about observable phenomena can be deduced. For a helpful account of this, see Clarke, "Descartes' Philosophy of Science and the Scientific Revolution."

real world that is described by the science of physics? The problem here is that the conception of nature affirmed by the physicists seems to entail a hopeless skepticism, since it renders nature, so conceived, inaccessible to the senses, which for the Aristotelian tradition were the primary means of cognition. Dealing with these and related problems was a task initially taken up by Descartes, who for that reason is generally regarded as the father of modern philosophy.

Descartes came to philosophy as both a scientist and a Christian, or, at least, a professed Christian. As a scientist, he was motivated by the dream of a "universal mathematics," an all-embracing science of order and proportion through which all fields of knowledge could be integrated into a single whole and mastered by a single method, that of mathematics. The first fruit of this endeavor toward a unified science was analytic geometry, in which Descartes showed that one and the same set of relations or proportions could be expressed either algebraically or geometrically. The attempt to apply this method to nature resulted in a purely geometrical physics, which, due largely to its evident inability to deal adequately with the dynamical aspects of nature, proved to be not nearly as successful.[5] As a professed Christian, Descartes conceived of human beings as possessing a free will and an immortal soul. He also tended to resolve any conflicts between faith and science or philosophy by assigning them to different realms, claiming that the sacred truths of the former are beyond the capacity of human reason, or, as it was frequently called, the "natural light."

As a philosopher, Descartes developed the split between mind and nature that was implicit in Galileo into a full-fledged metaphysical dualism, which became a focal point of Spinoza's critique. The key to this dualism is the conception of substance, a conception that also plays a crucial role in Spinoza's philosophy. In contrast to the hylemorphic Aristotelian conception, Descartes defined substance in purely ontological terms as "that which so exists that it needs no other thing in order to exist."[5] He also acknowledged, however, that, so defined, the term is used equivocally, since only God is dependent on no other thing for his existence, whereas all other substances, which for Descartes are corporeal, material, or extended substance (*res extensa*) and mind, or thinking substance (*res cogitans*), depend upon God's concurrence for their existence.[6]

[5] On this issue see Garber, "Descartes' Physics."
[6] It should be noted, however, that there is an ambiguity in Descartes' account of extended or material substance; for though he usually seems to suggest that there is only a single extended substance (*res extensa*) of which particular bodies are modes, while there are an indefinite number of thinking

Nevertheless, since the latter two kinds of substance are independent of everything except God for their existence, Descartes also characterized them as substances, a view for which, we shall see, he was sharply criticized by Spinoza. Moreover, for Descartes, each of these kinds of substance has one principal property, or attribute, which constitutes its essence and was likewise a subject of Spinoza's critique. As its characterization suggests, the essence of *res extensa* is extension in length, breadth, and depth, while the essence of *res cogitans* is thought, and all other specifically mental functions, e.g., imagining, willing, and feeling, are claimed to be merely diverse forms of thinking.[7]

Having split the worlds of mind and matter (which includes the human body) in so uncompromising a fashion, Descartes was faced with the problem of explaining their relationship. This problem is itself complex, however, and takes at least two forms. The first, the epistemological form, requires an explanation of how a thinking substance, which has immediate access only to its own thoughts, can ever attain a certain knowledge of the physical world. The second, the metaphysical form, concerns the inter-action between two distinct substances. Here the questions are: how can events in nature affect the mind and how can thoughts and free volitions have any effect in the corporeal world; e.g., how can my decision to raise my arm lead to the physical act? The latter issue, or set of issues, has come to be known as the "mind–body problem."

Descartes' solution to the epistemological problem, as presented in his *Meditations on First Philosophy*, is the best-known aspect of his thought. Its most characteristic and controversial feature is the attempt to overcome skepticism from within by doubting everything until one arrives at some-thing that simply cannot be doubted. The operative assumption is that the indubitable truth at which one will arrive by this process would not only be able to stand firm against any skeptical attack but also serve as the "Archimedean point" on the basis of which one could confidently proceed to erect the edifice of scientific knowledge. The first beliefs to be rejected by this method are those based on sensory evidence, including the belief in the existence of one's own body. Since it is evident that the senses sometimes deceive and that they do not of themselves provide any sure criterion for distinguishing between veridical and nonveridical perceptions, Cartesian doubt applies to every belief based on sensory evidence. But far-reaching as

substances (*res cogitans*), he sometimes indicates that he held that the material world consists of an indefinite number of material substances. For a discussion of this issue see Schmaltz, "Descartes on the Metaphysics of the Material World."

[7] Descartes, *The Philosophical Writings of Descartes*, vol. 1, 210–211.

it may be, this doubt does not stop here; for by means of the hypothesis of a deceiving God or evil genius, Descartes found it possible to doubt even the basic truths of mathematics, thereby apparently undermining the certainty of *any* cognitive claims.

Accordingly, the problem, as Descartes envisioned it, is to determine what, if anything, one could confidently claim to be the case on the assumption that one is being systematically deceived in this manner. And his famous answer is his own existence as a thinking, and in this case doubting, being. As he concisely puts it, "[A]fter considering everything very thoroughly, I must finally conclude that this proposition, *I am, I exist*, is necessarily true whenever it is put forward by me or conceived by my mind."[8] Descartes points out, however, that this does not take him very far, and in order to progress to other truths, the acceptance of which had been temporarily suspended by the process of methodical doubt, he concludes that it is necessary to determine what it is about this proposition – as well as others about which, apart from this hyperbolic doubt, he had taken to be certain, e.g., those of mathematics – that accounts for his assurance of their veracity. His answer is that they were clearly and distinctly perceived to be true. And since the only basis for doubting such propositions is the possibility that he was being systematically deceived by an evil genius, Descartes proceeds to eliminate this possibility by demonstrating the existence of a non-deceiving God. In short, since God functions for Descartes as the guarantor of his clear and distinct perceptions, the assurance of the existence of God justifies a similar assurance of the veracity of these perceptions.

Descartes' reasoning here has been the subject of intense debate from his time to the present, with the issue being its apparent circularity, as the result of which it has been dubbed the "Cartesian circle." The problem was clearly formulated by Antoine Arnauld, who in the fourth set of objections to the arguments of the *Meditations* wonders "how the author avoids reasoning in a circle when he says that we are sure that what we clearly and distinctly perceive is true only because God exists. – But we can be sure that God exists only because we clearly and distinctly perceive this. Hence, before we can be sure that God exists, we ought to be able to be sure that whatever we perceive clearly and evidently is true."[9]

Although he did not deal with the circularity problem as such, in both the DPP and the TdIE Spinoza rejected the Cartesian program of a radical doubt as the path to certainty, which underlies the worry about circularity.

---

[8] Descartes, *The Philosophical Writings of Descartes*, vol. 2, 17. [9] Ibid., 150.

Spinoza's basic claim in both works is that just as we can have a clear and distinct idea of a triangle without knowing whether we are being deceived by a Cartesian demon, so, too, we can have such an idea of God. Moreover, since it is self-evident that God is not a deceiver, once we have such an idea, there can no longer be a rational basis for doubt concerning God's nature, from which it follows that there is likewise no basis for doubting anything that we clearly and distinctly perceive to be the case (TdIE 79; G2 30; C1 35). And while this conclusion does not differ substantively from Descartes' view, Spinoza puts it to an opposite use. For rather than taking possession of the clear and distinct idea of God as the means for overcoming the hyperbolic doubt instituted by Descartes as a necessary condition of the possibility of arriving at certainty, he takes it to undermine both the need for and the basis of such doubt.

Descartes' proposed solution to the mind–body problem is less systematic. It basically amounts to an admission that the problem is insoluble, at least in terms of the appeal to clear and distinct perceptions, which is the standard of scientific evidence for Descartes. But since it was this appeal that initially led Descartes to the separation of mind and body, it could hardly enable him to explain the union between the two radically disparate substances. Instead, Descartes appeals to experience, claiming that "Everyone feels that he is a single person with both body and thought so related by nature that the thought can move the body and feel the things which happen to it."[10] Accordingly, Descartes' view seems to be that this unity must be accepted as a brute fact, even though it cannot be explained adequately. Nevertheless, Descartes did not abandon all efforts to explain how mind and body interact, and he even tried to provide a physiological account of their interaction. This account is based on the hypothesis, later ridiculed by Spinoza, that the pineal gland in the brain is the "seat of the soul," and that it serves as the point of union between the immaterial thoughts, passions, and volitions of the mind and the "animal spirits," which are the small particles of matter by which messages are allegedly relayed from the brain to the rest of the body, and vice versa.[11] Through this rather fanciful explanation, Descartes evidently hoped to unite his mechanistic physiology (the conception of the human body as a machine) with his conception of an immaterial, independent, and immortal soul, or thinking substance. But though Spinoza emphatically rejected Descartes'

---

[10]   Descartes, Letter to Princess Elizabeth, 28 June 1643, *Descartes' Philosophical Letters*, 142.
[11]   Descartes, *The Passions of the Soul*, pt. 1, articles 34–38, *The Philosophical Writings of Descartes*, vol. 1, 340–342.

account of the mind–body relation, we shall see that here, as well as in many other areas, the Cartesian account provided the framework in terms of which Spinoza articulated his own view and in relation to which this view must be understood.

2.2   Some Central Themes in Spinoza's Philosophy

In his editorial preface to the DPP, Lodewijk Meyer, speaking for Spinoza, notes several areas in which his philosophy differs from that of Descartes. These include the conception of the will and its alleged freedom and the notion that the human mind constitutes a distinct thinking substance. Special attention is given, however, to the Cartesian notion "that this or that surpasses the human understanding." As Meyer points out in reference to Spinoza:

> He judges that all those things, and even many others more sublime and subtle, can not only be conceived clearly and distinctly, but also explained very satisfactorily – provided only that the human Intellect is guided in the search for truth and cognition[12] of things along a different path from that which Descartes opened up and made smooth. (DPP; GI 132; CI 230)

Thus, in opposition to the Cartesian appeal to the limits of human cognition, an appeal that was undoubtedly motivated by theological considerations, Spinoza affirms an absolute rationalism. Given the proper method, reality as a whole is intelligible to the human mind, and Spinoza claims in his *Ethics* to have done nothing less than demonstrate this truth.[13] Indeed, as Michael Della Rocca aptly puts it in his study, which explicates Spinoza's rationalism in terms of an uncompromising commitment to the principle of sufficient reason, "For Spinoza, to be is to be intelligible."[14]

Above and beyond this, however, the greatest single difference between the philosophies of Descartes and Spinoza and the root of most of the others lies in the fact that the main thrust of Spinoza's philosophy is ethical. He was before all else a moralist, concerned with determining the true good for human beings. This is not to suggest that Descartes was unconcerned

---

[12] Following the translation of Silverthorne and Kisner (*Spinoza: Ethics – Proved in Geometrical Order*), I am rendering *cognitio* as used by Spinoza as "cognition" rather than as "knowledge," which is the rendering of Curley and most of the other English translations. The reason for this is the same as that for rendering Kant's "*Erkenntnis*" as "cognition" rather than as "knowledge," namely that both thinkers use these terms broadly to encompass false or inadequate cognitive claims, whereas "knowledge" is usually taken in a normative sense as implying truth.

[13] See Gueroult, *Spinoza* I, 11ff.   [14] Della Rocca, *Spinoza*, 9.

with ethical issues, but only to point out that they were never as central to his thought as they were to Spinoza's.[15] For while questions about the nature and the limits of human knowledge, the nature and existence of God, and the relationship between the human mind and body are given considerable attention in the *Ethics*, and will be the focus of the next two chapters, it must never be forgotten that Spinoza's treatment of these issues is based on, and often colored by, his ethical concerns, or, more precisely, the determination of the true good for human beings and the necessary conditions of its attainment.

Speaking in general terms, Spinoza's moral philosophy can be seen as an endeavor to unify the fundamental tenets of two distinct traditions of ethical thought. On the one hand, it falls squarely within the intellectualistic tradition, which goes back to the classical Greek moralists: Socrates, Plato, Aristotle, and, perhaps most germanely, the Stoics. Common to all these thinkers is the identification of virtue, or in the case of Aristotle the highest virtue, with knowledge. Otherwise expressed, the highest virtues are intellectual, whereas the so-called moral virtues – that is, virtues of character, such as self-control, courage, and benevolence – are seen within this tradition as either effects of intellectual virtue or preparatory stages necessary for its realization. Spinoza accepts this doctrine in an unqualified form and contends that it is only through knowledge that one can overcome the bondage to the passions that constitutes the essence of human misery. On the other hand, Spinoza's moral philosophy contains an equally firm adherence to the fundamental principle of the naturalistic-egoistic tradition, the major modern representative of which is Hobbes, for whom all human endeavor is motivated by and ultimately justified in terms of self-interest; though we shall also see that this is somewhat softened by Spinoza's view that an essential ingredient in a life governed by the dictates of reason is a concern with the well-being of others.

With respect to the overall structure and argument of the *Ethics*, however, the intellectualist strand of Spinoza's moral theory is clearly dominant. And in at least verbal agreement with Maimonides and other representatives of the medieval Jewish, Christian, and Islamic

---

[15] In the preface to the French edition of his *Principles of Philosophy*, Descartes famously compares the whole of philosophy to a tree of which "The roots are metaphysics, the trunk physics, and the branches emerging from the trunk are all the other sciences, which may be reduced to three principal ones, namely medicine, mechanics, and morals," *The Philosophical Writings of Descartes*, vol. 1, 186. However, in fairness to Descartes, it must be noted that he adds that by "moral" he understands "the highest and most perfect moral system, which presupposes the complete knowledge of the other sciences and is the ultimate level of wisdom."

religious traditions, Spinoza regarded God as the prime object of knowledge. The attainment of a genuine knowledge of God is, therefore, viewed as the ultimate goal of human life and the key to the achievement of blessedness. Moreover, not only did Spinoza see human existence as culminating in the knowledge of God, he also claimed, again in agreement with the religious tradition, that this knowledge necessarily leads to love. Thus, the entire argument of the *Ethics* culminates in the "intellectual love of God" (*amor intellectualis Dei*), through which the human mind is allegedly able to transcend its finitude and be united with the eternal. This conception constitutes Spinoza's purely philosophical alternative to the beatific vision appealed to by elements of this tradition and it provides much of the religious, perhaps even mystical, tone that some have found in his philosophy.

The ground of this conception lies, however, in Spinoza's uncompromising rationalism rather than his religious sensitivity. Although much of his language is reminiscent of the religious tradition, his overall point of view is diametrically opposed to it. The God that functions as the first principle of knowledge and is the object of a purely intellectual love for Spinoza has very little in common with the God of Abraham, Isaac, and Jacob. The latter is a personal being, who created humanity in his own image and manifests a providential concern for each individual, as well as for the human race as a whole. By contrast, Spinoza's God is defined as "a being absolutely infinite, i.e., a substance consisting of infinite attributes, of which each one expresses an eternal and infinite essence" (E1d6), and which in the famous formula "*Deus seu Natura*" (E4P) is identified with nature. This identification, however, is not with nature considered as the sum total of particular things, but, rather, with nature considered as an infinite (in the sense of all-inclusive) and necessary system of universal laws, in which all things have their determinate place and with reference to which they must be understood. The "divinity" of nature, so conceived, thus consists in its infinity and necessity. As truly infinite, or, in Spinoza's technical language, "absolutely infinite," there is nothing beyond it on which it depends; that is, no "creator" God, or any purpose that it embodies. As a necessary system of universal laws, nothing in it is contingent, which is to say that nothing could possibly be other than it is. Moreover, cognition of such a God is equivalent to cognition of the infinite and necessary order in which human beings, like everything else in nature, have their determinate place, while the intellectual love that supposedly springs from this cognition is the joyful acceptance and affirmation of the very same order, which is akin to the Stoic conception of the *amor fati*, which was later reaffirmed in a somewhat different fashion by Nietzsche.[16]

This complex activity of cognition, acceptance, and affirmation constitutes, for Spinoza, our highest destiny and chief good. It is not a means to happiness, but happiness itself in its most authentic and lasting form, namely blessedness. Similarly, virtue, so conceived, is its own reward, rather than, as traditional religions affirm, merely a means for acquiring future rewards or avoiding future punishments. Finally, Spinoza tells us that this very same activity is the source of human freedom. But freedom for Spinoza is not to be conceived, as Descartes and others have conceived it, as some mysterious power that in some inexplicable way exempts man from the laws and power of nature. Rather, it consists entirely in the apprehension of the necessity of these very laws. Accordingly, Spinoza's point is essentially the one that was later brought home so forcefully by Freud, namely that we gain control of our emotions and achieve freedom only by acquiring an adequate cognition of these emotions and their causes.[17]

This view, which I have attempted to sketch in only its broadest outlines, may be seen as the most fully developed defense of the ideal of scientific objectivity as a life task that is to be found in the history of Western thought. The maxim "Know thyself," which for Socrates expressed the sum and substance of human wisdom, but which led him to the ironic conclusion that the only thing one can know about oneself is that one knows nothing, became for Spinoza the demand to become aware of one's place in the infinite and necessary scheme of things, which he combined with the decidedly non-Socratic claim that such knowledge is attainable for at least some. Moreover, this demand is grounded in the conviction that things are, indeed, necessary and determined; that the course of nature is completely indifferent to human purposes; and, consequently, that moral and religious categories such as good and evil, sin and grace have no basis in reality, but are merely products of human imagination and desire. It is also based, however, on Spinoza's firm conviction that the recognition of these truths is the source of peace and satisfaction; not, to be sure, the "peace that passes understanding" of traditional religion, but the true and lasting peace that does not so much derive from as actually consist in understanding.

---

[16] The most fully developed "Nietzschean reading" of Spinoza is by Deleuze, *Spinoza: Practical Philosophy*. For an illuminating discussion of the Spinoza–Nietzsche connection that focuses on the conception of *amor fati*, see Yirmiyahu Yovel, *Spinoza and Other Heretics*, 104–135.

[17] For an insightful comparison of Spinoza and Freud on this point, see Hampshire, *Spinoza*, 106–109.

Spinoza provides the clearest statement of his basic standpoint in the critique of final causes, which he appended to the first part of the *Ethics*. Final causes there stand for almost everything Spinoza opposed and his critique is twofold. First, in agreement with the Cartesians and other proponents of the new science, he rejects any appeal to such causes on the grounds that they constitute an inadequate, unscientific mode of explanation, a view he expresses by noting that the doctrine of final causes "turns nature completely upside down. For what is really a cause, it considers an effect, and conversely what is an effect it considers as a cause" (G2 280; C1 442). But, second, unlike most of his contemporaries, at least in their published pronouncements, he uses this critique as a vehicle for attacking the theistic worldview that he considered as standing in the way of achieving the true understanding of ourselves and our place in nature.

According to Spinoza's analysis, all the prejudices, which stand in the way of attaining the requisite understanding, stem from the fact that human beings "commonly suppose that all natural things act, as men do, on account of an end," which he identifies with their perceived advantage (G2 77; C1 439). More specifically, the root of the problem is the view that God created all things for the benefit of human beings. For Spinoza, such a belief is the result of viewing things through the imagination, rather than the intellect, which alone grasps things through their true causes. Spinoza further maintains, however, that given human nature as it is, such a procedure is inevitable, since "all men are born ignorant of the causes of things, and ... they all want to seek their own advantage, and are conscious of this appetite" (G2 78; C1 440). And he claims that it follows from this that all human beings think themselves free and act with an end in view, which is whatever they consider to be useful. Moreover, being ignorant of true causes, they tend to judge other natures by their own, and when they find many things in nature that prove useful to them, such as "eyes for seeing, teeth for chewing, plants and animals for food, the sun for light, the sea for supporting fish, etc. . . . they consider all natural things as means for their own advantage." And being aware that they did not create all these great conveniences themselves, Spinoza suggests that they were led by their imagination to the belief that "there was a ruler, or number of rulers of nature, endowed with human freedom, who had taken care of all things for them and made all things for their use" (G2 78; C1 440). But Spinoza points out that it was soon realized that these benefits are not distributed equitably; that "conveniences and inconveniences happen indiscriminately to the pious and the impious alike" (G2 79; C1 441), which gave rise to the problem of reconciling the apparent evil in the world with the goodness of God. And, as Spinoza suggests, this problem is generally dealt with by an appeal to ignorance in the form of the pious claim that "the judgments of the Gods far surpass man's grasp," and he reflects that "This alone . . . would have caused the truth to be hidden from the human race to eternity, if Mathematics, which is concerned not with ends, but only with the essences and properties of figures, had not shown men another standard of truth" (G2 79; C1 441).

Although Spinoza's appeals to mathematics, particularly geometry, as the model discipline usually focus on the on the apodictic certainty of its results, his focus here seems to be on the nonteleological nature of its reasoning. Moreover, he provides a clear illustration of what he understood by this in the preface to part III of the *Ethics*, where he states that he will "consider human actions and appetites just as if it were a question of lines, planes, and bodies" (G2 138; C1 492). Not only is such a mode of explanation scientific, but even more important for Spinoza, it is the way in which we have to regard our own actions and desires, as well as those of others, if we are ever to achieve virtue, happiness, and freedom, all of which he regarded as basically equivalent.

2.3   The Geometrical Method

The privileged status that Spinoza gave to the geometrical manner of demonstration is mirrored in the form in which he cast the argument of the *Ethics*. This order or manner of demonstration is modeled on that of Euclid's *Elements*. Following this model, each of its five parts begins with a set of definitions and axioms, and the argument is presented in a series of propositions, each with its own demonstration, which in some cases are followed by corollaries and lemmata. Although it also contains numerous scholia in which Spinoza abandons the formal manner of presentation and adds significant illustrative material and occasional criticism of opposing views, while the last four parts of the *Ethics* have prefaces and the first and fourth appendices, which likewise are not presented in a geometrical manner, the great bulk of the work is cast in this austere form. This is equivalent to what Descartes had called the "synthetic method of demonstration," which he had contrasted with the "analytic method of discovery." But though Descartes made brief use of this method in his reply to the second set of objections to the *Meditations* at the request of his friend Marin Mersenne, he also there stated that he considered analysis, which was the method he employed in the *Meditations* itself, to be "the best and truest method of instruction."[18] It is clear from the form of the *Ethics*, however, that Spinoza, who had put the whole of his DPP and a portion of the KV in geometrical form, thought otherwise.

Not surprisingly, the significance of Spinoza's casting of the argument of the *Ethics* in this form has been the subject of considerable dispute. The basic issue is whether this form is required by the content of the work, or whether the connection between the two is more external, with the choice of a geometrical form being motivated purely by extrinsic factors, such as its pedagogical value. Moreover, there are distinguished scholars on both sides of the issue.[19] Nevertheless, I believe that if we are to take Spinoza seriously as a philosopher, we must also take his chosen manner of presentation seriously. And since the viability of his procedure depends largely on the definitions and to a lesser extent the axioms on which the demonstration of the propositions of the *Ethics* is based, I further believe that the best way to address this issue is through a consideration of the way in which Spinoza viewed these definitions and axioms and the role they play in its argument.

The most problematic feature of Spinoza's procedure in the *Ethics* is clearly the weight he placed on his definitions, for the obvious worry is that he had "cooked the books" by arbitrarily defining key terms in a way that would yield the desired conclusions. But regardless of how one ultimately judges the matter, it is clear that Spinoza was well aware of the problem and thought that he had dealt with it adequately. Thus, in a letter to his young friend Simon Joosten De Vries, who had queried him on the matter on behalf of a society of followers of Spinoza of which he was a member, and which had been discussing portions of the manuscript of what was to become the *Ethics* that he had given them, Spinoza distinguishes between two kinds of definitions in a way that parallels the traditional distinction between nominal and real definitions. The former kind stipulates what is meant by a word, or what is thought in a given concept. Such a definition can be conceivable or inconceivable, clear or obscure, helpful or unhelpful, but since it is arbitrarily concocted by the human mind, it cannot, strictly speaking, be called either true or false. By contrast, the latter kind of definition (real definition), which in Spinoza's terms "explains a thing as

---

[18] Descartes, Reply to the Second Set of Objections, *The Philosophical Writings of Descartes*, vol. 2, 110–112.

[19] Those in favor of the intrinsic connection include Freudenthal, *Spinoza Leben und Lehre*, pt. 2, 110–111; Joachim, *A Study of the Ethics of Spinoza*, 12–13; Gueroult, *Spinoza I*, 15ff.; and Delahunty, *Spinoza*, 8–12. Those against such a connection include Roth, *Spinoza*, 37–39; Hampshire, *Spinoza*, 21; and especially Wolfson, *The Philosophy of Spinoza*, vol. 1, 32–60.

it exists outside of the understanding," defines a thing, rather than a name.
It therefore can be either true or false; and it is, in fact, a proposition,
differing from an axiom only in its specificity (L9 G4 43; C1 194).

At first glance the definitions in the *Ethics* appear to be of the former
variety. They are introduced by expressions such as "by ... I mean that," or
"a thing is called ...," which specify how the term in question is being
used, and it is just this feature of Spinoza's definitions that gives rise to the
above-mentioned objections. The actual course of the argument makes it
clear, however, that Spinoza intended his definitions to be considerably
more than that, for merely nominal definitions cannot provide us with any
information about reality.[20] Like the definitions found in Euclid, Spinoza's
are designed to describe not only the names used, but also the objects
named. Accordingly, they are presented as true propositions. And just as
mathematicians deduce the properties of a figure from its real definition, so
Spinoza, the metaphysician, deduces the basic properties of nature from his
fundamental real definitions.[21]

The obvious question, however, is: how does Spinoza know that he has
arrived at a real or true definition, one that, in his own terms, provides us
with an adequate, or clear and distinct, idea of the object in question? Here,
perhaps more than in any other area, we can discern the influence of the
geometrical way of thinking on Spinoza. For what he does is, in effect, to
ask how the mathematician knows that he has arrived at a real definition of
a figure, and the proposed answer is when he is able to construct it. In other
words, the geometer's definition is essentially a rule for the construction of
a figure, what is often called a "genetic definition," and from such
a definition alone all the properties of the figure can be derived.[22] To cite
Spinoza's own example, the nominal definition of a circle as "a figure in
which the lines drawn from the center to the circumference are equal" is
rejected in favor of the genetic definition as "the figure that is described by
any line of which one end is fixed and the other movable." This definition
tells us how such a figure can be constructed, and from the rule for
construction, we can determine all of its essential properties.

Spinoza's central claim is that the same principles that apply to our
knowledge of nature also apply to our knowledge of abstract entities such
as mathematical objects. Thus, we can have a real definition: an adequate,
true, or clear and distinct idea of a thing (all these terms being more or less

---

[20] For an interesting defense of the opposite view, see Delahunty, *Spinoza*, 91–96.
[21] This interpretation is most forcefully presented by Gueroult, *Spinoza* I, 21ff.
[22] The significance of genetic definitions for Spinoza is emphasized by Gueroult, *Spinoza* I, 33ff., and
by Cassirer, *Das Erkenntnisproblem in der Philosophie und Wissenschaft der neueren Zeit*, vol. 2, 90ff.

interchangeable) insofar as we know its "proximate cause" and can see how its properties necessarily follow from this cause. "For really," Spinoza writes, "cognition of the effect is nothing but acquiring a more perfect cognition of its cause" (TdIE G2 34; C1 39). Moreover, in such instances there is no room for doubt of the kind envisaged by Descartes. For when the mind has a true idea (*any* true idea, not merely the idea of God), it immediately knows it to be true, since it grasps the necessity with which the properties of the object follow from the idea. Accordingly, the metaphysician, as well as the mathematician, can arrive at real definitions of things, and it is through such definitions that one acquires rationally grounded cognition.

If, however, the cognition of a thing is equivalent to the cognition of its cause, which Spinoza identifies with its logical ground, or the principle in terms of which it is understood, then either we find ourselves involved in an infinite regress, which would lead to a hopeless skepticism, or the whole cognitive enterprise must be grounded in a single first principle. Furthermore, this first principle in terms of which everything is to be explained obviously cannot itself be explained in terms of anything else. It must, therefore, have the reason or ground of its existence in itself, or, in the language of the schools, which Spinoza adopts, it must be *causa sui* (self-caused). The first principle is, of course, God; and we can thus see how Spinoza's method leads necessarily to his concept of God. Thus, Spinoza writes:

> As for order, to unite and order all our perceptions, it is required, and reason demands, that we ask, as soon as possible, whether there is a certain being, and at the same time, what sort of being it is, which is the cause of all things, so that its objective essence may also be the cause of all our ideas, and then our mind will ... reproduce Nature as much as possible. For it will have Nature's essence, order, and unity objectively. (TdIE G2; C1 41)[23]

Now, however, the problem becomes how we can be certain that our thoughts are arranged in the proper logical order – that they "have Nature's essence, order, and unity objectively." Spinoza's answer is that we know this in precisely the same way in which the mathematician knows that she has arrived at the correct idea of a circle. In both cases, the properties follow with strict logical necessity from the cause, and the mind is able to see that nothing is undetermined, nothing left unexplained. The argument of the

---

[23] The expression "objective essence" is used by both Descartes and Spinoza. It means the essence of a thing as grasped by thought, which is equivalent to the adequate idea of the thing. The topic will be discussed in Chapter 4 in connection with Spinoza's account of ideas.

Ethics is intended to lead us to understand nature as a whole in just this way. The aim is to enable those capable of following the argument to see "that from God's supreme power, *or* infinite nature, infinitely many things in infinitely many modes, i.e., all things, have necessarily flowed, or always follow, by the same necessity and in the same way as from the nature of a triangle it follows, from eternity and to eternity, that its three angles are equal to two right angles" (E1p17s1). Accordingly, the argument turns on an assumed isomorphism between two relations: that between the real, i.e., genetic, definition of geometrical figures such as a circle and a triangle and the figures themselves, on the one hand, and between the real definition of God, which for Spinoza is "a being absolutely infinite, i.e., a substance consisting of an infinity of attributes, of which each one expresses an eternal and infinite essence" (E1d6), and the order of nature, on the other. Moreover, in both cases the form of the relation consists in the logical necessity of the connection between the relata.

In his use of the geometrical method, however, Spinoza derives the propositions of the *Ethics* not only from definitions, but also from axioms. And though they are clearly subordinate to definitions in the proof structure of the work, they still play an ineliminable role.[24] Moreover, unlike definitions, which concern kinds or species of things (hence they are also called "common notions"), or, in the case of God, an individual, axioms purport to be universal truths; while unlike empirical generalizations, such as "all men are mortal," axioms purport to be necessarily true. More specifically, they purport to be self-evident, which makes it possible to use them in the demonstration of the propositions of the *Ethics*, which also purport to be necessarily true, though not self-evident. A look at the actual axioms that Spinoza provides, however, suggests that they are very much a mixed bag; for whereas some may be regarded as axioms in this sense, e.g., "The cognition of an effect depends on, and involves, the cognition of its cause" (E1a4) and "If two contrary actions are aroused in one subject, a change will necessarily have to take place in both of them or in one alone, until they cease to be contrary" (E5a1), which has the status of a law of nature, some seem to be logical truths or in Kant and post-Kantian thought

---

[24] In the *Ethics* Spinoza introduces fifteen main axioms: seven in part I, five in part II, one in part IV, and two in part V. In addition, he introduces two evidently subordinate axioms after the demonstration of P13 of part II, which deal with the nature of the human body. And to complicate the picture further, Spinoza also introduces six postulates: four in part II and two in part III concerning the nature of the human body, which, as such, would seem to be empirical propositions. Moreover, in commenting on the first postulate in part III Spinoza remarks that it could also be considered an axiom.

analytic judgments, e.g., "What cannot be conceived through another must be conceived through itself" (EIa2). Still others seem to be obvious empirical truths, e.g., "Man thinks" (E2a2) and "We feel that a certain body is affected in many ways" (E2a4).[25]

Setting aside the ambiguous character of Spinoza's axioms, the role he assigns to definitions, particularly his appeal to a strong analogy between geometrical definitions, conceived genetically, and his own philosophical definitions, suggests that he considered the geometrical form of the argument of the *Ethics* to be intimately related to, if not actually inseparable from, its content. This is not to say that the geometrical form of presentation is "demanded" or "required" by the argument in the strong sense that its basic conclusions cannot even be accurately expressed apart from it. Nevertheless, given the assumptions about the nature of cognition we have just touched on and shall examine in more detail later, the geometrical form is arguably the best vehicle for presenting this philosophy. Not only does it allow Spinoza to deduce, or at least attempt to deduce, all his conclusions from a single first principle, namely the concept of God, and to illustrate the absolute necessity governing all things; it also, for these very reasons, presents his account of nature in the form in which, according to his view of cognition, it can be adequately grasped by the intellect. Finally, and most importantly, such a form is from Spinoza's point of view best suited for the realization of the practical goal of the *Ethics*, by means of what might be termed an "emendative therapy,"[26] where what is emended is the understanding and its capacity to lead human beings, or at least those capable of it, to a condition of blessedness – which for Spinoza consists in "the satisfaction of mind that stems from the intuitive cognition of God" (E4 appendix) and which is equivalent to what he calls the "*intellectual love of God*" (my emphasis).

---

[25] I am here largely following the account of Nadler, *Spinoza's Ethics: An Introduction*, 48–50.

[26] I am borrowing the expression from Aaron Garrett, who uses it repeatedly in *Meaning in Spinoza's Method*. The view of Spinoza's *Ethics* as providing a kind of therapy, in this case Freudian, was introduced by Stuart Hampshire, *Spinoza*, and elsewhere.

CHAPTER 3

God

The first part of the *Ethics*, entitled "Concerning God," is devoted to an analysis of the nature of God and to the delineation of the main outlines of the relationship between God and the world. It contains Spinoza's analysis of the basic structure of reality and his criticisms of the Judeo-Christian or, more broadly, theistic conception of God as an omnipotent and omniscient personal being, who freely created the world for the sake of certain ends, which prominently includes the welfare of human beings. The argument, which, like that of every part of the *Ethics*, is preceded by a set of definitions and axioms, can be broken down into three parts, supplemented by an appendix dealing with final causes, which was discussed in the preceding chapter. Accordingly, the present chapter will be divided into three parts, corresponding to the three parts of Spinoza's argument. The first part (E1p1–p15) offers an exposition of the nature of God together with a set of demonstrations that God, so conceived, exists necessarily. Here Spinoza introduces his fundamental category of substance, in light of which he develops his conception of God as "a being absolutely infinite, i.e., a substance consisting of an infinity of attributes, of which each one expresses an eternal and infinite essence" (E1d6). It is on the basis of this conception that Spinoza argues that God is the only substance. The second part (E1p16–p29) is concerned with the divine power, or causality, which for Spinoza is equivalent to the infinite power of nature. This leads to an analysis of the relationship between God and the world; and within the context of this analysis, Spinoza characterizes particular things in nature as finite modes. The third part (E1p30–p36) makes explicit many of the results that have already been established and uses them as the basis for a polemic against the Judeo-Christian religious tradition and the theistic conception of God that underlies it.

3.1   **God as Substance**

We have already seen that by developing his doctrine of God in light of his concept of substance, Spinoza made an original use of one of the most important concepts in the history of Western philosophy. The concept arose with the Greeks in their endeavor to understand the nature of change. Explanation of change was thought to require the recognition of something abiding that underlies it and in relation to which it can be understood. The concept of substance served this function. It was introduced to refer to the permanent element or elements in the universe, the abiding substrata, whereas the changing features of experience were viewed as its states or qualities. Aristotle, who provided the first systematic treatment of this concept, states that "the most distinctive mark of substance appears to be that, while remaining numerically one and the same, it is capable of admitting contrary qualities."[1] But Aristotle not only claimed that substances are the substrata of change, he also insisted that they are the subjects of predication.[2] Accordingly, for Aristotle and the long tradition that followed him, intelligible talk about nature requires expressions both for qualities and for things or subjects, which have these qualities as properties. Moreover, since we can conceive of a thing or subject without at least some of its properties, which are, therefore, called "accidents," but we cannot conceive of a property except in relation to a thing or subject, it was thought to follow that the latter are more fundamental. The various subjects of predication – that is, the particular things in nature, such as human beings, horses, and trees – were viewed by Aristotle as substances in the primary sense, the basic elements in the universe in terms of which everything else is to be understood, while the various species or kinds of thing were regarded as substances in a secondary sense, because they too are subjects of predication, since the properties that pertain to all the members of a species are predicated of them.[3]

Although we have seen that by the time of Descartes, the concept of substance had changed considerably, and in a way that accords with the development of the mathematical science of nature, it retained its dual functions as the substratum of change, i.e., the enduring basis in terms of which change is to be understood, and as the subject of predication, i.e., that to which properties or qualities are attributed. The former may be considered its real or metaphysical and the latter its logical function. Descartes, it will be recalled, defined substance primarily in terms of

[1] Aristotle, *Categories*, chap. 5, 4a.   [2] Ibid.   [3] Ibid.

independent existence, as "a thing which so exists that it needs no other thing in order to exist."[4] Each substance, so conceived, has one fundamental attribute, or property, which constitutes its nature or essence and through which it is known. As we have seen, the essential property of corporeal substance for Descartes is extension, and it is on the basis of this conception that he argued for the possibility of a completely geometrical physics. Like Aristotle, Descartes used the concept of substance or, more precisely, corporeal substance (*res extensa*) to refer to what is fundamental in the physical world, that in terms of which everything else is to be explained; but in accordance with his radically different view of scientific explanation, he conceived of what is fundamental or "substantial" in a very different manner. Nevertheless, there is a residue of Aristotelianism in Descartes' conception; for in addition to the account that we have just considered, he gives another account in which substance is defined as "everything in which there resides immediately, as in a subject, or by means of which there exists anything that we perceive, i.e., any property, quality, or attribute, of which we have a real idea."[4] Thus, like Aristotle, and presumably because of the scholastic tradition in which he was educated, Descartes also conceived of substance as a subject of predication, as a *thing* that has *properties* and is, in fact, only known in terms of these properties, which is the logical function of the concept of substance. Moreover, it is in light of this conception that he used the words *attribute*, to designate the principal, or essential, property through which each substance is known, and *mode*, to refer to the nonessential properties, which cannot be conceived without substance, but without which substance or its principal attribute can be conceived.[5]

Spinoza's definitions of these terms, though not the conclusions that he derives from them, are broadly Cartesian, and as such retain significant Aristotelian elements. *Substance* is defined by Spinoza as "what is in itself and is conceived through itself, i.e., that whose concept does not require the concept of another thing, from which it must be formed" (E1d3). So defined, substance is distinguished both from *attributes*, by which Spinoza means "what the intellect perceives of a substance as constituting its essence" (E1d4), and from *modes*, by which he understands "the affections of substance *or* that which is in another through which it is also conceived" (E1d5). Leaving aside for the moment the definition of *attribute*, the most

[4] See Chapter 2, note 5.
[5] Descartes, Reply to the Second Set of Objections, *Philosophical Works*, vol. 2, 53. This point is emphasized by Melamed, *Spinoza's Metaphysics*, 12–17.

striking way in which Spinoza's conception of substance differs from Descartes' is that it includes conceptual as well as ontological independence. Thus, unlike Descartes, for Spinoza a substance must not only "exist in itself," but must also be "conceived through itself." Correlatively, the attributes and modes of substance are dependent in both senses; that is, they both exist in and are conceived through the substance of which they are predicated and in which they inhere.

Moreover, these differences turn out to be more significant than they might initially appear, since they lead directly to the demotion of Descartes' created substances to the status of attributes of the one genuine substance, which Spinoza identifies with God. One might think that this follows simply from the fact that the former are created, since this undermines their ontological independence. We have seen, however, that Descartes endeavored to avoid this consequence by characterizing a created substance as independent of everything except God – that is, of any other created substance – which is to say that thinking and extended substances are independent of each other. Presumably, then, in order to complete his case for a substance-monism Spinoza thought it necessary to include conceptual as well as ontological independence in his definition of substance. Since Cartesian created substances are conceived through their attribute, not through themselves, they do not satisfy the conceptual independence condition.[6] The essential point, however, is that ontological and conceptual independence are not merely contingently conjoined characteristics of substance for Spinoza, since for him only that which can also be conceived – that is, explained through itself – can also exist in itself, and vice versa.[7]

In addition to entailing Spinoza's substance-monism, by making conceptual independence or explanatory self-sufficiency a criterion of substance, this conception makes it possible for substance to fulfill the function it was evidently intended to but does not actually fulfill in the Cartesian scheme, namely to provide an ultimate ground of explanation, a source of the intelligibility of things. Spinoza's basic assumption, which will be considered in more detail in connection with an analysis of his demonstration of the existence of God, is that only that which is conceived through itself can fulfill this function, because nothing else is capable of providing a resting place for thought, a place where the explanatory buck stops. For the present, however, it suffices to note that what prevents

[6] I am here following the analysis of Curley, *Spinoza's Metaphysics*, 14–15.
[7] See Curley, *Spinoza's Metaphysics*, 15.

Cartesian created substances – that is, particular minds and bodies[8] – from fulfilling this function is their dependence on God, since this precludes attributing to them anything like explanatory self-sufficiency.

The demotion of Cartesian created substances to attributes of the one substance is not, however, the only significant demotion in Spinoza's account. Of equal, if not greater, import is that of Aristotelian primary substances to the status of mere modifications or affections of this substance, which Spinoza identified with God. In fact, this demotion was the focal point of what has historically been the most influential critique of Spinoza's metaphysics, namely that of Pierre Bayle. In what is perhaps the meatiest passage in his lengthy and deeply influential article on Spinoza in his *Historical and Critical Dictionary*, which in typical Baylean fashion is located in a note, he wrote:

> (The most monstrous hypothesis . . . the most diametrically opposed to the most evident notions of our mind.) He supposes that there is only one substance in nature, and that this unique substance is endowed with an infinity of attributes – thought and extension among others. In consequence of this, he asserts that all the bodies that exist in the universe are modifications of this substance insofar as it is extended, and that, for example, the souls of men are modifications of this same substance insofar as it thinks, so that God, the necessary and infinitely perfect being, is indeed the cause of all things that exist, but does not differ from them. There is only one being, and only one nature; and this nature produces in itself by an immanent action all that we call creatures. It is at the same time both agent and patient, efficient cause and subject. It produces nothing that is not its own modification. There is a hypothesis that surpasses all the heap of all the extravagances that can be said. The most infamous things the pagan poets have dared to sing against Venus and Jupiter do not approach the horrible idea that Spinoza gives us of God, for at least the poets did not attribute to the gods all the crimes that are committed and all the infirmities of the world. But according to Spinoza there is no other agent and no other recipient than God, with respect to everything we call evil of punishment and evil of guilt, physical evil and moral evil.[9]

The central text underlying Bayle's critique is E1p15, where Spinoza claims that "Whatever is, is in God, and nothing can be or be conceived without God." In subsequent notes, Bayle develops his critique of this "monstrous hypothesis" by arguing that it entails a threefold absurdity. First, it entails the ascription of contradictory properties to God, e.g., if

---

[8] On the ambiguity in Descartes' account of *res extensa* or material substance, see Chapter 2, note 7.
[9] Bayle, *Historical and Critical Dictionary*, 300–302.

Peter and Paul, as finite modes, are properties of God and Peter loves x and Paul hates x, then God both loves and hates x. Second, it denies that God is immutable, since finite modes, which according to Spinoza's "monstrous hypothesis" are in God, are obviously mutable. Third, since evil is supposedly the product of human actions, if human beings are merely finite modes of God, it makes God responsible for evil. Since addressing the last charge requires a consideration of Spinoza's moral theory, I shall reserve a consideration of it for Chapter 5 and focus here on the first two.

To begin with, it should be clear from the above that the first aspect of Bayle's critique turns on the assumption that the one substance, which Spinoza identified with God, is to be understood according to the model of an Aristotelian primary substance, and that the particular things, including human beings (their minds and their bodies), are demoted to mere qualities, accidents, or properties of this substance, which in the Aristotelian-scholastic terminology adopted by both Descartes and Spinoza became its modes or affections. Given this state of affairs, there appear to be two possible lines of response for a defender of Spinoza against this critique: one can either deny that it depicts Spinoza's actual view or admit that it does, but deny that it has the untoward consequences that Bayle contends.

The former alternative has been forcefully advanced by Edwin Curley, who attempts to avoid these consequences by denying that Spinoza considered finite modes as properties of God, even though his substance-monism entails that there is a sense in which they are "in God."[10] Since Spinoza claims immutability only for God and God's attributes (E1p20c2), this addresses the mutability objection as well. According to Curley,

> Spinoza's modes are, prima facie, of the wrong logical type to be related to substance in the same way as Descartes' modes are, for they are particular things (E1p25c), not qualities. And it is difficult to know what it would mean to say that particular things inhere in a substance. When qualities are said to inhere in a substance, this may be viewed as a way of saying that they are predicated of it. What it would mean to say that one thing is predicated of another is a mystery that needs solving.[11]

In rejecting Bayle's reading of Spinoza and the critique based upon it on the grounds that Spinoza's modes are of "the wrong logical type" to be viewed in the manner assumed by this critique, Curley is implying that this reading attributes a category mistake to Spinoza. Presumably, this is because as properties or qualities predicated of a substance, e.g., Socrates'

[10] Curley, *Spinoza's Metaphysics*, esp. 1–82 and *Behind the Geometrical Method*, 36–39.
[11] Curley, *Spinoza's Metaphysics*, 18.

snubnosedness, modes are universals, while the substances of which they are predicated or in which they inhere are particulars. And since Bayle's entire critique rests on the assumption that Spinoza was guilty of this error and Spinoza is widely recognized as a great philosopher, the principle of charity leads us to reject his reading. But while Curley endorses the principle of charity, he fortunately does not rest his case on it. Instead, he provides an alternative reading in which the relation between substance and the finite modes for Spinoza is that of cause to effect rather than of substance to quality or property. Accordingly, on this reading, E1p15, which underlies Bayle's critique and is generally considered as the quintessential statement of Spinoza's conception of divine immanence or pantheism, is understood as claiming merely that finite modes are in God in the sense of being causally dependent on God, which does not yield the consequences that Bayle avers.

The second line of defense of Spinoza's account of the substance–mode relation against Bayle's critique dismisses Curley's position on the grounds that it fails to do justice to the complexity and distinctiveness of Spinoza's account, since a traditional theist would affirm that all things are causally dependent on God. Here the underlying assumption is that one of the major things that makes Spinoza's philosophy interesting and historically important is that he emphatically rejected the theistic view, which led him to be widely considered an atheist. Instead, this alternative approach bites the bullet by accepting Bayle's premise that Spinoza's conception of substance effectively reduces Aristotelian primary substances, including human beings, to modes or affections of the one substance, while denying both that this entails that Spinoza is guilty of the logical error that Curley maintains he would be, if he construed the finite modes of the one substance as its inherent properties, and that this leads to the horrendous consequences that Bayle drew from it. The response to Curley's worry about particulars being of the wrong logical type to be predicated of substance (whether as properties, qualities, or states) has been addressed by John Carriero, who points out that within the Aristotelian-scholastic framework within which, despite significant deviations, Spinoza operates, there is in fact a recognition of individual accidents of a substance – that is, of accidents as individuals themselves rather than universals – e.g., it is *Socrates'* snubnosedness that is predicated of Socrates, not simply snubnosedness as such or in general.[12]

[12] See Carriero, "On the Relationship between Mode and Substance in Spinoza's Metaphysics," esp. 257–259. This aspect of Carriero's critique of Curley's account is endorsed by Della Rocca, *Spinoza*, 62–63.

The main thrust of this line of response to Bayle's critique, however, consists in the denial of the insidious nature of the consequences of the view that Spinoza's finite modes, including human beings, are in God in the way in which its qualities, states, or properties are in an Aristotelian substance. And while there are considerable differences in the details of this response, their common core is the claim that the thesis that finite modes are in God in this way does not introduce contradiction into Spinoza's conception of God because they are predicated of God qua considered in certain respects, rather than simply of God in an unqualified sense. Perhaps the staunchest advocate of this line of defense is Yitzhak Melamed, who, appealing to Spinoza's ubiquitous use of the modifier "*quatenus*" (insofar as), notes that Spinoza frequently states a thing may have a certain property insofar as it is X and a different or even opposite property insofar as it is Y. To cite Melamed's example: "While God qua Napoleon loves [honey], God qua Josephine hates it."[13] Accordingly, pace Bayle, there would be no contradiction in predicating contradictory properties of God, since they are not predicated of God in the same respect.[14]

Curley's critics are correct in maintaining that it is not necessary to reduce the relation between Spinoza's substance and its finite modes – that is, the view that these modes inhere in this substance as its properties – to that of cause and effect in order to counter Bayle's critique, since the alleged contradiction can be avoided in the manner suggested above. But it is also the case that for Spinoza the inherence relation between God as the one substance and these modes is inseparable from their causal relation, according to which God is their immanent cause (E1p18).[15] Moreover, it is evident from E1a4 ("The cognition of an effect depends on, and involves, the cognition of its cause") that this causal relation, like all such relations for Spinoza, is conceptual in nature.[16] The key text is E1p16, which states that "From the necessity of the divine nature there must follow infinitely many things in infinitely many modes (i.e. everything which can fall under an infinite intellect)." And in the demonstration of this proposition Spinoza writes:

> This proposition must be plain to anyone, provided he attends to the fact that the intellect infers from the given definition of any thing a number of properties

---

[13] Melamed, *Spinoza's Metaphysics*, 35.
[14] In addition to Melamed, those who voice this line of response to Bayle's charge of contradiction include Jarrett, "The Concept of Substance and Mode in Spinoza"; Carriero, "On the Relationship between Mode and Substance"; Della Rocca, *Spinoza*, 65–68; and Nadler, "Substance and Things in Spinoza's Metaphysics," esp. 54–59.
[15] The conception of an immanent cause will be discussed in Section 3.2.
[16] I take it that this is what Della Rocca had in mind when he wrote that "in an important way Curley is right after all." *Spinoza*, 67.

that really do follow necessarily from it (that is from the very essence of the thing); and that it infers more properties the more the definition of the thing expresses reality, that is, the more reality the essence of the thing defined involves.

The definition to which Spinoza here alludes is the previously cited definition of God as "a being absolutely infinite, i.e., a substance consisting of infinite attributes, of which each one expresses an eternal and infinite essence" (E1d6). Setting aside for the moment the notions of attribute and essence, the crucial point is that the necessity that Spinoza has in mind here is logical or conceptual in nature. In case there is any doubt on this matter, Spinoza makes this clear in a scholium to the next proposition, where he writes:

> [F]rom God's supreme power, *or* infinite nature, infinitely many things in infinitely many modes, i.e., all things, have necessarily flowed, or always follow, by the same necessity and in the same way as from the nature of a triangle it follows, from eternity and to eternity, that its three angles are equal to two right angles. (E1p17s)

Since for Spinoza the necessity with which the equality of its three angles follows from the nature of a triangle is logical, the necessity with which things, including finite modes, follow from the nature of God must also be logical. And this, in turn, enables us to see how Spinoza's core thesis of the inherence of all things in God is to be understood, namely in the sense in which the conclusion of a deductive argument follows from its premises. Moreover, pace critics of the causal understanding of the relation between Spinoza's God/substance and its finite modes, this does not blur the distinction between Spinoza's view and traditional theism, since the latter did not conceive of the relation between God and his creation in this way. On the contrary, as will be considered in more detail in Section 3.3, such a theist could hardly accept Spinoza's account of the relation between God and the entities that constitute nature (Spinoza's finite modes), since it undermines the core theistic conception of creation.

It must also be noted, however, that Spinoza's full account of the relation between finite modes and the God in which they inhere and is their immanent cause is far more complex than the above suggests; for though these modes follow necessarily from God for Spinoza, rather than being the products of a free creative act as traditional theism maintains, they do not follow directly. As we shall see in the next section of this chapter, their relation to God is mediated in two distinct ways: first by a series of eternal and infinite modes, which do follow directly from an attribute of God, and second by their relation to other finite modes, which serve as their proximate causes.

However, before examining the actual arguments of the first part of the *Ethics*, it is necessary to consider Spinoza's conception of an attribute and its relationship to the one substance. The conception is essential for Spinoza, as it was for Descartes, because modes are not predicated directly of substance per se, but of substance qua considered under an attribute. Thus, Spinoza cannot make do simply with substance and modes. The distinctiveness of Spinoza's conception of an attribute vis-à-vis Descartes' consists in the fact that he promotes thought and extension, which for Descartes are attributes of the two distinct kinds of created substance to attributes of a single, uncreated substance, i.e., God. The most striking consequence of this is that it makes Spinoza's God an extended being, and a good deal of the argumentation of the first part of the *Ethics* is concerned with his endeavor to explain and justify this highly heterodox view. But of more immediate import is the fact that Spinoza's radical modification of Descartes' position gives rise to two questions, the answers to which are central to his metaphysics. The first concerns the nature of the relationship between the one substance and *any* of its attribute, and the second the nature of the relationship between these attributes. That Spinoza assigns to God not merely a plurality of attributes but an infinite number of them is a third issue; but this, like the attribution of extension to God, will be discussed in the context of the analysis of the propositions of the first part of the *Ethics*.

The question of the relationship between *any* attribute and Spinoza's substance arises directly from his definition of *attribute* as "what the intellect perceives of a substance, as constituting its essence" (E1d4). The problem is that this qualifying phrase is ambiguous, because "perceiving as" ("*percipit*," "*tanquam*") can mean either truly perceiving or perceiving as if constituting its essence.[17] Moreover, this ambiguity has given rise to an ongoing debate in the literature between what are called objectivist and subjectivist interpretations of the relationship between Spinoza's substance and any of its attributes. The former takes Spinoza to mean that an attribute is whatever the intellect *truly* perceives to pertain to or constitute the essence of substance, while the latter takes him to mean what the intellect takes or assumes to pertain to or constitute its essence, with this taking reduced to a merely subjective interpretation or projection by the finite intellect rather than something that pertains to substance as it is in itself.[18]

---

[17] This ambiguity is pointed out by Shein, "Spinoza's Theory of Attributes."
[18] The definitive account of the debate, a focal point of which is Hegel's Spinoza-interpretation, is provided by Gueroult, *Spinoza* I, 428–461.

Since the substance at issue for Spinoza is God, the subjectivist interpretation is motivated by an endeavor to reconcile the unity or, better,
simplicity of God with the assignment of a plurality of attributes. The
model for this way of reading Spinoza is provided by medieval theologians,
most notably Maimonides, who insisted upon the absolute simplicity of
God, which presumably precluded predicating distinct attributes of God.[19]
Spinoza affirms this simplicity, albeit in the guise of an expositor of
Descartes rather than as presenting his own view, when he affirms that
"God is an entirely simple being," on the grounds that God cannot be
considered as composed of parts, since in that case the parts would be prior
in nature to the whole (PPC p17 G177; C260). And he discusses it more
expansively in the appendix to this work, where he argues that the divine
simplicity is preserved on the grounds that the distinctions between God
and any attribute of God, as well as between various attributes of God, are
distinctions of reason drawn by the intellect, rather than real distinctions,
which would be incompatible with the divine simplicity (CM G1 257–259;
C1 323–325). Accordingly, on the subjectivist interpretation, which finds its
strongest textual support in these passages rather than in the *Ethics*,
Spinoza reconciles the simplicity of substance with the diversity of its
attributes by assigning the latter to the human intellect.

By contrast, the objectivist interpretation maintains that the attributes
are distinct aspects of the divine essence; though, for the reasons noted
earlier, they are not parts out of which it is composed. This is reconciled
with divine simplicity, which Spinoza likewise maintains, by taking the
latter to exclude merely the generally discredited compositionalist view.
Given the uncompromisingly rationalistic thrust of Spinoza's thought, it is
not surprising that the objectivist interpretation is favored in the secondary
literature. In fact, it seems to be required by Spinoza's definition of God as
"a substance *consisting of* [my emphasis] an infinity of attributes" (E1d6)
and particularly by his bold claim (to be analyzed in the next chapter) that
"The human mind has an adequate cognition of God's eternal and infinite
essence" (E2p47). In addition, one may also appeal to the demonstration of
E1p4, where Spinoza remarks that "there is nothing outside the intellect
through which a number of things can be distinguished from one another
except substances, *or* what is the same by D4, their attributes and their
affections." Since Spinoza here characterizes the attributes of substance as

---

[19] This medieval model seems to have been the main justification for Wolfson's subjectivist reading of
Spinoza's attributes. See *The Philosophy of Spinoza*, 112–157.

"outside the intellect," this could be taken as decisive evidence for the objectivist interpretation.[20]

Clearly, the main challenge to the objectivist interpretation is to explain how a plurality of distinct attributes, each of which can be conceived independently of the others (if not from the substance to which it is attributed), can be predicated of a single substance, without undermining its simplicity. Spinoza's answer to this challenge lies in the qualifying clause in his definition of God as "a substance consisting of an infinity of attributes, each one of which expresses an eternal and infinite essence" (E1d6). The key term here is "express" (*exprimere*), which Spinoza uses frequently in his accounts of the relationship between substance and its attributes. For example, after claiming in E1p10 that "Each attribute of a substance must be conceived through itself," in a scholium attached to this proposition Spinoza remarks by way of explanation that, "[I]t is of the nature of a substance that each of its attributes is conceived through itself, since all the attributes that it has have always been in it together, and one could not be produced by another, but each expresses the reality or being of substance." Here and elsewhere, by the claim that attributes are expressions of substance I take Spinoza to mean that each attribute exemplifies substance; that is, each is a particular instantiation of it, so that to say that substance has several attributes is to say that it has several different expressions.

Although it is not clear whether he was influenced by Spinoza on this point, it is worth noting that Spinoza's claim that the attributes are different expressions of a single substance has its counterpart in Leibniz's thesis that every monad expresses or represents the universe from a particular point of view.[21] The key difference is that, whereas for Leibniz these different expressions share a fundamental commonality as distinct perspectives on the same rational order of things, which leads him to use the analogy with a mirror to depict the relationship between different monads, for Spinoza, despite being expressions or instantiations of the same substance and therefore rational order, these attributes are considered radically distinct, since they can have nothing in common with one another, which means that "the concept of one does not involve the

---

[20] The relevance of this text to the issue of the objectivity of the attributes was emphasized by Gueroult, *Spinoza* 1, who in addition to providing an overview of the dispute argues for the objectivist reading. In the more recent literature, this passage has been also cited by Melamed in support of the objectivist interpretation of the attributes. See "The Building Blocks of Spinoza's Metaphysics, Substance, Attributes, and Mode," 95.

[21] See, for example, Leibniz, "Discourse on Metaphysics," §16 and "Monadology," §56.

concept of the other" (E1a5). But since Spinoza does not deal thematically
with the issue of the relationship between the only attributes that the
human intellect cognizes, namely thought and extension, until part II of
the *Ethics*, where it underlies his account of the relationship between the
human mind as a finite mode under the attribute of thought and the
human body as a finite mode under the attribute of extension, further
consideration of this important topic will be reserved for the next chapter.

So far we have been concerned mainly with Spinoza's definitions and
axioms in the first part of the *Ethics*, which are foundational for the work as
a whole. We shall now turn to the propositions based upon them. As
previously noted, the initial task, to which the first fifteen propositions are
addressed, is to demonstrate that there can be in the universe only one
substance; that this substance possesses infinite attributes; and that it exists
necessarily. Spinoza proceeds in a systematic manner. The first step is to
argue for the singleness or unicity of substance, which he does by eliminating the two possible forms of substantial pluralism: a plurality of substances with the same nature or attribute and one of substances with
different natures or attributes. As we have seen, Descartes was committed
to both forms of pluralism, since he affirmed both a plurality of thinking
substances or minds and (presumably) of extended substances (or bodies),
while also insisting that these two types of substance have radically distinct
natures.

The argument against the first form of pluralism is contained in E1p4
and E1p5. It turns on the premise that a defense of the thesis that there are
a number of distinct substances of the same kind would require providing
a basis for distinguishing between them. E1p4 specifies the possible bases
for such a distinction. It states that "Two or more distinct things are
distinguished from one another, either by a difference in the attributes of
the substances or by a difference in their affections," which is essentially
a straightforward statement of the substantivalist framework in which
Spinoza, like the Aristotelian-scholastics and Descartes, structured his
metaphysics. Given this, E1p5 then claims that "In nature there cannot
be two or more substances of the same nature or attribute." Because it not
only directly challenges both the Aristotelian-scholastic and Cartesian
conceptions of substance, which allow for a plurality of substances with
the same nature or attribute, but also plays a crucial role in the demonstration of subsequent propositions, this is one of the most important propositions in the first part of the *Ethics*. It proceeds by rejecting both of the
alternatives specified in E1p4. Spinoza summarily dismisses the first alternative on the grounds that there could not be more than one substance

with the same attribute. He rejects the second on the grounds that, since a substance is prior in nature to its affections (by E1p1), "if the affections are put to one side and the substance is considered in itself . . . there cannot be many, but only one [of the same nature or attribute]."

Although Spinoza does not cite any definition, axiom, or proposition in support of the rejection of the first alternative, stating only that "it will be conceded," it seems clear that he is appealing to what since Leibniz has been called the "identity of indiscernibles"; that is, the principle that two substances cannot resemble each other completely and differ only in number.[22] Nevertheless, Spinoza's claim was challenged by Leibniz, who argued that it overlooks the possibility that two (or more) substances might have some attributes in common and others that were distinct, in which case they would be distinguishable and hence distinct. For example, substance A might have attributes x and y; and substance B, attributes y and z.[23] A possible response is to suggest that, at this stage of the argument for substance-monism, Spinoza is assuming a Cartesian framework, which means that he is considering only substances with one attribute. But though the fact that Spinoza fails to consider the possibility posed by Leibniz strongly suggests that he is here considering only substances with a single attribute, resting one's whole defense on this only postpones the day of reckoning, since he appeals again to this proposition in E1p14, where it is clear that it must apply to substances with more than one attribute.[24]

Leibniz's objection, which has become a focal point in the recent literature, concerns only the relationship between the concepts of substances and their attributes and does not mention the affections of these substances. Nevertheless, I believe that the best response to it turns on the rejection of the possibility of setting the affections aside.[25] Admittedly, this may seem wildly counterintuitive, since Spinoza stipulates that the affections should be set aside. But, like the proposition as a whole, this

---

[22] Leibniz, "Discourse on Metaphysics," §9.
[23] See Leibniz, "On the Ethics of Benedict de Spinoza," 305.
[24] As we shall see, in addition to E1p5, E1p14 also appeals to E1p11, which assumes that God is a substance consisting of infinite attributes, each of which expresses eternal and infinite essence and argues for its necessary existence.
[25] Recent commentators who address E1p5 in some detail and offer significantly different analyses and/ or defenses of its argument include Hooker, "The Deductive Character of Spinoza's Metaphysics"; Bennett, *A Study of Spinoza's Ethics*, esp. 66–70; Curley, *Behind the Geometrical Method*, 9–19; Donagan. *Spinoza*, esp. 70–71; Nadler, *Spinoza's Ethics*, 59–63; and most expansively Don Garrett, *Nature and Necessity in Spinoza's Philosophy*, 62–90. My present account of this proposition differs significantly from the one contained in the 1987 version of this book and it at least in part reflects an endeavor to deal with Garrett's criticisms of that account.

stipulation is directed primarily at the Cartesians, and presumably rests on the view that any difference in the affections of two or more substances must rest on a difference in the essences of the underlying substances. In the demonstration of E1p5 Spinoza expresses this obliquely by stating that if one sets the affections aside and considers the substances "truly" – that is, as they are in themselves independently of their affections – they would share the same essence and, therefore, by the identity of indiscernibles, they could not be considered distinct substances. Thus, the setting aside of the affections turns out to be essential to Spinoza's response to the Cartesian view that there are a plurality of distinct substances with the same nature or essence. But since Leibniz's objection to E1p5, which Spinoza did not address and evidently did not anticipate, is quite distinct from the Cartesian response, which he both anticipated and addressed, there would be no inconsistency in appealing to the necessity of not setting the affections aside in addressing the latter. On the contrary, I shall argue that it is precisely by the appeal to the affections of substance that Spinoza could have countered the Leibnizian objection.

To begin with, it seems clear that if we set aside the affections of substance, Leibniz would be correct. For in that case Spinoza could not block the possibility of the predication of the same attribute of two or more substances as the Cartesians maintain. A possible objection might be based on the definition of an attribute as what the intellect perceives as constituting the essence of substance; for then it might be argued that, since attribute x constitutes the essence of substance A, it could not also constitute the essence of substance B, because two distinct substances would then share the same essence, which, setting the affections aside, would render them indistinguishable. But though this works against the Cartesians, it would not suffice against Leibniz, since he could respond that substance A and B would not share the same essence because there is a part of B's essence, namely the part constituted by attribute y, that is not shared by A. Alternatively, it might be claimed that, since attribute x constitutes the essence of substance A, it could not *also* constitute the essence of substance B, since, *ex hypothesi*, the latter also has attribute y, which must likewise constitute its essence, and this would mean that the same substance had two distinct essences. But while this might seem to be a plausible response to Leibniz's objection, it is clearly one that Spinoza could not make, since it conflicts with E1p11, which states that "God, or a substance consisting of infinite attributes, each of which expresses eternal and infinite essence, necessarily exists."

Admittedly, there may be other possible Spinozistic responses to this objection; but the main point is that if we include the affections, Spinoza has the tools for a response to it. Moreover, this response is simple and direct, since it turns on Spinoza's definition of a mode or affection of substance as "that which is in another through which it is understood" (E1d4). The essential point is that the nature of an affection must be understood in terms of the essence of the substance of which it is an affection. Consequently, if there were a difference in the affections of two substances, it must correspond to one in their essences, while if there were no difference in the affections of two substances, there would not be any basis for distinguishing between their essences. And while the former provides the basis for Spinoza's actual response to the anticipated Cartesian objection to E1p5, the latter provides the basis for a possible response to the unanticipated Leibnizian objection.

Having thereby eliminated the possibility of a plurality of substances with the same attribute, Spinoza next considers the possibility of a plurality of substances with different attributes. This possibility is particularly important for Spinoza because it is reflected both in Descartes' distinction between extended and thinking substances, which, apart from their dependence on God, have nothing in common, and in the Aristotelian-scholastic conception of created substance. Spinoza's critique of this alternative has two parts. In the first (E1p8), he attempts to show that no substance can be finite, which eliminates both Aristotelian-scholastic substances and Cartesian created substances (or at least minds). In the second (E1p9–p10), he argues that any substance must be infinite in the absolute or eminent sense; that is, it must consist of "an infinity of attributes, each of which expresses an eternal and infinite essence" (E1d4). Although of itself the latter entails merely that only God, as defined by Spinoza, could count as substance, it enables him to complete his argument for substance-monism by demonstrating that God, or substance, so defined, exists necessarily (E1p11), and that no other substance can either be or be conceived (E1p14).

The first step in this line of argument is E1p6, which claims that "One substance cannot be produced by another substance." The demonstration turns largely on E1p5, which, as we have seen, rules out the possibility of two substances having the same attribute. Given this, together with the propositions that two substances having different attributes would have nothing in common (by E1p2), and that things that have nothing in common cannot be the cause of one another (by E1p3), it follows that there cannot be any causal connection between two substances, much less the creation of one by another. Since according to E1d6 God is a substance consisting of infinite attributes, this concise line of reasoning effectively undermines the Judeo-Christian conception of creation, at least if what is created are considered substances, as they were for both the Aristotelian-scholastics and the Cartesians.

The next step is to show that "It pertains to the nature of a substance to exist" (E1p7), or, equivalently, that "its essence necessarily involves existence." According to Spinoza's extremely cryptic argument, the unique relationship between the essence of a substance and its existence is a direct consequence of the preceding proposition. Since a substance cannot be produced by another substance, he argues that "it will be the cause of itself," which (by E1d1) means that "its essence necessarily involves existence *or* it pertains to its nature to exist." Moreover, Spinoza argues that a cause, or reason, must be assigned not only for the existence but also for the *nonexistence* of anything (E1p11, second proof). Consequently, nothing can simply exist or not exist; either way, there must be a rational ground, or cause, through which its existence or nonexistence is determined and can be understood. Simply put, in the Spinozistic universe there are no brute facts.[26] And in light of this principle, Spinoza reasons that, since substance cannot have the cause or reason for its existence in anything external to itself, for then it would not be substance, it must have it in itself. Substance, therefore, is self-caused, or self-sufficient, being, which entails that existence belongs to its very nature. Here the principle of sufficient reason is taken in its strongest form, since it requires an explanation not only for the existence but also for the nonexistence of a supposedly possible state of affairs.

Spinoza further claims that this entails that "Every substance is necessarily infinite (E1p8). Since by E1p7 existence pertains to the nature of substance, it follows that it must exist as either finite or infinite. The conclusion that it must exist as infinite is arrived at by rejection of the alternative. To assume that substance is finite is to assume that it is limited by something of the same nature, which presumably would also have to exist necessarily. But this contradicts the principle that there cannot be more than one substance with the same attribute. Consequently, substance must exist as infinite. Although it might seem that by showing that existence pertains to the nature of substance and that substance is infinite, Spinoza had already established the basic principle of his substance-monism, this is not the case. Like many

---

[26] This is the central thesis of Della Rocca's *Spinoza*, who argues for the ubiquity in Spinoza of the principle of sufficient reason.

philosophers of his time, Spinoza distinguished between different senses of "infinite."[27] In particular, he distinguished between something being "infinite in its own kind" – that is, nonfinite or unlimited – and something being "absolutely infinite" – that is, all-inclusive or, as Spinoza puts it, having infinite attributes (see the explanation added to E1d6). The former sense pertains to individual attributes and, as we shall see, to certain modes. Although unlimited, things that are infinite in this sense leave room for realities existing outside themselves, which means that they are not infinite in the absolute sense that Spinoza requires in order to make the case for his substance-monism.

Since up to this point the argument has shown only that substance is infinite in the first sense, it remains necessary to prove that it is also infinite in the second or absolute sense. This is needed to eliminate the possibility that there are a number of distinct substances with nothing in common. To put the point somewhat differently, it must be shown that all putatively distinct substances are attributes of a single, all-inclusive substance. Since such a proof is directed explicitly at the Cartesians, it must also deal with their contention that a substance cannot have more than one attribute. The basis for this new argument is the claim that "The more reality or being each thing has the more attributes belong to it" (E1p9). Although in support of this proposition Spinoza merely refers to his definition of "attribute," it is possible to understand his point if we keep in mind the interpretation of Spinozistic attributes as expressions of substance, perspectives from which it can be considered. On this interpretation, the claim that something possesses more reality than something else is equivalent to the claim that there are more perspectives from which it must be viewed, or more descriptions under which it must be taken, if it is to be conceived adequately. For example, consider a simple human action such as the raising of an arm. Presumably, one could give a complete neurophysiological account of this action in terms of impulses sent to and from the brain, the contraction of muscles, and so forth. But no matter how detailed the description, it could never exhaust the reality of the action; indeed, one could never even come to understand it as an action (as opposed to a mere bodily movement). For to understand it as such requires, or at least is generally thought to require, a psychological description in terms of the beliefs, intentions, desires, and so on of an agent. In that sense, then, there

---

[27] Spinoza's fullest discussion of the topic is in his famous letter to Meyer entitled "On the Nature of the Infinite," Letter 12, G4 52–62; C1, 200–205. An English translation of Gueroult's authoritative account of this letter (*Spinoza I*, 500–528) is provided in *Spinoza: A Collection of Critical Essays*, 182–212.

is "more reality" to an action than can be given by a purely neurophysiological account, no matter how complete. And for Spinoza this "greater reality" is understood as the possession of a greater number of attributes.

Continuing this line of argument, it follows that a being that possessed all reality (the *ens realissimum* of the tradition) could be described from every conceivable perspective, each of which, in Spinoza's language, would yield an expression of its "eternal and infinite essence." Consequently, though Spinoza does not argue explicitly this way, he could claim at this point that the Cartesian must either admit that a single substance could possess more than one attribute or deny the possibility of an *ens realissimum*. The orthodox Cartesian could not opt for the latter alternative, since this would amount to atheism; but nothing said so far seems to preclude the possibility that a more radical champion of the one substance–one attribute doctrine might deny God's existence in this way.[28] In order to block this possibility, Spinoza must, therefore, establish the existence of an *ens realissimum* and prove that it is the only substance.

Before turning to this, however, it is necessary to say a word about the controversial topic of the infinite attributes. The systematic function of this conception in Spinoza's argument for his substance-monism is clear: it precludes the possibility of a plurality of substances with different attributes. Since a substance with infinite attributes would possess all conceivable attributes, there would be none available for any other substance. Combining this with the proposition already examined that no two substances can share an attribute, it follows that the possibility of any other substance (apart from the *ens realissimum*) has been eliminated. This is the explicit argument of E1p14, which states that "Except God, no substance can be or be conceived." The crucial point, however, is that the argument requires merely that Spinoza's substance possess all conceivable attributes, so that "infinite" here serves as the functional equivalent of "all." Moreover, it has been noted in the literature that this argument for substance-monism is compatible with the possibility that there are only two attributes, namely thought and extension, which are the only attributes with which Spinoza maintains that we are acquainted.[29] But despite this and certain difficulties it creates for his epistemology and theory of mind (to be considered in the next chapter), there is considerable textual evidence that Spinoza believed that there were more than two attributes.[30]

---

[28] This was noted by Donagan, "Essence and the Distinction of Attributes," 173.
[29] This is argued by Bennett in support of his "dualistic" reading of Spinoza: *Spinoza's Ethics*, 75–79.
[30] See the KV appendix 2 (G1 114–116; C1 50–152) and the correspondence with Schuller and Tschirnhaus, Letters 63–66 and 70 (G4 274–280; C2 435–441).

In any event, Spinoza's next task is to establish the existence of an *ens realissimum*. This is attempted in EIp11, which states that "God or a substance consisting of infinite attributes, each of which expresses eternal and infinite essence, necessarily exists." In support of this claim, Spinoza provides four proofs modeled after arguments for the existence of God found in Descartes and other philosophers; though, given the unorthodox nature of Spinoza's God, these proofs are put to a rather different purpose. I shall focus only on the first two, however, since these are the most important, whereas the latter two were clearly regarded by Spinoza as supplementary rather than essential.[31]

The first of these proofs is Spinoza's unique version of the ontological argument, which was first developed by St. Anselm and later reformulated by Descartes. The distinctive feature of this famous argument is that it attempts to derive the necessity of the divine existence from the mere concept of God. One of the many difficulties with this argument in its various formulations is that it is often not clear whether what is being claimed is merely that it is necessarily true that God exists (a *de dicto* necessity), or that God exists in a unique way, namely necessarily (a *de re* necessity). Descartes' version invites the first reading. He maintains that it is necessary that God exist on the grounds that "existence can no more be separated from the essence of God than the fact its three angles equal to two right angles can be separated from the essence of a triangle, or the idea of a mountain can be separated from the idea of a valley."[32] This contention is based on the definition of God as an all-perfect being and the assumption, which has often been challenged, that existence is a perfection. If existence is a perfection (or, as it is sometimes put, a [real] predicate) and God (by definition) possesses all perfections, we cannot, without contradiction, deny God's existence, which is equivalent to saying that it is necessarily true that God exists.

Spinoza's version of this argument makes reference neither to the notion of perfection, which he equates with reality (E4 Preface), nor the definition

---

[31] The third proof, which Spinoza characterizes as a posteriori (understood in the traditional sense meaning proceeding from effects to causes, rather than the now familiar Kantian sense as proceeding on the basis of experience), turns on the principle that existence is a power and lack of existence a lack of power. From this Spinoza reasons that if only finite beings were to exist, then they would be more powerful than an absolutely infinite being, which he dismisses as absurd. In the fourth proof, which is contained in a scholium and, therefore, presumably assigned a merely supplementary role, Spinoza argues that God's existence follows from the same foundation as in the third proof, namely that being able to exist is a power. For a detailed analysis of the four proofs see Garrett, *Nature and Necessity in Spinoza's Philosophy*, 31–61.

[32] Descartes, *Meditations on First Philosophy, Philosophical Works*, vol. 2, 46.

of God, and the necessity that it affirms is clearly of the *de re* variety. Instead, it simply draws the logical consequence of the already established principle that "It pertains to the nature of a substance to exist" (E1p7) and applies it to the conception of substance, which by means of E1p8, p9, and p10 has been enriched to that of an *ens realissimum* and is here equated with God. Moreover, since the demonstration is essentially parasitic upon E1p7, like that proposition, it really turns on the principle of sufficient reason, which, having already been applied to anything that may be considered as substance (the genus), is now applied to the conception of substance at which Spinoza has arrived by the subsequent argumentation (the species).

Whereas the principle of sufficient reason was latent in the first proof of the existence of God, in the second it occupies center stage. Applying this principle, Spinoza claims that a cause or reason (these being taken as equivalent) must be assigned for either the existence or the nonexistence of a thing, and that it must be found either outside the thing or within its own nature. As examples of things whose cause or reason for existence are found outside their natures, Spinoza cites the mathematical examples of a triangle and a circle, where the cause or reason for their existence is attributed to "the order of the whole of corporeal nature." And as an example of something whose nonexistence follows from its nature, he cites that of a square circle, which does not exist because its very nature involves a contradiction.[33] Applying this line of reasoning to God, understood as an absolutely infinite and supremely perfect being – that is, as *ens realissimum* – Spinoza argues that any cause or reason for the nonexistence of God, so defined, would have to be either in God or in a substance of another nature. The latter alternative is ruled out in two steps. First Spinoza notes that a substance of another nature than God would, *ex hypothesi*, have nothing in common with God; then, invoking E1p3, he concludes that things that have nothing in common cannot stand in a causal relation. The former alternative is summarily dismissed on the grounds that, unlike a figure that is both square and circular, it would be absurd to suppose that an absolutely infinite and supremely perfect being – that is, an *ens realissimum* – could harbor a contradiction. And having thus ruled out the possibility of a cause of the nonexistence of God, so defined, Spinoza concludes that God necessarily exists.

---

[33] The *de re* or metaphysical nature of Spinoza's account is evident from the fact that the contradiction is not said to lie in the concept of a square circle but in its very nature. Given the identity of the order and connection of ideas and of things, this contradiction would apply to the idea/concept, but only because the contradiction already lies in the thing itself.

Although it as an open question whether Kant had Spinoza in mind, I believe that the above-considered proofs for the necessary existence of God or substance fall prey to his critique of the argument for an *ens realissimum* in his discussion of the Ideal of Pure Reason in the *Critique of Pure Reason*.[34] The main point of Kant's critique, which is all that is possible to consider here, is that by characterizing his target as *the ideal* rather than an *idea* of pure reason, Kant endeavored to make the point that the *ens realissimum* is taken as a higher-order individual. Simply put, the problem is that the positing of such an individual is the result of the illicit transformation, or what Kant calls the "hypostatization," of the *omnitudo realitas* or all of reality, into an *ens realissimum*.[35] Expressed in non-Kantian terms, this could be characterized as a category mistake in which one moves surreptitiously from the claim that every occurrence or state of affairs in nature has a sufficient cause or reason for its existence to the claim that nature as a whole must likewise have such a cause of reason for its existence. And since, *ex hypothesi*, there is nothing outside nature that could be the cause of its existence, it must be self-caused or *causa sui*.

To stop at this point, however, would ignore not only the full "critical" thrust of Kant's critique of the argument for the necessary existence of an *ens realissimum*, but also what he considered might be termed "the moment of truth" in this argument, a form of which he himself once endorsed.[36] For present purposes, the essential point is that for Kant a conclusion, such as the one Spinoza arrived at on the basis of the principle of sufficient reason, is not simply a garden-variety error that can simply be set aside, after which the metaphysician can proceed with business as usual. Rather, this fallacy is grounded in what for Kant is an unavoidable illusion ("transcendental illusion"), which is inseparable from the use of reason (as distinct from the understanding) in its explanatory role. According to Kant, this illusion is the result of the appeal in the explanation of phenomena to the require-ment of reason: "find the unconditioned for the conditioned cognitions of the understanding, with which its unity will be completed" (CPR A307/

---

[34] That this was Kant's target is the thesis of Boehm's *Kant's Critique of Spinoza*. According to Boehm, Kant was committed to Spinozism already in his 1763 essay *The Only Possible Basis for the Existence of God*, in which he defended the very argument for an *ens realissimum* that he criticizes in the *Critique of Pure Reason*. I discuss this essay, albeit without relating its argument to Spinoza, in *Kant's Transcendental Deduction*, 23–31 and in more detail in *Kant's Conception of Freedom*, 55–73. I analyze Kant's explicit criticisms of Spinoza in my paper "Kant's Critique of Spinoza."

[35] See CPR A580–583/B608–661.

[36] The major text in which Kant not only develops but defends this line of argument is his essay, *The Only Possible Basis for a Demonstration of the Existence of God* (1763). For my analysis of this argument see *Kant's Transcendental Deduction*, 23–31 and *Kant's Conception of Freedom*, 55–72.

B364), which might be characterized as the intellectual categorical imperative. As a requirement of reason, there is nothing illusory or fallacious in
this rule itself. The problem lies rather in the metaphysical, as contrasted
with the merely logical, use of this rule; that is, in an attempt to use it as
a principle for the explanation of nature. For in using it in this manner it is
necessary to assume that "[W]hen the conditioned is given, then so is the
whole series of conditions subordinated one to the other, which is itself
unconditioned, also given (i.e., contained in the object and its connection)" (CPR A307–308/B364). Moreover, in so doing one unavoidably
makes the above-mentioned category mistake.

Once again, I am not claiming that Kant had Spinoza specifically
in mind when he formulated this critique of the argument for an *ens
realissimum*, since I believe that he had a broader target, which
prominently included his own earlier view. Nevertheless, I think it
evident that this critique does address in a powerful way the core of
Spinoza's argument in a telling fashion. In fact, I think it fair to
claim that in appealing to the principle of sufficient reason in both of
the arguments sketched above, Spinoza is taking it as warranting the
inference that when the conditioned is given, the totality of conditions and with it the unconditioned is likewise given in the sense of
being inferable through reason, which for Kant is precisely to suc-
cumb to transcendental illusion.

This does not mean, however, as Hume famously put it, that we
should "[c]ommit … to the flames" Spinoza's argument because it
"contain[s] nothing but sophistry and illusion."[37] To begin with, since
it is endemic to the theoretical use of reason (as distinct from the
understanding), transcendental illusion, as understood by Kant, is
quite distinct from the species of illusion summarily dismissed by
Hume. Moreover, even if the force of this objection is acknowledged,
it must at least be recognized that Spinoza's argument answers what
many philosophers, including Kant, have considered a deep metaphysical need for something that both serves as the ultimate ground or
condition on the basis of which everything else can be explained and
is itself unconditioned in the sense of being self-grounded or

---

[37] Hume, *An Enquiry Concerning Human Understanding*, 211. In this famous concluding passage to the
Enquiry Hume was not, of course, referring explicitly or solely to Spinoza, since he levels this
dismissal at all works that contain neither "abstract reasoning concerning quantity or number or
experimental reasoning concerning matter of fact or existence." It is clear, however, from what he
says about the "hideous hypothesis" of Spinoza in the *Treatise of Human Nature* (1.4.5 159) that he
included him in this dismissal.

explanatorily self-sufficient.[38] Most philosophers in the Western philo-sophical tradition have found such an unconditioned condition in God the creator. We have seen that Spinoza repudiated this concep-tion of God as a figment of the imagination; but neither his rational-istic method nor his concern for a true and lasting good allowed him to stop there. It was not enough for him simply to show that nature, conceived under the category of substance, cannot possibly depend on a transcendent God and that there are no brute facts in nature. He likewise could not accept the view that nature as a whole, i.e., the universe, is itself a higher-order brute fact, for this would in effect introduce contingency at the very heart of things, which would not only render nature unintelligible, but in so doing undermine any possibility of human beings achieving a lasting good, which consists for Spinoza in the intellectual love of a God that is identified with the necessary order of nature.[39]

Moreover, if nature is not just there, so to speak – if its order, from which all things necessarily follow, is itself a necessary order – then it must be the only conceivable order. When reason recognizes this, all questions cease; for to see that no alternative is even conceivable, that the matter could not possibly have been otherwise, is to understand in the fullest possible sense. Consequently, we should not be surprised to find Spinoza claiming, after two propositions dealing with the indivisibility of sub-stance, that "Except God, no substance can be or be conceived" (E1p14). The importance of this proposition in the argument for substance-monism and its reliance on a proper interpretation of E1p5 has already been noted. In the present context, the emphasis is on the addendum that another substance cannot even be *conceived*. If we keep in mind what we have already learned about substance in Spinoza, we can see that he is here providing the strongest possible affirmation of the rationality and necessity of the order of nature. The only remaining question concerns the all-inclusiveness of this order; that is, whether there may be things or events (presumably not substances) that somehow stand outside it and are not subject to its laws. Spinoza answers this question in E1p15, where he asserts

[38] The "critical" Kant evidently recognized this point when he wrote that "The ideal of the highest being is, according to these considerations, nothing other than a *regulative principle* of reason, to regard all combination in the world *as if* it arose from an all-sufficient cause, so as to ground on that cause the rule of a unity that is systematic and necessary; but is not an assertion of an existence that is necessary in itself (CPR A619/B647). Boehm, *Kant's Critique of Spinoza*, 7 and passim cites this passage in support of his thesis that the "critical" Kant was committed to a "regulative Spinozism."

[39] In "Kant's Critique of Spinoza," 218–220, I note that in the *Critique of the Power of Judgment* Kant explicitly criticizes Spinoza for his denial of any contingency in nature.

that "Whatever is, is in God, and nothing can be or be conceived without God." Given the argument up to this point, this claim does not require any further analysis.

3.2   Divine Causality and the Modal System

With the above proposition, we have arrived at the decisive expression of Spinoza's substance-monism. Nothing exists or can even be conceived to exist apart from this one, self-contained system, which may be characterized as God, substance, or nature. Nevertheless, the very formulation of this thesis involves a dualism of sorts. In giving up the distinction between God *and* nature, we are forced to distinguish between two aspects of God *or* nature. For Spinoza, this is understood as the distinction between God *or* nature, as the self-sufficient source of things and their intelligibility, and the same God *or* nature as the system of particular things that are dependent on and conceived through this source. Spinoza terms the first of these two aspects *natura naturans* (active, or generating, nature), and the second *natura naturata* (passive, or generated, nature). The former refers to God as conceived through himself – that is, as substance with an infinity of attributes – and the latter to the modal system, which is conceived through these attributes (P29S). Furthermore, this distinction within God or nature entails a similar distinction with regard to divine causality. In his treatment of this subject, Spinoza first considers this causality as it is in itself – that is, in its inherent nature as *natura naturans* (E1p16–p20) – and then as it is expressed in the modal system, as *natura naturata* (E1p21–p29).

Spinoza establishes the essential features of his theory of divine causality at the very beginning of his analysis. "From the necessity of the divine nature," he asserts, "there must follow infinitely many things in infinitely many modes, i.e., everything which can fall under an infinite intellect" (E1p16). With this Spinoza determines both the nature of the divine causality, or power, affirming that it operates through the "necessity of the divine nature," and its extent, maintaining that it not only produces "infinitely many things in infinitely many modes" – that is, an infinite number of things, each of which is reflected in each of the infinite attributes – but that it also includes "everything which can fall under an infinite intellect"; that is, everything conceivable. By locating the power of God in the "necessity of the divine nature," Spinoza is not only rejecting any appeal to the "will of God" as a causal force, he is also conceiving of the causal relation between God and the world in terms of the model of the logical relation between ground and consequent. This reflects Spinoza's equation of causes and reasons and it means that God for Spinoza is at once the logical ground and the unconditioned cause of the series of finite modes. As we have seen, things follow from the nature of God in the same way as the conclusion of a valid deductive argument follows from its premises. Indeed, such a conception of causality is not only consistent with but is actually required by Spinoza's deductive model of explanation. If genuine knowledge involves the realization of the necessary consequences of our adequate ideas, and if these ideas are themselves ultimately grounded in the idea of God, then these same ideas are derivable from the idea of God as conclusions from a premise. Moreover, since "A true idea must agree with its object" (E1a6), if this logical chain of reasoning is to be something more than a consistent dream, it must reflect the structure of reality.

In light of the above considerations, it is understandable why Spinoza bases his demonstration of the infinite extent of the divine causality on his theory of definition. From the proper definition of a thing, Spinoza reasons, it should be possible to infer several properties of that thing. Furthermore, the more reality the essence of the thing defined involves, the more properties can be derived from its definition. This contention was questioned by perhaps his most astute correspondent, Ehrenfried Walter von Tschirnhaus, who claimed on the basis of geometrical examples that from the definition of a thing taken alone, only one property can be deduced (L82 G4 333; C2 486). Spinoza responded by granting that this may be true with regard to "the most simple things" or to "things of reason" (including geometrical figures), but that it does not apply to "real things." Spinoza endeavors to illustrate the fecundity of the latter species of definition by noting the possibility of deriving several properties such as necessary existence, immutability, infinity, and uniqueness from the definition of God as a "Being to whose essence belongs existence" (L83 G4 334–335; C2 365). Spinoza is here invoking the same conception of degrees of reality that he utilized in his argument for an infinity of attributes. Given this conception, which identifies a thing's degree of reality with the number of attributes it possesses, it follows that the more reality a thing has, the greater the number of consequences that can be derived from its definition. And since it has been established that God has an infinity of attributes, it follows that an infinite number of things must necessarily follow from the divine nature.

The subsequent propositions in this section specify more precisely the nature of divine causality. Spinoza first argues that "God acts from the laws of his nature alone, and is compelled by no one" (E1p17). As the demonstration indicates, the assertion that God acts from the laws of his nature means precisely the same as the claim just established that things follow from the necessity of the divine nature. The further qualification, that God acts *only* in this manner and is compelled by no one, follows from the proposition that there is nothing outside God. Thus, Spinoza concludes that nothing could possibly move God to act "except the perfection of his own nature" (E1p17c1); and that "God alone is a free cause" (E1p17c2). The latter point reflects Spinoza's definition of *free* as what is self-determined (E1d7). Continuing his analysis, Spinoza next claims that "God is the immanent, not the transitive, cause of things" (E1p18). A transitive, or transient, cause is one that is separable from its effects, whereas an immanent cause is inseparable. Thus, by characterizing divine causality in this manner, Spinoza underscores the point that God (*natura naturans*) is not a being distinct from nature (*natura naturata*), but the immanent ground of its intelligibility.

A traditional theological doctrine that Spinoza does retain, albeit in a manner consistent with his own views, is that "God is eternal, or all God's Attributes are eternal" (E1p19). The crux of the demonstration is the definition of eternity as "existence itself, insofar as it is conceived to follow necessarily from the definitions alone of the eternal thing" (E1d8). In his explanation of this definition, Spinoza notes that "eternity" here means essentially necessary existence, so that the existence of something eternal is itself an "eternal truth"; that is, a logically necessary truth. Moreover, eternity, so construed, is absolutely opposed to time or duration, even though the latter may "be conceived without a beginning or end." The eternity of God is, therefore, conceived as the logical consequence of his necessary existence, rather than being construed imaginatively as endless duration. And since the attributes express the "essence of the divine substance," they likewise are eternal in precisely the same sense.

On the basis of the above proposition, Spinoza concludes his analysis of *natura naturans* with the assertion that "God's existence and his essence are one and the same" (E1p20). This is another traditional theological formula and Spinoza uses it to make the point that God does not just happen to exist. Not only does existence follow from God's nature, but God's very nature or essence is to exist. For Spinoza, this is really nothing more than another expression of the eternity of God, but he draws two consequences from it: first, that the existence of God is an eternal truth – that is, a logically necessary truth (E1p20c1) – and, second, that "God *or* all of God's attributes, are immutable" (E1p20c2). Consequently, any change in God's mode of existence would also be a change in the divine nature. And if God could change in this manner, he would no longer be God.

Traditionally, this doctrine has been used to prove that God does not change his mind; that the divine decrees are inviolable. But for Spinoza, for whom God is identical with the order of nature, and the "decrees of God" are equivalent to the laws of nature, the unchangeableness of God really means nothing more than the unchangeableness and necessity of these laws.

This doctrine of the eternity and immutability of God both completes the discussion of *natura naturans* and serves as a transition to *natura naturata*, the modal system that exists in and is conceived through God. Spinoza's treatment of this theme seems to have been explicitly modeled on the theory of emanation, which was developed by Neoplatonic philosophers and their medieval followers in the Jewish, Christian, and Islamic traditions.[40] Expressed in its simplest terms, this theory held that the universe "flowed," or followed, from God in a series of necessary stages, beginning with immaterial beings such as the "intelligences," and ending with the material world. This notion of the progression, or emanation, of things, and especially of the material world, from God was intended to provide an alternative to both the orthodox theory of creation, according to which the material world was created by God *ex nihilo*, and the kind of dualism advocated by the Gnostics, which allowed for a preexisting matter out of which the world was fashioned. The problem with the first view is that it does not explain how something finite and allegedly "imperfect" (matter) could be produced by an infinite and perfect deity. The difficulty with the second view is that it grants to matter an existence independent of God (thereby denying divine omnipotence). By making matter ultimately dependent on God, yet conceiving of this dependence as mediated by several stages, and thus as indirect, the emanationists hoped to overcome the difficulties of both alternatives.

Spinoza, as we have seen, likewise rejected the doctrine of creation, as well as any view that would grant either matter or the material world an existence independent of God, which essentially reduces God to the Platonic demiurge. Furthermore, he can be said to have viewed the relationship between *natura naturans* and *natura naturata* in terms of emanation, albeit with the quasi-mythical notion of "flowing" replaced by the strictly logical relationship of ground and consequent. This view is expressed in his highly complex and often obscure theory of infinite and eternal modes, which in contrast to other aspects of his metaphysics does not seem to have had any immediate medieval or scholastic predecessors.

[40] See Wolfson, *Philosophy of Spinoza*, vol. 1, 331–346.

Unlike the emanationists, however, Spinoza did not use his doctrine as a device to connect an infinite God with a world of finite things, since he did not consider them to be essentially distinct. Instead, his theory of modes offers both an explanation of the relationship between the basic principles and categories of scientific explanation and the order of nature (as expressed in the attributes of thought and extension) and an account of how finite things express and are related to this order.

Modes, it will be recalled, were defined by Spinoza as "affections of a substance, *or* that which is in another through which it is also conceived." A mode is, therefore, by definition, a dependent being, and what it depends on is God or substance. But not all modes depend on God in the same way or have the same status. Spinoza's first concern is to establish the eternity and infinity of modes that follow directly from God. To this end he writes: "All the things which follow from the absolute nature of any of God's attributes have always had to exist and be infinite, or are, through the same attribute, eternal and infinite" (E1p21). The point is that whatever follows directly from God partakes to some extent of the nature of that from which it follows. Such modes must, therefore, like substance, or, more precisely, an attribute of substance, be eternal and infinite. Yet they obviously cannot be eternal and infinite in precisely the same way as substance, for this would mean that they were themselves substances. Spinoza indicates this difference by asserting that they are eternal and infinite through an attribute; that is, in virtue of their cause. And he further maintains that this holds not only for modes that follow immediately from some attribute of God, but also for modes that follow directly from these; that is, those that are "modified by a modification, which, through the same attribute, exists necessarily and is infinite" (E1p22). Spinoza thus distinguishes between "immediate" and "mediate" eternal and infinite modes, with the former derived directly from an attribute, and the latter directly from the former (E1p23).

Unfortunately, Spinoza gives us precious little information about these modes. The only one explicitly referred to in the *Ethics* is "God's idea," or the "idea of God" (*idea Dei*) (E1p21d), which is presumably equivalent to the previously mentioned infinite intellect. In the KV Spinoza mentions two: "motion" in the attribute of extension and "intellect" in the attribute of thought.[41] He is a bit more expansive, however, in response to a query on this point by his friend Schuller, where he distinguishes between the immediate and the mediate eternal and infinite modes. As examples of

---

[41] KV, part I, chapter IX, GI 48, C 92.

the former he gives "motion and rest" in the attribute of extension and "absolutely infinite intellect" in the attribute of thought. The only example he provides of the latter is the "face of the whole universe" (*facies totius universi*), which pertains to extension, and of which he states: "although it varies in infinite modes, yet remains always the same" (L64, G4 278; C2 439).

Of somewhat greater help for an understanding of Spinoza's doctrine is his account in the TdIE of the "fixed and eternal things," which are generally regarded as equivalent to the eternal and infinite modes of the *Ethics*. Spinoza's concern there is with the proper ordering of our ideas; and his main point is that they must be deduced from "true causes," or "real beings," as opposed to abstract universals such as the genera and species of Aristotelian-scholastic science. He is careful to point out, however, that by "real things" he does not mean the objects of ordinary experience – that is, "the series of singular changeable things" – but, rather, "the series of fixed and eternal things." An empirical approach, which would attempt to ground knowledge in the former, is rejected as both impossible and unnecessary. It is impossible because this series is infinite in both extent and complexity, which would mean that the human intellect could never arrive at adequate knowledge of any particular thing by tracing its causal ancestry. It is unnecessary because the essence, or true nature, of these things is accessible in a different manner. According to Spinoza:

> That essence is to be sought only from the fixed and eternal things, and at the same time from the laws inscribed in these things, as in their true codes, according to which all singular things come to be, and are ordered. Indeed, these singular, changeable things depend so intimately and (so to speak) essentially, on the fixed things that they can neither be nor be conceived without them. (TdIE G2 36–37; C1 41)

As this passage makes clear, Spinoza's claim is that we can only arrive at adequate knowledge of particular things through, and in terms of, the series of fixed and eternal things. His highly metaphorical characterization of these things as "codes" in which the laws of nature are inscribed calls attention to their status as ultimate principles, or categories, of scientific explanation. It may seem strange that Spinoza should here characterize these principles as "things" and later, in the *Ethics*, as "modes"; but he presumably did this to underscore their difference from Aristotelian class concepts. The latter, as we shall see in the next chapter, are viewed as mere products of the imagination, without adequate basis in the nature of things. The fixed and eternal things, by contrast, are more real than the particular things, since they are the source of the very essences of these things in the sense that they are that in terms of which their natures are to be understood. As such, they are rather like what Hegel later called "concrete universals"; that is, universals that, as unique wholes, contain the particulars within themselves.[42] At least, Spinoza suggests as much when he writes: "So although these fixed and eternal things are singular, nevertheless, because of their presence everywhere, and most extensive power, they will be to us like universals, *or* genera of the definitions of singular, changeable things, and the proximate causes of all things" (TdIE G2 36–37; CI 41).

This extremely schematic account is made more intelligible by a consideration of the designated eternal and infinite modes of extension. As Spinoza makes clear in his account of the elements of corporeal nature in the *Ethics*, each particular body is conceived of in terms of its proportion of motion and rest.[43] This, in turn, is tantamount to claiming that "motion and rest" functions as a basic category of scientific explanation, which is perfectly in accord with Galilean-Cartesian physics. Furthermore, by giving it the status of an eternal and infinite mode, Spinoza was endeavoring to overcome a basic difficulty in Cartesian physics. Having identified matter with extension, Descartes concluded that it could not contain a principle of motion (force) and hence of individuation within itself. Consequently, he found it necessary to introduce the action of God in order to explain the origin of motion and the division of matter into distinct bodies. We have seen that such a view was completely unacceptable to Spinoza; and his conception of motion and rest as derived directly from the attribute of extension (which follows from its status as an eternal and infinite mode) can be understood as his attempt to correct this aspect of Cartesian physics.[44]

The "face of the whole universe" can be understood in a similar manner. As a mediate eternal and infinite mode of extension, it follows directly from motion and rest. Like all eternal and infinite modes, motion and rest is immutable; but since the proportion of motion and rest in particular regions of corporeal nature is constantly changing, this immutability can hold only of corporeal nature as a whole, which Spinoza identifies with the "face of the whole universe." Consequently, it is in terms of this holistic

---

[42] For a useful and informative account of the Hegelian conception of a concrete universal, see Stern, *Hegelian Metaphysics*, esp. 143–176.

[43] This account is located in a series of lemmata located between propositions 13 and 14 of part II. The topic will be discussed in the next chapter.

[44] See Joachim, *Ethics of Spinoza*, 84–85, and Gueroult, *Spinoza* I, 324.

conception that Spinoza endeavors to "deduce" the principle of the conservation of motion, which is a basic principle of Cartesian physics.[45]
Moreover, in the portion of the *Ethics* to which Spinoza refers Schuller
with regard to this conception, he argues that precisely because it maintains
a constant proportion of motion and rest, corporeal nature as a whole can
be regarded as a distinct individual "whose parts, i.e., all bodies, vary in
infinite ways, without any change of the whole Individual" (E2p13l7s). And
since it is identical with corporeal nature as a whole, the same may be said
of the face of the whole universe. Accordingly, like the other fixed and
eternal things, the latter must be conceived as a "universal individual," or,
in Hegelian terms, a concrete universal, which includes its particulars
within itself and in terms of which these particulars must be understood.

The doctrine of eternal and infinite modes, which is constructed on the
basis of a few hints scattered throughout a variety of texts, raises problems
enough in its own right. Certainly, many (but not all) contemporary
philosophers would have difficulty with the idea that the fundamental
laws of nature have the kind of necessity Spinoza ascribes to them by
linking them directly to the attributes of God. The most problematic
feature of Spinoza's account, however, concerns his attempt to connect
this general framework with the particular things, processes, and events in
nature; that is, the series of finite modes. The basic problem can be
formulated in either metaphysical or scientific terms. Speaking metaphysically, it is clear that for Spinoza, particulars, or finite modes, cannot be
derived directly from either the attributes or the eternal and infinite modes,
because they then would themselves be eternal and infinite. Speaking
scientifically, it is equally clear that particular occurrences cannot be
deduced solely from a set of universal principles and laws. Consequently,
Spinoza must explain how, in spite of this, particulars (finite modes) do,
nonetheless, depend on God and in some sense participate in the divine
necessity.

Spinoza begins his attempt to deal with this problem by noting that
"The essence of things produced by God does not involve existence"
(E1p24), and that "God is the efficient cause, not only of the existence of
things, but also of their essence" (E1p25). The first of these propositions
follows from the analysis of what it means to claim that the essence of
something involves existence, namely that it is self-caused (E1d1). Given
this, it is self-contradictory to say of something both that it is produced
by God and that its essence involves existence. The second proposition is

---

[45] See Höffding, *Spinozas Ethica*, 41ff.

equally clear. Its negation entails that the essences of things could be conceived apart from God, which contradicts the theorem that "Whatever is, is in God, and nothing can be or be conceived without God" (E1p15). Moreover, from the second claim, Spinoza infers that "Particular things are nothing but affections of God's attributes or modes by which God's attributes are expressed in a certain determinate way" (E1p25c). This is the first explicit reference to particular things, or finite modes, in the argument. Its significance is not immediately apparent, however, because instead of developing his account of such modes, Spinoza continues with his general account of the divine causality. Thus, he argues that everything that has been determined to act in a certain way must have been so determined by God, and that anything that has not been so determined cannot determine itself (E1p26). Correlatively, once determined, a being cannot render itself undetermined (E1p27). Only after completing the outlines of his general account of the dependence of all things on God does Spinoza return to the problem of the specific nature of the dependence of finite modes or "singular things" modes. He writes:

> Every singular thing, or any thing which is finite and has a determinate existence, can neither exist nor be determined to produce an effect unless it is determined to exist and produce an effect by another cause, which is also finite and has a determinate existence; and again, this cause also can neither exist nor be determined to produce an effect unless it is determined to exist and produce an effect by another, which is also finite and has a determinate existence, and so on, to infinity. (E1p28)

At first glance, this picture of an infinite causal chain of individual things, which never gets back to God as its starting point, seems to contradict the doctrine of the dependence of all things on God. But this contradiction is only apparent. First, since each of these things is a finite mode, in depending on other finite modes it is still depending on God, albeit on God qua modified in a determinate way. Second, since each individual thing, as a "modification of a modification," is an instantiation of a general law, or principle (an eternal and infinite mode), it is also the case that each is governed by these general laws, or principles, and therefore ultimately by God.

The upshot of the matter is that, within the arcane metaphysical framework in which Spinoza presents his doctrine of divine causality, there is at least the outline of a thoroughly modern conception of nature and of scientific explanation.[46] According to this conception, every natural

---

[46] See Curley, *Spinoza's Metaphysics*, chap. 2.

occurrence or event is understood in terms of two intersecting lines of explanation: a set of general laws, which for Spinoza are logically necessary (since they are derived from the attributes and eternal and infinite modes of God), and a chain of antecedent conditions, which instantiate these laws and serve as the causes of subsequent occurrences. For example, in order to explain the phenomenon of thunder, it is obviously necessary to appeal to the laws of physics, but these laws alone cannot explain the occurrence of a particular clap of thunder at a particular time.[47] This requires that we refer also to the antecedent state of the atmosphere. Nevertheless, given the appropriate atmospheric state at t_1 (as specified by the laws of physics), the clap of thunder follows necessarily at t_2. And it appears that Spinoza had something like this in mind when he claimed that "In nature there is nothing contingent, but all things have been determined by the necessity of the divine nature to exist and produce an effect in a certain way" (E1p29).

Although there can be no doubt that the conception of nature sketched above is deterministic, there is a question as to whether this is *all* that Spinoza intended by the denial of contingency. This is because other propositions, particularly the already considered E1p16 ("From the necessity of the divine nature there must follow infinitely many things in infinitely many modes, i.e., everything which can fall under an infinite intellect") and E1p33 ("Things could have been produced by God in no other way and in no other order than they have been produced"), suggest a stronger doctrine. This has been termed "necessitarianism" and it maintains that things could not have been otherwise; that the actual order of nature is the only conceivable (logically possible) order; or, as it is sometimes put, that the actual world is the only possible world, which underscores the contrast with Leibniz's famous claim that the actual world is the best of all possible worlds. Both views maintain that the laws of nature and particular occurrences within nature are necessary; but they differ in that the former (determinism) maintains it is possible that the entire order of nature could have been different if there had been a different first occurrence or initiating condition, e.g., if (referring to the above example) the atmospheric conditions at t_1 had been different, while the latter (necessitarianism) denies this.[48] The latter view has also traditionally been referred to as "fatalism," a doctrine of which Spinoza has frequently been accused and which Leibniz took great pains to deny.

[47] This example is borrowed from Bennett, *Spinoza's Ethics*, 113.
[48] In the recent literature the main advocate of the deterministic view is Curley, *Spinoza's Metaphysics* and Curley and Walski, "Spinoza's Necessitarianism Reconsidered," 241–262. The main advocate of the necessitarian view is Garrett, *Nature and Necessity in Spinoza's Philosophy*, 98–148.

Interestingly, E1p33 could be appealed to in support of either alternative. As noted above, the necessitarian (or fatalistic) position is strongly suggested (if not required) by the formulation of the proposition itself. Spinoza's remark in the first scholium to this proposition that "A thing is called necessary either by reason of its essence or by reason of its cause" might seem to support the weaker deterministic position, since it suggests a distinction between two kinds of necessity: with the laws of nature being necessary by reason of their essence (the eternal and infinite modes in which they are engrained), while particular occurrences are only necessary by virtue of their cause, i.e., causally necessary. And this, it could be argued, is incompatible with the view that Spinoza recognizes only a strict or logical necessity, such as is exemplified in mathematics. But against this it must be noted that for Spinoza the above distinction is not between two kinds of necessity (absolute or unconditional and relative or conditional), but between two grounds on the basis of which something may be deemed necessary, with the necessity in both cases being of the strict sort. Spinoza expressed his basic view on the matter concisely in CM, where he remarks that "if men understood the whole order of Nature, they would find all things just as necessary as are all those treated in Mathematics" (G1 266; C1 332).[49]

It seems, however, that the main resistance to reading Spinoza as a necessitarian is the counterintuitive nature of the view, particularly its denial of alternative possibilities, which is unambiguously expressed in E1p33. For while determinism maintains that every occurrence, including human actions, is causally necessitated, it leaves open the possibility that things could have been different if a different choice had been made. To be sure, the determinist would insist that any given choice (or natural occurrence) is causally necessary and that the causal chain goes all the way up without any breaks; but this leaves open the possibility that the whole chain or series of occurrences could have been different if the first occurrence had been different. Moreover, it could be argued that Spinoza should have acknowledged this, since we have seen that for him no finite mode is determined directly by an eternal and infinite mode and the attribute it expresses – that is, by the laws of nature – but only by another finite mode *ad infinitum*. And, again, in support of this view one could appeal to Leibniz, who was clearly a determinist, since he famously held that nothing could occur without its sufficient reason, but who equally famously also

---

[49] The bearing of this passage on the issue of Spinoza's necessitarianism was noted by Nadler, *Spinoza's Ethics*, 108.

maintained (on the basis of the principle of sufficient reason) that God created the actual world because it was the best of all possible worlds as determined by the divine intellect.

Although he was visited by a younger Leibniz in 1676, Spinoza did not live to see the work of the mature Leibniz; but even setting aside his critique of final causes discussed in the preceding chapter, it is not difficult to discern the essence of his response to this view in the demonstration of the key E1p33, where he writes:

> For all things have necessarily followed from God's given nature [by p16], and have been determined by the necessity of God's nature to exist and produce an effect in a certain way [by p29]. Therefore, if things could have been of another nature, or could have been determined to produce an effect in another way, so that the order of Nature was different, then God's nature could also have been other than it is now, and therefore [by p11] that [other nature] would also have had to exist, and consequently, there could have been two or more Gods, which is absurd [by p14c1]. So things could have been produced in no other way and in no other order, etc., q.e.d.

Spinoza's argument has the form of a classical reductio. The possibility that the order of nature – that is, the series of finite modes – could have been different in even the slightest detail is dismissed on the grounds that it entails that God, the ground of this order, would have been different. And though Spinoza locates the absurdity in its implication of polytheism, it seems clear that the real point is that a different order of nature would entail a different God (not an additional God or Gods). Unlike Leibniz, Spinoza does not frame the argument in terms of perfection; though given his identification of perfection with reality, he easily could have done so, since the absurdity in the hypothesis of a different order of nature would consist in the fact that it entails that God would have less reality, which is to say that God would not be God, and this involves a contradiction.

Nevertheless, there is a problem with the necessitarian view, which does not apply to its deterministic alternative, at least not directly, namely its underlying conception of the order of nature as a totality. This is, of course, the very problem previously noted in connection with Spinoza's proofs of the existence of God on the basis of the principle of sufficient reason. And it reappears at a different level with Spinoza's conception of the face of the whole universe, which, as noted earlier, functions as a universal individual. Since classical determinism focuses on the causal necessity of particular occurrences within nature, it can remain silent on the question of nature as a whole, whereas this seems to be the very raison d'être for Spinoza's necessitarianism. But while this may be a strong, if not fatal, objection to the view that Spinoza held, it is not an objection to the thesis that he held it. In short, for better or worse, Spinoza was a necessitarian (or, if you will, a fatalist), not simply, like Leibniz, a determinist.

3.3   Some Theological Implications

The traditional conception of God as a person endowed with intellect and free will and the associated doctrine of the creation of the world have been left far behind by the relentless progress of Spinoza's argument. Nevertheless, apart from a brief aside (E1p17s), in which Spinoza affirms that he will show later that "neither intellect nor will pertain to God's nature," his repudiation of the traditional doctrine of God, as well as some of the other doctrines we have already touched on, has remained more or less implicit. The main function of the final section of the first part of the *Ethics* (P30–P36) and the previously discussed appendix dealing with final causes is to make all this perfectly explicit and to underline the radical distinction between the God of the *Ethica ordine geometrico demonstrata* and the God of the theistic religious traditions.

Spinoza's initial target is the notion of the divine intellect, which has traditionally been viewed as archetypal; that is, as the source of the plan in accordance with which the world was created by an act of divine will. This is contrasted with the ectypal human, or finite, intellect, which derives its ideas from preexisting objects. We have already seen that Spinoza does not completely reject the notion of a divine, or infinite, intellect; but he does deny it any creative or archetypal function and he carefully interprets it so as to avoid any anthropomorphic implications.

The first of these tasks is accomplished through the proposition that "An actual intellect, whether finite or infinite, must comprehend God's attributes, and God's affections, and nothing else" (E1p30). This innocent-sounding assertion is based on the truism that "a true idea must agree with its object" (E1a6), and the already established contention that there are literally no other objects for any mind to consider except the attributes of God and their modifications. The significance of this lies in the fact that it effectively undermines any attempt to establish a difference in kind, between a human or finite, and a divine or infinite intellect. Any intellect, whether human or divine, finite or infinite, must relate to its objects in precisely the same way. Thus, to the extent to which it possesses adequate ideas, the human intellect apprehends its objects in precisely the same manner as an infinite intellect; though they, of course, differ dramatically in the extent to which they are equipped with adequate ideas. The key point, however, is that for Spinoza, far from being archetypal or creative in the traditional sense, the infinite intellect is not an actual intellect at all. It is rather the idea of the sum total of possible cognition, or the cognition of the whole order of nature, as expressed in and through each of the infinite attributes. Nevertheless, because it refers to the complete cognition of a unique whole (nature), Spinoza attributes to it a certain specificity and concreteness. In other words, for Spinoza the infinite intellect, like other fixed and eternal things, is a kind of universal individual, and as such has a reality above and beyond that of the items of which it is composed, which again calls to mind the Hegelian conception of a concrete universal.

This implies that the infinite intellect is a mode, belonging to *natura naturata* rather than, like the attribute of thought, to *natura naturans*. Spinoza makes this explicit by claiming that "The actual intellect, whether finite or infinite, like will, desire, love, etc., must be referred to *Natura naturata*, not to *Natura naturans*" (E1p31). The point is that Spinoza cannot consistently attribute an intellect to God (at least not to God understood as *natura naturans*) and affirm, in the manner of the religious tradition, that "God has an intellect." Yet, given the fact that he regards thought as a genuine attribute of God, it would also seem that Spinoza cannot completely exclude intellect from the divine nature.

Spinoza's argument for the merely modal status of the infinite intellect turns on the distinction between thought as an attribute, or "absolute thought," and intellect. As Spinoza affirms in the scholium to E1p31, by "intellect" is meant "intellect itself"; that is, the act of understanding, and not some mysterious capacity or potentiality, for example the "potential intellect" of Aristotle. But this act, as well as other modes of thought, such as volitions and desires, depends on, and can only be conceived through, thought itself. Spinoza thus seems to view the act of intellection or understanding as the affirmation of a particular, determinate portion of the total realm of thought, which, therefore, presupposes this realm as a pregiven totality, precisely in the manner in which a particular body presupposes the whole of extension for Descartes. The limitation to a particular affirmation applies only to a finite intellect, but since Spinoza has just shown that the infinite intellect does not differ in kind from the finite variety, but rather affirms, in precisely the same manner, the whole realm of adequate ideas, it too can be said to presuppose the attribute of thought and thus to be a mere mode.

As the formulation of the above proposition makes clear, this conclusion holds not only for intellect but for other modes of thought too, including will. Nevertheless, Spinoza proceeds to argue that "the will cannot be called a free cause, but only a necessary one" (P32). The point here is to show that even if one wished to attribute a will to God, one could not conclude that God acts from freedom of the will. Although God has been characterized as a "free cause" (E1p17c2), and this has been shown to be equivalent to being self-determined, we now see that God is not such a cause by virtue of a free will. This follows from the definition of will as "only a certain mode of thinking." Since a mode will, whether finite or infinite, requires a cause that conditions it to act, it cannot (by E1d7) be called a free cause, but only a necessary, or constrained, one.

Moreover, if things follow necessarily from the nature of God, rather than from an act of free choice, it also follows that "Things could have been produced by God in no other way, and in no other order than they have been produced" (E1p33). We have already considered this proposition at some length in connection with the account of Spinoza's necessitarian, and have seen that, together with E1p29, it plays a key role in the overall argument of E1. We have not discussed, however, the second scholium to this proposition, where Spinoza spells out its theological implications. These concern the question of whether God may be considered a being that created the world through an act of free choice and that, if he had so willed, he could have created a different world, or perhaps none at all. The latter view is arguably the central tenet of traditional theism, since it underlies the attribution of personal qualities to the deity, and we have seen that Spinoza's rejection of it lies at the heart of his thought.

Continuing with the reductio form of the proposition, in this scholium Spinoza assumes for the sake of argument that God acts from free will, and he points out that to claim that God could have decreed a different order of nature is to assume that God's intellect and will and, therefore, his very nature could have been different. But the problem is that it is also assumed that God's nature, as it is, is supremely perfect; so that to attribute a different nature to God is in effect to deny that God is supremely perfect. Spinoza notes that in response to this line of attack it might be objected that there is no intrinsic perfection or imperfection in things, and that what is perfect or imperfect depends solely on the will of God. Thus, it might be claimed that "if God had willed, he could have brought it about that what is now perfection would have been the greatest imperfection, and conversely" (P33S2). This was the view of Calvin and Descartes, and Spinoza is easily able to show that it succumbs to precisely the same dialectic. Since God necessarily understands what he wills, Spinoza reasons, this view amounts to the claim that God might understand things differently from the way in which he does understand them, which leads to the same absurdity as before. God's will, after all, cannot be different from God's perfection, and, therefore, on the theologians' own assumption, things could not be different.

Although Spinoza totally repudiates the theory that "subjects all things to a certain indifferent will of God, and makes all things depend on his good pleasure," he nevertheless suggests that it is preferable to the theory that holds that "God does all things for the sake of the good" (E1p33s2). Despite its rationalist pedigree, Spinoza treats this doctrine, which is at least as old as Plato's *Euthyphro* and found a systematic expression in Leibniz, with the utmost contempt, arguing that conceiving of God as acting for the sake of some preestablished goal (the good) submits God to a kind of external control. And this, he suggests, is to subject God to fate, which, as we have seen, is precisely the charge that was raised by Leibniz and others against Spinoza's own view.

Even granting, however, that God could not have created a less than perfect world, it does not follow that he had to create any world at all. Perhaps, then, the traditional theologian might argue, we can locate the cherished element of divine choice in the sheer contingency and unfathomable mystery of the decision to create. But to such a claim Spinoza has a ready answer, namely: "God's power is his essence itself" (E1p34). This conclusion is derived from the principle that things follow from the very nature or essence of God. Its clear implication is that the suggestion that God might not have exercised his power – that is, that he might not have created at all – is once again equivalent to the absurd claim that God has the power not to be God. Spinoza thus concludes against the theologians that "Whatever we conceive to be in God's power, necessarily exists" (E1p35), which amounts to an explicit denial of the suggestion that the world might not have come into existence. The final proposition of the first part of the *Ethics* (E1p36) states that "There is no cause from whose nature some effect does not follow." Although this does not seem to further the argument, it reflects Spinoza's view that every particular thing participates in or expresses the infinite power of God, or nature, in a conditioned manner.[50] Moreover, it also serves as a transition to the discussion of final causes, which are in fact regarded by Spinoza as causes from which no effects follow.

Taken together, these concluding propositions show that, despite his diametrically opposed point of view, Spinoza had no qualms about

---

[50] This is suggested by Höffding, *Spinozas Ethica*, 45. It should also be noted, however, that the only subsequent appearances of this proposition are in E2p13, E3p1, E3p3, and E5p4s.

meeting theologians on their own ground, showing either that their views could be reduced to absurdity or that they entailed his own. In so doing, he completed his project of replacing the traditional conception of God as a superhuman person with the scientifically inspired conception of nature as an infinite, necessary, self-contained, and, above all, thoroughly intelligible system. It is important to realize, however, that Spinoza did not merely wish to keep the word "God" while emptying it of all significance. Rather, his intent was to show that, properly understood, it referred to nature, and to nature alone. This nature does not possess an intellect or a will, and thus it does not act for the benefit of humanity. But though it is not *intelligent*, it is *intelligible*, which the God of the theologians is not. Moreover, since there is literally no power apart from it that can in any way limit it, this nature is in the fullest sense of the word *omnipotent*. Thus, no matter what one may think of Spinoza's logic, there can be no doubt about his sincerity and the depth of the conviction with which he identified God and nature. For Spinoza, as for other thinkers of a similar persuasion such as Goethe, who have no use for the traditional conception of God, the features of nature mentioned above suffice to qualify it as divine.[51]

---

[51] For an account of Goethe's understanding of Spinoza see Förster, "Goethe's Spinozism."

CHAPTER 4

The Human Mind

In his brief preface to the second part of the *Ethics*, entitled "On the Nature and Origin of the Mind," Spinoza writes:

> I pass now to explaining those things which must necessarily follow from the essence of God, or the infinite and eternal Being – not, indeed, all of them, for we have demonstrated [EIp16] that infinitely many things must follow from it in infinitely many modes, but only those that can lead us, by the hand, as it were, to the cognition of the human Mind, and its highest blessedness.

This sets the agenda not only for the second part, but also for the remainder of the *Ethics* as a whole. It also provides a clear indication of the ultimately practical orientation of the work. Although self-contained, the account of *Deus seu Natura* in the first part lays the foundation for Spinoza's account of its most important finite modification, the human mind. Even this account, however, which is the subject of the second part, is not undertaken for its own sake, but as a necessary prelude to the analyses of the human emotions, virtue, and freedom, which are the concerns of the final three parts. The argument of the second part can itself be divided into three parts: an analysis of the nature of the mind and its relation to the body (E2p1–p15); an analysis of the intellect and of the nature and extent of human cognition (E2p16–p47); and an analysis of the will, its alleged freedom, and its relation to the intellect (E2p48–p49). Accordingly, the present chapter will be similarly structured.

4.1   The Mind and Its Relation to the Body

In spite of its extreme crypticness, which has generated wildly different interpretations, Spinoza's analysis of the mind and its relation to the body is one of the most intriguing aspects of his philosophy. Moreover, far from being a historical curiosity, it has proved to be of considerable relevance to contemporary discussions of the topic.[1] Spinoza's theory is designed primarily to account for the unity of human nature and to show that the mind, as well as the body, is part of the universal nature and, therefore, subject to its necessary laws. As such, this theory contrasts sharply with Cartesian dualism – with its conception of mind and body as two distinct, yet interacting, substances. It is also opposed, however, to a materialistic theory, such as that of Hobbes, who allowed only bodies and motion in the universe and identified thought with a physical process.[2] Although many aspects of Spinoza's psychological theory owe a great deal to Hobbes,[3] he staunchly resisted any attempt either to reduce thought to its physical correlate or to explain ideas in terms of anything in the realm of extension.[4]

Spinoza endeavors to avoid both Cartesian ontological dualism and Hobbesian reductive materialism by appealing to his doctrine of attributes. This allows him to affirm the autonomous, self-contained nature of thought, without making mind into a distinct substance. As two of the infinite attributes of the one substance, thought and extension are not separate entities, but distinct aspects or expressions of the same reality. Moreover, since the human mind and the human body are both finite modifications of these attributes, the same can be said of them. The general principle is that, just as "the thinking substance and the extended substance are one and the same substance, which is now comprehended under this attribute, now under that ... a mode of extension and the idea of that mode are one and the same thing, but expressed in two ways" (E2p7s). Later, after having characterized the human mind as the idea of the body (E2p13), Spinoza remarks in passing that "the Mind and the Body are one and the same Individual, which is conceived now under the attribute of Thought, now under the attribute of Extension" (E2p21s). He thus advocates a form of mind–body identity theory, albeit one that differs from the usual materialistic versions of such a theory in its insistence on giving equal weight to the mental.[5]

[1] This has been a central theme of the work of Della Rocca. See his *Representation and the Mind–Body Problem in Spinoza*, and *Spinoza*, 89–136.
[2] See Matson, "Spinoza's Theory of Mind," 53–54.
[3] The importance of Hobbes in this regard is emphasized by Cassirer, *Das Erkenntnisproblem*, vol. 2, 99–102.
[4] This fairly standard view has been challenged, however, by Bernadette, "Spinozistic Anomalies." In addition, it has been argued by Hampshire, *Freedom of Mind*, 225–226, and Curley, "Behind the Geometrical Method," 50–56, that Spinoza can be read as a materialist of a nonreductive sort. For a critique of the materialist reading of Spinoza, see Delahunty, *Spinoza*, 196–197.
[5] The most important contemporary statement of this view is the anomalous monism of Donald Davidson. For an account of the important similarities of their views see Della Rocca, *Spinoza*, 103–104.

As already indicated, Spinoza's argument for this identity thesis moves deductively from general principles concerning the attributes of thought and extension to specific conclusions concerning the human mind and body as finite modifications of these attributes or, better, as finite expressions of substance conceived under the attributes of thought and extension. The first thing to be established is that thought and extension are two of the infinite attributes of God (E2p1 and E2p2). From this Spinoza deduces several basic claims. To begin with, since thought is an attribute of God, and hence an expression of his infinite essence, "In God there is necessarily an idea, both of his essence and of everything that necessarily follows from his essence" (E2p3). This proposition serves a twofold function. First, it underscores the all-inclusiveness of the attribute of thought and its immediate eternal and infinite mode, the infinite intellect. Since such an intellect stands for realization of all possible cognition, i.e., the complete comprehension of nature, it encompasses everything that follows from the nature of God, which, given Spinoza's necessitarianism, means everything conceivable. Second, it entails that there is an idea, or modification, in the attribute of thought corresponding to the modifications of substance in each of the infinite attributes. As will become apparent later, this is not only a crucial ingredient in Spinoza's account of the mind–body relationship, it also raises questions about the overall coherence of his position.

The next thing to be established is the self-containedness of the attribute of thought. This is already implicit in the claim that, since God is one, God's idea – that is, the infinite intellect – is one (E2p4). It is made fully explicit, however, in the next proposition:

> The formal being of ideas admits God as a cause only insofar as he is considered as a thinking thing, and not insofar as he is explained by any other attribute. That is, ideas, both of God's attributes and of singular things, admit not the objects themselves, or the things perceived, as their efficient cause, but God himself, insofar as he is a thinking thing. (E2p5)

Since God, insofar as he is a thinking thing, is equivalent to thought viewed as an attribute, Spinoza's point is simply that each idea must be caused by another idea, and that this is what makes the realm of thought a self-contained whole. But, as he proceeds to remind the reader, this by no means reflects any special privilege for thought, since it holds for all the attributes, each of which can be conceived as a self-determined, self-contained whole (E2p6).

Having established the all-inclusiveness and self-containedness of the attribute of thought, Spinoza's next task is to spell out the implications of these characteristics for the understanding of the relationship between thought and the only other attribute known to us, extension. More specifically, what he must show is that "The order and connection of ideas is the same as the order and connection of things" (E2p7). This is generally referred to as Spinoza's "parallelism thesis," and since it is the essential statement of how the substance-monism of E1 is expressed in the different attributes, it provides the foundation for his subsequent account of the mind–body relation and, therefore, for both his epistemology and psychology, as developed in the remainder of E2 and E3. Given the systematic importance of this proposition, it is noteworthy that Spinoza treats it as virtually self-evident. Thus, rather than linking it with the definitions, axioms, and first six propositions of E2, the demonstration consists simply in an appeal, without further explanation, to E1a4, which, as he here characterizes it, maintains that "the idea of each thing caused depends on the cognition of the cause of which it is an effect." The problem, however, is that this is not so much a demonstration of the proposition as an explication of it, since it seems to assume the very parallelism or isomorphism between the order of the modes under the different attributes that it is supposed to explain.

However, Spinoza provides considerably more information concerning how he understood the proposition, if not its demonstration, in the corollary and scholium that he attaches to it. In the former, he notes that it means that God's power of thinking, or capacity to generate ideas, is equal to his power of acting, or capacity to produce the corresponding modes in each of the attributes. Spinoza explains that he means by this that "whatever follows formally from God's infinite nature follows objectively in God from his idea in the same order and with the same connection." Moreover, even more germane is the scholium in which Spinoza spells out how this parallelism is to be understood. Referring back to E1, he remarks that "the thinking substance and the extended substance are one and the same substance, which is now comprehended under this attribute, now under that. So also a mode of extension and the idea of that mode are one and the same thing expressed in two ways." And after alluding to the view of some unnamed Jewish philosophers that God, God's intellect, and the things understood by God are identical,[6] he follows his customary procedure of illustrating the point using a geometrical example:

> [A] circle existing in nature and the idea of the existing circle, which is also in God, are one and the same thing, which is expressed through different

---

[6] According to Wolfson, *The Philosophy of Spinoza*, vol. 2, 24, the reference is to Maimonides.

attributes. Therefore, whether we conceive nature under the attribute of extension, or under the attribute of thought, or under any under attribute, we shall find that one and the same order, or one and the same connection of causes, that is, that the same things follow one another. (G2 90; C1 451)

It seems useful to interpret the claim that a mode of extension and the idea of this mode are one and the same thing expressed in two ways by appealing to the analogy of a sentence expressed in two languages. For, example, "Snow is white" and "*Schnee ist weiss*" express the same propositional content in English and German. Alternatively, an analogy, which would likely have appealed to Spinoza, is drawn from Descartes' analytic geometry, where the same set of relations or proportions may be expressed either algebraically or geometrically. But while either analogy, and perhaps others, work well enough when the discussion is limited to the attributes of thought and extension and their corresponding modes, they seem to fall short when one factors in Spinoza's oblique reference to "other attributes," by which he evidently understood his doctrine of infinite attributes. Even setting aside the infinity issue, however, there are two problems. The first is that *any* additional attributes threaten the parallelism thesis, because Spinoza's account seems to require that there be an idea in God or, more precisely, in the infinite intellect, corresponding not only to a mode of extension, i.e., a body, but also to a mode in each of the other attributes. At the heart of the problem is the intentionality of thought.[7] Since a thought – that is, an idea – is by its very nature of some object, it follows that there must be a distinct idea of the corresponding mode and each of the other attributes, and this undermines the parallelism between the attributes by overpopulating the attribute of thought. Moreover, we shall see later that the problem is compounded by the fact that, in addition to intentionality, thought for Spinoza also has reflexivity; so that the attribute and its most significant finite mode, the human mind, contains not only ideas but also ideas of ideas. The second problem is understanding why, as Spinoza acknowledges, the human mind is not able to cognize the other attributes and their modes.

Both problems were posed to Spinoza by Tschirnhaus (mainly through Schuller in their three-way correspondence). And though Spinoza briefly addressed the second question, claiming that the infinite ideas by which the infinite intellect of God is expressed "cannot constitute one and the same mind of a singular thing, but infinitely many minds," which have no connection with each other (L66 G4 280; C2 440–441), he never responded

---

[7] The problem is posed in terms of the intentionality of thought by Nadler, *Spinoza's Ethics*, 126–127.

to the first. But while it is undoubtedly an intriguing question, since it does not bear directly on the subsequent course of Spinoza's argument, I shall not attempt to address it here.[8] Rather, the focus will be on other, not yet discussed aspects of E2p7, which are closely connected to the subsequent argument of this part, as well as the remainder of the *Ethics*. The main issue posed by this proposition is the ambiguity in Spinoza's multifaceted account of ideas. He defines an idea as "a concept of the mind which the Mind forms because it is a thinking thing" (E2d3). By distinguishing between conception (*conceptum*) and perception (*perceptionem*) in his explanation of this definition, Spinoza emphasizes the activity of the mind. Insofar as the mind has ideas, it does not passively perceive but actively conceives its object. Moreover, since we shall see that to conceive of something is to form a belief about it, ideas can be equated with beliefs.[9] Accordingly, to have an idea of something is to have a belief about it, not simply a mental picture in the manner of a Humean impression. Although further discussion of this topic must await consideration of Spinoza's actual arguments, we can already see how this conception of an idea makes it possible for him to identify the mind with its ideas (strictly speaking, with a single complex idea). Insofar as ideas are essentially acts of conceiving, or believing, this identification amounts to the claim that the mind is nothing above and beyond its activity; that its unity and individuality are the unity and individuality of this activity. We shall also see that this conception has its precise parallel in Spinoza's conception of body.

Unfortunately, things do not remain quite so simple, if we consider some of the other things that Spinoza says about ideas. At times, particularly when he is referring to ideas "in God," he seems to equate ideas with propositions; that is, with the content of beliefs, rather than with actual acts of belief. Carried to its extreme, this results in what has been called the "logicizing" of the attribute of thought, by which is meant the reduction of this attribute to the sum total of true propositions.[10] At other times, particularly when he is considering the mind as the idea of the body, Spinoza seems to treat ideas as if they were nothing more than mental correlates of physical occurrences or states, without any propositional content whatsoever. Insofar as ideas are considered in the latter manner, their "object" is identified with their physical counterpart, which in the case of the human mind is the human body; whereas insofar as they are

---

[8] For extensive treatments of this issue see Curley, *Spinoza's Metaphysics*, 144–153 and Melamed, *Spinoza's Metaphysics*, 153–204.
[9] For a discussion of ideas in Spinoza as beliefs see Bennett, *Spinoza's Ethics*, 162–167.
[10] Ibid., 129.

considered as beliefs, it is assumed that they can refer to any number of objects. Not surprisingly, then, Spinoza has frequently been accused of a gross confusion or equivocation in his account of ideas.[11]

This problem, in its various forms, will be with us throughout this chapter and will reemerge on steroids in Spinoza's account of the eternity of the mind (Chapter 7). But we can begin our consideration of it by noting the contrast made by Spinoza between the "formal" and the "objective" reality of ideas. This is a traditional scholastic distinction, which is also found in Descartes and which Spinoza adapts to his own purposes. In brief, the formal reality of an idea is its reality as a mental episode, or occurrence, whereas its objective reality is its reality as a representation with a propositional content. Thus, construing ideas as beliefs, every idea can be described as both a mental episode with its own psychological reality (a believing) and a propositional content that is affirmed in such an episode (what is believed). Construed as mental occurrences, ideas have causes, which, according to Spinoza, are always other ideas (E2p5); while construed as beliefs, they have grounds, or premises, which again must always be other beliefs. At least part of the confusion surrounding Spinoza's account of ideas can be removed simply by keeping this distinction in mind.

Of more immediate relevance is the fact that this distinction enables us to see just what is so perplexing in Spinoza's identification of the order and connection of ideas and things. One wants to know whether this applies to ideas considered formally, objectively, or both. A consideration of the uses to which the proposition is put in the subsequent argument makes it clear that it is intended to apply to ideas taken in both ways. In other words, it is to be taken both as a psychological claim about the causal sequence of mental occurrences (the formal reality of ideas) and as a logical claim about the inferential ordering of our conceptions or beliefs (the objective reality of ideas). There seems to be little difficulty with this claim taken in the latter sense. Since the objective reality of an idea is its conceptual content, and since this is equivalent to the reality of the object of which it is an idea qua grasped in thought, the order and connection of ideas, so construed, is identical to the order and connection of things. At least this is the case

[11] The classic formulations of this charge are by Pollock, *Spinoza: His Life and Philosophy*, 124ff.; Barker, "Notes on the Second Part of Spinoza's Ethics, II," 140ff.; and Taylor, "Some Incoherencies in Spinozism, II," 305. Some recent and sophisticated variations on this theme are offered by Wilson, "Objects, Ideas, and 'Minds': Comments on Spinoza's Theory of Mind." Among the defenders of Spinoza on this issue are Hallett, "On a Reputed Equivoque in the Philosophy of Spinoza," and Radner, "Spinoza's Theory of Ideas."

insofar as we are considering true or adequate ideas; that is, the order of ideas as contained in the infinite intellect of God. It is by no means obvious, however, that the same can be said about the formal reality of ideas; for there would seem to be no reason why the causal sequence of ideas considered as mental occurrences should have to mirror the causal sequence of the things of which they are ideas.

The problem is exacerbated by the proof that Spinoza provides of this proposition. As we have seen, it consists solely in an appeal to E1a4, which he here takes as maintaining that "the idea of each thing caused depends on the cognition of the cause of which it is an effect." For while this axiom can be taken to support the logical reading of the proposition, which doesn't really need it, it hardly seems to support the psychological reading. Why, after all, should a claim about the dependence of the cognition of an effect on the cognition of its cause have anything to do with the causal order of ideas considered as mental occurrences?

Although this is one of many places in the *Ethics* where it is difficult for an interpreter to be confident about any proposed solution, the basis for a possible explanation lies in the recognition of the fact that Spinoza is here talking specifically about the ordering of ideas in the infinite intellect of God, which, as such, is the logically correct ordering. As we shall see in the next section, insofar as it has adequate ideas, the human mind also conceives things in this manner, which means that in such cases the ideal logical order is also an actual psychological order. Since the logical order of ideas mirrors the causal order of things (E1a4), and (in this situation at least) the psychological order is identical with the logical order, the psychological order of ideas must likewise mirror the causal order of things. In other words, insofar as the human intellect conceives things adequately, its ideas not only causally condition one another, e.g., the belief that A at t_1 is the cause of belief that B at t_2, but the causal order is also a logically correct order of inference, e.g., the belief that A provides "adequate" (logically sufficient) grounds for the belief that B. And if this, or something like it, is Spinoza's view, then one can see why he could take E2p7 to apply to ideas considered as formal, as well as objective, realities, and even why he might appeal to the E1a4 axiom in support of this claim.

The situation is considerably more problematic in the case of inadequate ideas, where, by definition, the ordering is not logical; that is, where the belief that A precedes and causes but does not provide adequate grounds for the belief that B. That the parallelism thesis is also supposed to apply here is evident from Spinoza's account of our inadequate imaginative and perceptual cognition (which will be considered in the next section). To anticipate, Spinoza will claim that the causal order of our imaginative or perceptual ideas (considered with respect to their formal reality as mental episodes) mirrors the causal order of the states of our own body, which is itself determined by the order in which the body is affected by external bodies. Given its centrality to Spinoza's whole account of the human condition (our status as finite modes), it is not difficult to see why he would want to claim this. But what *is* difficult to see is just how the above axiom is applicable to this claim. One can easily make it applicable by taking it to entail the desired result; but then the "axiom" would stand as much in need of justification as the proposition it is supposed to support.

The situation is not as confused as it might appear, however, for this aspect of E2p7 can be shown to follow from Spinoza's conception of substance, as developed in E1, together with the earlier propositions of E2, quite independently of any appeal to the axiom. The reasoning goes roughly like this: if thought is an attribute of God (E2p1) – that is, if it is one of many expressions of the necessary and universal order of nature – and if there must be an idea or mode of thought corresponding to the modes expressed in each of the other attributes (including extension) (E2p3), and if these ideas, or modes of thought, considered with respect to their formal reality constitute a self-contained causal order (E2p5), then this causal order must correspond to the causal order as it is expressed under the attribute of extension (or any other attribute for that matter). The key to the argument is the move from the claim that there is a one-to-one mapping of modes as expressed in thought to modes as expressed in each of the other attributes to the claim that there is a similar mapping of the causal order of these modes as expressed in the various attributes. Although it is not easy to cite specific definitions, axioms, or propositions that license this move, which is perhaps why Spinoza felt compelled to press the axiom into service, it is likewise not easy to see how it could be denied without denying the unity of substance.

Nevertheless, even granting the main claims of proposition E2p7, more work must be done before Spinoza is in a position to develop his conception of the human mind as the idea of the human body. One point to be considered is the ideas of nonexistent things. These fall into two broad categories: merely possible things, which never were and never will become actual, though they might be said to inhere as possibilities in the mind of God, and things that either had existed in the past or will exist in the future according to the order of nature. While it is clear that Spinoza's necessitarianism has no place for the former, it is also clear that the all-encompassing nature of his conception of God/nature requires him to find a place for the latter. Spinoza refers to these, together with things that actually exist, as "singular things" and he defines them as "things that are finite and have a determinate existence" (E2d7). Since the ideas of these things must be contained in the infinite intellect of God, and the order and connection of things corresponds to the order and connection of ideas in that intellect, the non-occurrent, i.e., past and future, as well as the occurrent, singular things must have places in the other attributes (besides thought), which correspond to their place in the attribute of thought. And, given the distinction between formal and objective reality, this means that Spinoza must attribute a formal reality to the non-occurrent singular things in the attributes other than thought, which corresponds to the objective reality they possess in the infinite intellect of God.

Spinoza addresses this issue directly in E2p8, where he claims that "The ideas of singular things, or of modes, that do not exist must be comprehended in God's infinite idea in the same way as the formal essences of the singular things, or modes, are contained in God's attributes." Since, *ex hypothesi*, the things in question do not exist, Spinoza is presumably here referring to their formal essence rather than to the things themselves. Thus, rather than actual existents, what is supposedly contained in the attributes other than thought must be the essential nature of these singular things, i.e., "that which being given, the thing itself is necessarily posited and which, being taken away, the thing is necessarily taken away" (E2def. 2). Inasmuch as these things are not "given," the question is how their formal essences are contained in God's attributes; and the answer seems to be in a latent manner as infinite modes. It is clear that they must be contained in a latent manner because they lack actual existence, which for Spinoza means duration, i.e., "an indefinite continuation of existence" (E2d5). And since they are modal essences – that is, unchanging natures – this suggests they must have the status of finite eternal modes. Admittedly, this seems odd, since Spinoza's official ontology appears to divide modes into two classes, finite and eternal and infinite, thereby leaving no place for those that are both finite and eternal; but the combination of their lack of duration and their status as formal essences seems to require attributing this hybrid status to such modes.[12]

In the scholium to this proposition, Spinoza illustrates this thesis by means of a geometrical analogy, though he admits that it is inadequate because of the unique nature of the point he is trying to express. The nature

---

[12] Don Garrett, *Nature and Necessity in Spinoza's Philosophy*, 147 also characterizes the formal essences of singular things as eternal modes.

of a circle, he points out, is such that if any number of straight lines intersect within it, the resulting rectangles will be equal to one another. Although none of these possible rectangles actually exist unless the circle exists, given the circle, an infinite number of rectangles exist in the sense that they can be constructed in the circle. Moreover, since each of these possible rectangles can be conceived, and thus *is* conceived by the infinite intellect, the same can be said of the ideas of these rectangles. If, however, we suppose that of these infinite rectangles two actually exist, i.e., are constructed, then, Spinoza concludes, "their ideas also exist now not only insofar as they are only comprehended in the idea of the circle, but also insofar as they involve the existence of those rectangles." And he adds that "By this they are distinguished from the other ideas of the other rectangles" (E2p8s). While this captures the latency of the mode of existence of the non-constructed rectangles (they are constructible, though not actually constructed), it fails to capture, because of its geometrical nature, the temporal dimension of the scenario with which Spinoza is concerned. Simply put, geometrical figures, as contrasted with, say, physical sketches of them, which can be erased or otherwise obliterated, cannot be said to have any duration.

Spinoza's central concern, however, is not with geometrical figures, or even nonexistent singular things per se, but with an actually existing singular thing, namely the human mind or, more precisely, the idea that constitutes the human mind, which he will identify as the idea of the human body. Accordingly, our tasks are first to understand the line of reasoning that leads to this result and then to examine Spinoza's account of the relation between this idea and its object. Following his top-down procedure, Spinoza's first step is to determine the relation of all ideas of actually existing things to God. Since, like all things, they follow from God, though as finite they cannot follow directly, he claims that:

> The idea of a singular thing which actually exists has God for a cause not insofar as he is infinite, but insofar as he is considered to be affected by another idea of a singular thing which actually exists; and of this [idea] God is also the cause, insofar as he is affected by another, and so on, to infinity. (E2p9)

Since this is a direct consequence of the modal status of these ideas, it is not surprising. Of considerably more interest is the corollary, which states that "Whatever happens in the singular object of an idea, there is cognition of it in God, only insofar as he has the idea of the same object." This likewise sounds innocent enough on the face of it; but since to be in God just means to be in the corresponding finite mode, it entails that whatever is in the object is reflected in its corresponding idea and nowhere else. The significance of this will soon become apparent.

The next step is to establish the connection between the mind and the idea of an actually existing thing. Since a human being is not a substance (E2p10), and it is an undeniable fact that "man thinks" (E2a2), it follows that the essence of a human being must be constituted in part by certain modifications of the attribute of thought. But since for Spinoza, as for Descartes, ideas are the fundamental modifications of thought, in the sense that other modifications, e.g., desires and volitions, presuppose ideas of their objects, it also follows that the basic modification constituting the mind must be an idea. Finally, since it is clear that human beings actually exist, it must be the idea of an actually existing thing. Combining these points, Spinoza concludes that "The first thing that constitutes the actual being of a human Mind is nothing but the idea of a singular thing which actually exists" (E2p11).

On the basis of this contention, Spinoza adds, in a significant corollary, that the human mind is "part of the infinite intellect of God." We have already seen enough to realize that this mystical-sounding claim, which is central to Spinoza's epistemological and moral theories, is merely his way of making the point that the human mind is a member of and participates in the absolute, or total, system of thought. It is a finite, limited member, however, and Spinoza expresses this point by noting that statements of the form "The human mind perceives this or that" are equivalent to metaphysical statements of the form "God has this or that idea, not in so far as he is infinite, but in so far as he is displayed through the nature of the human mind" (E2p11c). This, again, is Spinoza's way of saying that perception follows from the particular nature of the perceiving mind, rather than from the absolute system of thought. We should note, however, that the word "perception" is used here, as elsewhere, in a very broad sense, to refer to all mental events, of which conscious apprehension is merely one particular manifestation.

This broad sense of perception, together with the principle of the identity of the order and connection of ideas with the order and connection of things, forms the basis of Spinoza's contention that "Whatever happens in the object of the idea constituting the human Mind must be perceived by the human Mind, or there will necessarily be an idea of that thing in the Mind, i.e., if the object of the idea constituting a human Mind is a body, nothing can happen in that body which is not perceived by the Mind" (E2p12). This is one of the more paradoxical-sounding propositions in the *Ethics*, since it seems to commit Spinoza to the absurdity that the mind must be consciously aware of everything that occurs in the body (down to the submicroscopic level). Nevertheless, there is no need to read Spinoza in this way, since his point is rather that the mind reflects the state of the body as a whole. Consequently, given the identity of the two orders, it follows that the state of the idea constituting a human mind must be a function of the state of the entire body. In other words, the mind varies in accordance with variations in the physical organism, and nothing occurs in the organism that does not have its mental correlate. It is in this sense, and this sense alone, that the mind can be said to "perceive" everything that occurs in the body.[13]

One might still ask, however, how this can be reconciled with the characterization of ideas as beliefs. For it seems to be as paradoxical to claim that the mind has a belief about everything that occurs in the body as it is to contend that it perceives everything that occurs in it. One possible way of overcoming this difficulty is to saddle Spinoza with the rather problematic notion of unconscious belief, which would commit him to the claim that there are an indefinite number of unconscious beliefs regarding various bodily occurrences. Another, more promising, way is to take the proposition to imply merely that the beliefs the mind has (all of which are consciously held) reflect the state of the entire body. This would commit Spinoza only to the thesis that everything that occurs in our body has its ideational counterpart, rather than the thesis that we actually have beliefs (conscious or otherwise) *about* everything that occurs in the body.

The nature of the connection between the mind and the body becomes fully explicit in the next proposition, in which Spinoza asserts that "The object of the idea constituting the human Mind is the Body, or a certain mode of extension which actually exists, and nothing else" (E2p13). Although the demonstration of this proposition, which turns on the distinction between ideas being in God qua constituting our mind and qua constituting some other mind, is highly obscure, the basic point seems clear enough. Since the human mind has an immediate, sensitive awareness of its own body and of its own body alone (I feel my own pain and not someone else's), the object of the idea constituting my mind must be my body. Far more problematic, however, is the scholium attached to this proposition, where, presumably referring to the entire argument up to this point, Spinoza remarks:

> For the things we have shown so far are completely general and do not pertain more to man than to other Individuals, all of which, though in

---

[13] See Parkinson, *Spinoza's Theory of Knowledge*, 110–111.

different degrees, are nevertheless animate. For of each thing there is necessarily an idea in God, of which God is the cause in the same way as he is of the idea of the human Body. And so, whatever we have said of the idea of the human Body must also be said of the idea of any thing. (E2p13s)

The refusal to exempt human beings from the universal order of nature is both characteristic of Spinoza and readily understandable, given his overall approach. What is perplexing, however, is the claim that all things, or at least all "Individuals," are animate (*animata*).[14] Since the Latin adjective *animatus* is cognate with the French *âme* (soul), as well as the English "animate," it would seem that Spinoza is attributing not merely life (which would be paradoxical enough) but also a soul in some sense analogous to a human mind (*mens*) to all things. In short, it appears that Spinoza was led by a reasonable concern not to exempt human beings from the universal order of nature to affirm a wildly implausible panpsychism.[15]

An initially attractive way of dealing with this problem is to rid Spinoza's claim of its paradoxical character by maintaining that all he means by it is that for every thing, or individual, x, there is in God an idea in the sense of a set of true propositions about x. This solution amounts to the previously mentioned logicizing of the attribute of thought. It seems attractive at this point because Spinoza holds that for every x there must be some such set of true propositions and he identifies this set with the idea of x in God. The difficulty, however, if this is construed as a *complete* account of what Spinoza means by the attribution of a "soul" to a thing, is that it effectively eliminates the mental from the Spinozistic universe.[16] For if the claim that x has a soul, or mind, means merely that there is a set of true propositions about x, then the claim that human beings have minds reduces to the claim that there is a set of true propositions about their individual bodies. Although this is a consequence with which an eliminative materialist would be quite content, for the reasons already given, it does not seem plausible to attribute such a view to Spinoza.

---

[14] The issue is whether by "individual" Spinoza means the same as "thing," or whether he reserves the former for entities with a certain level of complexity. The latter view is advocated by Gueroult, *Spinoza* II, esp. 164–165. Bennett seems to give tentative approval to this (*Spinoza's Ethics*, 138–139), but then goes on to criticize Gueroult's account. A quite different view is offered by Matheron, who argues that simple bodies are the limiting cases of individuals, so that the claim applies to all things, including simple bodies (*Individu et Communauté chez Spinoza*, 22). A similar view is expressed by Curley, *Behind the Geometrical Method*, 49.

[15] See Bennett, *Spinoza's Ethics*, 138. For a more charitable discussion of this topic see Della Rocca, *Spinoza*, 108–118.

[16] This is argued forcefully by Bennett, *Spinoza's Ethics*, 53–54, 128–129.

A more plausible reading is to take the claim that all things are animated to mean simply that there is a sense in which all things are alive.[17] Although such panvitalism might seem to be almost as outrageous as the panpsychism it is intended to replace, it is actually in accord with the main thrust of Spinoza's thought. Thus, in his appendix to the DPP, where he is presumably speaking in his own voice, Spinoza defines life as "the force through which things persevere in their being" (CM 1 260; C1 326). Moreover, later in the *Ethics*, he states that "Each thing, as far as it can by its own power, strives to persevere in its being" (E3p6). Given the above definition, this entails that everything is "alive"; and from this it is but a short step to the conclusion that everything has a "soul" in the sense of a principle of animation. The implications of this will become clearer in the next chapter, where we shall consider Spinoza's doctrine of conatus. For the present it must suffice to note that, although on this interpretation minds or souls are not limited to rational beings (the Cartesian position), it does not commit Spinoza to the doctrine that every individual thing has a mental life that is even remotely analogous to that enjoyed by the human mind.

Nevertheless, Spinoza still has the problem of explaining the superiority of the human mind to the "minds" of things lower down in the order of nature. He has a ready and ingenious solution to this problem, however. It turns on the distinction between different degrees of animation, or levels of mind, with the precise degree or level being a function of the nature and capacity of the body. As he puts it in the same scholium:

> [I]n proportion as a Body is more capable than others of doing more things at once, or being acted on in many ways at once, so its Mind is more capable than others of perceiving many things at once. And in proportion as the actions of a body depend more on itself alone, and as other bodies concur with it less in acting, so its mind is more capable of understanding distinctly. (G2 97; C1 458)

In spite of his arcane terminology, Spinoza here arrives once again at a thoroughly modern view, namely that mind is a function of organic complexity. The more a body is able to interact with its environment, both to affect it and be affected by it, the greater the power of mind to perceive this environment. On this view, then, conscious awareness and rational insight are located on a continuum of "mental" powers, rather than being

---

[17] See Curley, *Behind the Geometrical Method*, 49–50. The present account is based largely on his analysis. See also Della Rocca, *Spinoza*, and Nadler, *Spinoza's Ethics*, 134–137 for discussions of this point.

regarded as properties of a distinct thinking substance, as in the Cartesian view.

Although such a conception has many interesting implications, Spinoza largely ignores them in order to concentrate on the primary object of his concern: the human mind. As his functional approach makes clear, however, in order to understand the human mind, we must first acquire a more accurate cognition of the nature of the human body. Moreover, given Spinoza's deductive method, any such cognition must be based on general considerations concerning the nature of all physical bodies. Consequently, Spinoza found it necessary to interrupt his analysis of the human mind and its cognitive capacities in order to make a brief foray into the realms of physics and biology. This occurs in a series of lemmata, with attached axioms, and postulates that immediately follow E2p13 and that have been referred to in the literature as the "physical interlude."[18]

The discussion is divided into three parts. The first deals with the properties of the simplest bodies; the second is concerned with complex, organic bodies, or "individuals"; and the third consists of a series of postulates dealing specifically with the human body. As one might expect, the principle underlying the analysis is that all bodies are combinations of motion and rest. Accordingly, "bodies are distinguished from one another by reason of motion and rest, speed and slowness, and not by reason of substance" (l1). Moreover, it follows from this that all bodies must agree in certain respects; that is, all bodies are conceived in terms of the same attribute and its principal modification (l2). And since every body is a finite mode, "a body which moves or is at rest must be determined to motion or rest by another body, which has also been determined to motion or rest by another, and that again by another, and so on, to infinity" (l3), from which Spinoza derives one of the basic principles of physics, the law of inertia: "A body in motion moves until it is determined by another body to rest; and ... a body at rest also remains at rest until it is determined to motion by another" (l3c).

The discussion then shifts to complex bodies, which are compounded from the simple bodies, and it is in this context that Spinoza deals with the notions of individuality and life. The first question to be considered is the problem of identity. More specifically, in light of what principle can one claim that a number of distinct, simple bodies constitute a single individual? Spinoza's answer, which is based on the preceding analysis, is in terms of the contact and preservation of the same proportion of motion and rest.

---

[18] For an analysis of the "interlude" see Peterman, "The 'Physical Interlude.'"

Insofar as any given group of bodies is compelled by other bodies to remain in contact with one another, or insofar as they move in such a way as to communicate their motions to each other "in a certain fixed manner," Spinoza contends, "they all together compose one body or Individual, which is distinguished from others by this union of bodies" (G2 100; C1 460). A complex body, or individual, can thus retain its identity throughout a change in its component parts; and this principle provides the basis for Spinoza's schematic account of organic unity or individuality.

The subsequent lemmata (l4–l7) deal in terms of motion and rest with the basic biological functions of metabolism, growth, motion of the limbs, and locomotion. Spinoza argues that the unity of a living being consists in its ability to remain identical, not only in spite of but actually by means of a constant change in its component parts and an ongoing interaction with its environment. What is noteworthy here is that within the confines of a brief space Spinoza succeeds in developing the outlines of a speculative theory of organism that goes much further than Descartes' purely mechanistic account of the body and gives promise of dealing with the nature of life in a far more adequate manner.[19]

The discussion concludes with a series of postulates, which apply these principles to the human body. We are told that this body is an individual of a very high degree of complexity, composed of a number of parts, which are themselves complex individuals (post. 1). Some of these parts are fluid, some soft, and some hard (post. 2), but each of them, and consequently the body itself, is affected in a number of distinct ways by external factors (post. 3). Not only is the human body so affected, it also requires for its preservation "a great many other bodies, by which it is, as it were, continually regenerated" (post. 4). Finally, since it contains soft and fluid parts, it is capable of forming and retaining impressions when affected by external bodies (post. 5), while at the same time it can also affect external bodies in a variety of ways (post. 6). In short, and this is the whole point of Spinoza's analysis, since the human body is an extremely complex individual, which stands in a complex and reciprocal relationship with its environment, it turns out to be a suitable correlate for the human mind.

This suitability is explicitly affirmed in the next two propositions, which conclude the discussion of the mind–body relationship and prepare the ground for the analysis of human cognition. Spinoza here points out that, since the human body is capable of affecting and being affected by a large number of bodies in a variety of ways, the human mind, as the idea of that

---

[19] See Jonas, "Spinoza and the Theory of Organism."

body, "is capable of perceiving a great many things, and is the more capable, the more its body can be disposed in a great many ways" (E2p14). The perceptual power of the mind is thus a function of the sensitivity of the body. And just as the human body is a complex individual composed of a great number of bodies, so, Spinoza concludes, "The idea that constitutes the formal being [esse] of the human Mind is not simple; but composed of a great many ideas" (E2p15).

4.2 Human Cognition

In contrast to Descartes, Spinoza's account of human cognition – that is, his epistemology – is grounded in his metaphysics and encompasses the doctrine of God in the first part of the *Ethics* and his account of the human mind and its relation to the body in the just considered first fifteen propositions of the second part. Moreover, like the *Ethics* as a whole, Spinoza's epistemology is oriented toward the attainment of blessedness, which, since it consists in the intellectual love of God, requires cognition of God. Accordingly, the goal of Spinoza's epistemology is nothing less than to demonstrate the seemingly audacious thesis that "The human Mind has an adequate cognition of God's eternal and infinite essence" (E2p47). Although neither Descartes nor any other early modern thinker would have dared venture such a thesis, its audacity is lessened considerably if we keep in mind Spinoza's identification of God with nature.

One of the keys to Spinoza's account is the notion of adequacy, in particular the conception of an adequate idea, which we have already touched on in passing. As he tells us at the beginning of E2, "By adequate idea I understand an idea which, insofar as it is considered in itself, without relation to an object, has all the properties or intrinsic denominations of a true idea" (E2d4). In the explanation that follows this definition, he further notes, "I say intrinsic to exclude what is extrinsic, viz. the agreement of the idea with its object." Much the same point is made in response to Tschirnhaus' query concerning the relationship between truth and adequacy, where Spinoza writes: "I don't recognize any difference between a true idea and an adequate one, except that the term 'true' concerns only the agreement of the idea with its object, whereas the term 'adequate' concerns the nature of the idea itself" (L60 G4 270; C2 432).

These statements indicate that for Spinoza truth and adequacy are reciprocal notions. All true ideas are adequate, and vice versa. They differ only in that truth is defined in terms of the agreement of the idea with its object, or ideatum. Because of this definition, Spinoza is usually regarded as advocating a version of the correspondence theory of truth; that is, the view that construes truth as the correspondence with, or agreement between, beliefs or propositions and states of affairs or facts.[20] A major difference between Spinoza's view and the correspondence theory, as traditionally construed, is that he regards idea and ideatum as one and the same thing expressed in two ways, rather than as distinct entities. Moreover, partly for this reason and partly because of his conception of the attribute of thought as a self-contained whole, which does not involve reference to any extrinsic reality, Spinoza is also sometimes thought to hold a coherence theory of truth.[21] Reduced to its simplest terms, this theory maintains that the truth of a belief or proposition is a function of its place within the total system of true beliefs or propositions. Such a conception is generally associated with certain forms of idealism, wherein it is maintained that in some sense the structure of reality reflects the structure of thought (rather than vice versa). But just as Spinoza's view differs from the correspondence theory as commonly understood in that he regards idea and ideatum as one and the same thing, so, too, it differs from the coherence theory in that he maintains that the order of true thoughts (the content of infinite intellect) reflects the order of reality (as expressed in extension and the other attributes).

In light of this, it seems more fruitful to approach Spinoza's account of truth by way of his conception of adequacy. As the passages cited above suggest, adequacy is an intrinsic property of an idea by virtue of which it is judged to be true. This can also be expressed by saying that adequacy functions as the criterion of truth. The basic feature of an adequate idea is its completeness. As we saw in our preliminary discussion of Spinoza's method, an adequate idea is simply one from which the properties of its ideatum can be deduced. For example, the mathematician's idea of a triangle is adequate because all the mathematically relevant properties of the figure can be derived from it. Correlatively, the conception of a triangle possessed by someone ignorant of geometry is inadequate precisely because it does not allow for this. Such a person may have a vague idea of a triangle as a figure with three sides; but since he does not know what follows from this, he does not possess the true concept or adequate idea of a triangle.

---

[20] For accounts of Spinoza as a correspondence theorist, see Mark, *Spinoza's Theory of Truth*, and Curley, *Spinoza's Metaphysics*, chap. 4.

[21] See Walker, "Spinoza and the Coherence Theory of Truth," for a rigorous statement of this view.

The conception of adequacy and its function as the criterion of truth provide the basis for Spinoza's response to the specter of radical skepticism produced by Descartes' methodical doubt. In discussing this issue in Chapter 2, it was noted that for Descartes this doubt was motivated by the worry that God or, more precisely, a hypothetical evil genius might be systematically deceiving us, so that even our greatest subjective certainty, such as we have with respect to the basic propositions of mathematics, might be illusory. And it was further noted that Descartes' endeavor to escape from this skeptical morass by demonstrating that God exists and is no deceiver generated what has become known as the "Cartesian circle," since the demonstration presupposes the veracity of our clear and distinct conceptions, which is supposedly the very point at issue. Finally, it was pointed out that, though not referring to the circularity issue, in both the DPP and TdIE Spinoza maintained, contra Descartes, that, just as we can have a clear and distinct (that is, adequate) idea of a triangle without knowing whether we are being systematically deceived, so, too, we can have such an idea of God. Once again, the key point is that if we have this idea, there can no longer be any rational basis for doubt regarding God's nature, since it is self-evident that God is not a deceiver.

The earlier analyses underlie Spinoza's typically cryptic account in the *Ethics*, where, presumably in response to the Cartesian skeptic, he states that "He who has a true idea at the same time knows that he has a true idea, and cannot doubt the truth of the thing" (E2p43). As Spinoza explains in the attached scholium, this is because "to have a true idea means nothing other than cognizing a thing perfectly *or* in the best way." We have already seen that cognizing a thing in this manner involves seeing how all its properties follow necessarily from its nature or definition. In such cases, nothing remains ambiguous, unexplained, undetermined, or uncertain. Consequently, there is no need to appeal to God, or, indeed, to anything outside the ideas themselves, in order to guarantee their truth. To cite Spinoza's appropriate and uncharacteristically elegant metaphor: "As the light makes both itself and the darkness plain, so truth is the standard both of itself and of the false" (E2p43s).

The reference to falsity in this context is likewise extremely significant, for it shows that the very same conception of adequacy that serves as a criterion of truth also provides the basis for determining the nature of error or falsity. At first glance, error would seem to be a major problem for Spinoza. Since the order and connection of ideas is the same as the order and connection of things, and since an idea and its object are not two distinct things between which disagreement or lack of correspondence is possible, but merely one and the same thing expressed in two manners, one might ask how an idea could fail to agree with its object or, correlatively, how, on the basis of Spinoza's metaphysical assumptions, such a thing as error or falsity is even conceivable.

Spinoza begins his brief, yet significant, treatment of this topic by acknowledging that there is a sense in which all ideas are true. Specifically, "All ideas, insofar as they are related to God, are true" (E2p32). As the demonstration of this proposition makes clear, this follows from the identification of the order and connection of ideas with the order and connection of things. But this still leaves us with the question of what it means to say that ideas are related to God. Presumably, this is intended to contrast with a situation in which these ideas are related to a human or some other mind and to suggest that in the former, but not the latter, case they necessarily agree perfectly with their object. In other words, the proposition seems to reduce to the not very informative claim that all ideas that agree with or adequately express their objects are true.

This proposition is not as empty as it first appears, however, since from the fact that, as a mode in the attribute of thought, an idea must necessarily agree with its object, we can infer that "There is nothing positive in ideas on account of which they are called false" (E2p33). Furthermore, since falsity is not a positive characteristic of any idea, which means that there simply are no ideas that do not agree with their objects, error can be due only to the way in which an idea is grasped by a particular mind. Any given mind can possess or conceive a particular idea either completely or only in part, as in our earlier example in which the mathematician possesses the complete, and hence adequate, idea of a triangle, whereas the person ignorant of mathematics does not. Thus, even though an idea that is conceived adequately, i.e., completely, by the human mind is true and is, in fact, conceived in precisely the same way as an infinite intellect would conceive it (E2p34), the problem is that not many ideas are conceived by the human mind in this manner. Those that are not are conceived inadequately, so that "Falsity consists in the privation of cognition which inadequate, or mutilated and confused ideas involve" (E2p35). Falsity, in other words, is really partial truth, which is mistakenly taken as the complete truth about a state of affairs. This typically occurs when the mind perceives the idea of an effect without considering the idea of its cause. In such cases our ideas are said to be "like conclusions without premises" (E2p28d).

Spinoza illustrates his conception of error with two examples. The first is his favorite *bête noire*: the notion of freedom of the will. Belief in such freedom, he points out, arises because people are ignorant of the true causes of their actions. This ignorance is due to the fact that their inadequate ideas of their actions do not include ideas of their determining causes. Consequently, they tend to explain these actions in terms of a mysterious faculty of will; but he notes that "these are only words for which they have no idea." The second example is even more revealing, and Spinoza's analysis is worth quoting in full:

> Similarly, when we look at the sun, we imagine it as about 200 feet away from us, an error that does not consist simply in this imagining, but in the fact that while we imagine it in this way, we are ignorant of its true distance and of the cause of this imagining. For even if we later come to know that it is more than 600 diameters of the earth away from us, we nevertheless imagine it as near. For we imagine the sun so near not because we do not know its true distance, but because an affection of our body involves the essence of the sun insofar as our body is affected by the sun. (E2p35s)

Spinoza here underscores the fact that this imaginative idea of the sun is not intrinsically false, since it contains an accurate description of how the sun actually *appears* under certain conditions, or, in Spinoza's language, how it is perceived by virtue of its affection of the body. Presumably, it still appears this way to someone who has an adequate idea of it; but the latter includes within it an explanation (in accordance with the laws of optics) of just why the sun appears as it does under given conditions. This is lacking in the inadequate, imaginative idea, which, accordingly, involves a confusion between how the sun appears and how it really is. This confusion, which could be remedied by a causal account of why the sun appears as it does, is the error. Spinoza's claim, which is never really worked out, is that *all* cases of error, or inadequate ideas, can be explained in a similar fashion.

As the above suggests, Spinoza's treatment of error is closely connected with his account of sense perception, which precedes it in the text. He characterizes such perception and the thought based on it as perception "according to the common order of nature," which is the order in which the mind actually receives its ideas in experience. Given the parallelism doctrine, this corresponds to the order in which the body is affected by the objects of these ideas. Spinoza contends that the mind is necessarily passive when it perceives in this manner, and we shall see in the next chapter that this constitutes one of the bases for his theory of the passions. For the present, however, the important point is that perceptual ideas reflect the condition of the body in its interplay with the environment, rather than the true nature of an independent reality. Thus, insofar as the mind takes such ideas to represent an external thing as it is in itself, rather than the manner in which that thing affects one's sensory apparatus, it inevitably falls into error. Correlatively, error is avoided insofar as one's thought follows the "order of the intellect." The latter is the order of logical dependence "by which the mind perceives things through their first causes." Since this order, unlike the former, depends on the activity of the mind, rather than external causes (which vary from situation to situation), Spinoza contends that it is "the same in all men" (E2p18s).

At the root of Spinoza's account of perception and, indeed, of his whole analysis of cognition is the principle that "The idea of any mode in which the human Body is affected by external bodies must involve the nature of the human Body and at the same time the nature of the external body" (E2p16). This follows from the status of the body as a finite mode, which, as such, is determined by its network of relations with external bodies, and from the conception of the mind as the idea of the body, which reflects in the realm of thought everything that occurs in the world of extension. The key implication of this principle is that the human body provides the focal point from and through which the human mind perceives the external world.

This, in turn, has two consequences, one positive and one negative, which Spinoza presents in the form of corollaries. The first and positive consequence is that "the human Mind perceives the nature of a great many bodies together with the nature of its own body" (E2p16c1), which implies that sense perception *does* provide an awareness of external bodies. This is crucial because it makes clear that Spinoza does not want his claim that the body is the "object" of the idea constituting the human mind to be taken as implying that the *only* object a human mind can represent is its own body. The point is rather that the mind represents other things on the basis of their relationship to its body. The second and negative corollary is that "the ideas which we have of external bodies indicate the condition of our own body more than the nature of external bodies." This is also the principle underlying Spinoza's account of error. Since the perceptual awareness of external bodies is a function of the state of one's own body or, more precisely, of one's sensory apparatus, this awareness provides information only concerning how a body appears, and this, strictly speaking, is a fact more about the constitution of one's own body than about the nature of the external body.

Moreover, since the ideas in the mind reflect the nature both of one's own body and of external bodies, and since the order and connection of ideas is identical with the order and connection of things, it follows that the laws determining the relations of ideas in the mind must reflect the laws determining the relations of bodies conceived under the attribute of extension. Consequently, a foundation is laid for a quasi-mechanistic psychology, which formulates universal laws concerning the relations of ideas. This provides the basis for Spinoza's account of imagination and memory and, as we shall see in the next chapter, for his theory of the passions as well.

Spinoza construes the imagination in a very broad sense to encompass all thought, including sense perception, in which the order of ideas in the mind reflects the order of affections of the body. Ultimately, this includes all thought that is according to the "common order of nature." The reason for using *imagination* in this way seems to be that the bodily affections are themselves characterized as "the images of things" and their corresponding ideas the "imaginations of the mind" (E2p17s).[22] In the present context, however, Spinoza's concern is mainly with imagination in the more limited sense of the mind's propensity to form ideas of absent objects. Depending on circumstances and the conclusions drawn, this propensity can be viewed as either a power or a defect of the mind. Moreover, in either case it is both perfectly natural and explicable in terms of a general principle that constitutes a psychological version of the law of inertia: "If the human Body is affected with a mode that involves the nature of an external body, the human Mind will regard the same external body as actually existing, or as present to it, until the Body is affected by an affection that excludes the existence or presence of that body" (E2p17).

Spinoza applies the same line of thought to memory, understood as the mind's ability to recall the idea of a past object on the basis of a present image or impression. The principle at work here, which is a consequence of the law governing the operation of the imagination, is that "If the human Body has once been affected by two or more bodies at the same time, then when the Mind subsequently imagines one of them, it will immediately recollect the others also" (E2p18). As Spinoza notes in the scholium to this proposition, memory, so construed, is really association, and the law he presents here regarding the operation of memory is basically equivalent to what has subsequently been called "the law of the association of ideas." For Spinoza, as for later "associationists," the importance of this law stems from the fact that it provides an explanation of how the mind moves from

---

[22] For a detailed discussion of Spinoza's conception of the imagination, see Parkinson, *Spinoza's Theory of Knowledge*, 138–162.

the thought of one thing to the thought of another that does not stand in a logical connection with the first. The basis is habit, which is itself the product of past associations. To cite Spinoza's own examples, a soldier, on seeing the tracks of a horse, will tend to think of a horseman and then of war, whereas a farmer, seeing the same tracks, will naturally proceed to the thought of a plow and a field. Since in neither case is the transition logical, it does not lead to genuine cognition. Nevertheless, in both cases it is natural and predictable; for, as Spinoza concludes, "each one, according as he has been accustomed to join and connect the images of things in this or that way, will pass from one thought to another" (E2p18s).

Having articulated the basic principle underlying sense perception and described two of the fundamental operations of the mind with regard to its sensible ideas, Spinoza proceeds to his treatment of perceptual cognition. He first points out on the basis of the preceding analysis that the mind's cognition of the body depends on the body's having been affected by external bodies (E2p19). But since the mind is the idea, or mental correlate, of the body, what holds of one holds of the other (they are both in God in the same manner) (E2p20). And given this, Spinoza contends that "The idea of the Mind is united to the Mind in the same way as the Mind is united to the Body" (E2p21). Thus, just as the mind is aware of the body, so it is also aware of itself; that is, "The human Mind perceives not only the affections of the Body, but also the ideas of these affections" (E2p22).

The doctrine of ideas of ideas, which stand to the original ideas in precisely the same way as those ideas stand to their ideata, is another of the more perplexing and controversial aspects of the *Ethics*. It is tempting to read Spinoza as here offering the basis for a theory of conscious awareness. The need for such a theory is already apparent from Spinoza's claims that the human mind somehow perceives everything that occurs in its object (the body), and that there is a sense in which all things are animated. One way of making sense of these claims is to hold that they do not entail conscious awareness, and that the latter occurs only when there is also an idea of an idea in the same mind.[23] There seems to be a fatal difficulty to such a reading, however, since Spinoza is committed by his doctrine of parallelism to the principle that there must be in God an idea of every idea, just as there is an idea corresponding to the modes expressed in all the attributes. Consequently, if Spinoza is claiming that wherever there is an idea of an idea, there is conscious awareness, then he would seem to be committed to the twin absurdities that we have conscious awareness of

---

[23] This view was advocated by Curley, *Spinoza's Metaphysics*, 126–128.

everything that occurs in our bodies and that all things possess some form of conscious awareness.[24]

It is clear that, within the framework of Spinoza's metaphysics, the best way to avoid these consequences is to make self-awareness, like intelligence, a function of organic complexity. Although Spinoza does not develop this point, there is at least a hint of it in the next proposition, in which he claims that "The human Mind does not know itself, except insofar as it perceives the ideas of the affections of the Body" (E2p23). The significance of this proposition and its demonstration lies in the implication that external stimuli are needed for the mind's awareness of itself, as well as for its awareness of its own body (by E2p19 and E2p20). Moreover, since (by E2p13s) in order for the body to be receptive to stimuli from other bodies that affect it in various ways, it must have a corresponding sensitivity – that is, a capacity to receive and process sensory data like that possessed by the human brain – it follows that such a capacity is also necessary for self-awareness. Admittedly, this is vague and speculative, since Spinoza himself never really attempts to provide an explicit account of self-awareness. Nevertheless, the considerations outlined above suggest the possibility of constructing such an account along Spinozistic lines.[25]

Moreover, it is clear that the ideas correlated with the "images" received by the human body as a result of its being affected by other bodies do not provide the mind with adequate ideas either of the parts of its own body or of the nature of the affecting bodies (E2p24 and Ep2p25). The former is the case because one's awareness of the parts of one's own body reflects the way in which this body is affected by external bodies (the sensory input), while the latter is true because we perceive these bodies only insofar as they "appear" to us; that is, by virtue of the manner in which they affect us, not as they are in themselves. At the same time, however, it is also the case that

[24] This criticism was made by Wilson, "Objects, Ideas and 'Minds': Comments on Spinoza's Theory of Mind," *The Philosophy of Baruch Spinoza*, 116. In a subsequent discussion of the topic, Curley seems to have accepted this criticism (see *Behind the Geometrical Method*, 49).

[25] In this context one might try to develop a suggestion made to Margaret Wilson by Peggy Nicholson. According to Nicholson, as reported by Wilson ("Objects, Ideas and 'Minds,'" 116), Spinoza might have intended to account for self-awareness by the following distinction: "The ideas of ideas belonging to the human mind are in God in so far as he constitutes the nature of the human mind, whereas the ideas of ideas of nonhuman minds are in God, but not in so far as he constitutes these minds." Although Wilson acknowledges that this is a "natural move to try," she claims to be unable to find any textual warrant for it. This is certainly the case if by such a warrant is meant an explicit reference in the text. If, however, one attributes to Spinoza something like the organic complexity doctrine sketched above, then it would be a reasonable next step to claim that the ideas of the ideas belonging to the human mind are in God qua constituting the nature of that mind because of the nature of the human body.

it is only by means of such ideas that the human mind can form the idea of the actual existence of external objects (E2p26). Such cognition, in other words, requires sensory input, or experience.

These considerations, however, lead to some initially unsettling conclusions. Since the idea of one's own body depends on the ideas of external bodies, and since it has been established that the latter ideas are inadequate, it follows that the same holds for the idea of one's own body (E2p27), which entails that the cognition of one's own body possessed in this manner is similarly confused (E2p28). Moreover, the difficulty does not stop here. For since what holds for the idea of the body applies equally to the idea of the idea, which has already been shown to be equivalent to the mind's idea of itself, it can also be concluded that such ideas do not provide adequate cognition of the human mind (E2p29). The outcome of the initial stage of Spinoza's analysis of cognition thus seems to be a radical skepticism, which is further extended to include cognition of the duration of one's own body and of external bodies (E2p30 and p31).

However, no sooner does Spinoza arrive at this result than he begins to qualify it. These consequences, he notes, follow only insofar as the mind

> perceives things from the common order of nature, i.e., so long as it is determined externally, from fortuitous encounters with things . . . and not so long as it is determined internally, from the fact that it regards a number of things at once, to understand their agreements, differences, and oppositions. For so often as it is disposed internally, in this or another way, then it regards things clearly and distinctly. (E2p29s)

By thinking being determined internally is understood that the mind is guided by its own thoughts, which are ordered inferentially as premises to a conclusion (the order of the intellect), rather than in the manner in which they occur in the mind as the result of the body's being affected by external bodies (the common order of nature). Thus, the immediate problem is to explain how the mind, as the idea of the body, whose every modification must correspond to a modification of this body, can ever be in a position to do this. The basis of Spinoza's answer lies in the claim that there are certain ideas that the human mind possesses completely and hence can conceive adequately, because, unlike the ideas derived from ordinary sense experience, they do not "involve" or logically depend on ideas of particular modifications of the body. These ideas fall into two classes corresponding to two levels of generality. Spinoza calls them respectively "common notions" and "adequate ideas of the common properties of things."

These two classes correspond to the innate ideas advocated by other philosophers, which were also referred to "common notions." Both Descartes and Leibniz appealed to the theory of innate ideas in order to explain the foundations of rational cognition. Their basic claim was that our cognition of necessary and universal truths, adequate cognition in Spinoza's sense, cannot be derived from experience. Rather, it was thought that the sources of such cognition must lie in the mind and reflect its very structure, since this is required to account for its putative necessity and universality. This theory was not construed in a naive psychological sense, however; that is, it was not maintained, as some critics of the theory charged, that it entails that the infant or the untutored savage, who were favorites of the philosophical literature of the time, were actually conscious of the "true concept of God" or the basic principles of mathematics. Instead, innate ideas were viewed as dispositions that pertain universally to the human mind, but of which any given individual is not necessarily conscious. As Descartes expressed the matter in response to a critic:

> I have never written or taken the view that the mind requires innate ideas which are something distinct from its faculty of thinking. I did, however, observe that there were certain thoughts within me which neither came to me from external objects nor were determined by my will, but which came solely from the power of thinking within me; so I applied the tern "innate" to the ideas or notions which are the forms of these thought in order to distinguish them from others, which I called "adventitious" or "made up." This is the same sense as that in which we say that generosity is "innate" in certain families, or that certain diseases such as gout or stones are innate in others: it is not so much that the babies of such families suffer from these diseases in their mother's womb, but simply that they are born with a certain "faculty" to contract them.[26]

Spinoza's conception of the mind as the idea of the body does not allow him to distinguish in the manner of Descartes between innate and adventitious ideas; that is, between those that come from the mind and those that come from experience. For him, all ideas are innate, since they are all modifications of the attribute of thought, and none is "caused" by anything in the realm of extension. Correlatively, all are adventitious in the sense that each must have its physical correlate. Nevertheless, Spinoza's conception of the mind as the idea of the body allows him to make an analogous distinction, which leads to much the same result. This is the distinction

---

[26] Descartes, "Comments on a Certain Broadsheet," *The Philosophical Writings of Descartes*, vol. 1, 303–304.

between ideas that are correlated with specific features of particular bodies and those whose correlates are common to all bodies or a large class thereof. Things that are common to all bodies and are "equally in the part and in the whole," Spinoza notes, do not "constitute the essence of any singular thing" (E2p37). Moreover, it follows from this that the common notions, which are the ideas that correspond to these things, do not arise in the mind in connection with the experience of any particular object. Thus, on the basis of the preceding analysis, Spinoza contends that the mind possesses these ideas in their totality and understands them adequately (E2p38). And since these ideas correspond to what is common to all bodies, like the innate ideas of Descartes and Leibniz, they are common to all minds (E2p38c).

Since we have seen that bodies for Spinoza are particular modifications of the attribute of extension and are constituted by a certain proportion of motion and rest, the latter must be common to all bodies and present equally in the part and in the whole. Thus, the ideas corresponding to them, which evidently include the axioms of geometry and the first principles of physics, must be included among the common notions. Furthermore, if we extend this line of reasoning to the attribute of thought and point to thoughts that are present equally in a part and in the whole – that is, in all thoughts – we arrive at the laws of logic, the first principles of thought, which must likewise be regarded as common notions.[27] This brings us to the second category of adequate ideas: those of the common properties of things. These have a lesser degree of generality than the common notions and refer only to properties shared by certain bodies. Specifically, they refer to properties that are common and peculiar to the human body "and certain external bodies by which the human Body is usually affected, and is equally in the part and in the whole of each of them" (E2p39). Although it is not clear just what Spinoza has in mind here, the implication, once again, is that the commonality of these ideas enables the mind to grasp them completely and, hence, adequately. Thus, in spite of the extreme sketchiness of the account, which Spinoza evidently intended to remedy in a future work dealing with epistemology,[28] the basic point emerges with sufficient clarity. It is simply that, insofar as the human mind possesses such ideas and deduces other ideas from them, it will know things truly or in an adequate manner (E2p40).

But one detail could not be left to the projected future work. In order to avoid complete misunderstanding, Spinoza found it necessary to

---

[27] See Parkinson, *Spinoza's Theory of Knowledge*, 165.   [28] See Gueroult, *Spinoza* II, 333–339.

distinguish between his common notions and adequate ideas of the common properties of things, which were for him the very foundations of
scientific reasoning, and the universals, or general terms, of the scholastics.
The latter are of two kinds. The first are the so-called transcendentals, e.g.,
Being, Thing, and Something, which are the most general concepts,
applicable to all genera. The second are the various genera and species
under which all substances in nature fall. As already noted, Aristotelian
science proceeded largely by classifying substances in terms of such universals, and Spinoza's basic contention is that not only do such concepts not
yield adequate cognition of the nature of things, they also reflect the limits
of the imagination rather than the power of the intellect. The human
mind, Spinoza points out, is only capable of imagining distinctly as many
things as its body can form images of simultaneously. When these images
become confused, the mind tends to form general ideas answering to these
confused images. The transcendentals are the most confused ideas of all,
since they reflect the intellect's inability to make distinctions. What, after
all, is emptier than the concept of a mere "something"? But the situation is
not much better with respect to class concepts, such as *man, horse, stone*, or
tree. Since for Spinoza they merely reflect the inability of the imagination
to capture the small differences between individuals, they can hardly serve
as vehicles for adequate cognition. In short, rather than answering to the
essence of things, as Aristotelians claim, these general ideas merely depict
what a particular individual happens to regard as important, which, in
turn, is a function of the condition of that individual's body. To cite
Spinoza's own example: "Those who have more often regarded men's
stature with wonder will understand by the word *man* an animal of erect
stature. But those who have been accustomed to consider something else,
will form another common image of man, e.g., that man is an animal
capable of laughter, or a featherless biped, or a rational animal" (E2p40s1).

   In the second scholium to E2p40, which might be considered the
centerpiece of his epistemology because it brings together all its essential
features, Spinoza first uses the contrast between the two radically different
types of general notions to distinguish between two kinds of cognition.
Those of Aristotelian science yield what Spinoza calls "cognition of the first
kind, opinion or imagination." This, in turn, is subdivided into two
species, corresponding to two distinct ways in which such notions can be
formed: either from the confused perception of particular things as they are
encountered in experience or from signs, which includes both sensory and
memory images. By contrast, Spinoza's common notions and adequate
ideas of the common properties of things yield "cognition of the second

kind" or "reason" (*ratio*). They differ in that the former (in both species) involves only inadequate, and the latter only adequate, ideas.

However, rather than presenting this as the culmination of his account, on the grounds that it provides the basis for distinguishing between adequate and inadequate cognition, Spinoza abruptly introduces the possibility of a third kind of cognition termed "intuitive cognition" (*scientia*), which "proceeds from an adequate idea of the formal essence of certain attributes of God to the adequate cognition of the essence of things." We initially encountered the conception of the formal essence of an individual thing in connection with the analysis of E2p8, where the focus was on the metaphysical status of nonactual singular things. The proffered explanation was that by this is understood an eternal finite mode in a given attribute, which expresses the essential nature of that thing; and it was suggested that this essence is latent in an attribute in a manner analogous to the way in which constructible but not actually constructed rectangles are latent in the nature of a circle. Since the reference is to the essence of a *singular* thing, this is often taken to refer to what individuates a thing from others, which would mean that *scientia intuitiva* is a cognition of what individuates particulars, whereas *ratio* (to be discussed further later) is cognition of what is common to a number of things.[29] But inasmuch as the reference is to thing*s* (plural) rather than to *a* thing and *scientia intuitiva*, as Spinoza here construes it, is a form of *human* (not divine) cognition, I believe it better to take the intuitive cognition of the formal nature of singular things to be cognition of what such a thing fundamentally or essentially is, namely a finite mode in a certain attribute, rather than of what individuates it from others with a similar nature.[30] Spinoza illustrates all three kinds of cognition using the following example:

> Suppose there are three numbers, and the problem is to find a fourth which is to the third as the second is to the first. Merchants do not hesitate to multiply the second by the third, and divide the product by the first, because they have not yet forgotten what they heard from their teacher without any demonstration, or because they have often found this in the simplest numbers, or from the force of the demonstration of P19 in Bk. VII of Euclid, namely, from the common property of proportionals. But in the simplest numbers none of this is necessary. Given the numbers 1, 2, and 3, no one fails to see that the fourth proportional number is 6 – and we see this much more clearly because we infer the fourth number from the ratio which, in one glance, we see the first number to have to the second. (E2p40s2)

[29] I interpreted it in this manner in the 1987 version of this book (187).
[30] A similar reading is advocated by Primus, "Scientia Intuitiva in the *Ethics*," 176.

The procedure of merchants illustrates the first kind of cognition based on memory and/or association, whereas the second and third illustrate the manner of dealing with the same problem on the basis of *ratio* and *scientia intuitiva*, respectively. As noted above, both of the latter manners of cognition are considered adequate by Spinoza because they are based on adequate ideas and draw the correct conclusion solely on the basis of these ideas. But they differ in at least three essential respects, which are only partially indicated by Spinoza's illustration. The first is the nature of the adequate ideas on which their inferences are based. As was also noted above, the adequate ideas underlying the inferences of *ratio* are the common notions or ideas of common properties of things, e.g., motion-rest, whereas those underlying *scientia intuitiva* are the ideas of the formal essence of an attribute of God. The second is the manner in which their inferences proceed from their starting points. *Ratio* proceeds discursively from the common notions with which it begins by introducing intermediate concepts in roughly the manner of Aristotelian syllogistics, which link the starting point with the conclusion. By contrast, as the name suggests, *scientia intuitiva* derives the conclusion, which consists in cognition of the (formal) essence of things, i.e., finite modes, directly from an adequate idea of the formal essence of an attribute of God, which the case of human cognition is either thought or extension.[31] The third and, from the perspective of the argument of the *Ethics* as a whole, most important way in which *scientia intuitiva* differs from *ratio* is in terms of power, understood in both an epistemic and a psychological sense. Epistemically, *scientia intuitiva* is more powerful than *ratio* in two respects. First, it grounds the common notions on the basis of which the latter proceeds by deriving them from the formal nature of an attribute of God. Without this grounding, the common notions would be in effect brute givens, without a sufficient reason, which is what only *scientia intuitiva* can provide. Second, *scientia intuitiva* provides cognition of the (formal) essence, i.e., essential nature of things, whereas *ratio* is presumably incapable of arriving at a sharp distinction between what are essential and what are merely accidental, though shared, properties of things. Finally, as Spinoza will argue in E5p36s in connection with the intellectual love of God, *scientia intuitiva* is more powerful than *ratio* in the psychological sense that it alone is capable of

---

[31] Thus, the contrast between the second and the third kind of cognition is not between inferential and non-inferential cognition, but between an immediate and a mediate inference. The point is put clearly by Parkinson, who claims that the third kind of cognition is "ordinary deductive knowledge," *Spinoza's Theory of Knowledge*, 186.

producing the intellectual love of God in which the condition of blessedness consists.

But before Spinoza can claim that the human intellect through *scientia intuitiva* can proceed from cognition of the eternal and infinite essence of God to the cognition of the formal essence of singular things, he must show that it does, in fact, possess an adequate idea of this essence and is, therefore, capable of such cognition. In support of this, he maintains that "He who has a true idea at the same time knows that he has a true idea, and cannot doubt the truth of the thing" (E2p43). Although it is not immediately evident how this claim, which reflects Spinoza's critique of Cartesian skepticism, bears on the present issue, I believe that the answer lies in the appeal to E2p11c in the demonstration of this proposition, where Spinoza claimed that "the human mind is part of the infinite intellect of God." In the previous discussion of this important claim, it was noted that by it Spinoza maintains that the human intellect is a finite and, therefore, limited member of the total system of thought, which is what is meant by the infinite intellect of God. Thus, the emphasis was on the finite and limited nature of the human mind, which is due to its nature as the idea of the human body. In the present context, however, the emphasis is reversed, since the focus is on the participation of the human intellect in the infinite intellect of God, rather than on the limited nature of this participation. And the distinctive, though seemingly paradoxical, aspect of Spinoza's account of the human mind is that he adheres to both theses.

Given the participation of the human intellect in the infinite intellect of God, Spinoza first notes that "It is of the nature of Reason to regard things as necessary, not as contingent" (E2p44). Moreover, since to regard things as necessary is to consider them as eternal, it follows that "It is of the nature of Reason to perceive things under a certain form of eternity" (*sub quadem aeternitatis specie*) (Ep44c2). And since to conceive things in this way is to conceive them in relation to God, it also follows that "Each idea of each body, or of each singular thing which actually exists, necessarily involves an eternal and infinite essence of God" (E2p45).

Although this, like much else in Spinoza's account of the human intellect, seems paradoxical, it is a logical consequence of metaphysical principles laid out in the first part of the *Ethics*. Since all things depend on God, both for their essence and for their existence, or "the force by which each one perseveres in existing" (which Spinoza is careful to distinguish from the duration of their existence), the idea of each thing that actually exists must necessarily involve the idea of God. Furthermore, since the idea of God, like the common notions, is involved in the idea of everything and can be apprehended either in the whole or in the part, Spinoza concludes by the same line of reasoning that he used in connection with the common notions that "The cognition of God's eternal and infinite essence which each idea involves is adequate and perfect" (E2p46). Finally, since every finite thing is part of that infinite system (*natura naturata*), which is grounded in God (*natura naturans*), it follows that, in the last analysis, the adequate idea of anything involves the idea of the whole, or of God. We thus return once again to the central tenet of Spinoza's thought: that the cognition of anything in nature depends ultimately on the cognition of God, which is a consequence of the principle that "The cognition of an effect depends upon and involves the cognition of its cause." And since it has already been established that the mind cognizes some things, or possesses adequate ideas, Spinoza concludes that "The human Mind has an adequate cognition of God's eternal and infinite essence" (E2p47).

The key to this conclusion, which again is highly paradoxical from the standpoint of both traditional theology and common sense, is Spinoza's conception of God. Insofar as God is identified with the universal and necessary order of nature, it is obvious that the adequate idea of anything must "involve" (in the sense of presuppose) a cognition of God. Why, then, do most people fail to realize this, believing instead that God is uncognizable? Spinoza's answer is that it is largely because they do not correctly apply names to things (E2p47s). Specifically, they erroneously apply the name "God" to what is in fact a product of their own imagination. Such a being is certainly not cognizable, but neither is such a being really God. Accordingly, the moral to be drawn from this is the need to be sure that one has a proper understanding of the meaning of one's terms, which in the present instance is accomplished by attending carefully to the argument of the first part of the *Ethics*.

4.3   The Will

In the last two propositions and concluding scholium of E2, Spinoza turns from the intellect to the will. This short, but important, section both completes the analysis of the human mind and provides a bridge between the metaphysical and epistemological doctrines of the earlier parts of the work and the psychological and ethical concerns of its later portions. Here Spinoza applies to the human mind many of the same conclusions that have already been established with regard to the divine mind. Just as we have previously seen that God does not act from freedom of the will, that his actions are coextensive with his power, and that his intellect is identical with his will, so we now come to see that precisely the same things can be affirmed about the human mind, which is just what we should expect, given its status as a finite mode in the attribute of thought.

Although freedom is one of the fundamental values of Spinoza's philosophy, it should be evident that he had no use for the traditional conception of a free will. He makes this explicit by declaring categorically that "In the Mind there is no absolute, or free, will, but the Mind is determined to will this or that by a cause which is also determined by another, and this again by another, and so to infinity" (E2p48). The demonstration indicates that this is supposed to follow from the nature of the human mind as a finite mode. As such, each of its particular volitions must be determined by a particular cause from which the volition necessarily follows. Accordingly, while a human being for Spinoza may be said to choose something, this choice must itself have a cause that determines it necessarily, and, therefore, it is not free. And since this is the case, it follows that not only can we not talk of "free will" in the traditional sense, as a capacity for free choice, we also cannot attach any meaning to the notion of the will as a faculty of volition. Here Spinoza is clearly following Hobbes, who had dismissed the scholastic conception of the will as a distinct appetitive faculty by redefining it as "the last Appetite in Deliberating."[32]

Moreover, as Spinoza adds in the scholium, precisely the same line of reasoning suffices to demonstrate that there is no "absolute faculty" of understanding, desiring, loving, or anything else. While there are particular acts of understanding, desiring, loving, and so on, there are no mysterious faculties that perform and exist apart from these activities. Simply put, human beings, like God, are what they do; their power is coextensive with their activity. Thus, there is no room in the Spinozistic universe for any unexercised power or potentiality. Although human beings believe in such things, and this is one of the basic factors underlying the prevalent belief in a free will, here, as elsewhere, they are the victims of their imagination. On the basis of their experience of particular volitions, they come to form an abstract idea of a volition in general and then proceed to reify this abstraction, thereby giving birth to the fiction of a distinct faculty.

Having established that there is no faculty of will above and beyond particular volitions, Spinoza turns to the question of whether one can find a role for volition in the affirmation or negation of propositions. As one might expect, Spinoza's answer is an unequivocal no. "In the Mind," he writes, "there is no volition, or affirmation and negation, except that which

---

[32] Hobbes, *Leviathan*, 1.6, 47.

the idea involves insofar as it is an idea" (E2p49). The equation in this proposition of volition with affirmation and negation is a clear indication that Spinoza's specific target is Descartes, who in the Fourth Meditation distinguished between the intellect and the will and located the source of the possibility of error in the will's infinite capacity to affirm or deny what the intellect conceives.[33] The thesis underlying this Cartesian division of labor is that the intellect conceives or forms the idea of something and the will decides whether or not what the intellect has conceived is to be believed. Error, on this view, arises when the will does not limit belief to what the intellect clearly and distinctly conceives.

In the demonstration of E2p49, Spinoza mounts a two-step argument against this doctrine and, more generally, against any attempt to distinguish between acts of assent or belief and acts of understanding. Each of these steps is based on his previously discussed conception of an idea. The first points out that any affirmation or belief presupposes an idea of what is affirmed or believed. To cite Spinoza's own example: the mind cannot affirm that the three angles of a triangle are equal to two right angles without already having the idea of a triangle. This follows from the conception of ideas as the fundamental modifications of thought, and it is a premise that Descartes would likewise accept. The second, and crucial, step is to claim that an idea, by its very nature, already involves an affirmation. Spinoza attempts to illustrate this by appealing once again to the idea of a triangle. The point is that we do not first entertain this idea and examine it, and then, by a distinct act of volition, affirm or decide to believe that the sum of its three angles is equal to two right angles. Rather, this affirmation is part of the content of the idea of a triangle; so, in conceiving of a triangle, one is already affirming this and denying it is contradictory. Moreover, Spinoza continues, since this example of a "volition" has been selected at random, what has been said of it can be said of any volition, namely "that it is nothing apart from the idea." Finally, since a volition is nothing apart from an idea, and, since, as we have also seen, the will is nothing apart from its volitions and the intellect nothing

---

[33] For a defense of Descartes against Spinoza's critique see Cottingham, "The Intellect, the Will, and the Passions: Spinoza's Critique of Descartes." In his defense of Descartes, Cottingham claims that Spinoza tends to exaggerate the differences between his views of freedom and the will from those of Descartes, since the latter in his more careful formulations expressed more guarded views, which are not diametrically opposed to Spinoza's. As Cottingham seems to have reluctantly acknowledged, however, this does not apply to their views on the divine intellect and will, since Descartes' notorious doctrine of eternal truths as products of the divine will, to which Cottingham apparently alludes but does not discuss (254), is clearly radically opposed to Spinoza's view.

apart from its ideas, it follows that in human beings, as in God, "the will and the intellect are one and the same" (E2p49c).

Although Spinoza discusses a number of possible objections to this view, which are shown to rest on a failure to distinguish between ideas and images, on the one hand, and abstractions (faculties) and realities (particular ideas), on the other, and adds a catalog of the advantages of his doctrine vis-à-vis morality, this really completes Spinoza's analysis of the human mind. The implications of this analysis are quite revolutionary. The human mind is removed from the special place given to it by Descartes, which served only to make its activities incomprehensible, and is fully integrated into nature. As the idea of the human body, it is not a separate substance, nor does it possess distinct and mysterious powers above and beyond its activities. Nevertheless, this does not render it totally powerless. The true power of the mind consists in its ability to understand, which is coextensive with its possession of adequate ideas. Spinoza claims to have shown not only that the human mind possesses such power and how that is so, but also that this is nothing more than its own limited portion of the infinite power of nature. This account is obscure at many points, especially in regard to details, and Spinoza himself, as we have seen, does not pretend to have provided an exhaustive treatment of the topic. He does claim, however, that this account is complete and clear enough for his purpose, which, as he tells us at the very end of the section, is to "have set out doctrines from which we can infer many excellent things, which are highly useful and necessary to know" (E2p49s). It is to these things that we now turn.

CHAPTER 5

The Human Emotions

A striking feature of Spinoza's analysis of the human emotions (*affectiones*), which is the subject of the third part of the *Ethics*, is its thoroughgoing naturalism. We have already seen this naturalism at work in connection with his analysis of the cognitive capacity of the mind, his mechanistic account of imagination and association, and his Hobbes-inspired rejection of the will in E2. He reaffirms it in the preface to E3, claiming that "the way of understanding the nature of anything, of whatever kind, must . . . be the same, viz. through the universal laws and rules of Nature." Spinoza gives graphic expression to this view in the same preface, when he announces that: "[he] shall treat the nature and powers of the Affects, and the power of the Mind over them, by the same Method by which, in the preceding parts, [he] treated God and the Mind, and [he] shall consider human actions and appetites just as if it were a Question of lines, planes, and bodies" (G2 138; C1 492).

On the basis of this naturalism, Spinoza ridicules those who in writing about the emotions treat them not as "natural things, which follow the common order of nature, but [as] things which are outside nature." And he further suggests that this treatment stems from a tacit metaphysic, accord-ing to which, rather than simply being parts of nature and, as such subject to its laws, human beings are considered as constituting "a dominion within a dominion" and, therefore, as having the capacity to alter rather than simply follow the order of nature, as the result of which they are thought to have "absolute power over [their] actions and [are] determined by [themselves]" (G2 137; C1 491). Although Spinoza certainly did not include Descartes among the more popular writers on the emotions, who, on the basis of this tacit metaphysic, erroneously treat them as phenomena to be lamented, ridiculed, or cursed at rather than simply understood and explained in naturalistic terms, he notes that "the celebrated Descartes," whose views he shall consider in the "proper place," likewise mistakenly "believed that the Mind has absolute power over its own actions" (Ibid.).

This place is the preface to E5, where Spinoza ridicules Descartes' appeal to the pineal gland as the vehicle for the interaction between mind and body. But Descartes' account of the emotions as contained in his last work, *The Passions of the Soul*, is also a focal point of Spinoza's attention in E3, since much of his discussion of particular emotions either follows, modifies, or takes issue with Descartes' account.

Spinoza tells us that by "affect" (*Affectus*) he understands "affections of the Body by which the Body's power of acting is increased or diminished, aided or restrained, and at the same time, the ideas of these affections" (E3d3). The latter species of affects correspond to what is ordinarily understood by the emotions. Thus, they are ideas in the mind corresponding to changes in the body's power of acting or level of vitality, which, given Spinoza's account of ideas, means that they are cognitions through which the state of one's body is expressed in the attribute of thought. Spinoza divides these affects into two kinds. One corresponds to the human body as it is affected by external bodies. These are the passive affects or passions; and since the ideas in the human mind corresponding to the manner in which the human body is affected are attributed by Spinoza to the imagination, this means that they are confused or inadequate cognitions. The other are the active emotions, which are termed such because they express the genuine power of the mind. Although the great bulk of E3 is concerned with the passions, we shall see that the active emotions are central to the overall argument of the *Ethics* because they provide the basis for Spinoza's moral theory.

The present chapter is divided into four sections. The first examines Spinoza's distinction between the actions and passions of the mind in the definitions and first three propositions of E3 by contrasting it with Descartes' account of the emotions in the aforementioned work. The second analyzes Spinoza's Hobbes-inspired conception of the conatus or the endeavor of each individual or singular thing in nature (including human beings) to preserve its being, which replaces the will of traditional theories as the moving force of the mind. The third contains Spinoza's account of the passions, while the fourth considers his brief but exceedingly important account of the active emotions.

5.1 Descartes and Spinoza on the Actions and Passions of the Mind

Since he presents his analysis of the emotions as a direct repudiation of the Cartesian account, it will prove helpful to preface our analysis with a brief consideration of the latter. Descartes begins his account by distinguishing between actions and passions. Following the traditional view, which goes back to Aristotle, he argues that these are not two distinct things, but merely two names for the same thing. Which name is used depends on the point of view from which it is being considered. The same occurrence can be viewed as an action in relation to the agent (cause) and a passion in relation to the patient (effect). Since for Descartes the body acts directly and immediately on the soul, it follows that what in the body is an action is in the soul a passion; from which he concludes that in order to determine the passions of the soul, it is first necessary to distinguish the soul's functions from those of the body.[1]

These functions are determined by means of the general Cartesian method of appealing to clear and distinct ideas. Whatever we experience as being in us but can also conceive as existing in wholly inanimate bodies is attributed to the body alone, whereas whatever we cannot possibly conceive of as pertaining to the body or corporeal nature is attributed to the soul. On the basis of this principle, all physiological functions are attributed to the body, which Descartes regards as a machine, and the only function granted to the soul is thought. Thoughts, however, are of two sorts, termed "actions" and "passions." The former includes all our volitions, or desires, which experience teaches us proceed directly from the soul and depend on it alone. The latter encompass "all those kinds of perceptions or forms of knowledge which are found in us, because it is often not our soul which makes them what they are, and because it always receives them from the things which are represented by them."[2]

The passions, or perceptions, are themselves divided into two classes. The first consists of those that have the soul itself as a cause and includes the perceptions of our desires and imaginings and of other thoughts that depend on them, i.e., the mind's awareness of its inner states. The second consists of those passions that have the body as their cause. These, in turn, are divided into three subgroups: those that relate to external objects, e.g., sense perceptions; those that relate to our own bodies and their parts, e.g., the sensations of hunger, thirst, pleasure, and pain; and those that are referred to the soul itself, e.g., feelings of joy and sadness, love and anger, or, in other words, affects. These are the "passions of the soul" of which Descartes endeavors to give an account.[3]

---

[1] Descartes, *The Passions of the Soul*, pt. 1, articles 1 and 2, *The Philosophical Writings of Descartes*, vol. 1, 328.
[2] Ibid., article 17, 335.   [3] Ibid., article 25, 337–338.

This account is developed in terms of the interaction between the soul and the body. As previously noted, Descartes held that this interaction, or mutual influence, occurs through the action of the pineal gland. By means of the "animal spirits," which are small particles of matter that it both sends through the nerves to the other parts of the body and receives back again, this gland functions as a kind of messenger service between the mind and the body. When the body is affected by external stimuli, it sends its messages through the animal spirits to this gland, which are relayed to the mind, producing perceptions in it. By reversing the process and sending messages through the gland to the rest of the body, the mind is able to influence the body. This is the basis of Descartes' account of voluntary action, which enables him, on the one hand, to provide a physiological analysis of how the various passions are produced in the mind as a result of changes in the body and, on the other hand, to show that "There is no soul so feeble that it cannot, if well-directed, acquire an absolute power over its passions."[4]

This latter claim, which he shared with the Stoics, is the fundamental tenet of Descartes' moral philosophy and, as already noted, the main object of Spinoza's critique. Descartes attempts to justify it on the rather questionable grounds that the connection between our thoughts and the motions of the animal spirits is a consequence of custom, not nature. Thus, while a given affect, e.g., fear, is generally produced in the mind as a result of particular messages sent by the body through the pineal gland, the mind has the power to break this connection and to establish in its place a connection between these affects and different ideas: e.g., the physiological condition that normally gives rise to fear could, with proper training, be connected with the idea of courage.

In contrasting his view with the Cartesian position, Spinoza's first step is to redefine the notions of action and passion. Whereas for Descartes they refer to two ways of looking at a single occurrence, for Spinoza they characterize two distinct states of affairs. According to his account:

> [W]e act when something happens, in us or outside us, of which we are the adequate cause, that is [by d1], when something in us or outside us follows from our nature, which can be clearly and distinctly understood through our nature alone. On the other hand ... we are acted on when something happens in us, or something follows from our own nature of which we are only a partial cause. (E3d2)

---

[4] Ibid., article 50, 348.

As these definitions indicate, for Spinoza the distinction between action and passion is a function of the distinction between an adequate and a partial cause, which in the case of the mind is explicable in terms of the distinction between adequate and inadequate ideas. An adequate cause, we are told in E3 def. 1, is one "whose effect can be clearly and distinctly perceived through it," whereas an inadequate, or partial, cause is one "through which, by itself, its effect cannot be understood." This leads, in turn, to the above-mentioned definition of the affects, to which Spinoza adds by way of explanation that "[I]f we can be the adequate cause of any of the affections, I understand by an affect an action; otherwise, a passion." Thus, at the very beginning of his account, Spinoza introduces the notion of an active affect, to which he will return in the final propositions of E3 and which, as noted above, is central to his moral theory.

The immediate problem, however, is to explain how the mind can be an adequate cause of something. Given his analysis, it is not surprising to find Spinoza affirming that "Our Mind does certain things [acts] and undergoes other things, viz. insofar as it has adequate ideas, it necessarily does certain things, and insofar as it has inadequate ideas, it necessarily undergoes other things" (E3p1). When the mind conceives something adequately, it possesses its ideas completely and independently of any external causes, which is why, when the mind has adequate ideas, it is determined from within and follows its own laws (the laws of logic), rather than the associations of things dictated by the common order of nature. And it follows from this that to the extent to which the mind possesses adequate ideas, it is the adequate cause of its states (affects) and does not merely reflect external events passively. But unlike Descartes, this activity of the mind does not entail any power to determine the body directly; nor does passivity entail any power of the body to determine the mind. Both are precluded by the doctrine of attributes, from which it follows that "The Body cannot determine the Mind to thinking, and the Mind cannot determine the Body to motion, to rest or to anything else (if there is anything else)" (E3p2).

As Spinoza notes in an important scholium to this proposition, the problem with Descartes and with all who believe that the mind can influence the body through some mysterious act of will is that they have not adequately understood the nature of the body. "No one," he writes, "has yet determined what the Body can do, i.e., experience has not taught anyone what the Body can do from the laws of nature alone, insofar as nature is only considered to be corporeal." In view of Descartes' efforts to provide a purely mechanistic physiology and his consequent conception of the body as a machine, one might question whether Spinoza is here referring to him. Nevertheless, this is precisely the case. What Spinoza seems to have specifically in mind is Descartes' claim that we can determine the functions of the mind or soul by attributing to it everything that we cannot clearly and distinctly conceive as pertaining to the body, which means everything that cannot be explained in mechanistic terms. From Spinoza's standpoint, this whole approach is far too facile, since it neglects a great truth that has already been established, namely "that infinitely many things follow from nature, under whatever attribute it may be considered" (E3p2s).

Against this one might object that ordinary experience provides ample evidence of the mind's ability to exercise control over the body. Spinoza, however, emphatically denies this. "Experience," he points out, "teaches all too plainly that men have nothing less in their power than their tongue, and can do nothing less than moderate their appetites." Moreover, people tend to believe they are free only with regard to the moderate appetites and desires that they are able to control, not with regard to their stronger desires and more violent appetites, which often prove irresistible. Yet this distinction is illusory, and it stems from an ignorance of true causes. The truth of the matter, according to Spinoza, who is again echoing the Hobbesian view as modified by his own theory of attributes, is that there is no such thing as a volition or mental decision distinct from a bodily appetite, through which an individual either resists or yields to that appetite. On the contrary, he asserts that:

> All these things, indeed, show clearly that both the decision of the Mind and the appetite and the determination of the Body by nature exist together – or rather are one and the same thing, which we call a decision when it is considered under, and explained through, the attribute of Thought, and which we call a determination when it is considered under the attribute of Extension and deduced from the laws of motion and rest. (E3p2s)

With this appeal to his account of the mind–body relation, Spinoza radically transforms the problem of understanding human action from the form it had assumed in Descartes. The question is no longer whether or how consciousness can effect changes in the bodily mechanism; for this possibility has been ruled out on metaphysical grounds. Instead, the central issue is whether the mind can ever be the sufficient, i.e., adequate, cause of its affects. Moreover, once the question is posed in this manner, it admits of an affirmative answer. This occurs whenever these affects follow from, or are caused by, adequate ideas. We can express the same point in non-Spinozistic terms by saying that the mind acts, as opposed to being merely the passive victim of circumstances, whenever its affects, and hence its decisions, are grounded in rational considerations, e.g., when it desires a particular food because of the knowledge (adequate idea) that it is nutritious. In Spinoza's own terms, "The actions of the Mind arise from adequate ideas alone; the passions depend on inadequate ideas alone" (E3p3).

5.2   The Conatus Principle

Having laid the groundwork with the last two propositions of E2 and the first three of E3 for an account of human volition and behavior that dispenses with the conception of a will as a distinct mental power or faculty, Spinoza's task is to supply an alternative principle that can adequately account for the dynamics of human behavior. This is provided by the aforementioned conception of conatus, by which, again under the influence of Hobbes, Spinoza understands a thing's endeavor to persist in its own being. He affirms this in E3p6, which states that "Each thing, insofar as it is in itself [quantum in se est],[5] strives to persevere in its own being."

Since for Spinoza this endeavor pertains to the nature of every "singular thing," i.e., a finite thing with a determinate existence (E2def7), it is not distinctive to humans or even living beings; though, given the ultimately practical concern of the *Ethics*, Spinoza's focus is on a certain kind of singular thing, namely human beings, who are conscious of this endeavor and for whom it takes the form of a desire for self-preservation. But while the basis for Spinoza's conatus principle is to be found in his conception of a singular thing as developed in the "physical interlude" in E2, his explicit argument for it is presented as the logical consequence of the two immediately preceding propositions of E3. The first of these claims is that "No thing can be destroyed except through an external cause" (E3p4) and the second is that "Things are of a contrary nature, i.e., cannot be in the same subject, insofar as one can destroy the other" (E3p5).

Although Spinoza claims that E3p4 is self-evident, he offers what appears to be an argument for it based on an analysis of the essence of a singular thing as expressed in its definition, which he characterizes as affirming and not denying such a thing's essence. And from this he concludes that "while we attend only to the thing itself, and not to external

---

[5] I am replacing Curley's rendering of "*quantum in se est*" as "insofar as it can by its own power" with the more literal rendering provided by Thomas Shirley, *The Ethics and Selected Letters*, 109.

causes, we shall not be able to find anything in it which can destroy it" (E3p4d). Since the only basis given for this conclusion is the appeal to the essence of a singular thing, it seems reasonable to assume that by the "thing itself" is understood its essence. Recall that by the essence of a thing Spinoza understood "that which being given, the thing itself is necessarily posited and which, being taken away, the thing is necessarily taken away" (E2d2). Otherwise expressed, the essence of a singular thing consists in what is both necessary and sufficient for it being the thing that it is or, alternatively, having the specific nature that it has. As we have seen, in the case of a body this is a determinate ratio of motion and rest. Thus, assuming that by the "thing itself" is meant the essence of thing, so understood, and by an "external cause" one that is not part of the essence of the thing, the claim is that since nothing can be destroyed by something that pertains to its essence, anything that tends to destroy it must be considered an external cause.

Formulated in these abstract terms, this claim hardly seems self-evident. But if we keep in mind that by a thing's essence is understood that by virtue of which a thing has the determinate nature that it has, it can be considered as intuitively true. John Carriero's illustration of the point by a consideration of water as H_2O is useful in this regard. Citing an earlier discussion by Curley, he writes:

> There is something intuitive about the idea that if you focus on a thing's structure . . . you won't find a destroyer of the thing. If you just focus on H_2O (whether hot or cold, whether liquid, frozen, or vapor) you won't find some anti-H_2O real tendency, some tendency in the water molecule to take itself out of existence.[6]

Even granting this, however, it may be objected that the focus on a singular thing's essence, identified with the thing considered *as it is in itself*, is too narrow to support Spinoza's denial of self-destructive behavior to things. In particular, it seems arbitrarily to preclude what appear to be clear examples of such behavior, most notably suicide, due, say, to a subject being in a despondent state, which would seem to pertain to the subject more broadly construed, if not to the subject's essence.[7]

The case of suicide and Spinoza's analysis of it will be considered later, but it is first necessary to account for his procedure in the blanket denial of

---

[6] Carriero, "Conatus," *Spinoza's Ethics: A Critical Guide*, 143. The reference to Curley is to his *Behind the Geometrical Method*, 111.

[7] This line of objection was raised by Bennett, *Spinoza's Ethics*, 231–237 and has become the focal point of much of the subsequent discussion of the topic.

self-destructive behavior of any sort to a singular thing, understood as a thing *quantum in se est*. At issue is the justification of the restriction of the claim to things so considered, which might seem to preserve intuitivity or self-evidence at the cost of applicability to real things, which presumably are more than their essences. I believe that in order to appreciate Spinoza's procedure, it is essential to recognize that, despite its Hobbesian roots, his conception of conatus as a striving for self-maintenance, for which E3p4 provides the essential premise, is modeled on Descartes' account of the endeavor of a body to preserve its state in general and its rectilinear notion in particular, unless acted upon by other bodies, which is sometimes referred to as Descartes' law of inertia.[8] The main difference is that whereas Descartes, with his mind–body dualism, applied this conception only to the body, Spinoza, with his monistic metaphysics, applied it to the mind as well; so that for him, considering a thing as it is in itself, when applied to a human being, involves considering both the mind and the body as engaged by their very nature in this striving. The main point, however, is that just as the Cartesian principle is an idealization, which specifies how a body would behave if, *per impossibile*, it were not acted on by other bodies, so Spinoza's psychological counterpart of this principle is an idealization, which specifies how the human mind (in coordination with the body) would behave under similar counterfactual conditions. In the case of the human mind (or any mind for that matter), the idealization consists in an abstraction from everything that does not pertain to the essential nature of such a mind, even though it may pertain to its total state or whole nature. Thus, any causal factor that does not pertain to the essential nature of the mind would be considered an external cause, even if it does pertain to its total state or whole nature. And just as the physical principle of inertia has an essential explanatory role for Descartes, even though it is based on an idealization, the same may be said of Spinoza's psychological principle of inertia.

The line of thought underlying Spinoza's demonstration of E3p4 is nicely illustrated by his discussion of suicide in the scholium to E4p20. The proposition itself (to be considered in the next section of this chapter) connects the striving to preserve one's being, which is equated with seeking one's advantage, with virtue, while in the attached scholium Spinoza concludes that "No one ... unless he is defeated by causes external, and

---

[8] For a helpful account of the Cartesian background of Spinoza's conception of conatus, which includes Spinoza's own discussion of it in his DPP, see Garber, "Descartes and Spinoza on Persistence and Conatus."

contrary to, his own nature, neglects to seek his own advantage, or to preserve his being" (G2 224; C1 557). What is presently germane, however, is Spinoza's account of the external causes that might compel one to take one's own life. He cites three examples, which are arranged in an order of decreasing externality.

The first is a case of someone "killing himself" when the hand in which he happens to be holding a sword is twisted by another, who forces it against his heart, thereby killing him. The second is the case of Seneca, the Stoic sage, who was forced by Nero to poison himself, presumably to avoid a greater evil. The third is the case of someone whose imagination and body are so affected by "hidden external causes" that Spinoza claims it "takes on another nature, contrary to the former, of which there cannot be an idea in the mind." What is peculiar about the first case is that Spinoza considered it an example of *self*-destruction, since the causal agent at work is obviously whoever is twisting the hand of the sword-holder, rather than the unfortunate recipient of its blade. The second case is more complex, since the subject, Seneca, is in a nominal sense the agent and the taking of the poison is said to be for a reason, namely to avoid a greater evil. Evidently, the taking of the poison of itself is regarded merely as the vehicle for carrying out the command of Nero, who is the real external cause, since it presumably would be contrary to the nature of Seneca, qua Stoic philosopher, to take such a course of action. In other words, there is nothing in Seneca, *quantum in se est*, that could bring about such an occurrence. But in saying that Seneca did it in order to avoid a greater evil, Spinoza introduces intentionality into the story, thereby suggesting that it is an act that the subject actually performs after all. Although Spinoza does not tell us what this greater evil is, it seems reasonable to assume that it consists in Seneca's loss of his power or agency for the sake of an extension of his biological existence, however brief, in a weaker state. In any event, Spinoza's characterization of the situation disabuses the reader of any propensity to understood self-preservation in the manner of Hobbes as the mere extension of the duration of one's biological existence.[9] In the third case, the "external cause," evidently an overheated imagination, is prima facie internal. But Spinoza's point appears to be that the imagination of the subject is, as it were, infected by the negative idea of self-destruction (a kind of psychological pathogen), of which there is no idea in the mind *quantum in se est*.

---

[9] Spinoza makes this clear later in the *Ethics*, where he famously claims that "A freeman thinks of nothing less than death, and his wisdom is a meditation on life, not on death" (E4p67).

Returning to the argument of E3, Spinoza claims that the next proposition, "Things are of a contrary nature, i.e., cannot be in the same subject, insofar as one can destroy the other" (E3p5), follows directly from the preceding. As he puts it, "[I]f they [things of a contrary nature] could agree with one another, or be in the same subject at once, then there could be something in the same subject at once which could destroy it, which is absurd." Clearly, the proposition that things that could destroy one another can exist in the same subject at the same time is not itself absurd, since there are any number of *apparent* counterexamples, e.g., suicide resulting from an overheated imagination. Rather, as Spinoza claims, its absurdity stems from its incompatibility with E3p4. And since we have also seen that Spinoza claims that the former is self-evident, the present proposition is regarded as the logical consequence of something that is self-evident.

Leaving aside the demonstration (or lack thereof) of E3p4, Spinoza's claim that E3p5 follows directly from it might be questioned on the grounds that it is one thing to claim that things do not tend to their nonbeing through their essence, which is what E3p4 maintains, and quite another to claim that they do not tend to their nonbeing at all. Consider again Spinoza's own example of a suicide caused by an overheated imagination. Surely it is the subject's own imagination, not that of some other subject, that is the "external cause." Obviously, then, there is a sense in which the contrary and potentially lethal agent is "in the subject." Indeed, this is a necessary condition of its being effective!

Since Spinoza could hardly deny that the imagination of the unfortunate subject who is driven by his toxic state to commit suicide is "in the subject," making sense of his account requires disambiguating the phrase "being in a subject." Accordingly, it appears to be necessary to distinguish between "being in the subject" proper in the sense of being part of what the subject *essentially is*, which for Spinoza means insofar as it is in itself, and in the extended sense of being part of the total state or whole nature of the subject at a particular time. And since the toxic imagination is "in the subject" in the former but not the latter sense, it may be claimed that there is no contradiction and 3p5 does follow from 3p4.[10]

This solution, however, seems too facile to be convincing. One way of posing the problem is that Spinoza is only able to rule out cases in which we would ordinarily claim that the destructive cause is in the subject, such as his own example of a suicide resulting from a diseased imagination, by

---

[10] See Bennett, *Spinoza's Ethics*, 243–246 and Della Rocca, *Spinoza*, 144.

understanding "being in the subject" in a highly restrictive and counterintuitive way. Another and philosophically more interesting way of posing
what is essentially the same problem is to maintain that Spinoza's inference
is trivially true because analytic. Thus, just as the proverbial "all bachelors
are unmarried" is true because having a spouse is excluded from the
concept of bachelorhood, so containing a destructive element is excluded
by Spinoza from the concept of a singular thing. But if this is the case, it is
difficult to see how it could support the heavy metaphysical weight that
Spinoza evidently places on it, which is to ground the conatus principle.
Spinoza, of course, was not privy to the analytic–synthetic distinction and
it may seem unduly anachronistic to impose it upon him. Nevertheless, it is
evident that he would have been concerned with the triviality charge and
I believe it instructive to consider how he might respond to it with
resources available to him.

Given the foundational role of definitions in the argument of the *Ethics*,
it seems that Spinoza's main resource would be the distinction between real
and nominal definitions. Presumably, conclusions validly derived from
merely nominal definitions would be considered trivially true, since there
need not be anything in *rerum natura* to which they correspond, whereas
those derived from real definitions would be true in the nontrivial sense
that they agree with their object, which is Spinoza's definition of truth. We
have seen that Spinoza's model is the role of definitions in geometry, where
real definitions are conceived genetically as rules for the construction of
their object. Applying this to the argument presently under consideration,
the focus would be on the claim (discussed above) that the non-self-
destruct thesis is based on the (real) definition of the essence of a singular
thing. Clearly, this also applies to most of the propositions of the *Ethics*,
since their demonstrations are in some way based on definitions, all of
which are presumably assumed to be real.[11] But though this general point
about Spinoza's method of proof seems to be highly germane here, it
cannot be the whole story. Of at least equal importance is the analogy
between Spinoza's claim in E3p4 and the Cartesian principle of inertia. As
was noted earlier, while this principle is an idealization, which specifies

---

[11] One of Kant's fundamental criticisms of Spinoza concerns his (for Kant misguided) endeavor to
apply the method of mathematics, with its appeal to arbitrary definitions, to philosophy. Kant's
main example is Spinoza's conception of substance, which he correctly sees as an outgrowth of
Descartes' definition of substance as "that which so exists that it needs no other thing in order to
exist." Kant also acknowledges, however, that Spinoza reasons correctly from this "faulty definition,"
which I am suggesting is how he probably would have viewed the passage currently under consideration. See "Lectures on the Philosophical Doctrine of Religion," 381. For my overall account of
Kant's views on Spinoza see my "Kant's Critique of Spinoza."

how a body would behave if, *per impossibile*, it were not acted on by other bodies, it is not vacuous or otherwise trivial, because it has an essential explanatory role in the physical domain. And we shall see that its psychological counterpart plays an analogous role for Spinoza in his account of the human affects, which are all grounded in the conatus principle.

First, however, we must consider Spinoza's explicit argument for the conatus principle, which is contained in the demonstration of the previously cited E3p6: "Each thing, insofar as it is in itself [*quantum in se est*], strives to persevere in its own being." In the demonstration of this proposition, Spinoza first appeals to the conception of a singular thing. Alluding to E1p25c, he notes that such things are "modes by which God's attributes are expressed in a certain and determinate way"; and, citing E1p34, he takes this to entail that they are "things that express, in a certain and determinate way, God's power, by which God is and acts." As Don Garrett aptly puts it, singular things are "finite approximations of substance," which accounts for their capacity (however limited) to act and, therefore, to endeavor to preserve their being.[12] Of course, for Spinoza this is true not only of human beings but of anything that can be considered a singular thing, which includes not only other living beings but also inanimate entities such as rocks insofar as they may be said to have an inherent nature or structure. And given this, the demonstration proceeds by appealing to E3p4 and p5. The former excludes from the essential nature of a singular thing anything through which its existence could be destroyed, while the latter states that a singular thing is opposed to anything that threatens its existence.

Against this, it has been objected that, since striving is always for the sake of some end, even if this is understood as self-preservation or self-maintenance, Spinoza is surreptitiously introducing teleological considerations into his account.[13] In response, it may be noted that, even though the conception of striving seems teleological, this does not conflict with Spinoza's dismissal of final causation, because that was addressed to the conception of nature as a whole and, therefore, does not preclude the possibility of applying teleological considerations to entities within nature.[14] And to this it might be added that if, as I have suggested, Spinoza's conatus doctrine is modeled on the Cartesian conception of inertia, then it need not be interpreted teleologically, since Descartes evidently did not understand his conception in this way.

[12] Don Garrett, *Nature and Necessity in Spinoza's Philosophy*, 365.
[13] See Bennett, *Spinoza's Ethics*, 244–250 and passim.
[14] This has been argued by Garrett, *Nature and Necessity in Spinoza's Philosophy*, 323–327.

A more substantive line of objection concerns the demonstration of E3p6. In addition to the fact that it relies heavily on the two preceding propositions, each of which has been subject to criticism, it has been charged that it involves an illicit slide from the claim that things (by their very nature or definition) are necessarily opposed to whatever can destroy them to the claim that things necessarily act in self-maintaining ways. And Spinoza, so it would seem, is entitled only to the former.[15] Against this, it can be retorted, first, that insofar as a thing acts, this opposition to whatever tends to destroy it is expressed as an actual resistance; and, second, that for a thing to act in such a way as to resist whatever tends to destroy it is to act in a self-maintaining way. Combining this with the definition of essence as "that which, being given, the thing is also necessarily posited and which, being taken away, the thing is necessarily also taken away" (E2d2), Spinoza can claim that "the striving [*conatus*] by which each thing strives to persevere in its being is nothing but the actual essence of the thing" (E3p7). Moreover, precisely because it constitutes the essence of the thing, this striving does not last for a determinate time, but continues for as long as the thing endures (E3p8).

Since this argument is completely general, applying to anything that counts as a singular thing, it still remains for Spinoza to apply the conatus principle to the human mind. And since this striving or endeavor constitutes the essence of the human mind, and this mind is composed of both adequate (clear and distinct) and inadequate (confused) ideas, including the idea of itself (idea of an idea), it follows not only that this endeavor must be reflected in all of its ideas, but that it must also be conscious of this endeavor. Spinoza expresses this complex line of thought in E3p9, which states that "Both insofar as the Mind has clear and distinct ideas, and insofar as it has confused ideas, it strives, for an indefinite duration, to persevere in its being and it is conscious of this striving it has" (E3p9).

The importance of this proposition stems from the fact that it affirms the universality of the conatus principle for the explanation of human behavior. All such behavior, whether it be an "act of the mind" – that is, a rational decision based on adequate ideas of the end to be achieved and the means to be employed – or a passive response to external stimuli based on blind impulse and imagination (merely inadequate ideas), is an expression of the effort of an individual to preserve its being. This suggests the

---

[15] See Bennett, *Spinoza's Ethics*, 244–245 and Garber, "Descartes and Spinoza on Persistence and Conatus," 6, who claims that Spinoza is inferring a genuine (positive) force from a principle of resistance and notes that a similar, supposedly illicit move was made by Descartes and criticized by Leibniz.

absolute impossibility for Spinoza of what other philosophers might describe as "disinterested" action. One can no more help striving to preserve one's being than a stone can help falling when it is dropped. It is simply one's being, and nothing can violate the laws of its own being. Viewed from a psychological standpoint – that is, with reference only to the mind – Spinoza notes that this endeavor can be called "will" (*Voluntas*). But though one can, in a manner of speaking, say that human beings "will" to preserve their being, we have seen that for Spinoza there is nothing undetermined or free about this volition. As before, it is nothing more than the mental decision accompanying the bodily appetite. As with Hobbes, the notion of appetite (*Appetitus*) is, therefore, basic in the characterization of an individual's conatus. It refers to the striving for self-preservation viewed in relation to both the mind and the body. Construing it in this broad sense, Spinoza claims that appetite is "nothing but the very essence of man, from whose nature there necessarily follow those things that promote his preservation. And so man is determined to do those things" (E3p9s). Appetite in this sense can also be called desire (*Cupiditas*). The only difference is that desire implies consciousness, which Spinoza indicates in his definition of desire as "appetite together with the consciousness of the appetite" (E3p9s). Finally, in view of his virtual identification of desire and appetite, Spinoza states at the end of his account of the affects that "desire is man's very essence, insofar as it is conceived to be determined, from any given affection of it, to do something" (da1; G2 190; C1 531).

At first glance, this conception of conatus as the endeavor on the part of a thing to preserve its being might seem to conflict with the description of it as the thing's effort to *increase* its power or force for existence. Moreover, this latter conception was already implicit in the definition of the affects, where Spinoza refers specifically to the increase or diminution in the organism's active power, or power of acting (*agendia potentia*). The explanation lies in the fact that Spinoza's initial account of a thing's conatus as an endeavor to preserve its proportion of motion and rest, which constitutes its essential nature, is, like the principle of inertia, an idealization or abstraction, which considers a thing apart from the causal nexus in which it is in its actual existence unavoidably enmeshed. But when a thing is considered with respect to its actual existence as enmeshed in this nexus, it becomes necessary to try to enhance its power for existence in order to avoid it being diminished by external forces.

This power is the force through which the body maintains its existence (its particular proportion of motion and rest) throughout its interaction with other bodies in its environment. Spinoza also equates this force with a thing's "perfection." In the case of living organisms, it can be understood as the organism's level of vitality. When this sinks below a certain level, the organism is overcome by its environment; its particular proportion of motion and rest is destroyed, and it dies. The striving of an organism to preserve its existence is thus identical with its effort to increase its perfection, power of acting, force for existence, or level of vitality. The only difference is that the initial formula refers to the organism in isolation, whereas the latter, which is much more relevant to the emotional life of a human being, considers it as involved in a constant struggle for existence with other beings in its environment. From this point of view, anything that lessens an organism's power lessens its ability to preserve its being, and anything that increases its power enhances that ability.[16]

5.3 Spinoza's Catalog of the Passions

With the conception of an individual's conatus as its foundation, the remaining propositions of E3 are devoted to an explanation of the human emotions understood as the ideas or mental states corresponding to the increase or diminishment of the power of the human body to preserve its essential nature; that is, to persist. As previously noted, Spinoza divides these into two sharply different kinds: passions based on inadequate ideas stemming from the imagination and active emotions based on adequate ideas stemming from the intellect. The present section is concerned with the former, the discussion of which occupies the bulk of E3.

Rather than introducing and defining the specific passions directly in the propositions of E3, Spinoza refers to them mainly in scholia or corollaries attached to various propositions, saving their systematic presentation for an appendix devoted to the definitions of the affects (both active and passive [G2 190–203; CI 531–543]). He introduces the primary passions – joy, sadness, and desire – in a scholium to p11. Spinoza there first defines joy (*Laetitia*) as "that passion by which the Mind passes to a greater perfection," and sadness (*Tristitia*) as "that passion by which the Mind passes to a lesser perfection" (E3p11s). And he adds that joy, when related to both the mind and body at once, is called pleasure (*Titillatio*) or

---

[16] Once again, this suggests the influence of Hobbes, who insisted that a person's quest for power never ceases, "because he cannot assure the power and means to live well, which he hath present, without the acquisition of more" (*Leviathan*, I, 11, 75). The point is that human beings (and, for Spinoza, everything in nature) must constantly endeavor to increase their power, merely to preserve their actual level of existence.

cheerfulness (*Hilaritas*) and sadness is called pain (*Dolor*) or melancholy (*Melancholia*). Accordingly, pleasure and pain are for Spinoza primary affects, though they are not strictly speaking passions, since they have a physiological side as well as a mental side.

The status of desire as a distinct primary affect is complicated by the ambiguity of Spinoza's account of it.[17] On the one hand, he defines desire as "appetite together with the consciousness of the appetite" (E3p9s), which suggests that it is equivalent to a thing's conatus. As such, it is certainly fundamental to the emotive life; though, so considered, it is not so much a distinct emotion as the basis of all the emotions, including joy and sadness.[18] In fact, at one point Spinoza states that "joy and sadness are the desire, *or* appetite itself, insofar as it is increased or diminished, aided or restrained, by external causes" (Ep57d). On the other hand, Spinoza recognizes specific desires directed toward whatever the mind regards as beneficial to the body and to itself; that is, toward whatever it sees as a source of joy or as a means of avoiding sadness. So construed, a desire is a distinct emotion; though, given its dependence on joy and sadness, it does not seem to be primary. But even granting this ambiguity, it still seems possible to make a case for the claim that desire in the second sense is a primary as well as a distinct emotion.[19] For while a particular desire depends on what the mind deems joyful or at least a means of avoiding sadness, the desire itself is not a joy or a feeling of sadness. We cannot, therefore, account for the emotive life of a human being simply in terms of joy and sadness; it is also necessary to include desire, which functions as the basic motivating force in human behavior. Spinoza makes this explicit when he states that "Desire is man's very essence, insofar as it is conceived to be determined, from any given affection of it to do something" (da1; G2 190; C1 531).

In characterizing joy, sadness, and desire as primary passions, Spinoza is claiming that all the other passions are species of these, differentiated by their objects. Thus, he states that "There are as many species of Joy, Sadness, and Desire, and consequently of each affect composed of these (like vacillation of the mind) or derived from them (like love, hate, hope fear, etc.), as there are species of objects by which we are affected" (E3p56). Love, hatred, hope, and fear are the most important of the derivative emotions or species of joy, sadness, and desire because of the

---

[17] For a detailed discussion of the ambiguity in Spinoza's account of desire, see Lebuffe, "The Anatomy of the Passions," 206–208.
[18] See Nadler, *Spinoza's Ethics: An Introduction*, 203–204.
[19] See Martineau, *A Study of Spinoza*, 260.

outsized role they play in human life. Spinoza defines love as "nothing but joy with the accompanying idea of an external cause" and hatred as "nothing but sadness with the accompanying idea of an external cause" (E3p13c), while hope is defined as "an inconstant joy which has arisen from the image of a future or past thing whose outcome we doubt," and fear as "an inconstant sadness which has also arisen from the image of a doubtful thing" (E3p18s2).

Like the primary passions from which they are derived, there are as many varieties of these as there are of objects that give rise to them. For just as anything can be the accidental cause of joy, sadness, or desire (E3p15), so anything can be the accidental cause of love, hatred, hope, or fear. To complicate the picture further, Spinoza adds that "Each affect of each individual differs from the affect of another as much as the essence of the one from the essence of the other" (E3p57). Although he refers in passing to an axiom associated with a lemma in the physical digression in E2 (G2 99; C1 460) from which this proposition supposedly follows, Spinoza's demonstration of it turns on the connection of desire with the essence of an individual and of joy and sadness as inseparably connected with desire. The point is that the specific form that the joy, sadness, or desire of an individual takes is a function of the particular nature or essence of that individual, with the same holding for the derivative emotions. Spinoza illustrates this by noting that, though both a horse and a man are driven by lust to procreate, "the one is driven by an equine lust, the other by a human lust" (G2 187; C1 528).

While Spinoza's catalog of the passions is open-ended, allowing for an indefinite number of possible variations of the primary passions and their derivatives, his account of the mechanisms by which these passions are produced in the human mind is not. Although he acknowledges that anything could be the cause of hope and fear (E3p50) and that different people can be affected differently by the same object and the same person differently affected at different times (E3p51), the great bulk of the explanatory work is based on two principles, which have been dubbed by Wolfson as the "law of the association of affects" and the "law of the imitation of affects."[20]

According to the former, an object that has never been itself a cause of joy, sadness, or desire may become one by being associated with one that has. Spinoza distinguishes two ways in which this can arise. One is on the basis of their temporal congruity. Spinoza affirms this in E3p14, which

---

[20] See Wolfson, *The Philosophy of Spinoza*, vol. 2, 213.

states that "If the mind has once been affected by two or more affects at once, then afterwards, when it is affected by one of them it will be affected by the other." The other is on the basis of the similarity of their objects. This is the claim of E3p16, which states that "From the mere fact that we imagine a thing to have some likeness to an object which usually affects the mind with joy or sadness, we love it or hate it, even though that in which the thing is like the object is not the efficient cause of these affects." In E3p17 Spinoza suggests that the similarity of their objects can not only produce love and hatred toward its object but a mixed emotion, maintaining that "If we imagine that a thing which usually affects us with an affect of sadness is like another which usually affects us with an equally great affect of joy, we shall hate it and at the same time love it."

According to the latter, a passion in someone else can incite a similar passion in oneself, if we become aware of it. Although Spinoza does not explicitly formulate this as a law, he refers to the "imitation of the affects" (*affectum imitatio*) in the scholium to E3p27, where he states that in relation to sadness this imitation becomes pity and in relation to desire emulation. This is clearly operative in E3p27, which states that "*If* we imagine a thing like us toward which we have no affect, to be affected with some affect, we are thereby affected with a like affect." Moreover, this is a pivotal proposition in Spinoza's account of the passions, because it provides the basis for an extension of our concern for the affective state of others to those with whom we do not stand in an immediate affective relationship, which, in turn, underlies his conception of a human community that grounds his social, moral, and political philosophies.[21]

However, before he can argue for this thesis, Spinoza must first show that one can be concerned with the affective state of others at all, apart from its perceived bearing on one's endeavor to preserve one's own being. This is presumably accomplished in E3p21, where Spinoza moves from the narrow egoism that seems to follow directly from the conatus principle to a concern with the affective state of other human beings with whom we already stand in an affective relationship of love or hatred. It states that "He who imagines what he loves to be affected with Joy or Sadness will also be affected with Joy or Sadness; and each of those affects will be greater or lesser in the lover as they are greater or lesser in the thing loved." Rather than a passion being a direct emotional response to whatever is taken to be the cause of joy or sadness in oneself, one's joy or sadness is now considered

---

[21] This is the central theme of Matheron, *Individu et Communauté chez Spinoza*, who assigns a pivotal role to E3p27 and its corollaries. See especially 150–159.

due to the joy or sadness of the object of one's love or hatred, which implies that this object must itself be capable of having such emotions. E3p22 and p23 then extend this transfer of affection to whomever is imagined to be the source of joy or sadness in someone we either love or hate. Thus, we tend to love whoever produces joy in someone we love and hate whoever produces sadness in the object of our affection; while, conversely, we love someone who produces sadness in someone we hate and hate someone who produces joy in such a person.

Given the importance of E3p21, the demonstration that Spinoza provides seems lame. It consists essentially in an appeal to E3p19 and the scholium to E3p11. The former claims merely that one will be saddened by imagining the destruction of what one loves and rejoice in imagining that it will be preserved; but it says nothing about one's view regarding the emotional state of the beloved. The latter merely defines joy and sadness in terms of a transition to a greater or lesser degree of perfection, but is silent on the question of why the emotional state of the object of our love or hatred could have any bearing on this transition in oneself. Nevertheless, it is evident from the subsequent propositions in E3 that the real basis for a reflexive emotional response to the emotional state of other human beings is that we share a common nature or essence. Moreover, this is the thesis of the previously cited E3p27, which, therefore, seems to be presupposed by the preceding propositions.

Although the phrase "like us" (*nobis similem*) in E3p27 is indeterminate, leaving open the possibility that *any* similarity, no matter how superficial, would be sufficient to trigger the affect in oneself, the demonstration makes it clear that by "like us" Spinoza understands individuals having a like nature. Thus, appealing to the conception of the human mind as the idea of the human body, Spinoza writes: "if the nature of the external body is like the nature of our Body, then the idea of the external body we imagine will involve an affection of our Body like the affection of the external body" (G2 161; C1 508). But this cryptic argument is itself puzzling. One problem is that Spinoza appears to confuse representation with imitation.[22] In other words, from the fact that my representation of the body of another being resembles my representation of my own body, it does not seem to follow that my mental affects (emotions) stemming from this representation must in any way resemble the affects pertaining to the

[22] This objection has been raised by Bennett, though he credits Broad with having initially raised it (*A Study of Spinoza's Ethics*, 281). It also has been reluctantly endorsed by Curley (*Behind the Geometrical Method*, 118).

idea (mind) of the being with the resembling body. A second and recurring problem is that Spinoza seemingly helps himself to the thesis that there is a common human nature or essence, which is difficult to reconcile with his critique of Aristotelian-scholastic essentialism as the product of inadequate ideas stemming from the imagination rather than adequate ideas stemming from reason. This problem goes well beyond the demonstration of this proposition, however, since we shall see not only that the great bulk of the subsequent propositions of E3,[23] which are concerned with the psychodynamics of interpersonal relations, rest on this essentialist premise, but that Spinoza's moral theory does as well.

Spinoza's moral theory is the subject of the next chapter. For the present it suffices to note the outsized role that the conception of the imitation of the emotions plays in his account of the passions. This is immediately evident from the scholium to E3p27, in which he claims that, when related to sadness, this imitation yields pity and when related to desire emulation. Although pity for Spinoza, like emulation, is a passion and, therefore, based on inadequate ideas, he links it with benevolence, which he characterizes as a "desire born of pity" (E3p27c3s). Similarly, Spinoza grounds ambition, which is likewise based on the imitation of the emotions and the associated essentialism, on the proposition that "We shall strive to do whatever we imagine men to look on with joy, and ... be averse to doing what we imagine men are averse to" (E3p29 and p29s).

Spinoza provides a fuller account of the dynamic of imitation in the scholium to E3p32. (The proposition itself does not bear directly on the scholium and will be discussed later.) After noting that for the most part human nature is such that we pity the unfortunate, while not only envying the fortunate, but hating all the more anyone who actually possesses what we desire, he concludes that "We see, then, that from the same property of

---

[23] The two exceptions are p46 and p52. The former states that "If someone has been affected with Joy or Sadness by someone of a class, or nation, different from his own, and this Joy or Sadness is accompanied by the idea of that person as its cause, under the universal name of the class or nation, he will, love, or hate, not only that person, but everyone else of the same class or nation." This is of some importance, since it accounts for various forms of prejudice and, therefore, profoundly affects interpersonal relations as a source of imagination-based loves and hatreds; though since it is based on the principle of the association of the emotions, it does not fit neatly into Spinoza's explanatory scheme, which endeavors to account for such passions under the rubric of the principle of the imitation of the emotions rather than their association. The latter, which is likewise based on the principle of the association of the emotions, states that "If we have previously seen an object together with others, or we imagine it has nothing in but what is common to many things, we shall not consider it so long as one which we imagine to have something singular." This has nothing to do with love or hatred between human beings and Spinoza evidently included it simply because he uses it to account for wonder, which, following Aristotle, played a large role in Descartes' account of the passions.

human nature from which it follows that men are compassionate, it follows that the same men are envious and ambitious" (G2 165; C1 513). As Spinoza makes clear later in the scholium, the property to which he is referring is the propensity to imitate the emotions of others of which we are presumably aware through corporeal signs, such as facial expressions.[24]

Moreover, according to Spinoza, we not only endeavor to affect the passions of others in self-enhancing ways, as exemplified by his account of ambition, we also find satisfaction in the belief that we have succeeded. This is the thesis of E3p30, which states that "If someone has done something which he imagines affects others with Joy, he will be affected with Joy accompanied by the idea of himself as cause, or he will regard himself with Joy. If, on the other hand, he does something which he imagines affects others with Sadness, he will regard himself with Sadness." This a key step in Spinoza's construction of a social nexus, since it builds into an individual's joy or sadness a sense of the effect of one's actions on others. Although Spinoza does not make it explicit, it can be assumed from the formulation of the proposition that the agent has a pro-attitude (love) toward those whom he believes to be affected by his actions; otherwise he would not feel joyful about producing joy in them and sad about producing sadness. In the scholium attached to this proposition, Spinoza complicates the picture by stating that the specific kind of joy or sadness in question arises not simply from the belief that one is the cause of the joy or sadness of other human beings, but also (and perhaps mainly) from the belief that this is *recognized* by those whom one has affected. Spinoza calls this joy "love of esteem" (*Gloria*) and the sadness "shame" (*Pudor*), both of which clearly depend upon one's being recognized as the author of the deed in question.

Spinoza further claims that the quality of one's emotional response to something is a function of one's beliefs concerning the response of others to the same thing. This is the thesis of E3p31, which states that

---

[24] That Spinoza had something like this in mind is evident from the latter portion of the scholium to E3p32, where he writes: "[I]f we wish to consult experience, we shall find that it teaches all these things, especially if we attend to the first years of our lives. For we find from experience that children, because their bodies are continually, as it were in a state of equilibrium, laugh or cry simply because they see others laugh or cry. Moreover, whatever they see others do, they immediately desire to imitate it. And finally, they desire for themselves all those things by which they imagine others are pleased – because as we have said, the images of things are the very affections of the human body *or* modes by which the human body is affected by external causes, and disposed to do this or that." This could also serve as empirical support for the claim of E3p27, though Spinoza clearly would not be satisfied with a merely empirical grounding, since that would amount to an appeal to a brute fact without a sufficient reason.

"If we imagine that someone loves, desires, or hates something we ourselves love, desire, or hate, we shall thereby love, desire, or hate it with greater constancy. But if we imagine that he is averse to what we love or the opposite, then we shall undergo vacillation of mind." This proposition is a clear statement of the power of affective imitation. As a direct result of it, the agreement of others with one's likes, dislikes, and desires reinforces them, while disagreement weakens them, thereby generating a vacillation in the mind. In the scholium to this proposition, Spinoza links this with ambition, which he there characterizes as the endeavor to bring it about that everyone should share one's valuations. Moreover, he notes that, rather than being the basis for social cohesion, the attempt to bring this about is the source of conflict, so that everyone ends up hating everyone else. Although Spinoza's account of the reasons for this reciprocal hatred born of the desire to have one's valuations shared by others is not completely clear, the key point is that these valuations, as products of one's imagination, are peculiar to the nature of the individual, so that conflict becomes unavoidable. We shall see in the next chapter, however, that rather than being the source of conflict, for Spinoza the same propensity of human nature to find reinforcement of one's own valuations in those of a community of likeminded individuals plays an essential role in producing the social cohesion or harmony that is an essential condition of human flourishing.

Spinoza introduces conflict into his account in E3p32, which claims that "If we imagine someone enjoys some thing that only one can possess, we shall strive to bring it about that he does not possess it." In support of this proposition, he appeals to E3p27, thereby suggesting that, like the others in this set, it is based on the imitative propensity of the imagination, which is here applied to a situation in which what is supposedly enjoyed cannot be shared. But while two people loving or desiring something, which for some reason cannot be shared, is obviously a potential source of conflict, it does not follow, as Spinoza's demonstration seems to suggest, that the mere fact that Peter desires something, say the last remaining piece of pie, is sufficient not only to make Paul desire it also, but actually to endeavor to make sure that Peter does not get it. Paul might simply not care for that kind of pie, and the fact that Peter loves it would not make Paul love it also; at least not to the extent that would lead him to attempt to deprive Peter of it. Clearly, if we suppose that Paul had a strong liking for that kind of pie, then Spinoza's conclusion would follow; but this is not what the text maintains.

The next set of propositions (E3p33–p35) concern love between "like" individuals, i.e., human beings; though Spinoza does not characterize it in these terms, referring instead in each case to the loved one as a "thing" (*res*). The first two constitute a pair. E3p33 claims that "When we love a thing like ourselves, we strive, as far as we can, to bring it about that it loves us in return." This is a direct consequence of E3p29, which we have seen maintains that we strive to do what we believe human beings will find beneficial and to avoid doing what we believe they will consider harmful. Aside from replacing "human beings" (actually "men" [*homines*]) with the indeterminate "things like ourselves," what is noteworthy is that Spinoza adds by way of explanation that the loved one whom we endeavor to benefit recognizes that one is the cause of this benefit and the ensuing joy. E3p34, which builds upon its predecessor, states that "The greater the affect with which we imagine a thing we love to be affected toward us, the more we shall exult at being esteemed." This indicates that for Spinoza the reason why we try to benefit those whom we love is to gain their esteem. Accordingly, the motivation is neither a straightforward concern with the welfare of the beloved nor a narrowly utilitarian quid pro quo, but, rather, as in the preceding proposition, a pure ego satisfaction.

E3p35 completes Spinoza's analysis of imagination-based love between two individuals by the addition of a third party. It states that "If someone imagines that a thing he loves is united with another by as close, or by a closer bond of Friendship than that with which he himself alone, possessed the thing, he will be affected with Hate toward the thing he loves and will envy the other." This is Spinoza's description of the phenomenon of jealousy, which involves a complex emotional response to both one's own beloved and to her/his beloved. With regard to the former, the initial love remains in place (otherwise the lover would not be jealous); but it is now combined with hatred toward the beloved for being the cause of sadness. With regard to the new object of the beloved's affection, the lover likewise feels hatred for being the source of her/his loss of joy, combined with envy for enjoying the affection that she/he has lost. And in case there is any doubt about the sexual basis of the emotion that Spinoza has in mind in his analysis of the components of jealousy, he makes it clear in the scholium attached to E3p35, where he notes that it

> is found, for the most part, in Love toward a woman. For he who imagines that a woman he loves prostitutes herself to another not only will be saddened, because his own appetite is restrained, but also will be repelled by her, because he is forced to join the image of the thing he loves to the shameful parts and excretions of the other. To this, finally, is added the fact that she no longer receives the Jealous man with the same countenance as

she used to offer him. From this cause, too, the lover is saddened. (G2 167; C1 514)

This brief passage, which stands in sharp contrast to the dispassionate tenor of the *Ethics* as a whole, speaks volumes about Spinoza's views on human sexuality. But also worthy of note is the suggestion that the sadness stemming from the loss of sexual pleasure is compounded by the loss of the attention of the former beloved. It is a matter of adding insult to injury, where the insult is to the lover's self-esteem, which further enhances the lover's hatred of the unfaithful beloved.

Spinoza's analysis of hatred largely parallels that of love, though it is not as fully developed. Whereas the latter is defined as joy, accompanied by the idea of an external cause (E13p3c and da6), the former is defined as sadness, likewise accompanied by the idea of an external cause (E13pc and da7). The focal point of Spinoza's analysis is E3p39, which states that "He who Hates someone will strive to do evil to him, unless he fears that a greater evil to himself will arise from this; and on the other hand, he who loves someone will strive to benefit him from the same law." As is clear from the demonstration, the "law" to which Spinoza is alluding is E3p28, which states that "We strive to further the occurrence of whatever we imagine will lead to Joy, and to avert or destroy what is contrary to it, or will lead to Sadness." In other words, we endeavor to reward our imagined friends and to punish our imagined enemies; the point being that these are two sides of the same coin, since in each case we try to do what we believe (perhaps erroneously) will satisfy our desire. In the case of love, the desire is to enhance the power of whomever is perceived to be the cause of one's joy; while in the case of hatred, it is to eliminate, or at least lessen, the power of whomever is perceived to be the cause of one's sadness. Evidently, the reason for the inclusion of the "unless" clause in the case of hate and its omission in the case of love is that the endeavor to harm a perceived enemy is likely to trigger a response in kind, whereas there is no corresponding worry in the case of a perceived friend.

The most fundamental cause of hatred is the belief that someone intends to do one harm, and this is presumably built into the definition. But Spinoza includes three propositions, which deal with other, less direct, causes of this passion. The first (E3p38) maintains that "If someone begins to hate a thing he has loved, so that the Love is completely destroyed, then (from an equal cause) he will have a greater hate for it than if he had never loved it, and this hate will be greater as the love before was greater." Spinoza here seems to be referring to the jilted lover's hatred for her/his former beloved, and the point is that the repression of the former joy increases the present sadness. Otherwise expressed, Spinoza is effectively denying that it is better to have loved and lost than never to have loved at all. The second (E3p40) asserts that "He who imagines he is hated by someone, and believes he has given the other no cause for hate, will hate the other in return." Since for Spinoza the belief that one is hated gives rise to sadness of which the perceived hater is deemed the cause, it will naturally lead one to hate the perceived hater as the cause of this sadness. But, Spinoza notes in the demonstration, this only occurs on the assumption that one is not the cause of this hatred by being the cause of the sadness that induced it. More interestingly, Spinoza remarks in the scholium to this proposition that if one believed that one was the cause of the hatred inducing sadness of another, one would feel shame rather than sadness; though he also notes that this rarely happens because, as he claims in E3p25, it runs counter to our propensity to affirm whatever we believe will be a source of joy and deny whatever we believe will be a source of sadness. The third (E3p45) states that "If someone imagines that someone like himself is affected with Hate toward a thing like himself which he loves, he will hate that [person]." Spinoza here seems to be saying that an enemy of a friend is also one's enemy. The problem is that the demonstration assumes that the friend is aware of this enmity and is, therefore, saddened by it. Presumably, however, the hatred of a hater of a friend would be in place even if the friend were blissfully ignorant of being hated.

A somewhat anomalous feature of Spinoza's account of hatred is E3p47, which claims that "The Joy which arises from our imagining that a thing we hate is destroyed, or affected with some other evil, does not occur without some Sadness of mind." Spinoza is here suggesting that even though we relish the destruction of those whom we hate, the enjoyment of their demise is mixed with a tincture of regret. In support of this, he refers to E3p27, which tells us that the proffered reason for this regret is that we share to some extent the suffering of even our enemies because we share a common human nature. But this seems problematic for at least two reasons. First, the demonstration does not accord with the proposition it is supposed to justify, since the latter does not maintain that the "thing" one hates must be another human being. It could be, say, a man-eating tiger, who was about to attack, or a poisonous snake, who was about to bite, and surely in each case I would experience considerable joy in its demise without a trace of sadness. Second, though it does not amount to a direct contradiction, it does not mesh well with Spinoza's account of vengeance (*vindicta*) as "a desire by which, from reciprocal hate, we are aroused to do evil to one who, from a like affect has injured us" (E3da37).

Spinoza's analysis of hatred concludes with a pair of propositions which treat it together with love as subject to the same conditions. The first (E3p48) maintains that "Love or Hate – say, of Peter – is destroyed if the Sadness the Hate involves, or the Joy the Love involves, is attached to the idea of another cause, and each is diminished to the extent that we imagine that Peter was not its only cause." As Spinoza notes, this follows from the definitions of these passions, according to which the joy or sadness pertaining to the passion is attributed to an external cause. Since this cause is either the beloved or the hated, it follows that detaching the joy or sadness from its imagined cause by attributing it entirely to another cause would totally destroy the passion, while weakening the causal link by introducing other contributing causes would correspondingly lessen it. The second (E3p49) states that "Given an equal cause of Love, love toward a thing will be greater if we imagine the thing to be free than if we imagine it to be necessary. And similarly for Hate." The proof is based largely on the preceding proposition and is straightforward. The claim is that if we imagine that the cause of our joy or sadness and, therefore, of our love or hatred is free, we will regard it as wholly responsible; whereas if we view the cause as itself necessitated, our passion will be weakened in proportion to the extent to which we consider it necessitated by external causes. The latter proposition is of particular interest because it underscores the grounding of the passions for Spinoza in inadequate, imagination-based ideas, of which we have seen free will is a prime example; though it is not clear that sexual love, which we have also seen is for Spinoza among the most dangerous passions, has much to do with the belief in free will.

5.4   The Active Emotions

The first fifty-seven propositions of E3 deal with the mind only insofar as it is passive; that is, insofar as it is the inadequate, or merely partial, cause of its affections. To the extent that it is passive, it is subject to external causes, as a result of which Spinoza claims that "we are driven about in many ways ... and ... like waves on the sea, driven by contrary winds, we toss about, not knowing our outcome and fate" (E3p59s). But while Spinoza repudiates the Cartesian conception of the power of the mind in terms of a free will, he no more believes that the above account tells the whole story of the emotive life of the mind than that the analysis of sense perception and imagination tells the whole story of the mind's cognitive life. Accordingly, at the end of his lengthy analysis of the passions, Spinoza briefly introduces and describes the active affects. This is announced in

E3p58, which states that "Apart from the Joy and Desire that are passions, there are other affects of Joy and Desire that are related to us insofar as we act" (E3p58).

Unlike the passions, the active affects are grounded in the mind's adequate ideas. The essential premise of Spinoza's account of these affects is that insofar as the mind conceives anything adequately, it is also aware of itself. Since this self-awareness includes an awareness of its power or activity, Spinoza claims that it gives rise to an active emotion of joy, which is really a joy in the mind's own activity. Similarly, desire as an active affect is simply rational desire, or the endeavor to preserve one's being insofar as that endeavor is guided by adequate ideas. Spinoza further maintains that all of a person's actions stemming from active affects can be ascribed to "strength of character [*fortitudo*]," which encompasses courage (*animositas*) and generosity (*generositas*).[25] Courage is defined as "the Desire by which each one strives, solely from the dictates of reason, to preserve his being." As we shall soon see, courage construed in this broad sense is equivalent to virtue as a whole, although it here refers solely to actions concerned with the good of the agent. As such, it is contrasted with generosity, which is defined as "the Desire by which each one strives, solely from the dictates of the reason, to aid other men and join them to him in friendship" (E3p59Ss).

Spinoza's account of the active affects is as notable for what it omits as for what it includes, namely sadness, the third of the primary affects. In fact, Spinoza calls attention to this omission in the demonstration of E3p59, where he remarks that, rather than being an expression of the power of the mind, sadness is an indication of the diminution of this power, which we have seen is the result of the superior power of external causes. Moreover, the elimination of sadness entails the exclusion from the active affects not only of hatred, which we have seen is defined by Spinoza as sadness accompanied by the idea of an external cause, but also of jealously, vindictiveness, and the whole panoply of negative, hate-based emotions portrayed in E3. And this, in turn, suggests that the view of love and hate as virtual mirror images of each other, which is the picture suggested by the bulk of the argument of E3, is somewhat misleading. For while there is no active counterpart of hatred or its derivative passions, we shall see that there is of love, and this active form of love plays the

---

[25] I am here following Shirley in translating *animositas* as courage and Kisner in translating *generositas* as "generosity." This is contrasted with Curley, who renders the former as "tenacity" and the latter as "nobility." For Curley's choice of "nobility" for *generositas* see C1 647 and for "tenacity" for *animositas* see C1 658.

leading role in the final two parts of the *Ethics*. In fact, we shall see that for Spinoza the happiness or eudemonia of an individual is a function of the nature of the object that an individual most fully loves, a view that, we shall see, is encapsulated in his location of human blessedness in the intellectual love of God.

CHAPTER 6

Spinoza's Virtue Ethic

Spinoza's moral theory, or, as it is sometimes dubbed, "the ethics of the *Ethics*,"[1] is best characterized as a form of "virtue ethic," since its fundamental category is virtue rather than duty or obligation, which are central to deontological theories such as Kant's. It is contained in its fourth part, which has the daunting albeit somewhat misleading title, "Of Human Bondage, or the Powers of the Affects." As one might expect, it is grounded in the naturalist program of the preceding three parts, which culminates in the psychological egoism embedded in the conatus doctrine. Spinoza characterizes the nature of his project in a scholium to E4p18. Having presented his account of human bondage, understood as slavery to the passions in the first eighteen propositions, which explains why the title is only somewhat misleading, Spinoza abruptly shifts gear and turns to a consideration of "what reason prescribes to us, which affects agree with the rules of human reason, and which . . . are contrary to these rules." And after providing a brief sketch of what reason prescribes, the full articulation of which will be the concern of the remainder of E4, he notes that his intent is "to win, if possible, the attention of those who believe that this principle – that everyone is bound to seek his own advantage – is the foundation, not of virtue and morality [*pietatis*], but of immorality [*impietatis*]" (G2 223; C1 556).

Assuming that those whose attention he endeavors to gain are proponents of the more traditional theories of virtue, which from Spinoza's perspective includes different forms of Aristotelianism, including the religious versions in both the Jewish and Christian traditions, e.g., followers of Maimonides and Aquinas, as well as various forms of Stoicism and neo-Stoicism, most notably Descartes,[2] his self-proclaimed task is to show that

---

[1] Michael Della Rocca, *Spinoza*, 175. Similarly, John Carriero refers to Spinoza's ethical views in the work as "The Ethics in the *Ethics*," *Essays on Spinoza's Ethical Theory*, 20.

[2] In the preface to E5 Spinoza lumps Descartes with the Stoic view of control of the passions (G2 278; C1 595).

a theory of virtue, which captures most, though not all, of what these theories considered essential to morality, can be erected on the basis of his explicitly egoistic principles.[3] In fact, we shall see that at the heart of Spinoza's virtue ethic is an affirmation of something very like the proverbial "golden rule" – namely, "Do unto others as you would have others do unto you" – which suggests that his project in moral theory is best seen as operating within a fairly traditional framework, as contrasted with readings that consider his project through Nietzschean spectacles as a fundamental attack on traditional morality.[4] Otherwise expressed, Spinoza endeavored to pour new wine into old bottles; though it must also be kept in mind that the wine is quite new, since it is based on egoistic principles.[5]

The discussion is divided into five parts. The first considers the preface, definitions, and the single axiom, which lay the foundation for the subsequent argument. The second (E4p1–p18) contains Spinoza's account of the causes of human bondage or servitude (*servitute*) to the passions. The third (E4p19–p46) deals with the rules or prescriptions of reason, which describe the modus operandi of those who live according to the guidance of reason (*ex ductu rationi vivunt*) and who to that extent are virtuous. The fourth (E4p47–p66) discusses Spinoza's valuation of the affects with respect to an individual's conatus. The fifth paints an idealized portrait of a "free person" considered as one who lives according to the guidance of reason in the maximal conceivable extent.

6.1   The Metaethical Foundation: A Model of Human Nature

Spinoza begins the preface to E4 by stating that by bondage he understands a lack of power to moderate and restrain the affects; that is, the passions analyzed in E3. Since he characterizes a person in this condition as one who recognizes the good (what is better for himself), yet does the worse, this corresponds to the classical conception of *akrasia* or weakness of the will; though in the Spinozistic version, which has no place for will as a distinct

---

[3] One prominent critic of Spinoza's project, if not of his actual argument, was Kant, who dismissed the principle of one's own happiness as the "most objectionable" of the conceivable foundations for morality (*Groundwork of the Metaphysics of Morals*, KGS 4: 442).

[4] See, for example, Deleuze, *Spinoza: Practical Philosophy*; Yovel, *Spinoza and Other Heretics*, 104–135; and Della Rocca, *Spinoza*, 292–303.

[5] It is not, of course, entirely new, since Spinoza had an important and deeply influential predecessor in Hobbes. But Hobbes' brief treatment of the issue of the relation between egoism and moral rules in *Leviathan* 1, 15 in the form of an answer to "the Foole, who hath sayd in his heart, there is no such thing as justice" is narrowly focused on the rules of justice, whereas Spinoza's account is much deeper, since it explores the very nature of self-interest.

power, it is understood as a weakness of the mind as a whole, which translates as a lack of self-control. And Spinoza further states that he will demonstrate the cause of this condition (the task of E4p1–p18) and explain what is good and bad (*malum*)[6] in the affects (the task of E4p19–p66).

As Spinoza envisions the latter task, determining what is good and bad for human beings requires a norm or model (*exemplar*) in terms of which human actions and affects may be evaluated, with the function of this model being the specification of what human perfection consists in. Spinoza approaches this task indirectly and somewhat confusedly, however, by first rejecting the traditional model, which is essentially teleological in the sense that it presupposes some final end for the sake of which human beings were supposedly created. But, despite his critique of teleology, Spinoza does not rule it out completely. Rather, he assigns it a place in the consideration of human artifacts such as houses, buildings, and towers, while denying that this way of thinking is applicable to natural things, which are not the products of human invention. The problem, as he sees it, however, is that this difference is not generally recognized, with the result that:

> They regard these universal ideas [ideas of what is essential to being a thing of a certain kind] as models of things, and believe that Nature (which they think does nothing except for the sake of some end) looks to them, and sets them before itself as models. So when they see something happen in nature which does not agree with the model they have conceived of this kind of thing, they believe that Nature itself has failed or sinned, and left the thing imperfect. (G2 206; C1 544)

Although Spinoza here seems to be characterizing the views of the proverbial "man in the street" rather than of some philosophers, it is clear that he intends his account to be applicable to the latter as well. Thus, when he adds that "men are accustomed to call natural things perfect and imperfect more from prejudice than from true knowledge of these things" (Ibid.), he is surely including the philosophers whose views he is contesting among these men. Moreover, in explaining this prejudice, Spinoza notes that "[p]erfection and imperfection are … only modes of thinking, that is, notions we are accustomed to feign because we compare individuals of the same species or genus to one another" (Ibid.), which is

---

[6] A major point of disagreement among translators is whether "*malus*" should be rendered in English as "evil" or "bad." Although Curley opts for the former, I am following Kisner and Shirley in preferring the latter on the grounds that Spinoza uses the term in an extremely broad rather than in a specifically moral sense.

a charge that could be leveled against philosophers in the Aristotelian tradition. And the same applies to good and bad, which for Spinoza are likewise modes of thinking, formed by a comparison of things, rather than inherent properties of the things deemed good or bad, which he illustrates by noting that the same thing can at the same time be good, bad, or indifferent, taking as an example the case of music, which he notes is good for one who is melancholy, bad for one who is in mourning, and neither to one who is deaf (Ibid.).

Taken by themselves, the claim that the contrasts between good and bad, perfect and imperfect, concern only modes of thinking suggests a radical subjectivism, which would hardly seem to be a secure foundation for a theory of virtue. Spinoza makes it clear, however, that this is not what he has in mind when, immediately after these dismissive remarks, he writes:

> But though this is so, still we must retain these words. For because we desire to form an idea of man, as a model of human nature which we may look to, it will be useful to us to retain these same words with the meaning I have indicated. In what follows, therefore, I shall understand by good what we know certainly is a means by which we may approach nearer and nearer to the model of human nature that we set before ourselves. By bad, what we certainly know prevents us from becoming like that model. Next, we shall say that men are more perfect or imperfect, insofar as they approach more or less near to this model. (G2 208; C1 545)

Although Spinoza clearly understands them as relational terms, rather than as designating intrinsic properties of things, the characterization of "good" and "bad" as "what we certainly know" respectively to be a means for approximating and an obstacle to approximating the proposed model of human nature[7] might seem to provide sufficient grounds for dismissing the view that he advocates a radical ethical subjectivism. Indeed, the qualification of the cognition involved as certain (*certo*) indicates that Spinoza had in mind the second and third kinds of cognition, which are based on adequate ideas. Nevertheless, one still might resist this conclusion on the grounds that the assessments at issue are based on a model that is a product of the human mind (Spinoza refers to it as what "we set before

---

[7] These characterizations of "good" and "bad" do not correspond precisely to the official definitions Spinoza provides at the beginning of E4. There he defines the former as "what we certainly know to be useful to us" (d1) and the latter as "what we certainly know presents us from being masters of some good" (d2). The point, I take it, is that these definitions are intended to be more general, since not everything that one might consider useful helps to bring us nearer to the proposed model or bad further from it.

ourselves" [*nobis proponimus*]). In other words, it is a construction, so that the viability of Spinoza's virtue ethic seems to turn on the adequacy of his model. This is a crucial problem for Spinoza and I take his best response would be to claim that, unlike the teleologically based model, which he treats as a product of the imagination, this yet unspecified model is based on an adequate idea of human nature; otherwise it could hardly perform the function he assigns it.[8]

In an attempt to understand Spinoza's exceedingly cryptic account of a model of human nature and its function in the determination of human goodness and perfection (or the lack thereof), it is useful to consider his earlier accounts of two closely related matters. The first is in the TdIE, where his concern was to specify the true good. After claiming, as he later did in the *Ethics*, that good and bad are predicated of things only in certain respects – that is, relative to some chosen end – and that nothing considered in its own nature can be considered perfect or imperfect, Spinoza remarks:

> [S]ince human weakness does not grasp that order [the eternal order of nature] by his own thought, and meanwhile man conceives a human nature much stronger and enduring than his own, and at the same time sees that nothing prevents his acquiring such a nature, he is spurred to seek means that will lead him to such perfection. Whatever can be a means to his attaining it is called a true good. (G2 8; C10)

This is not to suggest that Spinoza's position in this early work is precisely the same as in the *Ethics*. First, unlike the *Ethics*, Spinoza there seemed to have based the need to appeal to what is effectively a model of an ideal human nature, even though he did not characterize it as such, on "human weakness," by which he evidently understood an intellectual rather than a moral weakness, namely the inability to grasp the necessary order of things, which, since it has no place for ends, also has no place for perfection or imperfection with respect to the attainment of an end. By

---

[8] The basic problem is that the very idea of a model of human nature seems to fly in the face of Spinoza's nominalism on the basis of which he dismisses Aristotelian conceptions of genera and species as fictitious products of the imagination. Accordingly, the question is: why isn't Spinoza's conception of a common human nature or essence, which is central not only to the conception of a model of human nature but also, as we shall see, to his account of human sociality in the body of E4, likewise fictitious? It is impossible to deal with this question or, better, tissue of questions here; but a useful treatment of the matter is provided by Karolina Hübner, "Spinoza on Being Human and Human Perfection," *Essays on Spinoza's Ethical Theory*, 124–142. On her account, while the concept of a common human nature does not have formal reality (actual instantiation), it has objective reality or validity because it is formed by reason on the basis of the cognition of common properties of things (in this case of human beings).

contrast, in the *Ethics* Spinoza argues *ab initio* from an eternalistic stand-point, and his task is to bring the reader to this standpoint. Second, though further discussion of this point must await a consideration of the propositions in the *Ethics* dealing with the "free person," it is at least arguably the case that Spinoza does not there view this ideal as one that can be fully realized by a human being. Nevertheless, in another important respect Spinoza's position in the TdIE does anticipate a key element of the moral teaching of the *Ethics*, since he not only identifies the good at which he aims with "the knowledge that the mind has of its union with the whole of Nature," but also includes in this good the possibility of sharing this knowledge with other individuals (G2 8; C10–11). For this indicates that he had already arrived at that unique blend of intellectual achievement in the form of the comprehension of the unity of the mind with the whole of nature, i.e., with God, and concern for the well-being of others, which are the twin components of Spinoza's egoistically grounded virtue ethic.

Similarly, in the KV, after claiming that all things in nature are necessitated and that there are, therefore, in nature no good or bad (as inherent properties of things), Spinoza notes that if one nevertheless wants to say anything about goodness and badness with respect to human beings, it is necessary to conceive a perfect human being, even though such a product of the intellect is nothing but an *ens rationis* (G1 60; C1 103). The text is once again highly cryptic, but I take it that Spinoza is making the essentially Platonic point that in order to predicate good or bad (perfection or imperfection) of a particular individual, one must already be in possession of the relevant concept of the true good or perfection for individuals of that type, so that the crucial question is whether the concept is a genuine *ens rationis* or merely a product of the imagination without any cognitive import.

Although the notion of a model of human nature is the focal point of the preface to E4, Spinoza also there makes two important points about what is to be modeled, namely human perfection. The first is the equation of the passage of an individual from a lesser to a greater degree of perfection with an increase in that individual's power of acting, which is for Spinoza that individual's capacity to affirm his being. Moreover, this turns out to be crucial, since Spinoza equates this power with virtue and claims that the latter "is the very nature or essence of man, insofar as he has the power of bringing about certain things, which can be understood through the laws of his nature alone" (E4d8). Spinoza is not claiming that virtue (understood as power) is the nature or essence of a human being, since that could be said only of God; rather, his point is that human beings are virtuous to the extent to which they *act*; that is, they are adequate causes of their condition, which for finite beings is always limited. The latter point is expressed in the single axiom to E4, which states that "There is no singular thing in nature than which there is not another more powerful and stronger. Whatever one is given, there is another more powerful by which the first can be destroyed."

The second point is the separation of the question of the perfection of a singular thing from that of its duration. Referring to his previous equation of the perfection of a thing with its reality (E2d6), which he now glosses as "the essence of each thing insofar as it exists and produces an effect, and duration as an indefinite continuation of existing" (E2d5), Spinoza denies that the perfection of a thing, so understood, has anything to do with its duration. As we have seen, this is because the duration of a thing is entirely a function of external factors, by which a finite mode or part of nature is unavoidably affected, rather than a consequence of its intrinsic nature. Spinoza is here reiterating his controversial view that no singular thing or individual in nature, including a human being, can self-destruct, which he uses to frame his accounts of the nature of human servitude or bondage to the passions, on the one hand, and of liberation from this bondage or freedom, on the other.

6.2 Human Bondage

Although Spinoza's equation of virtue with power contrasts sharply with more traditional conceptions, it reflects the original meaning of the Latin term *virtus*, according to which virtue is the ability to act according to one's nature or to be self-determined. For Spinoza, the virtuous person is one who has power over her emotions and is not merely a slave to her passions. In Kantian terms, she is autocratic.[9] We have seen, however, that Spinoza did not attribute this power to the will, as had been done by Descartes and most moralists, since the concept of that faculty was for him a fictitious product of the imagination. Nor, it would seem, could this power be

---

[9] The concept of autocracy, understood as a self-mastery based on reason, plays a central role in Kant's account of virtue, which bears many similarities to Spinoza's. It is contrasted with autonomy, which is, of course, the more familiar term in Kant's moral theory. Expressed in terms of the political analogies to which Kant appealed, the former refers to the executive function of practical reason and the latter to its legislative function. Since (as will be discussed further later) for Spinoza the rules of reason stem from the conatus of an individual, rather than from reason itself (pure practical reason in Kant's sense), it does not have a legislative function in Kant's sense; but his account of its executive function is similar to Kant's. For an account of Kant's conception of autocracy and its central role in his theory of virtue see Baxley, *Kant's Theory of Virtue: The Value of Autocracy.*

attributed to the intellect; for while bondage to the passions is rooted for Spinoza in inadequate ideas, he also insists that "Nothing positive which a false idea has is removed by the presence of the true insofar as it is true" (E4p1). This suggests that truth qua truth is not a weapon against false or inadequate ideas; and since the passions for Spinoza stem from inadequate ideas, it seems to follow that it also cannot be a weapon against them. Moreover, Spinoza denies that it has such power when he claims that "An affect cannot be restrained or taken away except by an affect opposite to, and stronger than, the affect to be restrained" (E4p7). This indicates that Spinoza not only rejects the voluntaristic thesis, championed by Descartes, according to which the will has power over the passions, but also the intellectualist and broadly Platonic view that the intellect, through its capacity to cognize the truth, has such a capacity. In opposition to both views, Spinoza maintains that an affect, say the desire to become rich, can be constrained only by another stronger and contrary affect, say fear of punishment, which would limit the courses of action through which one might endeavor to become rich.

Of itself, however, this is insufficient to provide the foundation for a theory of virtue as autocracy, since, as the illustration indicates, it only accounts for the possibility of replacing one form of emotional bondage with another. Thus, what Spinoza needs to do is to determine an affective role for cognition based on reason, without assigning it the task of determining the will, since the latter has been dismissed as a philosophical fiction. His starting point is the proposition that "The cognition of good and bad is nothing but an affect of joy or sadness insofar as we are conscious of it" (E4p8). The demonstration of this crucial proposition turns on the conception of an idea of an idea. First, Spinoza reminds us that we call a thing good or bad insofar as it is either an aid or a hindrance to the preservation of our being. Since the affections of joy and sadness are the signs through which we recognize this, it follows that by the "cognition of good and bad" is meant nothing more than the mind's awareness of these ideas. Consequently, this cognition has the form of an idea of an idea. Moreover, as such, Spinoza argues, it is not actually distinct from the original idea (the emotion of joy or sadness), but is merely the same idea qua consciously apprehended. And from this, Spinoza concludes that such cognition possesses the entire emotive force of the joy or sadness that it apprehends.

On the basis of this principle, Spinoza first provides an analysis (E4p9–p13) of the relative strength or emotive force of affects, insofar as they stem from the first kind of cognition, i.e., cognition based on the imagination and, therefore, inadequate ideas. The claim is that the relative strength of these affects is a function of factors such as the physical and temporal proximity of their objects, and the perceived possibility, contingency, or necessity of their existence. And on this basis Spinoza constructs a calculus in accordance with which an affect toward an object viewed as present and necessary is stronger, other things being equal, than one toward an object viewed as future and merely possible, or contingent; again with these determinations being made by the imagination or the first kind of cognition rather than by reason.

Having explicated the emotive force of affects based on inadequate and imaginatively based ideas, the next item on Spinoza's agenda is to consider the force of affects based on adequate ideas or, as he now terms them, "true cognitions." To this end, he notes that "No affect can be restrained by the true cognition of good and bad insofar as it is true, but only insofar as it is considered as an affect" (E4p14). In other words, even though truth qua truth has no emotive force, a true cognition – that is, one based on adequate ideas – can have such force qua affect and thereby serve as a means to escape from or, more accurately, limit our bondage to the passions. Thus, it is at this point that Spinoza forges the connection between "true cognitions" – that is, adequate ideas yielding the second and third kinds of cognition – and the affects, on which the remainder of the argument of the *Ethics* is based.

Although he does not here refer to it, the real basis for Spinoza's claim is contained in his account of the active affects in E3. As we have seen, there is no active sadness or any negative affect such as hatred for Spinoza because these are all products of the imagination, which, as governed by inadequate ideas, are determined by causes that are external to the essential nature of the agent. And we have also seen that the active affects are deemed such because in their case the mind itself is their adequate cause. Moreover, since, according to Spinoza, "We act when something happens, in us or outside us, of which we are the adequate cause" (E3d2), it follows that, insofar as our affective state is caused by an adequate idea, we can be said to act. Accordingly, it is through the conception of active affects, grounded in adequate ideas, of which agents are the adequate cause, that Spinoza attempts to explain, without appealing to the fiction of the will as a distinct power, how rational individuals or singular things – that is, human beings – despite being merely parts of nature and, as such, causally determined are capable of escaping bondage to their passions and attaining freedom as autocracy.

Human reason, however, is at best a fragile power for Spinoza, and he illustrates this by applying the general principles of his account of the human emotions to "desire which arises from a true cognition of good and bad"; that is, to rational desire. This shows that in general such desire can be checked by many other desires by which we are often assailed (E4p15). More specifically, it shows that a rational desire for a future object can be overcome more easily than a similar desire for a present object (E4p16); that such a desire directed toward a contingent object is weaker still (E4p17); and that, other things being equal, a desire arising from joy is stronger than one arising from sadness (E4p18). By this means Spinoza attempts to explain in his own terms, again without recourse to either the philosophical conception of will or the religious conception of a sinful nature, a fundamental and lamentable fact of human experience, namely the great difference between cognizing what is good, right, or useful, and actually doing it; that is, *akrasia*.

6.3   The Prescriptions of Reason

After demonstrating that reason has some, albeit very limited, power over the passions and explaining why it so frequently fails to control them, the next item on Spinoza's agenda is to show "what reason prescribes to us, which affects agree with the rules of human reason, and which, on the other hand, are contrary to these rules" (E4p18s). These are the topics of the remainder of E4, which contains the basic tenets of Spinoza's virtue ethic.

The account begins with the proposition that "From the laws of his own nature, everyone necessarily wants, or is repelled by, what he judges to be good or bad" (E4p19). That everyone desires what they take to be good and to avoid what they take to be bad seems harmless enough, even when we factor in that by good is understood what is thought to produce joy and by bad what is thought to produce sadness. But since the laws, which Spinoza equates with the very nature or essence of a human being, stem from the conatus or endeavor of each individual to preserve its being, this entails a form of psychological egoism in which self-preservation is the ultimate end of all human endeavor. In support of this, Spinoza cites E3p28, which states that "We strive to further the occurrence of whatever we imagine will lead to joy, and to avert or destroy what we imagine is contrary to it, or will lead to sadness," and E4p8, where he connects joy with what we consider to aid and sadness with what we consider to hinder the preservation of our being.

On the basis of this *psychological* egoism, Spinoza mounts an argument for what, at least initially, appears to be a rather straightforward form of *ethical* egoism, in which virtue is equated with success in the attempt to preserve one's being. E4p20 lays the foundation for this form of egoism by claiming that "The more each one strives, and is able to seek his own advantage [*suum utile*], that is, to preserve his being, the more he is endowed with virtue: conversely, insofar as one neglects his own advantage, that is, neglects to preserve his being, he lacks power." The demonstration turns on the equation of virtue with power (E4d8), where power is understood as what a person can accomplish on the basis of her essential nature alone (*quae solâ essentia*); that is, her conatus, which Spinoza had defined as the essence of a singular thing (E3d7). E4p21 then maintains that "No one can desire to be blessed, to act well act and to live well, unless at the same time he desires to be, to act, and to live, i.e., to actually exist." By the desire to be blessed and to act and live well Spinoza evidently understands the desire to be virtuous, and he takes it as self-evident that no one would desire to be virtuous without also desiring to exist. But given Spinoza's conception of virtue, it would seem that the proposition is not merely self-evident but tautologous, at least if the desire to exist is just the desire to preserve one's being. Spinoza completes this chain of reasoning in E4p22, maintaining that "No virtue can be conceived prior to this [virtue] [viz. the striving to preserve oneself]," to which he adds in a corollary that "The striving to preserve oneself is the first and only foundation of virtue. For no other principle can be conceived prior to this one [by p22] and no virtue can be conceived without it [by p21]." In short, the endeavor to preserve one's being is a necessary condition of virtue and success in this endeavor is a sufficient condition; or, better, since finite individuals or singular things can never be completely successful in this endeavor, the degree of an individual's virtue is a function of the degree of success it achieves in this endeavor.

This raises the question of what Spinoza understands by self-preservation. If, as is suggested by a literal reading of these propositions, he means merely the preservation of one's biological existence, then the claim is both deeply counterintuitive and difficult to reconcile with his broader ethical project. It is the former not only because we tend to admire what is perceived to be self-sacrifice for a noble cause, e.g., the warrior who gives his life for his country or to save the lives of comrades, but also because it seems to deny, for example, that one could simply desire that the starving be fed independently of a desire to be the one doing the feeding.[10] And it seems incompatible with Spinoza's own agenda in E4 because it is

---

[10] The example is from Bennett, *Spinoza's Ethics*, 246.

difficult to ground any general concern for the well-being of others in a concern with the preservation of one's biological existence.

It is evident from E4p23, however, that this is not what Spinoza intended. The proposition states that "A man cannot be said absolutely to act from virtue insofar as he is determined to do something because he has inadequate ideas, but only insofar as he is determined because he understands" (E4p23). The key term here is "absolutely" (*absolute*), which means unconditionally or without exception.[11] In other words, acting to preserve one's being can be considered virtuous if and only if it is based on adequate ideas. Moreover, in the next proposition (E4p24), Spinoza expands on this, claiming that "Acting absolutely from virtue is nothing else in us but acting, living, and preserving our being (these three signify the same thing) by the guidance of reason, from the foundation of seeking one's own advantage." What is added is the notion of one's advantage as it is determined by reason, which is presumably more than mere survival. And, after noting in E4p25 that "No one strives to preserve his being for the sake of anything else," by which, since Spinoza is now talking about someone acting according to the guidance of reason, means what is considered truly useful or advantageous, he concludes in E4p26 that "What we strive for from reason is nothing but understanding, nor does the mind, insofar as it uses reason, judge anything useful to itself except what leads to understanding."

As Spinoza makes clear in his demonstration of this pivotal proposition, by "reason" (*ratio*) is meant not a discrete mental faculty, but "the mind itself insofar as it understands clearly and distinctly." Assuming that by "mind" is here understood the *human* mind, the claim is that understanding is the activity through which such a mind affirms its existence or, in more Aristotelian terms, actualizes itself. The argument for this claim consists in an inference from the general principle that everything strives to affirm or preserve its existence to the human mind as a particular instantiation of this principle. For Spinoza this means that, just as the endeavor to preserve oneself is for its own sake, rather than for any transcendent end, so the human mind's endeavor to understand is likewise for its own sake, rather than for any further end that may be attained or facilitated through understanding.

This proposition is pivotal because it radically intellectualizes Spinoza's underlying conception of conatus, seemingly elevating the development of the understanding from merely being a means for overcoming bondage to

---

[11] I am here following Curley, who renders the nominative form "*absolutus*" as "unconditional" or "without exception" (*The Collected Works of Spinoza*, 1, 624).

the passions to an end in itself. For while the understanding for Spinoza does serve as a means for escaping bondage or servitude, it is not *merely* a means, since it is also the vehicle through which alone the ultimate end of human endeavor, namely freedom from bondage, also characterized as blessedness (*Beatitudo*), is attainable. Accordingly, this is the Spinozistic version of the biblical claim that "The truth shall set you free" (John 8:32). And it is in light of this that we must understand Spinoza's claim that "We know nothing to be certainly good or bad except what really leads to understanding or what can prevent us from understanding" (E4p27). Moreover, since God for Spinoza is the ultimate ground of the intelligibility of things, it also follows that "Cognition of God is the Mind's greatest good; its greatest virtue is to cognize God" (E4p28).

This line of argument has led to the conclusion that the development of the understanding is the supreme good for an individual; but it has not addressed the question of how the pursuit of this good should involve any concern for the well-being of others. Moreover, it would seem that this is an issue that must be addressed, if Spinoza is to show that the core of traditional morality, in the form of a virtue ethic, can be erected on an egoistic foundation. But while Spinoza does not neglect this problem (in fact, it is among the main concerns of E4), he makes things difficult for the reader by casting his argument in a metaphysical form, deducing human beings' need and concern for other human beings from general principles concerning the relations between all individuals or singular things.

The starting point of what might be considered Spinoza's egoistically based argument for altruism is the principle that "Any singular thing whose nature is entirely different from ours can neither aid nor restrain our power of acting, and absolutely no thing can be either good or bad for us, unless it has something in common with us" (E4p29). This follows from the even more general principle that things that have nothing in common cannot enter in a causal relation (E1a5). Since this means that they cannot affect one another at all, they obviously cannot affect one another either advantageously or adversely. In E4p30 and E4p31 Spinoza slides from claims about the nature of individuals or singular things as such to claims about "our nature," presumably meaning thereby our nature as human beings. The former claims that "No thing can be bad through what it has in common with our nature; but insofar as it is bad it is contrary to us," while the latter contends that "Insofar as a thing agrees with our nature it is necessarily good," thereby ruling out the possibility that something that agrees with our nature might be simply indifferent to us. Then, after arguing that insofar as human beings are subject to the passions they not only do not agree, but are contrary to one another (E4p32–p34), Spinoza concludes that "Only insofar as men live according to the guidance of reason must they always agree in nature" (E4p35).

Moreover, in a series of corollaries to this proposition and scholia to these corollaries, which lean heavily on E4p31, Spinoza argues from the agreement of human beings insofar as they live according to the guidance of reason to their goodness in the sense of usefulness for one another. As he puts it in the first corollary, "There is no singular thing in nature which is more useful to man than a man who lives according to the guidance of reason." And it is but a short step from this to the conclusion that "The good which everyone who seeks virtue wants for himself, he also desires for other men; and this desire is greater as his knowledge of God is greater" (E4p37), which Spinoza justifies by appealing to the usefulness claim of E4p35c1 that "There is no singular thing in Nature which is more useful to man than a man who lives according to the guidance of reason."

This concise bit of argument constitutes Spinoza's bridge from his egoistically grounded intellectualism to an altruistic, or at least other-oriented, ethic based on the essential sociability of human beings, insofar as they live according to the guidance of reason. It has not gone unnoticed, however, that this bridge is somewhat less than sturdy. Its main support is the conception of a common human essence or nature, which calls to mind two previously discussed problems. One is the compatibility of this conception with Spinoza's "nominalism"; that is, the view that natural kinds are products of the imagination with no grounding in the nature of things.[12] The other, and more directly germane to our present concern, is the relationship between a particular individual and its nature or essence, which we have seen underlies Spinoza's argument that no one would commit suicide unless compelled by an external cause. It was argued that in arriving at this conclusion Spinoza distinguished in a seemingly arbitrary manner between the essence or essential nature and the whole nature of an individual, such that the "external cause" could be considered external to the former and internal to the latter. As is clear from E4p30 and E4p31, however, the present issue concerns the relationship between two distinct

---

[12] I have put "nominalism" in scare quotes to echo Bennett's pointed denial that Spinoza is a nominalist, at least if this is understood to mean the rejection of universal items in favor of particulars. I believe, however, that Bennett goes too far when he claims (*Spinoza's Ethics*, 302) that Spinoza "Usually . . . makes room for nothing but universal items – natures or essences – and has no particulars except for the grand all-encompassing one, God or Nature," since the argument of the last four parts of the *Ethics* turns on the conception of human beings as genuine individuals or singular things.

individuals (A and B) sharing an essential nature or property x. Moreover, there are at least two problems here. One is metaphysical and concerns Spinoza's conception of essence. Since by the essence of a thing is understood "that which being given, the thing itself is necessarily posited and which, being taken away, the thing is necessarily also taken away" (E2d2), it is hard to see how two things could be said to share the same essence without thereby becoming the same thing.[13] The other is that, even assuming that two things can share the same essence, it remains unclear why whatever is either beneficial or harmful to A in virtue of having or being an x is ipso facto also necessarily beneficial or harmful to B in virtue of likewise having or being an x.[14]

Matthew Kisner, in defense of the argument sketched above, admits that the latter claim "does look suspicious" for two reasons. First, there are shared properties that are beneficial for different individuals, e.g., being a king, without being mutually beneficial; and, second, the argument applies only to shared essential properties, though individuals can have both shared and distinctive essential properties.[15] His defense turns on the fact that the shared property in question is rationality. And while he admits that "Spinoza's argument does not succeed unless he holds that rationality does not direct us to competing goods," he maintains that Spinoza succeeds in showing this.[16] The problem, however, is that the argument just considered does not refer to rationality or understanding as a shared nature. On the contrary, it abstracts from the nature of the properties that are assumed to be shared in an attempt to establish general truths about the relationship between singular things as such, which are assumed to share any essential property; and it this general argument that Spinoza evidently marshals in order to ground his claims about human beings in his underlying metaphysical principles.

Nevertheless, rather than cavalierly dismissing Spinoza's argument because it rests on shaky metaphysical foundations, it may prove worthwhile to consider it on its own terms. The essential claim, which for the

---

[13] This difficulty is pointed out by Della Rocca, "Egoism and the Imitation of Affects in Spinoza," in *Spinoza on Reason and the "Free Man,"* esp. 128–134.

[14] Among commentators who have puzzled over this are Bennett, *Spinoza's Ethics*, 300–301 and Garber, "Dr. Fichelson's Dilemma: Spinoza on Freedom and Sociability," esp. 188–189.

[15] Kisner, *Spinoza on Human Freedom*, 140–141. A similar albeit somewhat lengthier list of the difficulties with Spinoza's argument is provided by Nadler ("The Lives of Others," 49–50), who nonetheless likewise defends Spinoza's basic claim that one guided by reason has a grounded self-interested concern for the well-being of others, which he likewise characterizes as benevolence despite Spinoza's own apparent disparagement of that emotion.

[16] Ibid., 140.

sake of convenience I shall cite again, is E4p37: "The good which everyone
who seeks virtue wants for himself, he also desires for other men; and this
desire is greater as his knowledge of God is greater." To begin with, it is
notable that Spinoza here refers to those who are seeking virtue (*virtutem
secantur*), since this suggests that his intended audience encompasses those,
like the young Spinoza of the TdIE, who are seeking the truth, rather than
those who are already virtuous and might, therefore, provide a model to
emulate. At the same time, however, it also seems that these seekers are
assumed to be already living according to the guidance of reason; otherwise
they would not be seeking a good that is universally shareable.

The significance of this proposition for Spinoza is indicated by the fact that
he provides two distinct arguments, as well as two lengthy scholia in which he
lays out the basic elements of his moral and political theory. One is strictly
utilitarian; the other is psychological and based on his theory of the emotions.
The utilitarian argument, which is implied rather than stated, holds that
whoever lives according to the guidance of reason, and thus pursues understanding as the highest good, necessarily desires that others do likewise. He
offers two reasons for this claim. The first is that similarly motivated individuals
will not molest them out of envy, jealousy, or fear (the emotions with which
philosophers have traditionally been greeted). The second is that like-minded
individuals may be of assistance in one's own pursuit of understanding. As
Steven Nadler succinctly puts it, "[T]wo heads are better than one, especially if
they are in agreement about such important matters as what is good and what is
bad."[17] The psychological argument, which is based on the analysis of love and
the principle of the imitation of the affects offered in E3, seems rather like an
appeal to what is now called "positive reinforcement." The claim is that a good
that one loves or desires for oneself will be loved more constantly and with
greater strength if it is believed that others love it also. Applying this to the case
of cognition, it follows that the pursuit of understanding by others serves to
increase the zeal with which we pursue it ourselves.[18]

Although at first glance this line of argument suggests a narrow intellectualism, in which the society of those seeking understanding might seem like
a latter-day version of Plato's Academy, a careful consideration of the overall
context of the argument indicates that this is not the case. Rather, given
Spinoza's psychological premises, particularly the "law" of the imitation of the
emotions, the claim is that members of a society of like-minded seekers after
virtue would be mutually supportive not only of the development of each
individual's cognitive capacity, but also of certain affects, e.g., strength of

[17] Ibid., 51.   [18] This argument is also favored by Della Rocca, *Spinoza*, 134–138.

character or fortitude, which in E3p59 he divides into generosity and nobility and which he attributes to the mind merely insofar as it understands. Moreover, contrary to what has been claimed, I believe that with regard to the concern for the well-being of others, generosity (rather than benevolence) would be the fundamental virtue for Spinoza, since it is an expression of the activity of the subject.[19] In other words, I am suggesting that Spinoza's basic argument for the necessity of a concern for the well-being of others by those living according to the guidance of reason is best seen as an argument for the practice of the virtue of generosity, where this is both sharply distinguished from pity, which Spinoza considered as both bad in itself and useless for one living in this manner (E4p50), and is to be understood in a broader sense than merely a willingness to share one's wealth and other material goods.

However, if not narrowly intellectualistic, Spinoza's analysis of virtue seems exceedingly elitist, since it focuses on the *modus vivendi* of those few who live according to the guidance of reason and who could, therefore, provide appropriate models for imitation. In fact, virtually the only places where Spinoza deals explicitly with the question of how those who live according to the guidance of reason should relate to those who are not so fortunate are E4p35c2s, where he laments that "it rarely happens that men live according to the guidance of reason. Instead their lives are so constituted that they are usually envious and burdensome to one another"; Ep46, where he claims that "He who lives according to the guidance of reason strives, as far as he can, to repay the other's hate, anger, and disdain toward him with love, or generosity"; and E4p70, which states that "A free man who lives among the ignorant strives, as far as he can, to avoid their favors." Moreover, the clear implication of at least the latter two passages is that those who live according to the guidance of reason should have as little to do with those who don't as possible.

Nevertheless, this is not a view that Spinoza consistently espouses. For after approving the traditional Aristotelian conception of human beings as social animals and insisting that we derive from society with fellow human beings many more advantages than disadvantages, he remarks in a passage of uncharacteristic emotion:

> So let the Satirists laugh as much as they like at human affairs, let the Theologians curse them, let Melancholics praise as much as they can a life that is uncultivated and wild, let them disdain men and admire the lower

---

[19] Although they acknowledge that Spinoza explicitly deprecates benevolence, defining it as the desire to benefit someone we pity, both Kisner (*Spinoza on Human Freedom*, 144) and Nadler ("The Lives of Others," 47) use the term to characterize the concern for others of those living under the guidance of reason, so that they characterize Spinoza's argument for the necessity of such a concern as an argument for benevolence.

animals. Men still find from experience that by helping one another they can provide themselves much more easily with the things they require, and that only by joining forces can they avoid the dangers that threaten on all sides – not to mention that it is much preferable and more worthy of our knowledge to consider the deeds of men, rather than those of the lower animals. (E4p35c2s)

This suggests that there is a tension in Spinoza's egoistically based argument for generosity or, if one prefers, an active concern for the well-being of others; between a narrow view, based on the "law" of the imitation of the affects, in which this concern is focused on those who are like-minded, and a broader view, which is independent of this principle and addressed to humankind as such. This tension is illustrated by the juxta-position of two claims that Spinoza makes: "To man . . . there is nothing more useful than man" (E4p18s) and "There is no singular thing in nature which is more useful to man than a man who lives according to the guidance of reason" (E4p35c1). Moreover, these texts cannot be reconciled by maintaining that the first is merely an abbreviated form of the second; for in the sentence immediately following it, Spinoza writes:

> Man . . . can wish for nothing more helpful to the preservation of his being than that all should so agree in all things that the minds and bodies of all would compose, as it were, one mind and one body; that all should strive together, as far as they can, to preserve their being; and that all, together, should seek for themselves the common advantage of all. (G2 223; C1 556)

The problem, then, is that, even granting the argument from the imitation of the affects, a further argument is needed to ground this broader claim, which Spinoza clearly endorses and which applies to all human beings, not merely those who live according to the guidance of reason. The key to this argument, which Spinoza does not explicitly mount, is that the mutual usefulness of human beings concerns the goods of the body as well as of the mind.[20] Although he does not link it directly to his claim about the mutual usefulness of human beings, we have seen that since for Spinoza the human mind is the idea of the body, whatever is useful for the latter is *eo ipso* also useful for the body and vice versa. Moreover, Spinoza explicitly affirms the usefulness to human beings of whatever is beneficial to the body, which he understands both in terms of affecting and being affected by external bodies in beneficial ways; that is, in its interaction with its environment (E4p38), and as preserving the

---

[20] This aspect of Spinoza's thought is emphasized by Susan James, "Spinoza, the Body, and the Good Life," *Essays on Spinoza's Ethical Theory*, 143–159.

requisite proportion of motion and rest among the various parts of the body, which is essential to the preservation of the body as a whole (E4p39).

Since Spinoza acknowledges that human beings can be genuinely useful to one another in ways other than by serving as conduits of information or intellectual inspiration, the inclusion of a consideration of the needs of the body, which is clearly an essential part of his thought about the human condition and the social relations between human beings, may be seen as a necessary corrective to the seemingly one-sided intellectualism suggested by his account of life according to the guidance of reason. Even granting this, however, one may still ask if this is sufficient to support Spinoza's more fundamental thesis that the principle of seeking one's advantage (no matter how high-mindedly this advantage is understood) can provide an adequate foundation for a virtue ethic capable of supporting something like the aforementioned golden rule.

Although it was not, of course, known to Spinoza, a subsequent and deeply influential attempt to deal with this issue is Kant's treatment of it in terms of his so-called formula of humanity, namely: "So act that you use humanity, whether in your own person or in any other always at the same time as an end, never merely as means."[21] While it may be assumed that Spinoza, like his many subsequent critics, would have rejected Kant's more familiar universal law formulation of the categorical imperative, namely "Act only in accordance with that maxim through which you can at the same time will that it become a universal law,"[22] on the grounds of its lack of content, this cannot be said of the formula of humanity, which is why it has been endorsed by many Kantians who reject the universal law formula. The "merely as means" clause assumes with Spinoza that as embodied, social beings, we necessarily use other human beings as means to our own subjective or personal ends, which, as natural beings, boil down to our own happiness or well-being; but it imposes a constraint on this use, which in effect means that we must recognize the subjective or personal ends of others as having equal legitimacy with our own and, therefore, as imposing a categorical constraint on the means that can be used to promote these ends. Otherwise expressed, we must treat other human, i.e., rational, beings with respect in the sense of recognizing their right to set ends for themselves and, therefore, not to be treated *merely* as means to the satisfaction of one's private or subjective ends, which is basically what Kant means by using, i.e., treating, humanity as at the

---

[21] Kant, *Groundwork of the Metaphysics of Morals* (KGS 4: 428).
[22] Kant, *Groundwork of the Metaphysics of Morals*, 421.

same time an end.[23] And the problem is that it is difficult to see how Spinoza's account, with its seemingly uncompromising appeal to self-interest, could find room for such a constraint, even though something like it seems to be an essential ingredient in the golden rule to which Spinoza is presumably committed.

Among recent commentators, Kisner has taken this possible Kantian critique of Spinoza's egotistically grounded moral theory seriously and proposes what amounts to a qualified defense. Focusing on the concept of respect, Kisner maintains that "Spinoza's love of God accords people a kind of respect." In support of this claim, he appeals to what he terms Spinoza's argument for benevolence (which I have characterized as generosity), which on his reading apparently amounts to the claim that people have "'unconditional' value" in the sense that "it is good to treat all people well, regardless of whether they are particularly situated to contribute to my good."[24] I have questioned above the cogency of this line of argument from Spinoza's egoist premises; but, setting that aside, it is hard to see how any kind of respect could be grounded in the premise that it is good to treat other people well, even if doing so is of no perceivable advantage to oneself; since, for example, one might say the same thing about feeding a stray dog, which presumably would not entail any notion (however weak) of respect. Rather, respect would seem to require treating the object of respect as an end in itself; that is, as a being with the capacity to set ends for itself and to select the means for their attainment, which, as Kant claims, imposes a rational constraint on one's own personal or subjective ends and the means that may be used in their pursuit insofar as they may infringe on those of others. And I fail to see how Spinoza's ethical theory can accommodate any such constraint on an individual's endeavor to preserve its being, even if this is understood as the preservation of one's rational nature, rather than one's physical existence.

6.4   Spinoza's Evaluation of the Affects

After spelling out the foundations of his moral theory in the first forty propositions of E4, Spinoza devotes a number of propositions (E4p41–p66) to a discussion of various affects with respect to their contribution to or impairment of an individual's conatus. His overall strategy is to divide these affects into three classes: those that are intrinsically good, those that

---

[23] For my analysis of Kant's argument for this famous claim see *Kant's Groundwork for the Metaphysics of Morals: A Commentary*, 218–229.

[24] Kisner, *Spinoza on Human Freedom*, 159.

are intrinsically bad, and a large group that are good in moderation, but bad if they become excessive.

As one might expect, joy heads the list of the first category and sadness the second. Following his earlier account (see E3p11s), under joy Spinoza lists cheerfulness (*Hilaritas*), by which he understands joy as it relates to both mind and body, though here the focus is on the latter, while under sadness he lists melancholy (*Melancholia*), which is sadness as it relates to both the mind and the body, though again the focus is here on the latter. One significant difference from the earlier account is that Spinoza now treats pleasure (*Titillatio*) and pain (*Dolor*) as distinct from cheerfulness and melancholy, respectively, where he had previously suggested that they were equivalent. This is significant because, while Spinoza consistently maintains that cheerfulness can never be excessive and pain never beneficial, he now claims that pleasure can be excessive and pain sometimes beneficial, insofar as it counters a pleasure or enjoyment that is bad (E4p43), which obviously requires that they be distinguished from cheerfulness and melancholy. But though he duly notes that pleasure can be excessive, Spinoza's overall positive attitude toward pleasure, with the exception of the erotic variety, gives a decidedly anti-ascetic tone to much of his moral philosophy. In a passage that clearly indicates the kinds of pleasure of which he approves, Spinoza writes: "It is the part of a wise man . . . to refresh and restore himself in moderation with pleasant food and drink, with the beauty of green plants, with decoration, music, sports, the theater, and other things of this kind, which anyone can use without injury to another" (E4p45s).

Among the three primary affects, Spinoza considers only sadness to be bad. He acknowledges, however, that both love and desire can be excessive and, therefore, harmful, though he maintains that this applies to them only insofar as they are passions, since it is absurd to think that an active affect could become excessive (E4p61). Moreover, Spinoza claims that this excess occurs if an affect is fixated upon an object that stimulates or gratifies a part of the body or one of its appetites, at the expense of the well-being of the body as a whole. This includes pathological states such as greed, ambition, gluttony, and drunkenness; but the main culprit is lust. Contrary to his generally anti-ascetic attitude, Spinoza tended to view sexual desire as an unmitigated evil. Thus, he states that "A purely sensual love . . . that is, a Lust to procreate which arises from external appearance, and absolutely, all love which has a cause other than freedom of mind, easily passes into hate – unless (which is worse) it is a species of madness. And then it is encouraged more by discord than by harmony" (G2

271; C1 591).[25] But his views on human sexuality are perhaps best illustrated by his highly qualified endorsement of marriage, which he acknowledges "agrees with reason, if the Desire for physical union is not generated only by external appearance but also by a love of begetting children and educating them wisely, and, if the Love of each, of both the man and the woman, is caused not by external appearance only, but mainly by freedom of mind" (G2 271–272; C1 591).

In addition to sadness and melancholy, which are more properly classified as moods rather than emotions, among the harmful affects Spinoza gives pride of place to hatred, which he maintains can never be good, though he limits this to hatred toward other human beings (E4p45). And, together with hatred, Spinoza condemns envy, mockery, disdain, anger, vengeance, and other, unnamed affects, which are either related to or arise from hatred (E4p45sc1). Moreover, in the previously cited E4p46 he claims that "He who lives according to the guidance of reason strives, as far as he can, to repay the other's Hate, Anger, and Disdain toward him, with Love, or Generosity," which is evidently the Spinozistic analog of the biblical injunction to love not only one's neighbors but also one's enemies.

We have seen that Spinoza disapproves of pity, even though he considers it the basis of benevolence. In fact, he claims that for someone living according to the guidance of reason, pity is not only intrinsically bad but useless (E4p50). While being a form of sadness is sufficient for Spinoza to consider pity bad, it seems paradoxical to deny that it is useful, since its connection with benevolence indicates that it can lead to the endeavor to help those in need. This denial, however, is limited to those who follow the guidance of reason, because we have seen that he claims that those who are guided by reason will aid those in need on self-interested grounds without pitying them. In fact, evidently addressing such a concern, Spinoza claims that "To every action to which we are determined from an affect which is a passion, we can be determined by reason, without that affect" (E4p59). Moreover, far from dismissing pity altogether, Spinoza calls attention to the fact that this dismissal is limited to those living according to the guidance of reason and that "one who is moved to aid others neither by reason nor by pity is rightly called inhuman" (E4p50c).

Hope and fear are other powerful affects related to desire, which Spinoza denies can be good per se (E4p47), though we shall see later that he

---

[25] It is noteworthy that Spinoza here equates sexual desire with the desire to procreate, though he had previously more accurately characterized it as "a desire for and love of joining one body to another" (G2 202; C1 541).

recognizes a sense in which they can be useful. Once again, his main reason for disparaging them is their connection with sadness, and while this clearly applies to fear, it seems strange to say this of hope, since it is traditionally viewed in a positive light. Spinoza justifies this on the grounds that there can be no hope without fear, which he explains by citing his definitions of these passions as respectively an inconstant joy and an inconstant sadness, which in both cases stem from the idea of a past or future occurrence about whose outcome we are uncertain (da 12 and 13). In a scholium to this proposition, Spinoza extends this claim to the pairs of confidence and despair, on the one hand, and gladness and remorse, on the other. Again this is surprising, since confidence and gladness are generally regarded as pro-attitudes; but Spinoza justifies this on the grounds that they presuppose hope. Accordingly, Spinoza's view is that to the extent to which we are able to live according to the guidance of reason, we shall not only be without fear but also without hope. Nevertheless, in a concession to human weakness, in which he links hope and fear with the putative religious virtues of humility and repentance, Spinoza acknowledges that,

> [B]ecause men rarely live from the dictate of reason, these two affects, Humility and Repentance, and in addition, Hope and Fear, bring more advantage than disadvantage. So since men must sin, they ought rather to sin in that direction. If weak-minded men were all equally proud, ashamed of nothing, and afraid of nothing, how could they be united or restrained by any bonds? (E4p54s)

Another important class of affects for Spinoza concern self-evaluation, and they have both positive and negative forms, which are linked respectively to joy and sadness. The main positive forms are pride and self-contentment (*Acquiescentia in se ipso*).[26] Despite its pedigree in joy, Spinoza strongly condemns pride. Moreover, this is one place where he agrees with the view of the religious tradition, though he breaks with it in also rejecting its preferred alternative to pride, humility, which he defines as "a sadness born of the fact that a man considers his own lack of power or weakness" (da 26; G2 196; C1 536) (see also E4p53). The importance that Spinoza assigns to pride as a harmful affect is indicated by the fact that he devotes three propositions to it (E4p55–p57). In the first two of these he contrasts it with despondency or self-abasement (*Abjectio*) on the grounds that the extreme forms of each indicate both great ignorance of oneself and

---

[26] I am following Shirley and Kisner in translating *Acquiescentia in se ipso* as "self-contentment" rather than Curley's "self-esteem." Another possible rendering is "self-approval," which is how it is translated by Elwes, or perhaps simply "self-acceptance."

great weakness of mind, though in E4p56cs he remarks that despondency can be corrected more easily. But Spinoza's most sustained critique of pride is contained in E4p57, where he claims that "The proud man loves the presence of parasites, or flatterers, but hates the presence of the noble." This love is based on the fact that the former reinforce the proud person's inflated self-image and the hatred on the fact that the latter threaten it. In a scholium to this proposition, Spinoza notes that it would take too long to enumerate all the evils of pride, though he does stop to point out that the label applies also to those who think less of others than is warranted, presumably because this helps to enhance the proud person's sense of self-worth.

One should not expect, however, that a philosophy such as Spinoza's, which is founded on a form of psychological egoism, would disparage all positive forms of self-evaluation, and the form of which Spinoza does approve is the aforementioned self-contentment, which he defines as "the joy that arises from a person's thinking about himself and his own power of action" (da 25; G2 196; C1 536). In fact, Spinoza claims that self-contentment, if it arises from reason, "is really the highest thing we can hope for" (E4p52s). Since self-contentment would seem to be a form of pride, Spinoza's endorsement of it clearly rests on the condition that it arises from reason; and this is because, so considered, he takes it to be simply the conscious awareness of one's virtue (E4p52s).

E4 also contains three propositions contrasting the stance regarding the good and the bad by those guided by reason with those who are not so guided. The first of these (E4p63) maintains that "He who is guided by Fear, and does good to avoid bad, is not guided by reason." Since fear is a passion and, therefore, based on inadequate ideas, this is a case of doing a good thing for a bad or, perhaps better, an insufficient reason. In a scholium attached to this proposition, Spinoza refers to the superstitious as those who behave in this manner, evidently alluding to those who perform good deeds only because of the hope of reward or fear of punishment in an imagined afterlife, while in a corollary he adds that in a desire arising from reason one directly pursues the good and only indirectly avoids the bad. Spinoza illustrates this in a scholium by contrasting a putatively sick person who, from fear of death, consumes food that he is repelled by (broccoli?) with a supposedly healthy person, who thoroughly enjoys her repast (G2 258; C1 582). The problem, however, is that if the healthiness of a repast is a necessary condition of its enjoyment by someone guided by reason, then it cannot be said that the bad (death or illness that might result from consuming it) is avoided only indirectly, since the belief in its unhealthiness would then be a sufficient condition to preclude its enjoyment.

In the next proposition (E4p64), Spinoza argues that the cognition of what is bad is inadequate and in a corollary he claims that if the human mind had only adequate ideas, it would not have a conception of what is bad. His argument for this proposition, which also applies to the corollary, is peculiar because it draws an epistemic conclusion (the inadequacy of an idea) from a psychological premise, namely that the judgment that something is bad (presumably bad for oneself) has as its necessary concomitant a feeling of sadness. Since this feeling is a passion, and all passions are based on inadequate cognitions, Spinoza reasons that any judgment that something is bad must rest on an inadequate cognition of the object or state of affairs deemed bad. At least at first glance, however, the claim that the cognition that something is bad must be inadequate seems puzzling, since for Spinoza, at least, one can surely have adequate knowledge that something that one enjoys, say eating large amounts of ice cream, is harmful. And it also seems obvious that the ice cream lover would be saddened by this bit of knowledge. Presumably, then, the key to Spinoza's claims lies in the inclusion of the term "only" in the corollary. Since for Spinoza having only adequate ideas is an ideal unattainable by human beings, it follows that the fragmentary bits of such cognition attainable by beings like us, even those living under the guidance of reason, are compatible with the retention of a considerable body of inadequate ideas and the concomitant feeling of sadness.

E4p65 states that "From the guidance of reason, we shall follow the greater of two goods or the lesser of two evils." Since it refers to a greater good and a lesser evil, this proposition is perhaps the best example of how the guidance of reason consists in general propositions stemming from the second rather than the third kind of cognition. It is also among the propositions that Spinoza might have considered self-evident. But what makes it worthy of discussion is its apparent conflict with the corollary to E4p63, which, as we have seen, claims that by following the guidance of reason we pursue the good directly and only avoid the bad indirectly. This is because in the demonstration of this proposition Spinoza claims that a good that precludes the enjoyment of a greater good is really bad, while a lesser bad is really good. Thus, whereas the former claim prioritizes the quest for good over the avoidance of the bad, Spinoza now presents them as correlative.

Moreover, in support of this he refers not to a proposition, definition, or axiom, but to his claim in the preface to E4 that the concepts good and bad are only applied to things insofar as we compare them to one another (G2 208; C1 545). Since in the passage to which Spinoza refers the comparison concerns the goodness or badness of something with respect to different subjects (x might be good for A and bad for B), while here the question evidently concerns the comparative goodness or badness of distinct properties with respect to the same subject (even though x is bad for A, it can still be considered good if it is better than y, or bad if it is worse than x), it is not clear how the former could be used to support the latter. But since, as I have suggested, E4p65 is self-evident, this is a detail that can be set aside, for the real problem remains the compatibility of this proposition with E4p63c, which does not consider them as correlative.[27]

A final important topic with which Spinoza deals in his account of life according to the guidance of reason is the role of temporal considerations in the weighing of the relative goodness and badness of states of affairs. This is the concern of E4p62, which states that "Insofar as the mind conceives things from the dictate of reason, it is affected equally, whether the idea is of a future or past thing, or of a present one," and E4p66, which claims that "From the guidance of reason we want a greater future good in preference to a lesser present one, and a lesser present bad in preference to a greater future one." These propositions are complementary. The former maintains that the affects of a mind governed by reason – that is, its active affects – are independent of the temporal location of the objects of these affects, while the latter claims that the relative strength of the preferences and aversions of such a mind are likewise independent of their temporal location. Moreover, Spinoza is clear that both propositions are based on the same principle, namely that to conceive things from the dictate of reason is to conceive them from an eternalistic standpoint (*sub eadam aeternitatis*) and, therefore, as necessary, in which case the temporal proximity of a conceived state of affairs would have no bearing on how the mind would consider its desirability or lack thereof, either itself or in relation to other possible states of affairs. Simply put, from this standpoint, a bird in the hand is *not* worth more than two in the bush. Spinoza also notes, however, that human beings, even those who endeavor to live according to the guidance of reason, are not fully capable of adopting an eternalistic perspective. As he remarks in a scholium to E4p62, this is because our cognition of the duration of things is dependent on the imagination and, therefore, is very inadequate, from which he draws two important conclusions: one theoretical and the other practical. The theoretical conclusion is

---

[27] We shall see later that E4p68 explicitly considers good and bad as correlative.

that it provides an explanation of why even our "true cognition" of good and bad, i.e., that based on reason, is only abstract or general, which presumably applies to the dictates of reason presented in E4. The practical conclusion, which is clearly the most important for Spinoza, is that it helps to explain why the estimation of a future good or bad state of affairs is often easily outweighed by the consideration of a present one, which is to say why, given human nature, a bird in the hand *seems* more desirable than two in the bush, even though, when seen from an eternalistic standpoint, it is not.

6.5 The Free Person

In the scholium to E4p68 Spinoza surveys what has been shown up to this point by comparing the results of the first eighteen propositions with those of the subsequent forty with respect to the power of the affects. He notes that the former propositions were concerned with human beings considered as led only by their passions and the latter with them considered as led by reason. And having shown that the former do things from ignorance, while the latter do only what they know to be in their own true interest, Spinoza declares that he shall call the former slaves and the latter free men. But though this suggests that he is basically closing the books on E4 and preparing to move on to E5, where he will deal with the topic of human freedom, Spinoza remarks that he wishes to note "a few things concerning the free man's temperament [*ingenio*] and manner of living."

These "few things" are the subject of the final seven propositions of E4, and they are among the most controversial in the *Ethics*. The controversy concerns, on the one hand, the relationship between these propositions and the model of a perfect human nature to which Spinoza appeals in the preface to E4, and, on the other, their relationship to the preceding account of human life according to the guidance of reason. As was previously noted, the appeal to a model of human nature is itself controversial because of its apparent tension with Spinoza's nominalism, according to which general ideas such as the idea of human nature are products of the imagination without any foundation in reality. In response to this worry, it was argued that Spinoza's conception of human nature is an adequate idea of the essential nature of a human being as such. But, assuming that Spinoza can appeal to a model of human nature based on an adequate idea of this nature, there is a further question about whether the final propositions provide this model. This seems problematic because a free person is, *ex hypothesi*, led by reason alone and has only adequate ideas (E4p68d), whereas Spinoza had insisted in E4p4 that "It is impossible that a man should not be a part of Nature, and that he should be able to undergo no changes except those which can be understood through his own nature alone, and of which he is the adequate cause." The problem, then, is that the free person, as Spinoza characterizes him, is not a part of nature, which is to say that he is impossible. And if this is the case, it is difficult to see how he could serve as the model. Rather, it seems more reasonable to locate the model to which Spinoza alludes in the preface to E4 in the account of human life according to the guidance of reason as depicted in E4p19–p66, since it is presumably the best humanly possible form of life.

This still leaves us, however, with the problem of what to do with these seven propositions, which constitute something of a hermeneutical dilemma. On the one hand, Spinoza clearly intends that they be considered as a set, which appears to support the view that they provide the proposed model, even though he nowhere explicitly claims this to be the case, while, on the other hand, the casual way in which he introduces them invites us to consider them more as an addendum, rather than a crucial part of his argument, which they would clearly be if they were intended to provide the proposed model. But while I do not claim to have a satisfactory solution to this dilemma, I believe it important to note that an examination of the propositions themselves indicates that not everything Spinoza claims about the free person seems problematic in the manner suggested above. Rather, considered from this point of view, these propositions fall into two camps: one in which what Spinoza claims about the free person accords with what he says about a human life according to the guidance of reason; the other in which what Spinoza says about the free person goes beyond what he says about the latter in a way that renders both their modeling function and their relationship with the earlier set of propositions about life according to the guidance of reason problematic.

The former camp consists of E4p69: "The virtue of a free man is seen to be as great in avoiding dangers as in overcoming them"; E4p70: "A free man who lives among the ignorant strives, as far as he can, to avoid their favors"; E4p71: "Only free men are very grateful to one another"; and E4p73: "A man who is guided by reason is more free in a state, where he lives according to a common decision, than in solitude, where he obeys only himself." Interestingly, the last of these does not even mention the free person, referring instead to one who lives according to the guidance of reason, which suggests that Spinoza considered these as identical. Moreover, it seems reasonable to claim that the other three propositions in this set could be applied to someone guided by reason as depicted in the preceding propositions. For example, inasmuch as Spinoza's demonstration of E4p71 appeals to E4p35, which maintains that human beings will always agree with one another only insofar as they live according to the guidance of reason, it clearly applies to all those to whom that characterization applies and not merely to a special subset of "free persons." And the demonstrations of E4p69 and E4p70 likewise appeal to considerations that would apply equally to anyone living according to the guidance of reason.

This cannot so easily be said, however, about E4p67, which states that "A free man thinks of nothing less than of death, and his wisdom is a meditation on life, not on death"; E4p68, which maintains that "If men were born free, they would form no concept of good and bad as long as they remained free"; and E4p72, which stipulates that "A free man never acts deceptively but always with good faith."[28] The problem with these propositions is that, unlike those considered above, their demonstrations rest on an idealized conception of a free person, which calls into question their suitability for evaluating the character and deeds of actual human beings. In the first case, the problem is that the demonstration assumes that a free person lives according to the guidance of reason *alone*, in which case she is by E4p63 without fear of death, or of anything else for that matter, though it does not seem possible that even a person living according to the guidance of reason could be totally without fear. In the second case, where Spinoza equates being free with being led by reason alone, the hypothesis underlying the proposition (that someone could be born free and without any concept of good and bad) indicates that it refers to an idealized perfectly free individual rather than to a possible human being.[29]

The last of the above-mentioned propositions, which maintains that a free person never acts deceptively, calls for a separate treatment because it concerns not only the question of idealization but also the more fundamental issue of the success of Spinoza's endeavor to ground his moral theory on an egoistic basis. Indeed, both the demonstration that Spinoza provides for this proposition and the scholium attached to it raise further

---

[28] I am substituting the English rendering of Shirley and Kisner for Curley's. The Latin text states "*Homo liber nunquam dolo, sed semper cum fide agit*," which Curley renders as "A free man always acts honestly, not deceptively." In addition to the word ordering, which I do not take to be significant, the important differences are in the rendering of "*dolo malo*" and "*cum fide*." The former is generally translated as "deceitfully" or "deceptively" and the latter as "faithfully." I am here following Don Garrett, who suggests that Spinoza's terminology here was chosen to echo Hobbes'. See *Nature and Necessity in Spinoza's Philosophy*, 504–522.

[29] As Nadler notes ("On Spinoza's 'Free Man,'" 15–16), such a hypothetical individual is outside of nature.

questions about the compatibility of the argument with this egoism. The demonstration has the form of a reductio and consists of the following steps:

(1) If a free person (insofar as she is free) acted deceptively, she would be acting in accord with a dictate of reason; for it is only insofar as one acts in this way that one may be considered free.

(2) In that case it would be virtuous to act deceptively, at least insofar as this is deemed necessary to preserve one's being. This follows from E4p24, where we have seen that Spinoza equates acting absolutely from virtue with preserving one's being according to the guidance of reason on the egoistic grounds of seeking one's advantage.

(3) Therefore, everyone would be better advised (*consultius esset*) to act deceitfully, i.e., it would be to everyone's advantage to agree verbally, though not in fact, if it is thought necessary to preserve their being.

(4) But this is absurd by E4p31c, which states that "[T]he more a thing agrees with our nature, the more useful, or better, it is for us, and conversely, the more a thing is useful to us the more it agrees with our nature."

(5) Therefore, a free person would never act deceitfully.[30]

Although the conclusion, like the proposition itself, directly applies only to the free person, the alleged absurdity to which deceitful practices supposedly lead is depicted as the consequence of *everyone* acting contrary to the manner in which a free person would act. This appeal to the hypothetical universalization of a practice to determine its reasonableness calls to mind Kant's appeal to universalizability in his formulation of the categorical imperative, and this comparison is further suggested by the fact that both philosophers appear to argue for an unconditional prohibition of deceitful practices or, in Kant's terms, lying.[31] The decisive difference is that, whereas Kant grounded this prohibition in a universal law, Spinoza, who evidently eschewed any appeal to abstract principles, grounded it instead in the normative status ascribed to the free person as an exemplar of human perfection. Thus, appealing to his version of the

---

[30] Spinoza's cryptic conclusion states only: "Therefore, a free person etc.," but given the nature of the proposition for which the demonstration is offered, it seems reasonable to assume that he intended thereby that such a person would not act deceptively.

[31] Kant's considered view is that truthfulness is a perfect duty to oneself, which, as such, is independent of the question of the effect of a lie on the rights or well-being of others. See, for example, *The Metaphysics of Morals* (KGS 6: 429–431; 550–552). Indeed, for Kant the worst form of lie is the lie to oneself, something that, as far as I can see, has no counterpart in Spinoza.

universalizability requirement, Spinoza argues that if a free person could act deceitfully to preserve her being, then it would also be virtuous for everyone to act likewise. And it is this universalization that leads to the consequence that is incompatible with a necessary condition of human flourishing, which is the proposed end of Spinoza's virtue ethic.

The main problem posed by this argument is not with its account of the behavior of the putative free person, since it is clear from E4p67 and, indeed, from Spinoza's account of the free person that she would not engage in deceitful behavior. It lies, rather, in the underlying assumption that the free person's behavior should be considered a norm or model for the behavior of actual and not completely free human beings. Moreover, Spinoza evidently had this problem in mind when in a scholium attached to this proposition he wrote:

> Suppose someone now asks: What if a man could save himself from the present danger of death by treachery? Would not the principle of preserving his own being recommend, without qualification [*omnino suadet*], that he be treacherous? The reply to this is the same. If reason should recommend that, it would recommend it to all men. And so reason would recommend, without qualification, that men should make arrangements to join forces and to have common laws only by deception – i.e., that really they have no common rights. This is absurd. (G2 264; C1 587)

Spinoza's reply to this easily anticipated objection is puzzling, since it appears to involve an *ignoratio elenchi* because it fails to address the question that was actually raised. This question concerns the reasonableness of engaging in deceitful behavior, if it is thought necessary to preserve one's life. In his response, however, Spinoza omits reference to the condition under which deceitfulness was offered as a reasonable course of action, presumably for someone other than a free person, who, *ex hypothesi*, would under no circumstances engage in such behavior. Instead, Spinoza appears to be asserting that a principle that deceitfulness is warranted for anyone, whenever it is deemed advantageous by that person, would be absurd, because it is incompatible with the possibility of something that is a necessary condition of human flourishing, namely a communal existence. But the problem is that, while one could admit that such a principle would be absurd for the reason given, and, therefore, would not be adopted by a free person, this has no bearing on the point at issue, since that concerned the reasonableness of such conduct for *anyone* (including the "unfree") on the condition that it is deemed necessary for self-preservation.

The root of the problem is the modeling role assigned to the concept of a free person in cases where there is a conflict between the behavior of the idealized free person and the endeavor of an actual human being to persevere. Moreover, the problem has not gone unnoticed. The most fully developed response of which I am aware is that of Don Garrett, who denies the premise that it is never good to act contrary to the way in which the free person acts,[32] and proposes that "we interpret Spinoza as holding *both* that the ideal or free man would never act deceitfully, *and* that deceit may under some circumstances nevertheless be good for actual human beings who have not fully achieved this ideal."[33] In a similar vein, Della Rocca maintains that the key to saving the consistency of Spinoza's argument is by distinguishing between degrees of freedom. On his reading, a maximally or perfectly free human being could never be in a situation in which deceit would be necessary (presumably because for such a purely hypothetical being no situation, not even one involving a threat of imminent death, would provide a sufficient reason to deceive), whereas actual and imperfect human beings (even virtuous ones) might find themselves in such a situation, in which case deceit could even be considered obligatory.[34]

Although I concur with both Garrett's proposal for interpreting Spinoza and Della Rocca's emphasis on degrees of freedom, I question their claims that lying under certain conditions, particularly those in which it is deemed necessary to save one's life, might be considered good, much less obligatory by Spinoza. Rather, I take his view to be that, since the endeavor to preserve itself is the essence of every individual or singular thing, lying under some conditions would be understandable and, therefore, not blamable. Nevertheless, there is a further issue raised by Spinoza's manner of dealing with the problem of deceitful promising in cases where it is deemed necessary for the preservation of life (of oneself or others) or perhaps other extreme situations. It concerns the apparent absence in his account of what intuitively might seem to be the most obvious answer to such dilemmas, namely that in certain circumstances deceit is permissible. In fact, the standard criticism of Kant's infamous denial of a right to lie, even when necessary to save lives, which has a superficial affinity with Spinoza's argument, is that he should have maintained that lying under certain conditions is permissible, a move he presumably could make within the

---

[32] Don Garrett, *Nature and Necessity in Spinoza's Philosophy*, 449.   [33] Ibid., 451.
[34] Della Rocca, *Spinoza*, 200–201.

framework of his deontologically structured moral theory.[35] But, as suggested by Garrett's proposed response to the dilemma posed by Spinoza's account, which consists in the claim that under certain conditions it might be *good* (not merely permissible) to deceive,[36] Spinoza's virtue ethic, with its radically anti-deontological thrust, did not provide him with the conceptual resources to make such a response.[37] This is, however, a complex issue in metaethical theory, which is beyond the scope of this study to adjudicate. For present purposes, I wish simply to note that this marks a decisive difference between Spinoza's moral theory and Kant's and, therefore, it casts further doubt on the attempt of interpreters such as Kisner to establish some significant common ground.

---

[35] The text in which Kant argues explicitly for this view is his late essay "On a supposed right to lie from philanthropy" (KGS 8: 425–430), which contains his off-the-cuff response to the objection raised against his view that there is a duty to tell the truth by Benjamin Constant. Kant's reply has been subject to frequent and sometimes mocking criticism as an example of a misplaced emphasis on duty. But it has also been misinterpreted because of a failure to recognize the explicitly political context in which Kant formulates his argument. For a useful discussion of the issue see Helga Varden, "Kant and Lying to the Murderer at the Door."

[36] Elsewhere, however, Garrett does depict Spinoza's response in terms of permissibility. See his "Promising Ideas: Hobbes and Contract in Spinoza's Political Philosophy," 206–209.

[37] This is not to say that Spinoza had no place for conceptions such as obligation and permission. As we shall see in Chapter 8, it is rather that they operate only in a civil context, where they are determined by the laws of a state or civil law, rather than by natural law, as more traditional "natural lawyers" (including Kant) maintained. Nevertheless, at one point in the *Ethics* Spinoza does appeal to the notion of the permissible (*licit*), when he states that "It is permissible for us to avert, in the way that seems safest, whatever there is in nature that we judge to be bad, *or* to prevent us from being able to exist and to enjoy a rational life . . . And absolutely, it is permissible for everyone to do, by the highest right of nature, what he judges will contribute to his advantage" (E4app8; G2 268; C1 589). And it could be claimed that permissibility in this sense would be applicable to the passage currently under discussion. But what is lacking in Spinoza is the notion of the "permissible" as an ethical category distinct from both the "obligatory" and the "forbidden." One might term this the "merely permissible," but it is clear that this is not what Spinoza had in mind in the above-quoted passage.

CHAPTER 7

Freedom and Blessedness

The fifth and final part of the *Ethics* is entitled "On the Power of the Intellect, or on Human Freedom." The title reflects Spinoza's relativized conception of human freedom, understood as control of the passions by the intellect. As the title suggests, it is intended to complement the fourth part, the full title of which is "On Human Bondage, or the Powers of the Affects." Like E4, E5 is divided into two radically distinct parts, only the first of which is indicated by the title. The first part (E5p1–p20) provides an account of how and the extent to which human reason is able to control the passions and achieve the kind of freedom of which human beings are capable, insofar as they live according to the guidance of reason, which I have characterized as autocracy, while the second part (E5p21–p40) is concerned with the state of blessedness or beatitude (*beatitudo*), which, as the term suggests, is for Spinoza at once the condition of victory in the struggle with the passions and his rationalistic-naturalistic counterpart to the traditional religious conception of blessedness. A noteworthy structural feature of E5 is that each part culminates in an appeal to a love of God that is grounded in an adequate cognition of God, which means that such love functions both as a weapon against the passions and, in the form of an intellectual love of God, as that in and through which the human mind enjoys the blessedness of which it is capable. They differ in that the former is grounded in a cognition based on reason (*ratio*), or the second kind of cognition, since it arises from an inference concerning the common properties of things, whereas the latter is grounded in intuition (*scientia intuitiva*), or the third kind of cognition, which means that the latter form of love is more powerful.[1] Spinoza gives voice to the bifurcated nature of his concern in the preface to E5, noting that he "shall treat of the power of

---

[1] At one point in the scholium to E5p20 (G2 294; C1 606) Spinoza refers to the superior power of the third kind of cognition with respect to its power over the passions; but we shall see that his account of the mind's power over the passions in the first twenty propositions of E5 is concerned with the power of reason or the second kind of cognition.

reason, showing what it can do against the affects and what freedom of mind or blessedness is" (G2 277; C1 594).

7.1 The Way to Autocracy

Apart from the closing reference to blessedness, the preface to E5 is concerned solely with the first of these topics. Spinoza first identifies the power of the mind with reason (*ratio*) and reminds us that its power over the passions is limited, which was also the lesson of the first eighteen propositions of E4. Then, appealing to experience, he summarily dismisses the Stoic view that the mind has absolute power over the passions, which they erroneously attributed to the will, rather than to reason. The bulk of the preface, however, is devoted to a sardonic critique of Descartes' appeal to the pineal gland to which Spinoza had alluded in the preface to E3, and which he here treats as a misguided attempt to rehabilitate the Stoic view by making it the vehicle through which the mind can gain control of the passions. As Spinoza sees it, Descartes, the great critic of the scholastics, who insisted on accepting nothing that is not clearly and distinctly conceived, here assumed "a hypothesis more occult than any occult quality" (G2 279; C1 596). Against this view, Spinoza claims that he will show how the power of mind, defined only by the intellect, and without reference to a separate faculty of will, can provide the needed remedy from the affects.

Spinoza begins his analysis by laying down the basic principle in terms of which the discussion will proceed: "In just the same way as thoughts and ideas of things are ordered and connected in the Mind, so the affections or the body, or images of things are ordered and connected in the body" (E5p1). This follows directly from the identity of the order and connection of ideas and the order and connection of things as affirmed in E2p7. It has been aptly called the "metaphysics of the remedy" because it allows Spinoza to claim that the mind can have control over the modifications of the body, even though they do not interact.[2] As the proposition makes clear, the modifications in question are the images of the external things that affect the body and determine its appetites. According to the above principle, it follows that insofar as the ideas in the mind are ordered in the manner of the "order of the intellect," the images and appetites, which are their physical correlates, will be similarly ordered. The task, therefore, is to produce the requisite ordering of ideas in the mind; and in order to

---

[2] See Wolfson, *The Philosophy of Spinoza*, vol. 2, 265.

understand how this is best achieved, it suffices to focus on a number of points that have already been established.

To begin with, despite his above-mentioned critique of Descartes' account of how the mind can control the passions, Spinoza follows Descartes in affirming that the key lies in the mind's ability to break established patterns of association and replace them with new ones. Unlike Descartes, however, Spinoza views these associations as holding between ideas, and not between ideas and corporeal states, e.g., Descartes' "animal spirits." His analysis of the remedies for excessive love or hatred is a case in point. These affects, it will be recalled, were defined respectively as pleasure and pain accompanied by the idea of an external cause. The imagined external cause of pleasure or pain is the object of the affect, and the way to overcome the affect is to sever it from *this* idea of the external cause (E5p2). This can be accomplished by uniting it to the thought of another cause. For example, hatred toward a particular individual who has done one some harm can be overcome, or at least be diminished, by thinking of the harmful action as only a contributing factor in one's pain and as itself conditioned by a prior cause, and this, in turn, by a prior cause, etc. In short, rather than focusing one's attention entirely on the unique object of hatred, one comes to see it as merely a link in a causal chain. Since doing this is equivalent to forming a clear and distinct idea of the affect, Spinoza claims that "An affect which is a passion ceases to be a passion as soon as we form a clear and distinct idea of it" (E5p3).

Moreover, Spinoza continues, since "There is no affection of the Body of which we cannot form a clear and distinct concept" (E5p4) – that is, none we cannot understand in terms of general laws or "common notions" – and since an affect is an idea of a modification of the body, it follows that there is no affect of which we cannot form a clear and distinct idea (E5p4c). This means that our affects are capable of being understood scientifically (by the second kind of cognition), and this possibility provides a basis for Spinoza's recommendation that we strive to cultivate a detached, objective attitude toward our own affective life. Although Spinoza acknowledges that there are limits to our ability to do this, he also insists that, to the extent to which we can attain such an understanding, we can gain control not only of our loves and hatreds but also of our desires and appetites.

This ability is allegedly enhanced by certain features of our affective makeup, which give some advantage to the rationally grounded and, therefore, active affects in their struggle with the passions. First of all, Spinoza points out that, all else being equal, our strongest affects are toward things we regard as free (E5p5). For example, we love or hate an individual with greater intensity if we believe that the person is solely responsible for our condition and acted out of free choice. Conversely, the knowledge of the necessity of a state of affairs, which is chiefly what we derive from a "clear and distinct conception," inevitably serves to weaken the force of an affect. Our tendency to respond passionately to things is based largely on a sense that they might have been otherwise. We feel saddened by the loss of a good that we believe we might have possessed, but this feeling is mitigated, if not completely overcome, by the recognition that the loss was inevitable. Furthermore, since rationally grounded affects are, by their very nature, directed toward the common properties of things, it follows that if we take their duration into consideration, these affects will be stronger than passions directed toward an absent object (E5p7). The object of the former kind of affect (nature and its universal laws) is always present, and the affect can remain constant. Thus, while obviously less intense at a given moment than the hope, fear, disappointment, or regret generated by the thought of an absent object, these affects can prevail over passions in the long run. In other words, the greater endurance of rationally grounded affects more than compensates for their lack of intensity.

Spinoza further argues that, while it is obviously true that "The more an affect arises from a number of causes concurring together, the greater it is" (E5p8), such an affect turns out to be less harmful than an equally powerful affect that arises from fewer causes or a single cause (E5p9). Once again, Spinoza seems primarily to have had sexual desire in mind. His point is that affects of this nature lead to an obsessive concern with a few objects, or one particular object, thereby hindering the mind from engaging in its characteristic activity, thought. Fortunately, however, an affect fostered by a large number of different causes is stronger, and since this is precisely the kind of affect associated with the scientific attitude that is operative in the exercise of *ratio* (which is concerned with what is common to all things), the healthy affect has the power to overcome obsessive concern with particular objects. On this basis, Spinoza concludes confidently that "So long as we are not torn by affects contrary to our nature, we have the power of ordering and connecting the affections of the Body according to the order of the intellect" (E5p10). The problem, however, is that we cannot always be in the idyllic condition of detached observation. Since we are part of nature, we cannot completely avoid being assailed by dangerous affects. Nevertheless, Spinoza maintains that it is possible to minimize the danger, if, while in a detached state, we prepare for the inevitable assault by forming and committing to memory a set of rules or principles for correct living, which we can then apply as rules of thumb, when the occasion demands it (E5p10s). This is Spinoza's therapeutic alternative to the training of the will advocated by the Stoics and Descartes. Its goal is to condition the imagination (not the will) to respond in appropriate ways to the threat to the freedom and equanimity of the mind posed by the passions.

These rules turn out to be mainly conventional bits of popular wisdom, though Spinoza gives them his own characteristic twist. For example, we have already learned that hatred should be overcome by love, and in order that "we may always have this rule of reason ready when it is needed," Spinoza suggests that we reflect often on human wrongs and how they may best be prevented by generosity. By so doing, he claims, we shall come to associate the idea of wrongness with that of love or generosity, so that, when a wrong is done to us, we shall tend to respond with the proper affects. Similarly, if we constantly reflect on the necessity of things, we shall be better able to control the anger or hatred in our reactions to personal injury; and if we reflect on courage as a means of overcoming fear, we shall be better prepared to meet the ordinary dangers of life. Most importantly, we must condition ourselves so that we are always moved to action by an affect of pleasure, since this is the ultimate expression of the power of positive thinking. Spinoza's point is that the proper way to free ourselves from an obsessive attachment, be it to a sexual partner, wealth, power, or whatever, is *not* to harp constantly on the harmful features of the object. The negative approach succeeds only in breeding an attitude of envy or resentment, and, as Spinoza acutely notes, all the faults that we have convinced ourselves are to be found in the lover who has jilted us miraculously disappear as soon as we find ourselves back in his or her good favor. Hence, the only way to overcome, as opposed to repress temporarily, these affects is to think positively about things – to concentrate on people's virtues rather than their faults (see E5p10s G2 287–269; C1 601–603).

As noted above, the ultimate positive thought, and, therefore, the ultimate remedy against the passions for Spinoza is a rationally grounded love of God. His argument at this point, which depends on both his conception of God and his definition of love as "joy accompanied by an external cause" (da 6; G2 192; C1 533), is that, given the nature of its object, this love provides the most powerful vehicle by means of which the human mind is able to maximize control over its affective life. Basic to the latter point is Spinoza's contention that the more things a given affect can be associated with, the more frequently it can be evoked, and, therefore, the more constantly it can occupy the mind (E5p11–p13). Since there is no modification of the body or physical state of which the mind cannot form some clear and distinct idea, and since to conceive something clearly and distinctly is to conceive it in relation to God, it follows that the mind is able to refer all of its bodily modifications to the idea of God (E5p14s). Accordingly, this idea can be associated with all of these modifications. Since this satisfaction is accompanied by the idea of God as its cause, Spinoza calls it the "love of God" and claims that "He who understands himself and his affects clearly and distinctly loves God, and he does so the more, the more he understands himself and his affects" (E5p15). Finally, since this love is fostered by and associated with all states of the body, Spinoza concludes that it must necessarily hold the chief place in the mind (E5p16).

In an effort to clarify the nature of this rationally grounded love of God, Spinoza calls attention to its unrequited character. The main point is that inasmuch as God is without passions, he (it?) cannot be said to either love or hate (5p17 and corollary). Consequently, one who loves God in this manner cannot expect to be loved in return, since this would entail that the God whom one loves is not God (E5p19). Moreover, appealing to E4p28, where he had claimed that cognition of God is the mind's greatest good and to E4p36 where he had claimed that this good is common to and shareable by all human beings, Spinoza argues that this love of God is immune to jealousy or hatred and that the more people share in this love, the more it is enhanced (E5p20). A more problematic feature of this series of propositions is Spinoza's denial that one could hate God (E5p18). This is because it might be objected that, as the cause of all things, God is also the cause of pain. Consequently, given Spinoza's definition of hatred as pain accompanied by the idea of an external cause, God could very well become an object of hatred. To this anticipated objection, Spinoza responds on the basis of his theory of the affects that, to the extent to which we understand the cause of pain, it ceases to be a passion and, therefore, ceases to be pain. Furthermore, insofar as we understand God to be the cause of pain, we feel satisfaction. Spinoza is not here making the absurd claim that one can get rid of pain simply by acquiring a knowledge of its cause. Nor is he merely claiming with the Stoics that the knowledge of the necessity or unavoidability of pain makes us better able to endure it. Although the latter is certainly part of what Spinoza had in mind, it is not all of it. He is also arguing that the adequate knowledge of a pain is not itself a pain; rather, like any adequate idea, it is an expression of the mind's activity and, as such, a genuine source of satisfaction.[3]

Finally, in a scholium to E5p20 Spinoza summarizes his account of the power of the mind over its affects. Two points in this summary are worth noting. The first is that this power is directly proportional to the extent of the mind's cognition of these affects, with this understood in terms of its possession of adequate ideas. Although I have emphasized in the preceding discussion that this power is to be understood as the power of reason or the second kind of cognition, Spinoza notes in passing that the third kind of cognition, the object of which is God, has even more power over the passions than the second kind (G2 294; C1 606). The second is that Spinoza characterizes this power of the mind over the passions in quasi-mereological terms. As he puts it, "Insofar as the affects are passions, if clear and distinct cognition does not absolutely remove them ... at least it brings it about that they constitute the smallest part of the mind" (Ibid.). While it seems strange to think of the mind, as contrasted with the brain, as composed of parts, this may be seen as a consequence of Spinoza's parallelism thesis. As will become clear later, however, the main import of this conception of the mind is its bearing on the argument of the second part of E5.

7.2   The Way to Blessedness

The transition to the second portion of the argument of E5 is both sudden and dramatic. It occurs at the end of a lengthy scholium to E5p20, wherein, after reviewing the nature and extent of the power of cognition, Spinoza proclaims, "With this I have completed everything which concerns this present life ... so it is now time to pass to those things which pertain to the Mind's duration without relation to the body" (E5p20s). This sets the agenda for the final twenty-two propositions, which are generally regarded as among the most perplexing of the *Ethics*. This perplexity stems in part from the extreme crypticness, even by Spinozistic standards, of his account of the mind's duration apart from its relation to the body, which taken literally would seem to mean its postmortem existence. But its main source is the apparent incompatibility of any such view with the starkly naturalistic tenor of the preceding four and a half parts of the *Ethics*. In fact, any such view seems incompatible not only with Spinoza's mind–body identity thesis, which together with his conception of God lies at the center of his

---

[3] For a very different interpretation, see Delahunty, *Spinoza*, 248–250.

metaphysics, but also with his ethical theory, where we have seen that the virtuous life, i.e., the life according to the guidance of reason, has no place for the hope or fear that are traditionally connected with the belief in a postmortem existence. Thus, for the argument of the *Ethics* to culminate in the affirmation of such a conception seems to be incompatible with both the letter and the spirit of the philosophy articulated in the rest of the work.

The range of interpretations of these propositions in the recent literature falls into three camps. One is composed of interpreters who, despite the above-mentioned problems, maintain that Spinoza's claims about the eternality of the human mind, understood in a fairly literal sense, are compatible with the overall argument of the *Ethics*.[4] A second camp, of which Jonathan Bennett is the major representative, dismisses this portion of Spinoza's argument as "an unmitigated and seemingly unmotivated disaster."[5] The third camp, which includes a number of the recent commentators on the topic, endeavors to defend the core of Spinoza's argument, at least in terms of its consistency with the central arguments of the *Ethics*, which is to say its naturalistic and rationalistic thrust, against Bennettian-type objections, while recognizing that the account of the eternality of the mind that Spinoza affirms is far removed from the traditional conceptions, which affirm a personal immortality in the form of the survival of the soul after the demise of the body.[6] My view, which I refer to as an epistemic interpretation of Spinoza's account of the eternality of the human mind or, more precisely, the intellect, falls loosely into the third camp. Simply put, my claim is that this eternality is to be seen as an epistemological accomplishment that is attainable to various degrees in this life by those capable of achieving the second but especially the third kind of cognition, rather than a mode of existence to be attained in an imagined hereafter.[7]

---

[4] Prominent in this group are Donagan, "Spinoza's Proof of Immortality," Kneale, "Eternity and Sempiternity," and Matson, "Body Essence and Mind Eternity in Spinoza."

[5] Bennett, *A Study of Spinoza's Ethics*, 357.

[6] This includes Don Garrett, "Spinoza on the Essence of the Human Body and the Part of the Mind That Is Eternal," *Nature and Necessity in Spinoza's Philosophy*, 243–262; Della Rocca, *Spinoza*, 254–274; and Nadler, *Spinoza's Ethics: An Introduction*, 248–274.

[7] Although it would unduly complicate matters to discuss the matter in any detail, I also believe that external support for this reading is provided by similarities between Spinoza's account of the eternality of the mind and those of two decidedly heterodox medieval Jewish philosophers with whose writings Spinoza was known to be deeply familiar, namely Maimonides and Gersonides. For example, as Nadler, summarizing the view of Gersonides, writes: "The immortality available to any human being consists only in this persistence, after the death of the body, of the knowledge that he or she has acquired in this lifetime," *Spinoza's Heresy: Immortality and the Jewish Mind*, 88. For a detailed account of the similarities between Spinoza's account of the eternality of the mind and the views of Gersonides see Julia R. Klein, "Spinoza and Gersonides on Intellectual Eternity." A central thesis of

To begin with, I believe that this reading finds significant textual support in the overall structure of E5, which, as noted, is concerned with the power of the intellect. Since we have seen that the first twenty propositions of E5 deal with the power of the intellect over the passions, one might expect that the remaining twenty-two propositions would deal with this same power as it is exercised independently of its relation to the passions. Moreover, since the intellect's relation to the passions is inseparable from its relation to the body, one might further expect that these propositions would deal with the power of the intellect considered independently of its relation to the body, which, given Spinoza's metaphysics, could only mean its power over itself. But while this is in fact the case, it is also the case that Spinoza's account is greatly complicated by the abrupt introduction of the issue of the mind's duration apart from the existence of the body. Thus, the task is to explain this seemingly discordant element in what is supposedly a seamlessly naturalistic account.

This element is introduced in E5p23, which states that "The human Mind cannot be absolutely destroyed with the Body, but something of it remains which is eternal." Since this proposition is central to any interpretation of Spinoza's views on the eternality of the human mind, it and its associated scholium call for careful examination. And perhaps the first point to note is his use of the term "remains" (*remanet*) in its formulation. For while this seems to suggest that Spinoza is using the term to refer to the literal postmortem survival of the intellect of a human being in a disembodied state, it has been noted by several commentators that *remanet* can also be taken as equivalent to "remainder" in arithmetic or "residue" in geometry. This suggests that the passage can plausibly be read as maintaining that there is some "eternal" aspect of the mind that has not yet been considered, namely the intellect, as contrasted with a literal reading in which the term refers to something that remains after the demise of the body.[8] Moreover, if this is granted, we are well on the way to the proposed epistemological interpretation of Spinoza's account of the eternality of part of the human mind.

Nadler's book, with which I concur, is the denial that Spinoza held a doctrine of personal immortality in even an attenuated sense. He also there argues that despite the lack of any canonical view on the matter in Talmudic and Rabbinic Judaism, the beliefs in personal immortality, together with eternal rewards for the virtuous and punishment for the wicked, were central tenets of the Amsterdam Jewish community in Spinoza's time.

[8] See Harris, "Spinoza's Theory of Human Immortality," 250; Hardin, "Spinoza on Immortality and Time," 310, and Delahunty, *Spinoza*, 293.

I shall argue that this reading is borne out by an analysis of the demonstration of this proposition and the attached scholium; but before examining them it is necessary to consider the two preceding propositions (E5p21 and p22), which may be considered as essential stepping stones to Spinoza's central claims. E5p21 states that "The mind can never imagine anything, nor recollect past things, except while the body endures" (E5p21). Since the mind is now being considered apart from its relation to the body, it follows that neither imagination nor memory can be attributed to it. Spinoza supports this claim by appealing to E2p8c, which distinguishes between two senses in which a singular thing may be said to exist: as comprehended in the attributes of God (wherein it presumably exists eternally) and as having a durational existence. The point is that the human mind (a singular thing) can only have imagination and memory insofar as it exists in the latter sense, which means that any existence that might be attributed to the mind apart from the actual existence of the body would be without either memory or imagination. The denial of imagination to the human mind, so considered, is nonproblematic, since for Spinoza, as well as Descartes, it is closely connected with the body. Memory, is another matter, however, at least if one wishes to speak of a disembodied personal existence, since it is widely thought that it is at least a necessary condition of personal identity, if not actually constitutive of it.[9] Moreover, although he only broaches the subject in passing in a scholium to E4p39, where, referring to an anecdote concerning a Spanish poet, who lost his memory through an illness and later recovered it, Spinoza suggests that he endorses the view that memory is essential to personal identity. And this naturally raises questions about the nature of the life beyond the present one that Spinoza will presumably attribute to the human mind apart from its relation to its body.

Having denied it memory and imagination, the question becomes what could be positively attributed to the human mind when considered apart from its relation to an actually existing human body. What makes this particularly problematic for Spinoza, as contrasted with not only traditional defenders of the doctrine of the immortality of the soul but also, closer to home, Descartes, is his denial of the substantiality of the mind/soul and his characterization of it as the idea of the human body. In fact, given this conception of the mind, it seems that Spinoza's only option is to link the mind's eternality with the essence rather than the actual existence

---

[9] Like Locke, Spinoza evidently regarded memory as at least a necessary condition of personal identity. See E4p39s.

of the body. He makes the first step in this linkage in E5p22, which claims that "in God there is an idea that expresses the essence of this or that human body, under a species of eternity." This presupposes the distinction between the essence and the existence of a singular thing, as well as the thesis that the former can exist in God as a formal, as opposed to an actual, essence; that is, as the essential nature of a non-occurrent, i.e., past or future, singular thing, which is contained in an attribute of God.[10] Thus, by the formal essence of the human body is understood its intrinsic nature or (its "formula," as it were), considered as a pure possibility, which subsists in God qua extended, i.e., in the attribute of extension, and, therefore, as eternal and involving no relation to duration, while its actual essence is this formula (a particular portion of motion and rest) considered as existing in the common order of nature.

The second and decisive step in this linkage is the identification of the human mind or, more precisely, the intellect, with the idea in God that expresses the essence of the human body under an aspect of eternity. This is accomplished in the aforementioned E5p23, in the demonstration of which Spinoza claims that the concept or idea, which expresses the essence of the human body, pertains to the essence of the human mind. Spinoza justifies this by appealing to E2p13, which maintains that the object of the idea constituting the human mind is the human body, understood as a certain mode of extension that actually exists. Since the human body, as the object of the idea that constitutes the essence of the human mind, is in God under the attribute of extension, it follows that the human mind, considered as this idea, must likewise be in God under the attribute of thought. Although E2p13 speaks of the mind and body *simpliciter*, rather than of their essences, since we have seen that by the essence of a thing is understood that which being given the thing itself is necessarily posited and which being taken away the thing itself is also necessarily taken away (E2d2), it follows that if a thing is in God in a certain respect, then its essence must likewise be in God in the same respect. Moreover, since this idea, considered as part of the eternal and infinite intellect of God, is eternal and pertains to the essence of the human mind, it follows that whatever pertains to this essence is likewise eternal.

A complicating and confusing feature of the demonstration of this proposition is that, rather than simply denying duration *tout court* to the human mind considered apart from its relation to the human body,

---

[10] Spinoza introduces the conception of the formal as contrasted with the actual essence of a singular thing in E2p8. For my discussion of this matter see Chapter 4, p. X.

Spinoza ambiguously denies only that it could have "any duration that can be defined by time" (*quae tempore definire potest*), which might be taken as leaving open the possibility that the human mind has a duration that is not so defined. And since the most plausible candidate for such duration is existence at all times, which could also be characterized as sempiternal or omnitemporal existence, this has led some commentators to find in Spinoza's account a robust doctrine of personal immortality, in the form of a sempiternal postmortem existence for the human mind, or at least a part thereof.[11] However, in addition to its obvious conflict with Spinoza's naturalism, this view seems difficult to reconcile with at least two passages. The first is the definition of eternity as "existence itself, insofar as it is conceived to follow necessarily from the definition alone of an eternal thing," in the explanation of which Spinoza notes that "such existence ... cannot be explained by duration or time, even if the duration is conceived to be without beginning or end" (E1d8). The second is in the scholium to E5p23 (to be discussed later), where Spinoza claims that "eternity can neither be defined by time nor have any relation to time." Since both of these passages strongly suggest that Spinoza adhered to a Platonic conception of eternity, which is disassociated from any reference to time, including the essentially Aristotelian conception of sempiternity, it does not seem that the above-quoted phrase can bear the weight that some interpreters have placed upon it.

In the scholium appended to E5p23, Spinoza characterizes the "something" to which eternality is ascribed in the proposition as a "certain mode of thinking." Since the idea of the essence of the human body is such a mode, this is not surprising. What is surprising, however, is the immediately following claim that "though it is impossible that we should recollect that we existed before the body ... we feel and know by experience [*sentimus experimurque*] that we are eternal," which Spinoza justifies by claiming that "the mind feels those things that it conceives in understanding no less than those that it has in memory. For the eyes of the mind, by which it sees and observes things, are the demonstrations themselves" (G2 296; C1 608). While this terminology, particularly the reference to feeling and experience, seems out of place for a staunch rationalist such as Spinoza, his appeal to the familiar metaphor of the eyes of the mind (*Mentis oculi*) suggests he is simply referring to the third kind of cognition (*scientia intuitiva*), which shares the immediacy of memory with the certainty of what is conceived through the understanding through the second kind of

---

[11] Slightly different versions of this view have been advocated by Kneale and Donagan. See note 4.

cognition (*ratio*). Alternatively, one might take Spinoza to be maintaining that some vague grasp of the eternality of the mind is available to everyone in the form of a feeling. But the operative question is: exactly what does Spinoza claim to be cognized in this manner? And the problem is that, though a literal reading of the phrase "we are eternal" suggests a robust conception of personal immortality, the underlying argument in support of this conclusion implies that what has purportedly been shown to be eternal is merely the concept or idea, which expresses the essence of the human body, and perhaps also the formal essence of the latter, considered as its no longer actualized essential nature, as defined by its particular proportion of motion and rest.[12]

Setting aside for the moment the question of the status of the formal essence of a human body, our immediate concern is with the interpretation of the claim that the concept or idea of this essence is eternal. In addressing this question, it is necessary to revisit the analysis of Spinoza's conception of an idea provided in Chapter 4. We saw there that Spinoza defines an idea as "a concept of the mind which the mind forms as a thinking being" (E2d3). Following Bennett, I argued that Spinoza's account of ideas is ambiguous because he gives them both a psychological sense as believings or cognitions and a logical sense as the contents of belief or propositions that are cognized, and that this is reflected in his adherence to the scholastic distinction adopted by Descartes between the objective and the formal reality of an idea. The former corresponds to the logical sense of an idea (what is cognized) and the latter to its psychological sense (the cognizing). I there appealed to this distinction in an attempt to explicate Spinoza's identification of the order and connection of ideas with the order and connection of things in the pivotal E2p7; and I argued that the complexity of Spinoza's account stems from the fact that this identification supposedly applies to the order and connection of ideas in both senses. In the present case, Spinoza has characterized the idea in question as "a certain mode of thinking," which pertains to the essence of the human mind. And since this is likewise ambiguous in the same way, the question becomes: in which of these senses may this idea be said to be eternal?

The claim that this idea is in God, specifically in the eternal and infinite intellect of God, suggests that it should be taken in the logical sense, since this intellect supposedly contains a set of true propositions about the essential nature of an individual human mind, as well as a set about the

---

[12] Matson, "Body Essence and Mind Eternity in Spinoza," 89, usefully characterizes the formal essence of the human body as its "formula" or "genetic code."

essence of the corresponding body. And, so understood, this idea is clearly eternal. The problem, however, is that when taken in this sense, eternality may be attributed to the ideas corresponding to the essence of every body, i.e., finite mode of extension, in the Spinozistic universe, not to mention the ideas of those modes in the unnamed attributes, all of which are supposedly contained in the eternal and infinite intellect of God. Accordingly, taken in the logical sense, the claim that the idea in the human mind of the essence of the corresponding body is eternal might be said to be trivially true in the sense that it has no bearing on the underlying issue of human blessedness, since it fails to differentiate the human mind from the "mind," i.e., expression in the attribute of thought, from the idea of any finite mode. Conversely, if this idea is taken in the psychological sense as a mode of thinking (a cognizing), it clearly is not eternal, even if what is cognized through this idea (its objective reality) is an eternal truth or set of eternally true propositions about the essence of the body, since this cognizing is directly correlated with the activity of the corresponding body (see E5p39). Moreover, this suggests that when Spinoza affirms the eternality of part of the human mind, he is either making a claim that is trivially true or guilty of a non-sequitur stemming from the failure to distinguish between the logical and psychological senses of the complex idea that constitutes the human mind.

The proposed epistemic interpretation of Spinoza's account of the eternality of part of the human mind, specifically the intellect, resolves this dilemma and provides a middle course between these unpalatable alternatives. So understood, Spinoza's claim is not simply that there is an idea in God and, therefore, an eternal truth about the essence of each human body, which is what the logical thesis maintains, but also that the human intellect has the capacity to grasp this truth and what it entails by the second and especially the third kind of cognition. This does not, however, entail that the actual cognizing of this truth or set of truths by the human intellect somehow enjoys a postmortem duration, which is presumably what ascribing eternality to the human mind understood in the psychological sense would entail. Moreover, I submit that the epistemic interpretation is strongly suggested by the final propositions of E5, where Spinoza identifies the eternality of part of the human mind with blessedness.

The most direct textual support for this reading contained in these propositions is E5p31, which states that "The third kind of cognition depends on the Mind, as on a formal cause, insofar as the Mind itself is eternal." By referring to the human mind as the formal cause of the third kind of cognition, Spinoza is presumably alluding to its inherent capacity to attain cognitions of this kind in view of its stock of adequate ideas. And if this is the case, it seems reasonable to assume that, when Spinoza claims that the human mind has this capacity *insofar as it is eternal* (my emphasis), he means that its eternality, qua formal cause, consists in this capacity. The only other interpretations of the ubiquitous "insofar as" that I can envision in this context require taking Spinoza to be claiming either that the human mind has this capacity only insofar as it literally is eternal (or sempiternal) or that enjoying an eternal (or sempiternal) existence is a necessary condition of having this capacity. But the first alternative, which amounts to attributing to Spinoza a version of the Platonic theory of recollection, seems to be ruled out by his evident rejection of this view in E5p23s, where he denies that we can recollect that we existed before our bodily existence (G2 296; C1 608), while the second can be dismissed on the grounds that the inference from a previous existence to the possession of this capacity would be a gross non-sequitur.

Moreover, I believe that further and, indeed, decisive support for the epistemic reading of Spinoza's account of the eternality of the human intellect is provided by the complete set of the final propositions of E5. These propositions are chiefly concerned with two topics: the connection between the intellectual love of God and the eternality of the human mind and the thesis that one can increase the extent to which one's mind is eternal by increasing the adequacy of one's cognition. I shall consider each in turn.

(1) *The intellectual love of God and the eternality of the human mind*: As was noted in the first part of this chapter, the love of God appears in two forms in E5, in each of which it is "intellectual" in the broad sense that it is based on an adequate idea of God, rather than the traditional conception of a personal God, which, according to Spinoza, is a product of the imagination and, therefore, pertains to the first kind of cognition. In its first appearance, this love of God was portrayed as a means for gaining victory over the passions; and I suggested that it stems from the second kind of cognition. By contrast, in its second appearance, where this love is labeled "intellectual," it is explicitly connected with the third kind of cognition. Moreover, rather than being considered merely a means to an end, albeit a highly important one, the love of God is now understood as the experience or condition in which blessedness is attained.

The connection that Spinoza makes between the third kind of cognition, the intellectual love of God, and human blessedness is quite direct.

Once again, the main point is that the understanding of anything in this manner is intrinsically satisfying because it involves the activity of the intellect; and since this understanding consists in comprehending the thing in question in relation to God, this satisfaction is accompanied by the idea of God as its cause (E5p32). The equation of the satisfaction connected with such a cognitive state with the love of God depends on Spinoza's conception of love as pleasure accompanied by the idea of an external cause. Given this conception, anything that can serve as a cause of pleasure can be an object of love. The pleasure or, better, mental satisfaction associated with the third kind of cognition is the pure joy of understanding. Spinoza's God is the cause of this joy in the sense that it is both the ultimate object of this cognition and the source of the very intelligibility of things. In the last analysis, then, the intellectual love of God turns out to be equivalent to a delight in the intelligibility of things that accompanies the mind's satisfaction with its own cognitive powers. And, not coincidentally, this same satisfaction also constitutes human blessedness for Spinoza.

This conception of intellectual love also helps us to understand Spinoza's mystical-sounding and paradoxical claims that "God loves himself with an infinite intellectual love" (E5p35) and that "The Mind's intellectual Love of God is the very Love of God by which God loves himself not insofar as he is infinite, but insofar as he can be explained by the human Mind's essence, considered under a species of eternity; i.e., the Mind's intellectual Love of God is part of the infinite Love by which God loves himself" (E5p36).

Having been told previously that, "strictly speaking, God loves no one" (E5p17c), one is taken aback by these propositions. In reality, however, there is no contradiction or change of doctrine, but merely another example of Spinoza's propensity to express his rationalistic thought in traditional religious terms. Since the human mind has been shown to be a finite modification of God expressed in the attribute of thought and, with regard to its adequate ideas, part of the infinite intellect of God, the mind's love of God is equivalent to God's love of himself, so modified. Spinoza's claim, in other words, reduces to an elaborately expressed tautology; and there is no reason to believe that he intended it to be construed otherwise. By expressing himself in this convoluted and paradoxical manner, Spinoza is, in effect, saying to theologians that this is the only way one can understand their central contention that God loves humankind.

The present issue, however, is the bearing of Spinoza's conception of the intellectual love of God on his account of the eternality of the human mind, particularly with respect to the proposed epistemic understanding of this eternality. The key text is E5p33, which states that "The intellectual love of God, which arises from the third kind of cognition, is eternal." This is a challenging proposition on any reading, particularly since Spinoza claims in the corollary that this love has no beginning, which seems to suggest that it is timeless or at least sempiternal. Nevertheless, Spinoza gives a clear indication of his understanding of it by basing it on his demonstration of E5p31 and E1a3, the relevant portion of which essentially claims that effects follow necessarily from determinate causes. In this case, the determinate cause of this love is the idea of God; and the claim is that it follows necessarily from the cognition of God through the third kind of cognition. Inasmuch as the second kind of cognition is supposedly also based on an adequate idea of God, it would seem that the love of God discussed in the first part of E5, which is presumably based on this kind of cognition, would likewise be eternal in the same sense, though for reasons already noted it would have less effect on the mind. This is perhaps why Spinoza does not mention it at this point, though he does claim that the desire to know things by the third kind of cognition can arise from the second (E5p28); and we shall see that in E5p38 he argues that both kinds of cognition function to mitigate the fear of death. But the main point is that the idea of God operative in both the second and third kinds of cognition would be eternal with respect to its objective reality, because it is an idea of what is *ex hypothesi* eternal, though, like any idea, as a finite mode under the attribute of thought, it would not be eternal with regard to its formal reality. Moreover, since the intellectual love of God (in both forms) is the product of an adequate cognition, it too would be eternal in the same sense.

   Spinoza expands further on the eternal nature of the intellectual love of God in a corollary to E5p34. In the proposition itself, he claims that the human mind is subject to the passions only as long as the body endures. This is nonproblematic, since the passions are grounded in the imagination and the latter is tied to the existence of the body, while in the corollary he maintains that it follows from this that no love except an intellectual love is eternal. Although this assumes rather than shows that an intellectual love is eternal, it points to a decisive difference between it and other forms of love based on the imagination or the first kind of cognition. In a scholium to this corollary, Spinoza further remarks that "If we attend to the common opinion of men, we shall see that they are indeed conscious of the eternity of their mind, but that they confuse it with duration, and attribute it to the imagination, *or* memory, which they believe remains after death" (C2 301; 611–612). Spinoza appears to be here reiterating the claim in E5p23s that "we feel and know by experience that we are eternal," where the "we" refers to ordinary human beings and not merely the Spinozist philosopher. Presumably the reason why "the common opinion of men," i.e., the ordinary, untutored understanding, is prone to this confusion, despite the fact that it is supposedly conscious of the eternality of the human mind, is that this consciousness is itself confused, since it is grounded in the imagination and, therefore, the first kind of cognition. The claim that the ordinary understanding is both conscious of the eternality of the human mind and deeply confused about it seems paradoxical, but it reflects Spinoza's claims that "All ideas, insofar as they are related to God are true" (E2p32) and that "Falsity consists in the privation of cognition which inadequate, or mutilated and confused ideas involve" (E2p35).

(2) *The possibility of increasing the extent to which one's mind is eternal by increasing the adequacy of one's cognition*: This is the topic of E5p38, p39, and the corollary and scholium to p40. Since the identification of the eternality of the human mind with the possession of the second and particularly the third kind of cognition is the best – indeed, the only – plausible explanation of why the extent to which a mind is eternal should depend upon the extent to which it achieves such cognition, it provides what is perhaps the strongest textual support for the epistemic interpretation of Spinoza's claims about the partial eternality of the human mind.[13]

   According to E5p38, "The more the mind understands things by the second and third kinds of cognition, the less it is acted on by affects which are evil, and the less it fears death." In justifying this claim, Spinoza argues that it is because the more we understand things in this manner, the less we have to lose by death, because the greater is the part of the mind that is eternal; or, as he puts it, "the greater the part that remains." Presumably, "remains" is to be understood in the same manner as in E5p23, to which Spinoza refers in the demonstration – that is, as what is left when one subtracts the affects stemming from the imagination, which are the source

---

[13] Matson, "Body Essence and Mind Eternity in Spinoza," 92–93, heroically attempts to defend something approaching a literal reading of Spinoza's account by providing an explanation of "How the Eternal Part of the Mind Grows." His intent is to show how, pace critics such as Bennett and Curley, it is coherent to claim that the eternal part of the mind can grow, which he does by denying that the eternal part of the mind for Spinoza is identical with the idea of the essence of the human body. But though this is correct, it is beside the point, since the issue concerns how the *eternality* of the eternal part of the mind is to be understood. Moreover, "growth" in the sense of an increase of an individual's cognitive capacity is perfectly compatible with the proposed epistemological interpretation, as long as this is not taken to entail a similar increase in the portion of the mind that survives death, which is what Matson claims. For my discussion of Matson's essay see Allison, "The Eternity of Mind: Comments on Matson on Spinoza."

of the fear of death – rather than as claiming that an increase in the extent of one's cognitions of the second and third kinds produces an increase in the extent to which one's mind survives the death of the body (which would be nonsensical). Moreover, proceeding from a claim that covers both the second and third kinds of cognition to one about the latter in particular, Spinoza adds that in this case "the part of the mind that perishes with the body is of no moment compared with what remains." In other words, while part of the mind of a subject who has acquired the second kind of cognition "remains" after the death of the body, much more, though presumably not all of it, "remains" if the subject has succeeded in acquiring cognitions of the third kind.

Continuing this line of thought, Spinoza claims in E5p39 that "He who has a Body capable of a great many things has a Mind whose greatest part is eternal." What this adds to the preceding proposition is simply that the portion of the mind that is eternal is a function of the complexity of the body. In response, one might well ask: why, given Spinoza's conception of mind–body identity, does this not entail that the body is likewise eternal in the same respect?[14] This is beside the point, however, since the main issue posed by this proposition is whether the capacities of the body could have any bearing on the extent to which the mind is eternal. Moreover, it is difficult to see how it could have any bearing if the eternality of the mind is understood to involve an eternal or sempiternal existence apart from its relation to the body, whereas it is entirely in accord with Spinozistic principles if the eternality of the human mind is understood in the aforementioned epistemic sense. Although this may seem a meager kind of eternality, we have seen that it is not a trivial one. In fact, Spinoza underscores both the mind–body correlation and the epistemic thrust of this proposition in the appended scholium, where he remarks that "Because human bodies are capable of a great many things, there is no doubt that they can be of such a nature that they are related to minds which have a great knowledge of themselves and of God, and of which the greatest, or chief, part is eternal" (G2 305; CI 614). Presumably, the part of the mind that is eternal is the one that contains (or consists in) the knowledge of itself and God, i.e., the intellect.

---

[14] This issue is addressed by Don Garrett ("Spinoza on the Essence of the Human Body," 252–255), who argues that for Spinoza the formal essence of a human body is a nonlocalized part of this body and is eternal. But this does not address the issue of the variability of the extent of this eternal part. For example, does it make sense to claim that one body could have more of a formal essence than another?

Since E5p40 deals explicitly with perfection rather than eternality, it might not seem to be germane to our present concerns. It asserts a direct correlation between the degree of activity of a thing and its perfection. The demonstration is straightforward, appealing to the identification of reality with perfection (E2d6) and Ep3 and its scholium, which together maintain that the actions of the mind arise entirely from adequate ideas, while the passions, since they depend entirely on inadequate ones, involve negation rather than reality. Its relevance, however, is found in its corollary, and particularly in the scholium added to the latter. The corollary states that it follows from the proposition that "the part of the mind that remains, however great it is, is more perfect than the rest." The part that remains and is more perfect because it is active is the intellect, while the part that is passive and perishes is the imagination. The key terms are again "remains" and "perishes," and once again everything turns on whether they are to be taken literally or simply as Spinoza's way of talking about the activity of the mind considered apart from its relation to the body, which would preclude the imagination, while leaving intact the intellect. Moreover, Spinoza addresses this point in the scholium, where, apparently reflecting on the entirety of the argument from E5p21, rather than merely on the corollary to which it is appended, he writes:

> These are the things I have decided to show concerning the mind, insofar as it is considered without relation to the body's existence. From them – and at the same time from 1p21 and other things – it is clear that our mind, insofar as it understands, is an eternal mode of thinking, which is determined by another eternal mode of thinking, which is determined by another eternal mode of thinking, and this again by another, and so on, to infinity; so that together, they all constitute God's eternal and infinite intellect. (G2 306; C1 615)

Since E1p21 speaks to the eternal and infinite nature of whatever follows from the absolute nature of the attributes of God – that is, the infinite and eternal modes – it is not clear why Spinoza cites it in support of a claim about the eternality of the human mind, a finite mode, which, as such, does not follow absolutely from an attribute of God, though this may be explained by the reference to "other things," which, as the latter portion of the passage indicates, are other finite modes of thought. The main point, however, is Spinoza's dual use of the ubiquitous "insofar as" (*quatenus*), since this once again underscores the highly qualified nature of Spinoza's claims about the eternality of the human mind. To predicate eternality of a human mind *insofar as* it is considered apart from the existence of the body is not to claim that it can exist independently of its relation to its body, much less that it can so exist eternally or "throughout all time";

rather, it is to make the essentially methodological point that, *so considered*, the operations of the human mind are independent of any functions of the body, not that they can actually occur apart from their relation to the body.[15] And, similarly, in claiming that the human mind is an eternal mode of thinking, which defines the sense in which it can be said to be eternal, insofar as it understands, Spinoza is again equating the eternality of the human mind with its capacity to understand, which is to say that the human mind is eternal insofar as it can cognize things by means of the second and third kinds of cognition.

Spinoza strikes the same note in the scholium to the final proposition of the *Ethics* (E5p42s), where, after noting that he has said what he wished to say about the mind's power over its affects and its freedom, he reflects that, in contrast to the ignorant person, who is troubled by external causes and unable to attain true peace of mind, "the wise man, insofar as he is considered as such, is hardly troubled in spirit, but being, by a certain eternal necessity, conscious of himself, and of God, and of things, he never ceases to be, but always possesses true peace of mind." Here, as elsewhere in the *Ethics*, by "freedom" Spinoza understands the mind's power over its affects. Moreover, as is indicated by the "insofar as" locution, the "wise man," like the "free man" of E4, is an idealization, since for Spinoza an actual human being, even one living under the guidance of reason, is never *completely* free from being troubled by external causes. And, again, it is *only* insofar as or to the extent that the wise man is conscious of himself and God "by a certain eternal necessity," i.e., is capable of the third kind of cognition, that he "never ceases to be," because to that extent he is an active rather than a passive being, which is also the extent to which his mind can be said to be eternal. Accordingly, I submit that the proposed epistemic interpretation of Spinoza's account of the eternality of part of the human mind provides a consistent reading of the texts without either trivializing it, dismissing it as based on fallacious reasoning, or rendering it blatantly inconsistent with the radically naturalist thrust of Spinoza's thought in the *Ethics*.

---

[15] There is a striking and to my knowledge hitherto-unexplored parallel between Spinoza's claims about the activity of the human mind considered apart from its relation to the body and Kant's notorious claims about things "considered as they are in themselves," by which is understood things considered as they are independently of the conditions of human sensibility (space and time). In both cases, the "considered as" (*consideratur, betrachtet als*) locution functions to make clear the methodological, as contrasted with substantive, nature of the claim. I have discussed this issue with respect to Kant; for my fullest treatment of it see Allison, *Kant's Transcendental Idealism: An Interpretation and Defense*, esp. 50–64.

CHAPTER 8

The Individual and the State

We have learned from the *Ethics* that, despite their conatus or fundamental drive for self-preservation, human beings for Spinoza are essentially social animals, and, as such, they can achieve, peace, security, and freedom (as autocracy) only in association with others. We have also learned, however, that these same human beings are, at best, imperfectly rational. Indeed, according to Spinoza, the great majority of them are hardly rational at all, since they are governed by their passions rather than reason, which entails that they cannot live in society with one another unless they are subjected to a common set of laws and a sovereign power to enforce them. Human society, in other words, is possible only in a state. But the problem is that, inasmuch as this subjection presupposes a high degree of socialization, this seems to preclude the possibility of achieving the very freedom that requires socialization. Together with peace and security, the problem of freedom is thus central to Spinoza's political thought, just as it was to his metaphysical and moral theory. Whereas the task of the *Ethics* (at least one of its most important tasks) is to investigate the nature and limits of human freedom and to show how it was possible in the face of the thoroughgoing determinism of nature, the major concern of Spinoza's political philosophy is to explain how this same conception of freedom can be realized in a state, which, by its very nature, demands absolute obedience to law.[1]

Spinoza's basic conviction as a political theorist is that such freedom is both possible and desirable; indeed, that "the end of the Republic is really freedom" (TTP G3 241; C2 346). But he also believed that this freedom can only be secured if each individual surrenders all their power to the state. Again, the parallel to the doctrine of the *Ethics* is striking. There, the great lesson was that one can only achieve freedom by realizing that one is a completely determined part of nature; that one has no free will; and

---

[1] The identity of the conception of freedom with which Spinoza was concerned in the *Ethics* and in his political writings is noted by Steinberg, *Spinoza's Political Psychology*, 68.

that all one's actions follow universal and necessary laws. Here, freedom and subjection to law are intrinsically connected, rather than opposed. And, as a consequence, Spinoza maintained that the most absolute state, meaning the state with the most power over its citizens, is the best state, and, paradoxically enough, that this condition is realized in a democracy.

These thoughts are developed in the TTP and the TP. Aside from the fact that in the former work Spinoza regards civil society or the state as originating through a social contract (the supposed historical example being the covenant of the Hebrew people under Moses), while the latter contains no reference to any such contract, the two works, though differing greatly in both style and tone, contain much the same doctrine. The TTP is a polemical piece, addressed to the events of the time. In the context of a devastating attack on the authority of the Bible (to be discussed in Chapter 9) and hence on the authority of the clergy, who were its self-proclaimed interpreters, Spinoza there provides a classical defense of the principles of freedom of thought and speech. By contrast, the TP, which Spinoza never finished, is basically a textbook of political science. Eschewing any reference to a social contract and adopting the dispassion-ate, analytic method of the *Ethics*, in which human behavior is considered as subject to a set of universal and necessary laws, the TP attempts to deduce from these basic laws of human nature the true causes and func-tions of the state. And, on the basis of these considerations, Spinoza endeavors to show how any regime must be organized, whether it be a monarchy, an aristocracy, or a democracy, if it is to endure and preserve the peace and freedom of its citizens.[2]

The present chapter, which is concerned with Spinoza's political theory as it is contained in the TTP and the TP, is divided into four parts. The first sketches the context in which Spinoza developed and articulated his views on the state and civil authority. Here two factors are directly germane to understanding these views. One is the natural law tradition and the associated conception of natural rights, which were sometimes combined with the conception of a social contract as the vehicle through which this law was applied and these rights secured for a given society. The other is Hobbes, who anticipated Spinoza in his critique of the natural law trad-ition and in contrast to whom Spinoza defines his own views. The second part discusses the points on which Spinoza differs from Hobbes and on the

---

[2] Melamed nicely captures the spirit of Spinoza's project in the TP when he suggests that the aim of the work is to sketch "fundamental laws that will run the state, as it were a political *perprteuum mobile*, for all three kinds of civil order," "When Having Too Much Power Is Harmful," 163.

basis of which, despite sharing considerable common ground, he arrives at a radically different conclusion. The third part analyzes the core elements of Spinoza's political theory in the form of his account of the proper uses and limits of political power as contained in both the TTP and the TP. The fourth part examines Spinoza's account in the TP of how the three main recognized forms of governance – monarchy, aristocracy, and democracy – can best be structured to maximize the security and freedom of a society's denizens.

8.1   Natural Law and the Social Contract: Hobbes versus Grotius

Although the notion of natural law has its roots in Stoic philosophy and Roman law, and during the Middle Ages was invoked in support of feudalism, it also played a central role in classical liberal thought, where it was closely associated with the theory of natural rights and the conception of a social contract. In this context, natural law was generally construed as a set of universally valid moral rules grounded either in reason or in the will of God, depending on whether the theory in question is secular or religious. These rules function as criteria for judging the morality of the actions both of individuals and of states. This doctrine holds that the "positive" – that is, actual – laws of every state *ought* to conform to these rules; and that the sovereign, who was often thought to be "above the law" in the sense of the civil, or positive, laws, is nonetheless obliged to follow these rules, which, therefore, constitute a "higher law." Correlatively, by "natural rights" were generally understood a set of inalienable moral entitlements, usually featuring the security of one's life and liberty, in the sense of freedom to pursue one's interests, as long as they do not conflict with the legitimate interests of others, and property in the sense of ownership of the legitimate fruit of one's labors, which in theory is possessed by all human beings, though in practice it was generally limited to adult male property owners, with a certain degree of fiscal independence.

  The conception of a social contract can be traced to the Greek sophists, who conceived of rules of justice as products of human agreement, and in this sense as arbitrary, rather than as grounded in the very nature of things. Subsequently, however, it was understood to include two distinct conceptions, which, while closely connected, were not always held together.[3] The first, which was called the "social contract proper," or "pact of association,"

---

[3] This account of the history of the conception of the social contract is taken from Gough, *The Social Contract*, 8–21.

asserts that the state or civil authority originates when a group of individuals living in a "state of nature," understood as a condition in which individuals are not bound by positive, i.e., civil, laws, agree to join together to form an organized society subject to a set of common laws binding on each of its members. It is, therefore, a theory of the origin of the state or civil authority. The second conception is that of a contract of submission. It presupposes an already formed governmental power and takes the form of an agreement between the sovereign power and the civic body or citizens concerning the extent of this power and the rights and duties of the citizenry.[4]

Since both Hobbes and Spinoza held absolutist conceptions of sovereign power and viewed the will of the multitude as the source of this power, their focus was on the conception of a social contract in the first of the above senses; that is, as a pact of association, which has the subjection to the sovereign power constituted by that association built into it. And for both, the most important representative of this way of thinking was the Dutch jurist Hugo Grotius. Although his monumental and influential work, *De Jure Belli ac Pacis* (*The Law of War and Peace*), is concerned primarily with international law, particularly, as the title indicates, laws governing the conduct of wars and an ensuing settlement of peace, both the lengthy prolegomena to this work and its opening chapter are devoted to providing a rational foundation for law as such, including the civil laws of a given society and of the rights of its individual members, against attacks on these conceptions stemming from a philosophical skepticism and antinomial theological views.[5] Since Grotius defended both an absolutist conception of sovereign power and individual rights as warranted moral claims, his position has been aptly characterized as "Janus faced."[6] Moreover, the complexity of his position is reflected in the fact that his view of individual rights is based on an essentially Aristotelian conception of human sociality, which was firmly rejected by Hobbes, though, as we have seen, affirmed by Spinoza in his *Ethics*, albeit on a decidedly non-Aristotelian basis.[7]

Although Grotius did not use contractual language in his accounts of the rational grounding of the laws governing a particular state and the rights

---

[4] With some terminological changes, I am following the distinction between the two senses of a social contract drawn by Gough, *The Social Contract*, 2–3.

[5] These two targets of Grotius' work are noted by Haakonssen, "Divine/Natural Law Theories in Ethics," 1327.

[6] Tuck, *Natural Rights Theories*, 79.

[7] Tuck, *Natural Rights Theories*, 63 characterizes Grotius' view that human society has its origin in nature in view of the essentially social nature of human beings, while civil society is derived from deliberate design as "schizophrenia."

and duties of its denizens, he may be said to have implicitly appealed to this conception.[8] Thus, in challenging the skeptical (Carneadean) view that social relations are merely a matter of expediency with no rational basis, and, therefore, that there are no objective, universally binding principles of justice, such as have supposedly been sanctioned by natural law, which had been advanced by modern-day skeptics such as Charon and Montaigne, he states that

> The very nature of man, which even if we had no lack of anything would lead us into the mutual relations of society, is the mother of the law of nature. But the mother of municipal law is that obligation which arises from mutual consent; and since this obligation derives its force from the law of nature, nature may be considered, so to say, the great-grandmother of municipal law.[9]

As a Christian, Grotius affirmed that natural law accords with divine law, but he also insisted upon their distinction, claiming that natural law and its consequent rights and duties would retain their validity, "even if we should concede that which cannot be conceded without the utmost wickedness, that there is no God, or that the affairs of men are of no concern to Him."[10] For Grotius, this is because by the law of nature is understood "a dictate of right reason, which points out that an act, according, as it is or is not in conformity with rational nature, has in it a quality of moral baseness or moral necessity; and that, in consequence, such an act is either forbidden or enjoined by the author of nature, God."[11] Moreover, for Grotius this law of nature or set of rational prescriptions is both demonstrable a priori from its agreement with the rational and social nature of humankind and a posteriori from its acceptance by all nations, or at least "among all those that are more advanced in civilization."[12]

Despite sharing an absolutist conception of sovereign power, Hobbes repudiated both Grotius' essentially Aristotelian conception of human sociality and his view of natural law as the source of universally binding rights and duties. This dual repudiation is clearly expressed in Hobbes' conception of the state of nature, understood not as an actual historical condition but as a hypothetical account of the human condition considered apart from the constraints imposed by civil law. Rather than conceiving of human beings as essentially social animals and, as such, capable of forming and maintaining cooperative social relations in their natural state (roughly the Grotian view), Hobbes famously described the

---

[8] This is asserted by Gough, *The Social Contract*, 80.   [9] Grotius, *The Law of War and Peace*, 15.
[10] Ibid., 13.   [11] Ibid., 38–39.   [12] Ibid., 42.

state of nature as a state of war of "every man, against every man," and life in such a state as "solitary, poore, nasty, brutish, and short."[13] This conception of a state of nature reflects Hobbes' egoistic psychology. The Hobbesian person is both thoroughly determined and thoroughly egotistical. As with Spinoza, who was clearly influenced by Hobbes on this point, the fundamental drive is for self-preservation, though, in contrast to Spinoza, Hobbes also grants a basic role to vanity or "vainglory" in the motivation of human behavior.[14] In the state of nature, Hobbes argues, an individual has a "natural right" to do whatever seems necessary for self-preservation. But since everyone else possesses this right, which is limited only by one's power, and since everyone else is motivated by the desire to appropriate everything necessary to preserve their being and impress others, it follows that this state is one of perpetual conflict, in which no one really possesses any rights in the sense of guaranteed protection.[15]

Assuming that such a condition would be intolerable, Hobbes concluded that it must be avoided at all costs. And he further maintained that reason provides certain rules, which, if followed, would make it possible to avoid it. With typical audacity, he equated these rules for survival with natural law, or the "laws of nature," and even with "divine law," thereby distancing himself from the normative conception of natural law advocated by Grotius and other more traditional "natural lawyers." Although Hobbes cites fifteen such rules, we need here only consider the first two, which form the basis of his theory of the social contract and consequently of his doctrines of sovereignty and political obligation. The first and most fundamental of these laws of nature is the maxim that "peace is to be sought after, where it may be found; and where not, there to provide ourselves for helps of war."[16] The basic question, then, is how peace is to be achieved, which is equivalent to asking how human beings can escape from the state of nature. The answer is provided by the social contract. The necessity for such a contract emerges when one realizes that the basic source of conflict in the state of nature is the unlimited right therein of all people to all things they deem necessary for their self-preservation. Given this state of affairs, Hobbes maintains that reason dictates that peace can be achieved only if everyone voluntarily relinquishes or transfers their rights to a sovereign power. Such a mutual transference of rights is a contract, and when it includes a promise of future performance, it is called a covenant. The formation of such a contracts or covenant is,

---

[13] Hobbes, *Leviathan*, pt. I, chap. 13, 97.   [14] Hobbes, *De Cive or The Citizen*, pt. I, chap. I, 24.
[15] Ibid., 28.   [16] *De Cive*, pt. I, chap. 2, 32.

therefore, seen by Hobbes as the means by which human beings can escape from the intolerable state of nature.

A central feature of Hobbes' contractarian thought is that covenants create obligations where none existed before; and since in the state of nature, as he conceived it, there could be no assurance that others would honor any such agreement, he maintained that in order for covenants to be valid, it is first necessary to have a sovereign power capable of enforcing them. But, according to Hobbes, this can be achieved only if the multitude covenant among themselves to surrender all their rights to such a sovereign power. By this act, which is what Hobbes understood by a social contract, the multitude of wills becomes one will. Moreover, this contract for Hobbes leads not to a limited but to an absolute sovereign, whose very will is law. The absolute nature of sovereign power follows from the absolute nature of the multitude's surrender of their rights. In contracting among themselves, the multitude voluntarily give all their rights or powers to the sovereign, thereby creating for themselves an obligation of total obedience. Underlying this severe theory, which seems to justify the most unyielding despotism, is the conviction that sovereignty must be either absolute or nonexistent, and that if it is nonexistent, chaos and civil war will necessarily result. Having experienced civil war in England, Hobbes evidently thought that it is the greatest conceivable social evil, and hence that any form of government, no matter how oppressive, is preferable to it.

8.2 Spinoza's Critique of Hobbes

At first glance, Spinoza's political philosophy seems to be an only slightly modified version of Hobbes'. As in the *Ethics*, human beings are viewed as parts of nature, completely subject to its laws; and, like everything else in nature, their basic endeavor is to preserve their own being. Since they do this according to the laws of their nature, rather than through free will, and the laws of their nature are, as the *Ethics* has shown, the laws of God, they may be said do this by "sovereign natural right." Thus Spinoza, like Hobbes, reinterprets the notion of natural right and construes it to encompass whatever an individual does in accordance with the laws of human nature. And since everything that an individual does is a necessary consequence of these laws, it follows that whatever an individual is capable of doing is right! Whether the individual in question acts according to the dictates of reason or is driven by passions, whether he/she is motivated by sympathy for other people or by sheer malice, are beside the point. Either way, that individual is acting according to the laws of nature and has no power to do otherwise. Moreover, given this deterministic, amoral starting point, Spinoza does not hesitate to conclude that "the Right and established practice of nature, under which all men are born and for the most part live, prohibits nothing except what no one desires and no one can do: it does not prohibit disputes, or hatreds, or anger, or deceptions, and it is absolutely not averse to anything appetites urge" (TP G3 279; C2 511).

This interpretation of "natural right," which is diametrically opposed to the view of Grotius, is even more radical than that of Hobbes, who limited the right of an individual to whatever is deemed necessary for self-preservation. This would seem to rule out at least some kinds of actions, such as those grounded in mere vanity, which the individual knows will not enhance their self-preservation. One might, therefore, contend that, despite his naturalism, there remains a trace of the old, normative meaning of natural right in Hobbes.[17] In other words, Spinoza is the more consistent or, perhaps better, more radical naturalist, and this will prove to be crucial for understanding his critique of Hobbes and the development of his positive alternative to the Hobbesian Leviathan state. For Spinoza, an individual's natural right is limited only by the power that said individual possesses and, indeed, is coextensive with this power.[18]

Spinoza's conception of the state of nature follows logically from this basic premise concerning natural right. Human beings in this condition strive, as they do everywhere, to preserve their own being. Here, however, there is no authority except that which is grounded in fear, and no basis for mutual trust. Human beings are, therefore, naturally enemies, and in such a situation literally "anything goes." Spinoza expresses this latter point by contending, against Hobbes, that people have a natural right to break promises, which again counters the Grotian view. Since there is no external authority to enforce obedience, it is both natural and rational for an individual to honor an agreement only insofar as it is profitable to do so. And since the individual is the only judge of this, Spinoza reasons:

> [I]f this person, who, by the Right of nature, is his own judge, has judged – whether rightly or wrongly (for since he is human, he may have erred) – that the assurance he gave will lead to more harm than good, he will think in his own mind that he ought to cancel his assurance. And by the Right of nature [by §9] he will cancel it. (TP G3 280; C2 512–513)

---

[17] Although he does not put it in quite this way, this view is suggested by McShea, *The Political Philosophy of Spinoza*, 138.

[18] That Spinoza's view is that right is coextensive with power rather than equivalent to it is emphasized by Curley, "Kissinger, Spinoza, and Genghis Khan," 315–342.

Although he does not go quite as far as Hobbes and equate the state of nature with a state of war, Spinoza affirms that in this situation human beings are always subject to the threat of war and, therefore, have no security. Ultimately, this is because, as was already noted by Hobbes, isolated individuals are really powerless, inasmuch as they are unable to preserve their being, either in the sense of fully protecting themselves from attack or adequately fulfilling their basic needs. Moreover, since right is coextensive with power, Spinoza can also say with Hobbes that, despite their supposedly unlimited natural rights, individuals in this situation really have no rights at all. Accordingly, for both thinkers the unsustainability of this condition renders necessary a transition to civil society, which they regarded as the only condition in which human beings can effectively exercise their rights or power. In his analysis of the benefits to be derived from membership in civil society, however, Spinoza goes considerably beyond Hobbes, by supplementing the latter's emphasis on security and escape from a state of war with a consideration of the more positive benefits of such membership. These range from an increase in material comfort, gained through the division of labor, to the possibility of philosophy itself, which reflects Spinoza's radically non-Hobbesian view that nothing is more useful to human beings than other human beings. But Spinoza's view of the actual mechanism of the transition from a state of nature to civil society is somewhat uncertain, since he offers divergent accounts in the TTP and the TP.

In the TTP Spinoza sides with Hobbes in appealing to the social contract as the means whereby human beings move from a state of nature to civil society. However, unlike Hobbes, Spinoza seems to have regarded it as an actual historical occurrence. For example, in repudiating the notion that, despite the lack of civil law, human beings in a state of nature still stood under an obligation to God – that is, to natural law – he asserts that the state of nature is prior both in time and in nature to religion (G3 198; C2 292). And, after reflecting on the misery inherent in this condition in which everyone must constantly be on guard against everyone else, he suggests that "They had to agree to rein in their appetites, insofar as those appetites urge something harmful to someone else, to do nothing to anyone which they would not have done to themselves, and finally, to defend another person's right as if it were their own" (G3 191; C2 285). But, continuing this line of thought, Spinoza further suggests that these same individuals came to realize that human beings can be expected to honor an agreement only as long as they deem it advantageous to do so and, therefore, that a lasting union of human beings cannot be built on a foundation as fragile as good faith. Consequently, he claims that they must have further agreed that everyone should transfer all their rights to society as a whole. Since society as a whole, rather than any individual or group therein, is given power by this agreement, the resulting state for Spinoza (though not for Hobbes) is called a democracy. Nevertheless, society, thus empowered, will possess the natural right or sovereign power to work its will on its individual members, "and each person will be bound to obey it, either freely, or from fear of the supreme punishment" (G3 193; C2 287).

By contrast, in the TP not only is all reference to such an agreement dropped, but it is affirmed that "because all men everywhere, whether Barbarians or civilized, combine their practices and form some sort of civil order, we must seek the causes and natural foundations of the state, not from the teachings of reason, but from the common nature, *or* condition, of men" (TP C2 506; G3 276). Accordingly, for Spinoza it is here not reason, but some common passion such as hope or fear, that leads men to join together, so that the origin of society is seen as the inevitable outcome of human passions, rather than as the product of deliberate design by rational human beings. Nevertheless, within this changed perspective, the requirement of complete submission and obedience to sovereign power is maintained, although it is now viewed as a necessary condition for the existence of an enduring state, rather than as a historical event through which a state is created.

This change has been viewed both as the result of a genuine development in Spinoza's thought and, contextually, as a reflection of factors such as the different circumstances under which the works were composed and their intended audiences.[19] Since the orientation of the TTP is to a large extent historical and in its political portions focuses on the Hebrew commonwealth, considered as a theocracy, which was alleged to have originated at a particular moment in time with an explicit covenant, it would be natural for Spinoza there to treat the origin of the state *as if* it were a historical event. The important point, however, is that the thesis that the state began with an explicit covenant between rational individuals is not only not required by but is actually incompatible with the basic

---

[19] Those affirming the former view include Matheron, *Individu et Communauté chez Spinoza*, 287ff.; and Vaughan, *Studies in the History of Political Philosophy Before and After Rousseau*, vol. 1, 71. Advocates of the latter view include McShea, *The Political Philosophy of Spinoza*, 85–90, and more recently Steinberg, *Spinoza's Political Psychology*, esp. 10–11. I believe that the latter view is strongly suggested by Spinoza's own remarks in the TP to the effect that he is merely explicating and giving a formal proof of doctrines already expressed in the TTP (G3 276; C2 507).

outlines of Spinoza's philosophy. We have already seen that it is a cardinal tenet of the *Ethics* that the life of reason is possible only in a society. Thus, one would hardly expect him to assume that the existence of rational, autonomous, "free" individuals was a precondition of society itself. Moreover, as Spinoza makes quite explicit, if human beings were in fact led by the dictates of reason, the sanctions imposed by a state would be unnecessary, and a society of rational human beings would never submit to them. Finally, and perhaps most importantly, we have seen that Spinoza rejects any notion of an obligation independent of utility, which seems to be required by the contract theory in its historical, or factual, form.[20]

Nevertheless, apart from the issue of a historical contract, the central tenet of Spinoza's political philosophy, which is common to both political treatises, is that the very possibility of a civil society requires the total surrender by all individuals of their right and power to society as a whole. Although in the resulting civil state, as in the state of nature, individuals are still governed by hope and fear and by the desire to preserve their being, the difference is that in the civil state "everyone fears the same things: for everyone, there is one and the same cause of security and principle of living" (TP G3 285; C2 518). Moreover, for this to be possible, Spinoza claims it is necessary that the surrender include the right to decide what is just or unjust. For, he reasons, if the multitude is to be guided "as if by one mind, and hence, the will of the Commonwealth considered the will of all, what the Commonwealth has decided is just and good must be thought of as having been decreed by each [citizen]" (TP G3 286; C2 519). Only by such means can anarchy be avoided. For if individuals retain the right of private judgment, there is no common standard of justice to which one can appeal, and, therefore, no unifying social bond. Thus, Spinoza concludes that "though the subject may think the decrees of the Commonwealth unfair, he's nevertheless bound to carry them out" (Ibid.).

A more uncompromising argument for absolutism could hardly be imagined. Individuals have no rights except those granted them by the state. Those who attempt to reserve additional rights for themselves, or who challenge the authority of the state, are to be regarded as enemies of the state and treated as such. Yet, we are struck by the paradox that the same philosopher who argues in this manner also claims that the goal of the state is liberty, champions the freedom of thought and speech, and maintains in at least one of his works that democracy is the best form of governance. The reconciliation of these claims is the basic task of any interpretation of Spinoza's political philosophy, and it is to this task that we now turn.

---

[20] This is noted by Wernham in his introduction to his edition of *Spinoza's Political Works*, 26.

8.3   The Proper Uses and Limits of Political Power

Having suggested that Spinoza arrived at these results through the adop-
tion of a more consistently naturalistic and "amoral" position than
Hobbes, it seems clear that the best place to begin our analysis is with
a consideration of Spinoza's own account of the relationship between his
thought and that of Hobbes. Fortunately, such an account is available, for
in a letter to his friend Jarig Jelles, who evidently requested information on
just this point, Spinoza wrote:

> As far as Politics is concerned, the difference you ask about, between Hobbes
> and me, is this: I always preserve natural Right unimpaired, and I maintain
> that in each State the Supreme Magistrate has no more right over its subjects
> than it has greater power over them. This is always the case in the state of
> Nature. (L 50; G4 239; C2 406)

By the claim that, unlike Hobbes, he preserves natural right unimpaired,
Spinoza evidently meant that he consistently maintains the coextensiveness
of right with power and that Hobbes failed to do so. Moreover, the point is
well taken, since it underscores a basic inconsistency in the argument
through which Hobbes establishes his absolutist conclusions. This inconsistency concerns the weight given to contracts, which, in turn, reflects an
inconsistency in Hobbes' conception of natural law. As we have already
seen, Hobbes equates natural law with a set of precepts or practical maxims
that rational beings ought to follow if they desire to escape from a state of
nature. Accordingly, they are essentially rules for self-preservation, maxims
of prudence, or, in more Kantian terms, hypothetical imperatives.
Obviously, this is quite different from the traditional conception of such
laws as a body of "higher laws," or moral principles, above and beyond the
civil laws of any state, to which both the citizens and the sovereign are
morally obligated, such as was maintained by Grotius. With his conception
of the state of nature and his correlative notion of sovereign power as the
source of all law and justice, Hobbes, like Spinoza, repudiates *this* conception of natural law. Nevertheless, when discussing the social contract,
Hobbes contends that it creates an unconditional obligation to obey,
which he justifies in terms of the "law of nature" that covenants ought to
be kept.[21] Such an obligation, it turns out, is independent not only of the
wisdom and justice of the sovereign's commands, but also of his power.
Thus, for Hobbes the very same law of nature that teaches us what to do for
our self-preservation places us under an absolute obligation to obey the

---

[21] Hobbes, *De Cive*, pt. 1, chap. 3, 43–44.

sovereign power, even when doing so is obviously not in our best interests. And this is precisely what Spinoza denies.

Hobbes' partial normativization of natural law was no doubt motivated by his deep conviction that civil war is an unmitigated evil, to be avoided at all costs. But given his conception of human beings as driven by a desire for self-preservation, he could not maintain this obligation to obey the sovereign in an unqualified form. Since, in his view, individuals enter into the social contract only in order to preserve their being, they could not be expected to abide by it when doing so would threaten their very lives. Hobbes is, therefore, forced to admit that individuals have a "right" to resist the sovereign power when their lives are in immediate danger.[22] Furthermore, he cannot stop with this single exception, but must acknowledge many other "rights," which individuals reserve for themselves and which the sovereign power cannot justifiably threaten. Thus, we are told that the subject reserves the right to resist for "bodily protection, free enjoyment of air, water and all necessaries for life";[23] that a subject cannot be commanded to kill a parent; and that "there are many other cases in which obedience may be refused."[24] These and other passages, which add further qualifications, reflect the tension between the naturalistic and the normative elements in Hobbes' theory of natural right and provide vivid illustrations of the contradictions that emerge when he attempts to unite both elements in support of his theory of absolute sovereignty.[25]

Spinoza avoids these pitfalls by the simple expedient of eliminating all reference to a moral element that creates an obligation above and beyond the actual arrangement of power, thereby breaking not only with the traditional Grotian view, but with Hobbes' somewhat mitigated naturalism as well. Once again, the key to his position lies in the recognition that the right of the sovereign, like that of everything else in nature, is coextensive with its power, and that since this power is not infinite, neither is its right. The sovereign, in other words, does not have the right to do what it does not have the power to do. And since sovereign power is largely exercised in the promulgation of laws and regulations, Spinoza's point is that there are some laws that a sovereign literally does not have the power to enforce. This conclusion is derived from the realization that everyone is motivated by the desire for self-preservation and, consequently, will always choose that course of action that is believed to be most advantageous. People who live according to the dictates of reason will recognize the

[22] Ibid., pt. 1, chap. 3, 39–40.   [23] Ibid., pt. 1, chap. 6, 51.   [24] Ibid., pt. 2, chap. 6, 79.
[25] For a discussion of this topic, see McShea, *The Political Philosophy of Spinoza*, 142.

desirability of obeying the law, but since such individuals are few and far between, the force of the law rests largely on its sanctions; that is, on fear of punishment or hope of reward. Although by properly applying these sanctions, a sovereign can gain considerable control over a populace, Spinoza contends that certain acts run so counter to human nature that no threat or promise of reward could lead an individual to perform them. As examples, he cites forcing people to testify against themselves, torture themselves, kill their parents, or make no attempt to avoid death (TP G3 282; C2 521). Since laws or commands requiring these or similar deeds are ineffective, one can claim, "keeping natural right unimpaired," that the sovereign has no right to promulgate them.

Spinoza, however, does not stop with such extreme cases, which by themselves do not go very far toward mitigating the evils of tyranny. He also shows a keen awareness of the inherent limitations of legislative power with regard to beliefs and private morality. Such things should not, because they cannot, be legislated. As he notes in the TTP, "Anyone who wants to limit everything by laws will provoke more vices than he'll correct" (G3 243; C2 348). And he reflects that if this holds true for obvious evils, such as extravagance, envy, greed, and drunkenness, which a government might legitimately wish to eliminate, "How much the more must we grant freedom of judgment, which not only cannot be suppressed, but is undoubtedly a virtue" (Ibid.; C2 348–349). Thus, rather than appealing to abstract principles in the manner of traditional natural right theorists, Spinoza's argument for freedom of thought and expression is thoroughly instrumental. It basically consists of two claims: that allowing such freedoms is beneficial to society and that a government is powerless to prevent it.

In addition, Spinoza notes that, while there are some things a government could accomplish by brute force, doing them would inevitably undermine its own authority. And given the thesis of the coextensiveness of right with power, he claims that they do not actually have the right to do them (TTP G3 240; C2 345). Underlying this view is the contention that for a law to be effective – that is, to command obedience – it must not do too much violence to the public's sense of what is to its own advantage. Although a government could for a time, by the use of force and propaganda, institute policies that run completely counter to prevailing public opinion, the attempt to do so would succeed only in arousing widespread opposition, which would lead in the end to the government's downfall. Public opinion, or what the majority regards as in its own best interests, thus functions for Spinoza as a real check on governmental power, which leads him to conclude that in order to function effectively, and even to stay in power, a government must consider the will of the people.

Spinoza's political philosophy, however, is not primarily concerned with specifying either what a government cannot do at all or what it could not do with impunity, but rather with determining what it *ought* to do, if it is to realize the end for which it was established. Although, like Hobbes, Spinoza defines this end as peace and security and acknowledges that this cannot be achieved without a force strong enough to guarantee compliance with the law, he understands these in a much richer and more positive way.[26] "A commonwealth," he writes, "whose subjects are restrained from revolting by fear must be said to be free from war rather than to enjoy peace." And, again, "When the peace of a Commonwealth depends on its subjects' lack of spirit – so that they're led like sheep, and know only how to be slaves – it would be more properly called a wasteland than a Commonwealth" (TP G3 296; C2 530). The point, then, is that for Spinoza, in contrast to Hobbes, peace is not construed primarily as the mere absence of war, for the sake of which almost any degree of tyranny and oppression would be tolerable; rather, it is regarded as a positive condition in which it first becomes possible for human beings to exercise their power, which is to say their virtue. Accordingly, the function of the state is to create this condition, and Spinoza gives clear expression to this view when he states that "When we say . . . that the best state is one where men pass their lives harmoniously, I mean that they pass a *human* life, one defined not merely by the circulation of the blood, and other things common to all animals, but mostly by reason, the true virtue and life of the Mind" (TP G3 296; C25 30).

By virtually identifying a fully human existence with the life of reason, Spinoza reaffirms the basic practical conclusion of the *Ethics*. But if human beings are to exercise their reason properly, and thereby achieve the freedom described in the *Ethics*, it is obviously necessary for them to develop independent judgment. Thus, a regime that proscribes opinions is not one in which people could readily realize their true nature and live fully human lives. This is the point of the previously cited claim in the TTP that "the purpose of the state is really freedom." Here freedom is understood primarily as freedom of thought and speech, which presupposes autocracy; and it is argued that, while governmental power can and ought to be used to limit the actions of subjects, it should not be used to limit their thoughts (which is impossible) or their freedom to express these

---

[26] This point has been emphasized by Steinberg, *Spinoza's Political Psychology*, esp. 72–76.

thoughts. Moreover, not only is suppression of these basic freedoms harmful to the individual who is attempting to live according to the dictates of reason, it is also harmful to the state itself. In recognition of the history of both the Dutch Republic and the Marranos in Spain and Portugal, Spinoza contends that attempts to suppress these freedoms succeed only in producing hypocrites and martyrs. Accordingly, one of the main lessons of Spinozistic political science is that "[I]f good faith, not flattering lip service, is to be valued, if the supreme powers are to retain their sovereignty as fully as possible, and not be compelled to yield to the rebellious, freedom of judgment must be granted. Men must be so governed that they can openly hold different and contrary opinions, and still live in harmony" (TTP G3 245; C2 351).

The emphasis on freedom of thought and expression leads Spinoza in the TTP to his conception of democracy, which he there defines as "a general assembly which has, as a body, the supreme right over everything in its power" (G3 193; C2 287). The focus is on the generality of the assembly to which legislative and presumably executive power is vested, as contrasted with a monarchy in which it is vested solely in a single individual and an aristocracy in which it is invested in only a few, though it is clear from his later fragmentary discussion of democracy in the TP (to be considered below) that this generality is far from universality, since it excludes women and servants. Spinoza here characterizes democracy as "the most natural state," meaning the one "which approached most nearly the freedom nature concedes to everyone" (TTP G3 195; C2 289). The point is that, even though a democracy, like any other form of governance, requires that all individuals transfer their natural right to the sovereign and agree to obey the laws, it at the same time gives them the greatest possible say in determining the laws that they are obliged to obey. Thus, in a democracy every citizen has, at least in theory, an equal voice in the affairs of the state, and "in this way," Spinoza claims, "Everyone remains equal, as they were before, in the state of nature" (Ibid.). Moreover, Spinoza notes that in no other form of governance are the benefits of freedom more apparent. Since every citizen has a stake in the decision-making process, and since the will of the majority becomes law, a democracy does not merely tolerate but actually requires freedom of thought and expression. A democracy, in other words, more than any other form of governance, has a vested interest in the liberty and rationality of its citizens; and for that reason it is for Spinoza the form of governance under which one could most readily lead the form of life described in the *Ethics*. The problem, however, is that because of the above-mentioned restrictions on citizenship, not every denizen of the commonwealth is a citizen and, therefore, eligible to participate in the form of life that is supposedly fostered by a democracy.

A distinctive feature of Spinoza's defense of democracy is that rather than grounding it in an appeal to abstract principles such as liberty, equality, or the inherent dignity of human beings in the manner of other republican thinkers, he grounds it naturalistically in the conception of human nature articulated in the *Ethics*, which accounts for the essential continuity between it and his political writings.[27] In addition to empowering individuals (at least those who are fortunate enough to be members of the general assembly), democratic institutions for Spinoza are superior to those of monarchies and aristocracies because they tend to maximize social harmony and foster a sense of interdependence, as expressed in the tenet of the *Ethics* that "To man ... there is nothing more useful to man" (E4p18s).[28] And by minimizing affective states such as envy and resentment and replacing them with positive ones such as love and a concern with the well-being of others, a democracy also provides individuals with a greater sense of security, which, as we have seen, was one of the major benefits of the civil condition as contrasted with the state of nature for Spinoza as well as for Hobbes.

Furthermore, democracy for Spinoza is not only affectively superior to other forms of governance, it is arguably intellectually superior as well, because the inclusion of many in the deliberative process underlying decisions of state tends to maximize the rationality of the process.[29] In short, in politics for Spinoza, the more the merrier! Admittedly, the latter claim seems wildly counterintuitive, given Spinoza's apparent disdain for the irrationality of the multitude, particularly as it was manifested in his own experience in the brutal murder of the De Witt brothers.[30] And this has led to the fairly widespread view in the literature that rather than being an application of a line of thought articulated in the *Ethics*, Spinoza's ardent defense of democracy in the TTP is incompatible with his harshly negative view of the masses or, in the language of the TP, the "plebeians."[31]

---

[27] This is a central thesis of Steinberg's book, *Spinoza's Political Psychology*.

[28] In E4p37s2 Spinoza provides a brief sketch of his political theory. For present purposes the most noteworthy feature of this discussion is the claim that in a civil state decisions about personal property and justice are decided by common consent (G2 238–239), since this suggests that Spinoza there equated the civil state as such with a democracy.

[29] I am here largely following Steinberg, *Spinoza's Political Psychology*, esp. 163–189, who maintains that Spinoza mounts both an affective and an epistemic case for the superiority of democracy. The latter point is also emphasized by Nadler, *A Book Forged in Hell*, 194–195.

[30] On the latter point see Feuer, *Spinoza and the Rise of Liberalism*, esp. 151.

[31] For a discussion of this issue see Steinberg, *Spinoza's Political Psychology*, esp. 164–165.

The point, however, is that irrational mob behavior, which Spinoza condemns, is the polar opposite of the deliberative process that he claims to be essential for a functioning democracy, since in such a process individual passions, if not totally set aside (as would be the case in Spinoza's ideal society of "free men" in E4), are at least balanced out, so that the result is more likely to be rational in the sense of expressing the genuine interests of the commonwealth. Clearly, given Spinoza's hardheaded pragmatic realism, there are no guarantees that such a result will incur in a particular case, but the claim is that the likelihood of a successful outcome is a function of the size of the deliberative body. As Spinoza succinctly puts it at one point in the TPP, "in a democratic state, absurdities are less to be feared. If the assembly is large, it is almost impossible that the majority of its members should agree on one absurd action" (G3 194; C2 288). We shall see later that he develops this view in the TP by insisting that a monarchy be supplemented by a council and that, other things being equal, an aristocracy composed of a large number of patricians is preferable to one with relatively few.

Even granting this, however, Spinoza's essentially Hobbesian absolutistic conception of sovereignty, which requires unconditional obedience to the commands of the sovereign power, even in a democracy, seems difficult to reconcile with the broadly democratic thrust of his political thought, with its emphasis on freedom of thought and expression. Consider, for example, the following passage from the TTP, in which he endeavors to reconcile the right of free speech with the demand for total obedience to the law:

> [I]f someone shows that a law is contrary to sound reason and therefore thinks it ought to be repealed, if at the same time he submits his opinion to the judgment of the supreme power (to whom alone it belongs to make and repeal laws) and in the meantime does nothing contrary to what the law prescribes, he truly deserves well of the republic as one of its best citizens. But if he does this to accuse the magistrate of inequity, and makes him hateful to the common people, or if he wants to nullify the law, seditiously against the will of the magistrate, he's just a trouble maker and a rebel. (G3 241; C2 347)

This passage expresses in graphic form the limits of Spinoza's political philosophy, limits that seem to follow from his rigid separation of thought and action. In particular, it makes clear that, despite his advance over Hobbes in finding room for the rights of the individual in an authoritarian state, Spinoza was unable to show how these rights could be fully reconciled with political power and the demand for total obedience to the law.

Although when confronted by an unreasonable or "unjust" law, an individual has the right to reason with the authorities and try to convince them of their folly, if he fails to persuade, he must remain silent and obey.[32] Moreover, on Spinoza's view, the rational person will do so voluntarily, and the state has the right to treat as an enemy and execute for the crime of treason anyone who does not.

Spinoza attempts to avoid some of the more unpleasant consequences of this harsh view by appealing to his pragmatic and Machiavellian analysis of the natural limits of governmental power. As previously noted, in order for a law to be effective, it must not clash too violently with the majority's sense of its own best interests. A law requiring universal suicide, for example, would be universally disobeyed, and any government that tried to enforce such a law would be "rightly" overthrown, given Spinoza's view of the coextensiveness of right with power. But the problem is that this has no bearing on the dissent of an individual or vocal minority, who feel that their legitimate rights are being violated and who have no real recourse. In short, perhaps because, like Hobbes, he saw the problem of political authority in terms of a conflict between the sovereign and the multitude, Spinoza's political theory, including his account of democracy, seems to have no answer to what has been called the tyranny of the majority. Instead he appears to have dismissed the very possibility of such a state of affairs on the seemingly overly optimistic grounds that the decision of the majority will generally be reasonable, which he combined with the Hobbesian view that even if it is not reasonable, it is better to submit than to rebel or resist.

Spinoza provides a clear statement of the latter part of his position in the TP, where, addressing the easily anticipated objection that, according to his own view, it would be contrary to reason to subject oneself unconditionally to an external authority, he writes:

> [S]ince reason teaches nothing contrary to nature, sound reason cannot dictate that each person remain his own master, so long as men are subject to affects . . . reason denies that this can happen [that reason should dictate that each person remain his own master].
>
> Moreover, reason teaches us without qualification to seek peace, which certainly can't be obtained unless the common laws of the Commonwealth are observed without violation. So, the more a man is free is led by reason . . .

---

[32] A somewhat similar view is affirmed by Kant in his famous essay "What Is Enlightenment?," where he cites with approval the presumed dictate of Frederick the Great: "*Argue* as much as you will and about whatever you will, *but obey!*" (KGS 8:37). As this passage indicates, the difference is that, unlike Spinoza, Kant does not place any limits on the right to express disagreement.

the more free he is, the more steadfastly he will observe the laws of the Commonwealth and carry out the commands of the supreme power to whom he is subject.

Furthermore, the civil order is naturally established to take away the common fear and relieve the common wretchedness. So what it aims at most is what everyone who is guided by reason would strive to do in the state of nature, but in vain [by ii, 15]. If a man who is guided by reason sometimes, by the command of the commonwealth, has to do something he knows is incompatible with reason, that harm is far outweighed by the good he derives from the civil order itself. For it is also a law of reason that we should choose the lesser of two evils. (G3 286; C2 519)

Spinoza's characterization of a voluntary submission to a law that one recognizes as contrary to reason as a choice of the lesser of two evils is both striking and difficult to square with his claim to have "preserved natural Right unimpaired." Moreover, this whole line of thought is epitomized by Spinoza's extremely negative views on revolution, which he shares with Hobbes. Although he notes that revolutions tend to occur whenever a tyrannical government seeks to extend its authority beyond its actual power, he denies that they are ever effective, in the sense of leading to a genuine amelioration of the human condition. On his view, which is largely based on appeal to history, all that ever happens is the replacement of one form of tyranny with another that is usually even more severe. In the TTP Spinoza explicitly draws this moral from his analysis of the history of the Hebrew nation and presents it as a warning to his contemporaries. While the people held power, he notes, there was only one civil war, and even this was not bitterly contested, which made possible a peaceful settlement. "But after the people, who were by no means accustomed to kings, changed the first form of the state into a monarchical one, there was hardly any end to civil wars, and they engaged in battles so fierce that they surpassed the reputation of all others" (G3 224; C2 325). Moreover, lest one believe that the problem lay with the monarchy, rather than with the change in the form of governance, Spinoza notes that it is equally dangerous to remove a monarch, even if he is universally regarded as a tyrant, because, having become accustomed to royal power, the multitude will refuse to acknowledge any lesser authority. The removal of one tyrant, therefore, leads inevitably to the installation of another; and Spinoza reflects: "That's how it happens that the people can often change the tyrant, but can never destroy him, or change a monarchic state into another of a different form" (G3 227; C2 329).

8.4 Forms of Governance

Although Spinoza denied the likelihood, if not the possibility, of a beneficial change in the form of the governance of any given state, he believed that each form could be constituted so as to maximize both the security of the state and the liberty of its subjects. The analysis and demonstration of the appropriate principles of organization (the constitutions) for each form of governance is the main task of the TP. The account is based on the division of these forms into monarchies, aristocracies, and democracies, which seems to have been founded on the principle that sovereign power must be vested in either one, some, or all.[33] The analyses of monarchy and aristocracy are complete, but the treatment of democracy remains a mere fragment. The entire discussion is based on the principle that for each form of governance "it's been necessary to set up a state, so that everyone – both those who rule and those who are ruled – does what's for the common well-being, whether they want it or not. That is, it's been necessary to set it up so that everyone is compelled to live according to the prescription of reason, whether of his own accord, or by force, or by necessity" (G3 297; C2 532).

8.4.1 Monarchy

According to Spinoza, the successful functioning of a monarchy depends on its limited, constitutional nature. Against Hobbes, and as a warning to the Orangists in his own country, Spinoza challenged the myth of the security and stability of an absolute monarchy. The inherent weakness of this form of governance lies in the fact that "the power of a single individual is quite unequal to bearing such a burden" (G3 298; C2 533). Accordingly, the monarch necessarily depends on others, so that the state that is believed to be a pure monarchy is in practice an aristocracy, which, since this is concealed, is of the very worst kind (Ibid.). Moreover, not only is such a monarch often ruled by his advisers, who are in turn ruled by their desire to please him, but in his efforts to preserve his power, he will come to fear and oppress his own subjects. As is generally the case, however, Spinoza maintains that oppressive policies by a monarch are counterproductive and would eventually lead to the monarch's demise.

Again, in the spirit of Machiavelli, the main goal of Spinoza's analysis of the monarchial form of governance is to specify those institutions that will

---

[33] This is the view of Hobbes. See *De Cive*, pt. 2, chap. 7, 87.

effectively limit the monarch, so that he will be able both to preserve his power and serve the best interest of the people. As one might suppose, the most important of these institutions is a large council, with members drawn from all clans and classes of the realm. Spinoza specifies that each member of this council be over fifty years of age and serve for a limited term. He further suggests that the council be so constituted that it reflects all shades of public opinion, since this would help to ensure that the private affairs and interests of its members depend on the preservation of peace. Here, again, Spinoza makes no optimistic assumptions about human nature. All of his recommendations are designed to maximize the chance that the members of the council serve the common good and are neither motivated by the desire for perpetual power nor corrupted by bribes. The primary function of the council is to defend the fundamental laws of the realm and to give advice about the administration of the state to the monarch, so that he may know what the common good requires. The king, for his part, "will not be permitted to decide anything about any matter unless he has first heard the opinion of this Council" (G3 301; C2 537). And since the makeup of the council supposedly ensures that its majority opinion reflects the views of the majority of the populace, the monarch is always obliged to confirm that opinion or, in the case of a badly split council, attempt to reconcile their differences (G3 312; C2 549). The institution of the council thus limits the power of the monarch in such a way that there is at least a reasonable guarantee that he will act in the public interest.

According to Spinoza, a second essential institution in a stable monarchy is state-owned land. He claims that all the land and, if possible, the houses should be public property, subject to the control of the sovereign, who should rent them to the citizens, who should not be subject to any further form of taxation in time of peace (G3 300; C2 535–536). This radical proposal, by virtue of which Spinoza has been described as a forerunner of Henry George, was formulated in the interests of peace and security.[34] The thought is that without a landed gentry and with all subjects engaged in commerce, everyone will have a basically equal risk in war. The majority of both the council and the people will, therefore, tend to oppose war unless absolutely necessary. And as a result, it is assumed that such a commonwealth would not involve itself in costly and destructive wars, which are among the chief causes of the undoing of states.

---

[34] See Feuer, *Spinoza and the Rise of Liberalism*, 188.

Finally, in agreement with Machiavelli, Spinoza argues for a citizens' militia and underlines the extreme danger of mercenary troops in a - monarchy.[35] Spinoza here shows a keen awareness of the dangers of militarism; that is, of a strong professional army, which could either lead the nation into unnecessary wars or be used by the monarch as a means of oppressing the people.[36] For Spinoza, then, a people's militia is the best protection of their liberty. Such a militia would fight only when necessary and even then only in defense of liberty, rather than out of desire for gain. Since no one would be exempt from service in this militia, everyone would have not only an equal stake but also an equal part in the preservation of the commonwealth. Given these as well as other institutions, which we need not consider, Spinoza concludes his discussion of monarchy with the reflection that "a multitude can preserve a full enough freedom under a King, so long as it brings it about that the monarch's power is determined by the power of the multitude, and is preserved by the multitude's support" (G3 323; C2 563). Thus, it seems that for Spinoza even in a monarchy, and without appeal to a social contract, the multitude remains the ultimate source of political power.

8.4.2 Aristocracy

Whereas Spinoza seems to have only grudgingly admitted that a properly constituted monarchy could function as a viable form of governance, his attitude toward aristocracy is far more positive, and his discussion thereof ends with the claim that if any state could last forever, it would be an aristocracy (G3 357; C2 600). In fact, his whole treatment of the subject could be seen as a defense of this form of governance, together with an analysis of why it failed in the Netherlands and how such failure could be avoided in the future.[37] This analysis consists largely of an appeal to certain features of the constitution of the Venetian republic, which are modified to fit the situation in the Netherlands.

Aristocracy, as defined by Spinoza, is a form of governance in which political power is held "not by one man, but by certain men selected from the multitude, whom we'll henceforth call Patricians" (G3 323; C2 564). Whereas an aristocracy differs from a monarchy in respect of the number of those who are in power, it differs from a democracy with regard to the

---

[35] See Machiavelli, *The Prince*, chaps. 12–13; *Discourses*, bk. 2, chap. 20.
[36] Feuer points out that the use of a professional army and the hiring of mercenaries were policies of the Orangist party in the Netherlands (*Spinoza and the Rise of Liberalism*).
[37] See Feuer, *Spinoza and the Rise of Liberalism*, 182–192.

method of selection, which presumably is why Spinoza thought that an aristocracy, though not a democracy, might last forever. The key point is that in an aristocracy the patricians are expressly elected by other patricians, whereas in a democracy the right to vote, and, therefore, political power, is automatically granted to every person who meets certain stipulated conditions. In practice, these conditions might be so stringent that very few could meet them – for example, a very considerable amount of wealth, whereas in an aristocracy those elected might constitute a substantial proportion of the population. Theoretically, therefore, an aristocracy might actually have a larger governing body than a democracy. Nevertheless, the former would still be a democracy and the latter an aristocracy. Indeed, a large number of patricians is not merely a theoretical possibility for Spinoza, but a practical necessity if the aristocracy is to avoid either degenerating into a monarchy or splitting into factions.

Spinoza's task, as already noted, is to determine the best constitution for an aristocratic form of governance; but before proceeding to do so, he stops to catalog the advantages that a properly constituted aristocracy has over a monarchy. He lists four. The first is that it has adequate numbers and hence sufficient power to govern. Consequently, unlike a monarchy, it does not require councilors. The second is that, whereas monarchs are mortal, councils are everlasting, which means that an aristocracy is not subject to periodic upheaval. The third is that, while because of old age, sickness, minority, or other causes, a monarch's power is often held only on sufferance, the power of a council always remains the same. The fourth and presumably most important for Spinoza is that an aristocracy does not suffer from the extreme disadvantage of having its laws based on the inevitably fluctuating will of a single person. Thus, he notes that, while in a monarchy, "every law is indeed the king's will made explicit; but not everything the king wills should be law," in an aristocracy with a sufficiently numerous council, "every declaration of its will ought to be law" (G3 325; C2 566).

Although theoretically, the power of an aristocracy is much greater than that of a monarchy for Spinoza, he notes that in practice aristocracies have been limited by the fact that the multitude has often maintained a certain independence and has, therefore, become an object of fear. Moreover, Spinoza concludes from this that the greatest need of an aristocratic regime is that the multitude be deprived of all power; that it "maintains no freedom except what must necessarily be granted it from the constitution of the state itself, which is therefore a right, not so much of the multitude itself, as of the whole state, which only the best proclaim and preserve as theirs" (G3 326; C2 567). As one commentator has pointed out, this amounts to the demand for a dictatorship of the commercial aristocracy, and all the constitutional safeguards and conditions for stability that Spinoza includes in his discussion of aristocracy work toward this end.[38] But though such a form of governance is in fact a dictatorship, Spinoza evidently thought that it could be a benevolent one and that the people would, therefore, have nothing to fear: "For the will of a Council so large cannot be determined so much by immoderate desire as by reason. Indeed, evil effects pull men in different directions. They can't be led by one mind except insofar as what they desire is honorable, or at least has the appearance of being honorable" (G3 326; C2 567).

Once again, then, the issue for Spinoza is how an aristocratic regime can best be constituted. The analysis of monarchy provides the point of departure and the guiding question is what changes must be made in monarchical institutions in order to establish a successful aristocracy. In dealing with this question, Spinoza shows a keen understanding of the organic connection between institutions in various types of states. What is appropriate in a monarchy is not necessarily so in an aristocracy. Moreover, he points out that one of the basic reasons for the demise of the Dutch Republic was the failure to realize this. Since it was mistakenly thought that all that was necessary was to get rid of the king, there was never any thought of changing the underlying organization of the state (G3 352; C2 594–595). Spinoza's analysis of aristocracies is complicated, however, by the fact that he recognized two distinct kinds. One, like the Venetian, comprises a single city and its territories; another, like that of the United States of the Netherlands, comprises several relatively autonomous cities. Although Spinoza felt that the latter was superior, largely because of its greater power, he devotes much of his attention to the former. Only after completing his analysis of the single-city form of aristocracy does he turn to the question of what modifications would be necessary in an aristocratic state composed of several cities.

For Spinoza it is absolutely essential to the success of an aristocracy of any form that the supreme council, which is composed of all the patricians, be sufficiently strong. His recommended size is 2 percent of the population. The function of this council, which must meet regularly at a fixed location, is to pass and repeal laws and to choose patrician colleagues as well as ministers of state (G3 328–330; C2 11–14). Moreover, since stable

[38] Ibid., 165.

government requires that nothing be left to chance or to the good faith and rationality of the governors, Spinoza also felt it necessary that there be a supplemental body of patricians, subordinate to the supreme council, charged with the duty of seeing to it that the constitution is preserved and order maintained in the supreme council. Such bodies are called syndics, and they are in effect the watchdogs of the council. Spinoza goes into great detail concerning the appropriate number, age, involvement, and length of service of the syndics, all for the purpose of ensuring that their self-interest will lead them to pursue the general good (G3 332–335; C2 572–576). Moreover, precisely the same principle is operative in determining the other institutions. Chief of these are the senate and the judiciary. The senate, which is a second council subordinate to the supreme one, is assigned the task of transacting public business. The most important part of this business is the ordering of the fortifications of the cities and the conferring of military commissions. Since it is directly involved with the military operations of the state, it is vital that it be composed of men who have more to gain from peace than from war (G3 336–339; C2 578–580). The judiciary has the job of deciding disputes between private parties. It must, therefore, be constituted so as to be as impartial as possible and not subject to bribes (G3 341–343; C2 582–584).

Moreover, for Spinoza a successful aristocracy differs from a monarchy in other areas besides the organization of its governing bodies. Thus, he proposes for an aristocracy two institutions, which he had deemed inappropriate for a monarchy: mercenaries and private property. Since an aristocratic government possesses absolute power, the danger, inherent in a monarchy, of hiring foreign mercenaries does not exist; and since the people have no power and are more appropriately termed "subjects" than "citizens," they can hardly be expected to serve in the army without pay (G3 327; C2 5658). A similar line of reasoning is used to justify private ownership. Since the people have no say in the governance of the state, without the possession of property they would have no interest in its survival. In an aristocracy, unlike a monarchy, private property, therefore, functions as an incentive to support the government (G3 328; C2 569).

Among the features of an aristocracy to which Spinoza devotes serious attention is religion. Alluding to his discussion in the TTP, he states that the members of the aristocracy (the patricians) should adhere to the same religion and it should be the simple universal faith described in that work (to be discussed in Chapter 9); that is, a minimal set of basic tenets or "dogmas" (3 345; C2 587). Spinoza is clear that the need for such a shared faith among the aristocracy is to avoid sectarian conflict such as was rampant in Europe at the time. And it is also clear that these tenets were not chosen by Spinoza because of their truth (they affirm a personal, providential deity), but because they are deemed necessary for the obedience of the multitude.[39] Spinoza further suggests that, rather than stifling freedom of thought, a universal religion, so constituted, would foster it, presumably by foreclosing the superstition, which he saw as an inevitable concomitant of sectarianism. For reasons that are not completely clear, however, Spinoza also goes into considerable detail concerning matters such as the size of the houses of worship (those of the national religion being "large and magnificent," while those of the other confessions must be small and distanced from one another). And he further maintains that only patricians should be permitted to perform the priestly functions such as marriage and baptism, which would effectively deprive the clergy of the various confessions of their traditional functions.

According to Spinoza, most of the above-mentioned institutions are relevant to aristocracies of both types. The greatest modification required for an aristocratic republic composed of several cities is in the supreme council. In the latter things must be organized so that the authority of each city in the union is strictly proportionate to its power. Each city should have its own supreme council and a good deal of autonomy. The senate and judiciary should be the main links between the cities, with the senate having charge of all intercity affairs. Although the state will have a supreme council, this should not have a role in the ordinary affairs of state; rather, it should only convene at moments of national danger, when the very union itself is threatened. Such an aristocracy, like the United States of the Netherlands, is more a loose federation for common defense than a genuine nation. Its weakness would seem to lie in the difficulty of joining together for conceited action and the danger of degenerating into a mere debating society. Spinoza was well aware of this weakness and of the charge that it was the cause of the demise of the United States of the Netherlands, but he denied that this was in fact the case, arguing instead that its demise was due to "the defective constitution of the state and the small number of its regents" (G3 352; C2 595).

8.4.3 Democracy

As previously noted, Spinoza's discussion of democracy in the TP is a mere fragment and does not provide an account of the specific institutions that

---

[39] My discussion of this topic is based largely on the discussion by Garber, "Religion and the Civil State in the TP."

he thought would be required for a viable democracy, such as he had done in his highly detailed discussions of monarchy and aristocracy. Whereas we have seen that in the TTP he had defined democracy as "a general assembly which has, as a body, the supreme right over everything in its power," in the TP he characterizes it as the form of governance in which the supreme council or ruling body is composed of everyone who qualifies for citizenship (G3 358; C2 602). This is contrasted with an aristocracy, in which the members of the governing body (the patricians) are selected on the basis of criteria such as wealth and primogeniture. More interestingly, whereas we have seen that in the TTP Spinoza claimed democracy to be the most natural and, therefore, also presumably best form of governance, in the TP, where he is functioning as political scientist rather than advocate, there is no such contention. Instead, Spinoza is content to note that, while aristocracy might seem superior to democracy on the grounds that it supposedly affirms rule by the best for the benefit of all, in practice this is not the case, since wealth and primogeniture are not reliable indicators of those who are best suited to rule (G3 359; C2 602). Thus, Spinoza here takes what appears to be at best a neutral stance on the virtues of democracy and aristocracy as forms of governance, though he evidently sides with aristocracy in view of its durability. Clearly, however, for Spinoza both are preferable to a monarchy on the grounds that sovereign power is divested in a collective body, rather than an individual, which maximizes the dangers of arbitrariness.

Although Spinoza notes that democratic governance can take many forms, he states that he proposes to consider only what we might call a broad-based democracy; that is, one in which all nonforeign residents who are independent and who live honestly have the right to vote in the supreme council and to hold offices of state. The exclusion of foreign residents is based on the premise that they owe allegiance to another state; and the qualification of independence is intended to exclude women and servants, who are subject to their husbands and masters, respectively, as well as children and wards, who likewise lack the requisite independence. Spinoza evidently considered all of these exclusions, except for women, obvious and, therefore, not in need of further explanation. But he acknowledges that the inclusion of women in the class of those who are denied participation in a democracy does require justification. Assuming that it would be granted that women are under the power of their husbands (thereby ignoring the whole class of adult, unmarried women and presumably widows), he defines the issue as whether this dependence is due merely to custom or to reason. Spinoza argues for the latter, though he notes that he does so by means of an appeal to experience rather than by reason (thereby implicitly acknowledging that he cannot provide an a priori grounding for this view). And dismissing as fanciful apparent counter-examples such as the all-female society of the Amazons, which had been cited by Hobbes in support of females' capacity to rule, and conveniently overlooking real-life counterexamples such as Queen Elizabeth, Spinoza argues that,

> If women were by nature equal to men, both in strength of character and in native intelligence – in which the greatest human power, and consequently right consists – surely among so many and such diverse nations we would find some where each sex ruled equally, and other where men were ruled by women, and so educated that they could do less with their native intelligence. (G3 360; C2 603)

Moreover, insisting that this state of affairs has never actually occurred, Spinoza concludes his "induction" by confidently claiming that "[W]e can say without reservation that women do not, by nature, have a right equal to men's but they necessarily submit to men" (Ibid.). And, finally, moving from an appeal to historical experience to his own account of the emotions, he concludes that

> [I]f we consider human affects, namely, that for the most part men love women only from an affect of lust, and that they judge their native intelligence and wisdom greater the more beautiful they are, and furthermore, that men find it intolerable that the women they love should favor others in some way, etc., we'll have no difficulty seeing that men and women can't rule equally without great harm to the peace. (G3 360; C2 603–604)

Although Spinoza never finished his discussion of democracy, the fact that he concludes his dismissive treatment of women by remarking: "But enough of these matters" (G3 360; C2 604) makes it clear that he had said all he had to say on this topic. Thus, any thought that he might have gone on to qualify his view if he had more time must be dismissed as wishful thinking.

Moreover, any attempt to mitigate, if not dismiss as immaterial, the unabashedly sexist nature of Spinoza's remarks about women as simply a reflection of the spirit of the time is obviated by the example of Hobbes, who explicitly argued that women, in a state of nature, have equal rights with men, and that their "inequality of natural force" is not so great as to undermine their basic equality with men. In support of this contention, as noted above, Hobbes points to the Amazon women, who actually waged war against men, and to the fact that "at this day in diverse places, women are invested with the principal authority."[40] But setting this aside, as well as Spinoza's acknowledgment that his views about women and their place in society would be considered controversial by his contemporaries, it is also the case that these views are in some tension with his account of human nature in the *Ethics*, which supposedly was not intended as applicable only to the male gender.[41] Accordingly, it is not surprising that this has proven to be a fertile topic for feminist Spinoza scholars to address.[42]

---

[40] Hobbes, *De Cive*, pt. 2, chap. 9, 106.
[41] This is noted by Moira Gatens, "The Condition of Human Nature: Spinoza's Account of the Ground of Human Action in the Tractatus Politicus," 56–57.
[42] In addition to Gatens ("The Condition of Human Nature"), this includes Amelie Rorty, "Spinoza on the Pathos of Idolatrous Love and the Hilarity of True Love"; Susan James, "Politically Mediated Affects Envy in Spinoza's Tractatus Politicus"; and Hasana Sharp, "Family Quarrels and Mental Harmony: Spinoza's Oikos Polis Analogy."

CHAPTER 9

The Theology of the Theological-Political Treatise

In the previous chapter we considered the political portion of the TTP, but the main import of the work and the basis of its great influence was its theological component, particularly its views regarding the interpretation of the Bible. The close connection between political and theological considerations is to be understood in light of the political situation in post-Reformation Europe, where political conflicts were closely intertwined with confessional ones and the toleration of those who did not adhere to the established Church in a particular state was a contentious issue. In Protestant states such as the United Provinces of the Netherlands, aka the Dutch Republic, this meant that the interpretation of the Bible played an outsized role, since, in contrast with Roman Catholic states, where supreme religious authority was placed in the teachings of the Church, the Bible was regarded as the sole basis of Christian faith. Moreover, Spinoza had an important predecessor and model for such a political-theological project in Hobbes' *Leviathan*, the second and today largely neglected second half of which is devoted to many of the same topics as the theological portion of the TTP, albeit from a vehemently anti-Catholic point of view, which reflected the political situation in England. Indeed, Hobbes is cited as having remarked about Spinoza's treatment of the Bible: "I durst not write so boldly."[1]

But while Spinoza's project in the TTP was akin to Hobbes' and some of his critical claims about the Bible were more radical than Hobbes dared to venture, his overall intent was quite different. This is evident from the lengthy subtitle of the TTP, which reads: *Several Discussions Showing that the Republic Can Grant Freedom of Philosophizing Without Harming Its Peace or Piety, and Cannot Deny It Without Destroying Its Peace and Piety* (G3 3; C2 65). This indicates that the argument is specifically applicable to

---

[1] The citation is from John Aubrey. It is taken from Curley, "'I Durst Not Write so Boldly,' or, How to Read Hobbes' Theological Political Treatise," 497.

a republic, and the essential claim is that in a republic the freedom to philosophize is not only compatible with but actually a necessary condition of the possibility of both peace and piety. Ostensibly, then, the intent of the TTP is to defend the freedom to philosophize or, more generally, the freedom of thought and expression; and the question is why mounting such a defense would require dealing with seemingly arcane theological issues, including biblical hermeneutics.

Although he was not asked about his motivation for composing the TTP, we have seen that Spinoza volunteered an answer in a letter to Oldenburg written five years prior to its publication in which he gave three reasons: (1) to expose the prejudices of the theologians; (2) to counter the accusation of atheism; and (3) to justify the freedom to philosophize.[2] Since the third of these reasons coincides with what Spinoza will maintain in the subtitle and preface to the TTP, it does not call for comment, except perhaps to note his blame of the clergy for opposing the freedom to philosophize. And since when Spinoza published the TTP he did not attach his name to it and listed a false place of publication (Hamburg rather than Amsterdam), it is clear that he had changed his mind in the intervening years regarding the second point. Moreover, if he had really thought that this work would defend him against the charge of atheism, subsequent events show that he was sadly mistaken. The most important of these proffered reasons, however, is clearly the first, since it is precisely the "prejudices of the theologians" that were Spinoza's main target. The theologians whom he targeted were mainly the Calvinist clergy, and their chief prejudice was the view that the Bible is to be regarded as the literal word of God, of which they were the self-appointed and authoritative interpreters.

The theological portion of the TTP contains Spinoza's systematic response to these theologians or, more precisely, to the principles on which their claim to spiritual authority was based. But though it cannot be gleaned from either Spinoza's letter to Oldenburg or the subtitle and preface to the work, with its focus on the Hebrew Bible and Judaism it also contains far more than this, namely Spinoza's belated response to his cherem from the Jewish community.[3]

Keeping both of these concerns in mind, the ensuing discussion is divided into four sections. Section 9.1 examines Spinoza's analysis and critique of the view that the Bible (mainly the Hebrew Bible, but also the New Testament) contains the revealed word of God. Its foci are Spinoza's

---

[2] See Chapter 1, p. 12–13.
[3] For this aspect of the TTP see Nadler, *A Book Forged in Hell*, esp. 1–16.

understanding of prophecy, considered as the vehicle through which the word of God is conveyed to human beings, and miracles as the means by which the authenticity of the prophetic messages is verified. Section 9.2, which bears directly on Spinoza's own relation to Judaism, considers his critique of the claim that the Jewish people were chosen by God for a special destiny. Section 9.3 discusses his hermeneutical principles, by virtue of which Spinoza became one of the founders of a scientific, historical approach to the interpretation of the Bible. Finally, Section 9.4 analyzes Spinoza's account of faith or "true religion," which he contrasts with superstition.

9.1   The Critique of Revelation

The distinction between natural and revealed religion was fundamental to the theological controversies of the seventeenth and eighteenth centuries. By natural religion was understood a body of truths about God and his providential concern for humanity that was accessible to unaided human reason, while revealed religions were those that are putatively based on a communication or revelation by God at a particular point in time, the essential contents of which were later codified in a holy book or Scripture. The major examples of these were, of course, Judaism, Christianity, and Islam, which for that reason have often been referred to as "religions of the book." Modeled on the basis of the traditional distinction between natural and positive law, the distinction was also framed as a contrast between natural and positive religion, with a positive religion being one that is posited, i.e., initiated, at a particular time through a divine revelation. Although Spinoza did not avail himself of this terminology in the TTP, which only became commonplace somewhat later with the advent of Deism, which under the influence of Spinoza (among others) argued for the sufficiency of natural religion, this basic line of thought underlies his argument, and we shall see that his account of faith or "true religion" in chapter 15 of the TTP can be read as presenting his version of a natural religion.

Spinoza's view of the claims of revealed religion should be clear from our consideration of the *Ethics*. Basically, belief in the teachings of these religions, as generally construed, is equated with superstition. The source of such belief is the imagination, and its hold on the mind of the multitude is explained in terms of its connection with the passions of hope and fear. Hence, not only does Spinoza maintain that this belief lacks any rational basis, but we have seen that he considered many of the "virtues" its proponents affirm, e.g., fear of God, a sense of guilt, repentance, humility, and so on, to be at variance with the dictates of reason.[4] Such a critique is external, however, and rests on philosophical assumptions that theologians would deny in the name of a superior revealed truth. Thus, in order to challenge this premise and the theoretical and political consequences derived from it, Spinoza recognized the necessity of addressing it directly, which meant that he must examine the central theological claim that Scripture, whether the Jewish or Christian version, contains the authoritative word of God to which reason must be subjected. Although Spinoza does not discuss Islam and the Koran, it would seem that the logic of his position is applicable to it as well.

Our present concern, however, is with Spinoza's critique of the claim that the Christian religion or, more specifically, the version of Protestantism defended by the Calvinist, Dutch Reformed Church is the true religion. And since this defense is based on an appeal to the Bible as containing the true and literal word of God, this is likewise the focus of his critique. Assuming for the sake of argument the standpoint of his theological opponents, Spinoza proclaims that the only way in which the authority of Scripture can be justified is by an appeal to Scripture. And, ignoring the obvious circularity of such an approach, he affirms as a fundamental exegetical principle that the sense of Scripture must be taken from Scripture itself (G3 9; C2 71). Spinoza's radical innovation consists in his use in the interpretation of Scripture of the basic principle of Cartesian method: that nothing may be claimed to be in the text that is not clearly and distinctly perceived to be contained in it. Moreover, in light of this governing principle, Spinoza rejects out of hand not only the Calvinist doctrine "that the light of nature has no power to interpret Scripture, but that a supernatural faculty is required for the task," but also the basic tenet of Maimonidean rationalism that "If it's found that its [Scripture's] literal meaning is contrary to reason – no matter how clear the literal meaning seemed to be – he thinks it should still be interpreted differently" (G3 113; C2 187). For Spinoza, both these approaches are not only dangerous politically because they lead to the establishment of spiritual authorities, they are also useless for determining the actual meaning of Scripture and, therefore, for justifying its authority.

---

[4] This is not completely true, however, for, as noted in Chapter 5, Section 5.2, Spinoza does accord a kind of provisional value to "virtues" such as repentance and humility for those not living under the guidance of reason. Thus, they are dictated by reason for those who are not themselves capable of full rationality.

Having rejected these approaches, Spinoza centers his attention on the evidence traditionally adduced for the divinity of Scripture. This evidence is of two sorts. First, there is the authority of the prophets, whom Spinoza construes broadly to encompass the apostles and even Christ, as well as the Hebrew prophets. Although his focus is clearly on the Hebrew Bible or Old Testament, this enables him to include the New Testament in his analysis and thereby address more directly the views of the Calvinist clergy. Second, there are miracles, which allegedly serve as signs of divine revelation in both the Jewish and Christian traditions. Spinoza's critique of revelation thus contains a systematic analysis of both prophecy and miracles.

Prophecy, which he equates with revelation, is defined by Spinoza as "the certain knowledge of some matter which God has revealed to men" (G3 15; C2 76). Echoing, though without alluding to, the view in the *Ethics*, Spinoza notes in passing that this definition could very well include natural knowledge, since this also depends on the knowledge of God, though in general such knowledge is not attributed to prophecy. Accordingly, his concern is solely with the extraordinary, superhuman knowledge that has traditionally been regarded as the unique result of prophetic insight. Following Maimonides, Spinoza agrees that prophetic insight is based on a superior imagination, rather than a superior intellect. But whereas Maimonides, as an Aristotelian, used the superiority of imagination to justify a real superiority of insight, Spinoza, in accordance with the basic principles of his theory of knowledge, uses it to draw just the opposite conclusion. Moreover, having established that the authority of the prophets depends *merely* on their superior imaginative capacity and not on their intellect, Spinoza concludes that their views are of no import in theoretical matters. The overall strategy and intent of the work, however, prevents him from simply deducing this from the metaphysical and epistemological doctrines of the *Ethics*, but requires instead that he derive them from a consideration of Scripture itself.

The first step in this derivation is to demonstrate that Scripture clearly teaches that prophetic power is a function of the imagination rather than the intellect. In line with the traditional Jewish insistence on the primacy of the Mosaic revelation, by considering a number of biblical texts, Spinoza shows that only Moses was held to have heard a real voice or received a direct revelation from God. All the other prophets encountered God through dreams and visions, which Spinoza takes to mean through the mediation of their imagination. The one exception is Christ, who in evident deference to his Christian readership Spinoza treated as a prophet, and to whom he claimed "the decisions of God, which lead men to salvation, were revealed immediately – without words or visions" (G3; C2 84), which enabled him to concede that Christ's knowledge of God (in contrast to Moses') stemmed from the intellect. And on the basis of what he takes to be the express teachings of Scripture, Spinoza argues at length that, with the exception of Moses and Christ, it was only by virtue of their vivid imagination and upright character, rather than their intellects, that the prophets were held to possess the "spirit of God," which is equivalent to being vehicles of divine revelation.

Spinoza's next and decisive step is to argue that precisely because the prophets relied on their imagination, they cannot be taken as authorities in theoretical or speculative matters. Although this is a logical consequence of the analysis of imagination found in the *Ethics*, we have seen that Spinoza's strategy does not permit him to present it in this fashion. It is also clear, however, that he could not very well maintain that the prophets themselves teach this conception of the imagination, since this would run counter to his claim that they are not to be relied upon in theoretical matters. Instead, he endeavors to demonstrate that not only the doctrines and conceptions but even the imagery and style of the various prophets differ markedly, and that these differences can be understood in terms of their dispositions, backgrounds, and ways of life. For example, Spinoza points out that the rustic prophets such as Amos and Ezekiel tend to depict God in rustic images and in a crude style, whereas a far different kind of imagery and a much more polished style are to be found in the prophecies of the "courtly Isaiah." Spinoza further shows that this explains the specific differences between the visions of Ezekiel and those of Isaiah, and he presents these differences as graphic examples of disagreement among the prophets. In his own cryptic language, which is intended to sum up the whole issue: "Isaiah saw seraphim with six wings, while Ezekiel saw beasts with four wings; Isaiah saw God clothed and sitting on a royal throne, while Ezekiel saw him as like a fire," from which Spinoza concludes that "each of them saw God as he was accustomed to imagine him" (C2 99; G3 34).

Such discrepancies were a potential source of embarrassment to biblical literalists and one standard tactic was to attempt to reconcile these differences by interpreting the passages in question in some nonliteral manner. Against this, Spinoza simply points out that by this means "It would be permissible to perpetrate and defend, without harm to the authority of Scripture, whatever evil, human malice can think up" (G3 37; C2 102). Consequently, Spinoza concludes that the only reasonable thing to do is to acknowledge frankly that the prophets disagree, and that their individual insights and visions reflect merely their own opinions and backgrounds and not some mysterious "higher truth." However, while Spinoza uses this obvious disagreement to undermine the authority of the prophets in speculative matters, he also points out that they all agree in teaching the virtues of justice and charity. He thus grants their moral teachings an authority that he denies to their speculative views. And we shall see that this result plays a central role in Spinoza's systematic attempt to separate theology from philosophy and genuine religion from superstition, which are among the central concerns of the TTP.

The appeal to miracles and to reports thereof constitutes the second traditional basis for establishing the divine origin and authority of Scripture. Miracles are here construed as events that violate, or at least transcend, the laws of nature. As such, they are assumed to function as signs or credentials, which authenticate the claims of a prophet to be revealing the authoritative word of God. Such a conception obviously runs completely counter to the whole tenor of Spinoza's metaphysics, which expressly rules out the possibility of anything contravening the universal laws of nature.[5] Once again, however, Spinoza's strategy does not allow him simply to refute this conception by a metaphysical argument; rather, his task is to demonstrate that this conception is not in accord with, or at least not derivable from, an unbiased reading of Scripture. Nevertheless, as Spinoza himself is forced to acknowledge, the question of miracles is not quite the same as that of prophecy. The nature of prophecy, he notes, is a "purely theological question," by which is meant a question as to what Scripture actually teaches, whereas the question of miracles is completely philosophical, namely: "[C]an we grant that something happens in nature contrary to its laws, or something which couldn't follow from them?" (G3 95; C2 167). Some metaphysical considerations are, therefore, necessary in dealing with miracles, but Spinoza is careful to separate these from the specifically anti-theistic tenets of the *Ethics*. Here, as elsewhere in the TTP, his concern is to formulate the argument in terms that theologians might accept, or at least not reject out of hand with cries of "atheism." Nevertheless, despite his conciliatory intent, Spinoza begins by describing the common attitude toward miracles in contemptuous terms. Central to this attitude, as he sees it, is the belief that the power of God is somehow

[5] As Nadler points out (*A Book Forged in Hell*, 90–91), Spinoza's critique of miracles differs sharply from that of the other great critic of this conception among early modern philosophers, David Hume, in that the latter, unlike Spinoza, regarded it as an epistemological question concerning what we have grounds to believe rather than a metaphysical one regarding what is intrinsically possible.

more evident and more worthy of adulation when manifested in unusual and inexplicable events than when it is found in the ordinary course of nature. This power is, therefore, distinguished from the power of nature, and God is viewed as a kind of royal potentate, who orders things for the benefit of humankind. Spinoza sums up his whole attitude toward the subject by reflecting: "What do the common people not foolishly claim for themselves, because they have no sound conception of God or of nature, because they confuse God's decrees with men's decisions, and finally, because they posit a nature so limited that they believe man to be its chief part!" (G3 82; C2 153).

As this passage indicates, Spinoza maintains that one of the underlying causes of the common belief in miracles is the failure to comprehend the infinity of nature and to recognize that "its laws are so broad that they extend to everything which is conceived by the divine intellect itself" (G3 83; C2 155). Students of the *Ethics* will realize that this failure is itself the result of an illicit separation between God and nature. In our analysis of that work we saw that the infinity of nature follows logically from the very conception of God, or nature, as the one substance that contains within itself everything that is possible. ("Whatsoever is, is in God, and nothing can be or be conceived without God" [E1Ip15].) Since nature contains within itself everything that is possible, miracles, which by definition violate the laws of nature, are both logically and metaphysically impossible. Moreover, Spinoza suggests that this same conception of nature as an infinite and necessary system of laws is the true meaning of Maimonides' assertion that the intellect and the will of God are identical. In arguing for this thesis, Spinoza begins with the acceptable theological formula, "we affirm the same thing when we say that God wills something as when we say that he understands it" (G3 82; C2 154); and he infers from this that the universal laws of nature reflect perfectly both the divine understanding and the divine will. He claims that once theologians admit this, they must also admit that anything that contravenes the laws of nature would also contravene the will (and intellect) of God. In willing a miracle, God would, therefore, be acting contrary to his own nature, which is absurd. Thus, by a process of argument based on accepted theological principles, Spinoza reduces the belief in miracles to an absurdity.

Furthermore, Spinoza continues, even if one were to acknowledge the existence of miracles, this could serve only to undermine, rather than to confirm, our knowledge of the existence of God. The point here is simply that an appeal to events that contravene the laws of nature casts doubt on the very principles of our reasoning, and this leads inevitably to a hopeless skepticism. If we cannot be certain of these laws, or "primary ideas" (the "common notions" of the *Ethics*), then we cannot be certain of anything, including the existence of God. But given these laws – that is, given the uniformity of nature – the existence of God can confidently be inferred. Thus, once again, Spinoza turns the argument of the theologians on its head, showing that it is the lawfulness of nature, not the alleged exceptions to this lawfulness, that provides a basis for inferring the existence of God.

There is, however, another conception of miracles that is not subject to these objections and that Spinoza had to consider. According to this conception, miracles are events that cannot be explained through natural causes because we, or whoever witnesses them, are not in possession of the requisite knowledge. Thus, they do not transcend the laws of nature, but merely our knowledge of these laws. This conception of a miracle is certainly meaningful. In fact, Spinoza claims that it is precisely the sense of miracle found in Scripture, which he characterizes as "a work of nature which . . . either surpasses men's power of understanding or is believed to surpass it" (G3 87; C2 159). But, as Spinoza points out, the problem with miracles, so understood, is that they cannot fulfill the function traditionally assigned to them. How, after all, could any such event, which by definition surpasses human understanding, serve as a source of knowledge? Moreover, even assuming that some inferences could legitimately be drawn from miracles conceived in this way, we could not appeal to them to infer the existence of God. For God is by definition an infinite being, while miracles are particular, finite events. And, Spinoza reasons, we cannot infer an infinite cause from a finite effect (G3 86; C2 157).

Finally, in accordance with his general strategy, Spinoza supplements his philosophical critique with a further consideration of the actual biblical teaching concerning miracles. As already noted, his view is that the Bible considers miracles merely as events that surpass human comprehension, rather than as occurrences that violate the laws of nature. Spinoza points out, however, that this means that what counts as a miracle is determined by the particular level of knowledge possessed by the narrator or witness. And since the ancient Hebrews had a very limited amount of scientific knowledge, they naturally regarded as miraculous many events which, from the superior standpoint of seventeenth-century science, could easily be explained. Moreover, Spinoza notes that the prevalence of miracles in the Bible is also explicable in terms of the poetic manner of expression and the religious intent of the various authors. This intent often led them to ignore secondary causes and to refer things directly to God. As a result, many events are described in ways that suggest miraculous intervention on

242   9 The Theology of the *Theological-Political Treatise*

the part of God, when the authors themselves had no such thought in mind. The moral that Spinoza draws from this is that the interpretation and evaluation of biblical miracle stories requires, among other things, an understanding of the level of knowledge, motivation, and manner of expression of their authors. Thus, rather than serving as a basis for claiming the authority of Scripture, or as a ground of faith, miracles are seen by Spinoza as a reflection of the limited understanding of the biblical authors.

9.2   The Critique of Jewish Exceptionalism

The analysis of prophecy and miracles constitutes the essence of Spinoza's general critique of revealed religion in the TTP. But he supplements this with a critique of Jewish claims of exceptionalism; that is, the belief that the Jewish people (or Hebrew nation) were chosen or elected by God on the basis of certain unique virtues for a specific destiny and in light of this given a special law or discipline (the Torah). In all probability, the basic elements of this critique date back to the time of his excommunication or cherem and reflect both the main reasons for it and his reaction to it.[6] Spinoza prefaces his treatment of this topic, however, with a reflection that lies at the very heart of his moral philosophy: "The true happiness and blessedness of each person consists only in the enjoyment of the good, and not in a self-esteem founded on the fact that he alone enjoys the good, all others being excluded from it" (G3 44; C2 111). As Spinoza sees it, the Jewish people would have been blessed nonetheless if God had conferred his favors equally on all human beings. Thus, the fact that the ancient Hebrews thought otherwise, that they prided themselves on being especially chosen, is for Spinoza merely a reflection of their childish understanding and crude moral standpoint.

Nevertheless, since the Bible does speak of the election of the Jews, Spinoza's overall hermeneutical strategy requires that he explain what legitimate sense this could have. As one might expect, this sense turns out to be consistent with the basic principles of his philosophy. First, he deals with the general question of the nature of divine aid, or grace. Since the "will of God" is perfectly manifest in (really identical with) the laws of nature, Spinoza claims that these very same laws may also be called "decrees of God." Accordingly, any and all human accomplishment, since it occurs in accordance with the fixed laws of nature, may, if one wishes, be seen as the result of

---

[6] For an account of the reasons for Spinoza's cherem and particularly the extreme form that it took, see Nadler, *Spinoza: A Life*, esp. 127–138.

divine aid. In other words, the notion of divine aid is allowed, but only in a form in which it is merely another name for purely natural occurrences.

On the basis of this principle, Spinoza explains the peculiar achievement of the Hebrew people by virtue of which they could be said to have been chosen by God. Denying that they possessed any superiority over other nations in either knowledge or virtue, he concludes that their "election" can refer only to their unique social organization, which enabled them to survive in a hostile environment for such a long period of time. This turns out to be far from complimentary, however, for the attribution of this organization to divine election merely reflects the fact that it is otherwise inexplicable how such a crude and ignorant people could have arrived at it by rational planning. Although there is nothing supernatural in such a state of affairs, in view of its evident incomprehensibility, Spinoza ironically notes that it could even be considered a miracle (G3 47; C2 114). Accordingly, for Spinoza this is the only sense in which one can meaningfully talk about the Jews as a "chosen people." Moreover, even the gift of prophecy, which was traditionally viewed as a sure sign of Jewish uniqueness, or divine favor, is of no significance in this regard. For, as Spinoza notes, Scripture itself clearly teaches, explicitly in the story of Balaam and implicitly in many other places, that the ability to prophesy was commonly attributed to individuals of other nations. Spinoza can, therefore, reaffirm his contention that the election of the Jews concerns only their social order, from which he concludes that "each Jew, considered alone and outside that social order and state, possess no gift of God which would place him above other men, and that there is no difference between him and a gentile" (G3 50; C2 118). And since this social order (the Hebrew commonwealth) no longer exists, Spinoza concludes that "today the Jews have nothing which they could attribute to themselves beyond all the Nations" (G3 56; C2 124).

In response, it might be objected that by arguing in this way Spinoza ignored the obvious fact that, despite all their oppression and suffering, the Jews had managed to survive as a people with a sense of identity and a common hope for the future. Just as Christian apologists often cited the incredible growth of Christianity in the oppressive atmosphere of the Roman Empire as a sign of divine favor, and hence as evidence of the truth of the Christian faith, so, too, Jewish thinkers have appealed to the very survival of Judaism as evidence of the divine election of the Hebrew people.[7] Spinoza

---

[7] The rapid spread of Christianity throughout the Roman Empire was one of the three "historical" proofs of the divine origin of the Christian revelation advanced by apologists (the other two being miracles and fulfilled prophecies). This argument was appealed to by Albert Blijenbergh (or Burgh) in his correspondence with Spinoza in an attempt to convince him of the truth of the Catholic faith

meets this issue head on, however, and his treatment might be considered an astute bit of sociological analysis. He cites two factors as jointly sufficient to account for Jewish survival, namely gentile hatred and circumcision. Far from destroying them, Spinoza claims that the experience of hatred and oppression unified the Jews and kept them in their traditional faith. He supports this claim by noting the different fate of the Jews in Spain and in Portugal. In both countries, Jews were compelled either to embrace Catholicism, the state religion, or go into exile. But whereas in Portugal they were forced to live apart and were considered unworthy of civic honors, and as a result they steadfastly maintained their traditional faith, in Spain the Jews who converted were made full-fledged citizens, with all the rights and privileges thereof, with the predictable result that they so intermingled with the Spaniards that "after a little while no traces of them remained, nor any memory" (G3 56; C2 124). Spinoza, however, seems to have attached even greater importance to circumcision, which he compares with the Chinese custom of keeping a tail on their head as a means of preserving their national identity. With regard to this traditional Jewish rite, he reflects: "I am convinced that this one thing will preserve this Nation to eternity. Indeed, if the foundations of their religion did not make their hearts unmanly, I would absolutely believe that some day, given the opportunity, they would set up their state again, and God would chose them anew" (G3 57; C2 124).

To complete his critique of traditional Judaism, Spinoza had to deal directly with the Mosaic law, or Torah. And in doing so, he also addressed one of the central issues that had led to his cherem some sixteen years earlier. For his claim, which certainly would not have pleased his Rabbinical instructors, is that it was largely because they were the recipients of this law, rather than by virtue of any special moral or intellectual powers, that the Jews lay claim to being a chosen people with a unique historical mission. Moreover, this law contains not only moral principles but also rules for worship, social organization, and diet. Indeed, it provides precepts governing almost every phase of daily life. During the Middle Ages, Jewish thinkers such as Maimonides attempted to explain and justify some of these rules, which did not seem to serve any explicitly moral purpose, e.g., the dietary laws, by suggesting that they had a spiritual significance. The goal of these efforts was to demonstrate that, apart from the laws concerning worship in the Temple, which obviously could not be observed after its destruction, all of these laws were obligatory for all Jews. The requirement

to which he had recently converted. For a discussion of this correspondence, which bears directly on Spinoza's views in the TTP, see Curley, "Spinoza's Exchange with Albert Burgh."

to observe a large number of apparently arbitrary laws concerning such morally indifferent matters as what one may or may not eat was ridiculous to a philosopher of the rigidly rationalist cast of mind of Spinoza. But rather than simply rejecting the entire corpus of Jewish law on the basis of an independent philosophical perspective, Spinoza attempts to analyze the actual significance of this law for the Hebrew people. Central to this analysis is the distinction between the divine and the ceremonial laws, both of which were presumably contained in the Mosaic revelation.

By "divine law" Spinoza understood those moral rules, dictated by reason, which describe what is necessary for the realization of human blessedness. This law is divine because blessedness, as we have seen from the *Ethics*, consists in the love of God and because it follows from the idea of God that is within us. The chief precept of this law for Spinoza is simply to love God as the highest good, rather than out of fear or in expectation of some further reward (G3 60–61; C2 128–129). Since this precept is universal and is, in fact, deduced from human nature, it is more properly described as an eternal truth than a command. According to Spinoza, however, though the prophets themselves wrote the law in the name of God, they did not adequately conceive God's dictates as eternal truths (G3 64; C2 132). Rather, because of their crude, anthropomorphic conception of the Deity, they viewed the divine law as the command of a sovereign. Thus, while the prophets taught the genuine divine law (love of God and one's neighbor), they did not present it in its proper, spiritual sense. Moreover, Spinoza suggests that it was Christ, who was sent to teach not only the Jews but the whole human race, who first taught the true sense of the law. That Christ was able to do this was because he possessed adequate ideas, or, in the carefully chosen language of the TTP, because he "perceived the things revealed truly and adequately" (G3 65; C2 133–134).

The situation with regard to the ceremonial laws is somewhat different. Ceremonies are defined by Spinoza as morally indifferent actions, which are called good or bad only by virtue of their institution; that is, by the fact that they have been commanded by God. Since ceremonies are by their very nature morally indifferent, they do not have an intrinsic or necessary role in the achievement of human blessedness for Spinoza. Consequently, the law commanding such practices (the ceremonial law) cannot, like the divine law, be viewed as an expression, however inadequate, of eternal truths. Nevertheless, Spinoza recognized that this law had great significance for the Jewish state, since its precepts constituted the civil legislation of that state. Moreover, in a manner analogous to his treatment of various institutions in monarchial and aristocratic forms of government in the TP, Spinoza shows in considerable detail how various aspects of this legislation, e.g., the laws concerning sacrifice and economic arrangements, were important in maintaining the stability of the state. The major upshot of the analysis, however, is that, since the significance of this law is limited to its function in the ancient Jewish state, and since this state no longer exists, Spinoza concludes that no contemporary Jew is under any obligation to keep the law (G3 69–80; C2 138–152).

9.3   The Interpretation of Scripture

Spinoza's thoroughgoing critique of revelation and of the special claims of Judaism rests, to a considerable extent, on an appeal to what he claims to be the express teachings of Scripture. The presentation and justification of the proper method for determining this sense is, therefore, an integral part of Spinoza's project, forming the subject matter of chapters 7–10 of the TTP. I have already noted that Spinoza proposed to approach Scripture like a good Cartesian, attributing nothing to it that cannot be clearly and distinctly seen to be contained therein, and we have now to consider what this means. Spinoza first (chapter 7) explains the basic principles of his exegetical method, then, in the succeeding chapters, applies these principles to the entire canon of the Old Testament and to some of the Epistles in the New Testament.

Although radical, Spinoza's approach to the Bible was not completely novel. As already noted, he had an important predecessor in Hobbes, who, despite some caution in his manner or presentation, expressed similar views regarding, prophecy, miracles, and the authorship and interpretation of biblical texts.[8] It appears, however, that the most important influence on Spinoza's understanding of the Hebrew Bible was the twelfth-century Jewish philosopher and commentator, Ibn Ezra, whom Spinoza himself cites as an authority and whose work was cited by Christian as well as Jewish commentators.[9] He is perhaps best known for arguing that Moses could not have been the author of the Pentateuch because, among other things, the final chapter of Deuteronomy depicts his death.[10] Another

---

[8] For a detailed analysis of Hobbes' views on the Bible, which includes a comparison with Spinoza's views, see Curley, "'I Durst Not Write so Boldly.'"
[9] For a discussion of Ibn Ezra's influence on Spinoza see Warren Zev Harvey, "Spinoza on Ibn Ezra's 'Secret of the Twelve.'"
[10] See Richard Popkin, "Spinoza and Biblical Scholarship," 386–387 and Nadler, *A Book Forged in Hell*, 108–109.

important critic of the historicity of the accounts in the Pentateuch was Isaac La Peyère, whose major work, *Prae-Adamitae* (Pre-Adamites), was in Spinoza's library, and where, as the title suggests, he argues by appealing to the Genesis account that Adam could not have been the first man, since it depicts Cain as having a wife.[11]

The essence of Spinoza's exegetical approach is concisely expressed in the famous formula: "[T]he method of interpreting Scripture does not widely differ at all from the method of interpreting nature, but agrees with it completely" (TTP 7 6; C2 171; G3 98). By this Spinoza meant that the Bible, which had been traditionally viewed as the literal word of God and hence as equally sacred in every syllable, is to be construed as a natural phenomenon, the product of purely human capacities and endeavors. In other words, it is to be interpreted in precisely the same manner as any other ancient text. With regard to any such text, the goal would be to arrive at the clear intent of the author, and any interpretation that twisted the sense of a given passage in order to make it conform to a previously accepted view would be rejected out of hand. Accordingly, Spinoza insists that the Bible is not to be considered as an exception to this rule, regardless of the consequences for traditional theology. Rather, just as Descartes, in his *Discourse on Method*, had argued that the proper method in the sciences must be clear and distinct conceptions, which serve as the foundation of all truth, so Spinoza, in what amounts to a discourse on the method for arriving at the true meaning of the Bible, points to the clear meaning of the text as the ultimate standard and source of its interpretation.

Assuming the above-mentioned analogy with nature, the first step in the development of a science of biblical interpretation is to determine the proper method for the interpretation of nature, which, as Spinoza tells us in typically oblique fashion, "consists above all in putting together a history of nature, from which, as from certain data, we infer the definitions of natural things" (G3 98; C2 171). By the "history of nature," Spinoza seems to have meant the sequence of actual events (in the language of the *Ethics*, the series of finite modes). He therefore appears to be describing an essentially Baconian inductive procedure, in which one moves from particular events to general laws ("certain fixed axioms") and from these back to the phenomena to be explained, rather than the deductive *more geometrico* of the *Ethics*. With regard to the Bible, the phenomena requiring explanation are the particular passages under consideration. The goal is to determine the true intentions of their authors and these intentions are to be

---

[11] See Popkin, "Spinoza and Biblical Scholarship," 390–391 and Nadler, *A Book Forged in Hell*, 118–120.

derived from fundamental principles; that is, general exegetical rules, which are themselves based on a consideration of the history of Scripture. By proceeding in this way, Spinoza reflects, "everyone – provided he has admitted no other principles or data for interpreting Scripture and discussing it than those drawn from Scripture itself and its history – everyone will always proceed without danger of error (G3 98; C2 171).[12] Under the rubric "history of Scripture," Spinoza had in mind three quite specific things. The first is a linguistic, or philological, analysis. Since the interpretation of any text requires an understanding of its language, it is necessary to investigate "the nature and properties of the language in which the books of the Bible were written, and in which their authors were accustomed to speak" (G3 99; C2 173). A thorough knowledge of the ancient Hebrew language is, therefore, the first prerequisite for accurate biblical exegesis, and it was no doubt with this in mind that Spinoza attempted to write a Hebrew grammar. Furthermore, Spinoza adds in a reflection, which suggests considerable historical insight, that this requirement holds not only for the Old Testament but also for the New, since the latter, though written in Greek, contains Hebrew modes of thought and speech (G3 100; C2 173).

Second, it is necessary to analyze each book and to arrange its topics under appropriate headings. This provides a general frame of reference for the interpretation of obscure passages. As an example of such a passage and of the proper way to handle it, Spinoza cites two statements attributed to Moses: "God is a fire" and "God is jealous." Although each of these statements is perfectly clear in and of itself, taken literally they are both absurd. The problem, therefore, is to determine whether they are in fact to be understood in a literal fashion. This requires a comparison of these passages with other relevant passages relating to Moses and a consideration of the ways in which these expressions were commonly used by biblical authors. The important point, which Spinoza emphasizes over against the defenders of the "reasonableness" of Scripture, which for Spinoza primarily meant the Maimonideans, is that if an alternative reading cannot be found by the above method, then the literal meaning must be accepted as the expression of the author's intent, no matter how absurd it may seem from the standpoint of a more "rational" conception of God. Applying this principle to the above statements, we find that since the notion of fire is used to denote anger and jealousy in the Old Testament, we can easily

---

[12] It seems that Spinoza's model for biblical exegesis is taken from Bacon's method of scientific inquiry. See Nadler, *A Book Forged in Hell*, 132–133.

reconcile the two statements and conclude that, in describing God as fire, Moses was merely trying to indicate, through a common metaphor, that God was jealous. The situation is somewhat different with regard to jealousy, however, since there is no textual evidence to support the claim that Scripture denies that God has passions. Hence, despite the completely unphilosophical nature of this doctrine, we must conclude that Moses actually taught that God was jealous and not try to read some more philosophically acceptable sense into the passage by interpreting it metaphorically or allegorically.

Third, one must consider certain topics relevant to the composition of each book. More specifically, we need information about the life, times, and situation of the author, as well as some knowledge of the purpose and occasion for which the book in question was written. The crucial importance of this kind of information is obvious from the analysis of prophecy, where it was shown that the teachings of the prophets reflect their dispositions, circumstances, and backgrounds, rather than either divine inspiration or exceptional acuity. Finally, Spinoza claims that it is also necessary to inquire into the history of each book, including how it was first received, how many different versions existed, and how it became part of the canon. In short, it is essential to have an accurate historical knowledge of both the author and the text, for it is only in light of such knowledge that the true meaning of the text can be determined and the "divinity" of Scripture established.

Although he acknowledges that a number of difficulties prevent the attainment of this knowledge, Spinoza is quick to point out that they concern only the interpretation of the speculative teaching of the prophets, for example their conception of God, and not their moral teachings, which are clear even to the unlearned (G3 III; C2 185). Paramount among these difficulties are the very limited nature of our historical knowledge and an almost total lack of knowledge of the nuances of the ancient Hebrew language. Moreover, above and beyond the difficulties arising from the limitations of our knowledge there is the problem that the very traditions and sources on which this knowledge is based are unsound. Spinoza is here referring to the received, orthodox views concerning the authorship of the various books of the Bible, the dates of their composition, their internal agreement, and the histories of the texts. The orthodox view of these matters, in both the Jewish and Christian traditions, was based on the assumption of the absolute infallibility of the text. Accordingly, each book in the canon was regarded as a unitary work, written in its entirety by the designated author. And in order to preserve their assumed inerrancy, it was necessary to maintain that the texts had remained unaltered from the time of their composition until the present. According to Spinoza, such views, which had been challenged by Ibn Ezra, Hobbes, La Peyère, and others, effectively reduce the Bible to nonsense. Thus, he includes within the TTP a detailed discussion of the authorship and history of the main books of the Old Testament, which is largely based on the work of Ibn Ezra and some brief considerations regarding some of the Epistles of the New Testament.

Typical of Spinoza's approach is his treatment of the Pentateuch, which had been traditionally ascribed to Moses and, therefore, referred to as the "Five Books of Moses." Following the views of the above-mentioned commentators, Spinoza rehearses the familiar reasons why Moses could not have been the author of the entire Pentateuch. And as an alternative explanation, he suggests that these books, as well as many others in the canon, were compiled from a variety of sources by Ezra, the scribe who, together with Nehemiah, is traditionally credited with the reconstruction of the Temple and the revival of the religious tradition after the exile. In defense of this hypothesis, Spinoza suggests that it explains the unity of theme and language found in the various books. But since this unity is far from complete and the various books contain a number of alternative and incompatible narratives, Spinoza also suggests that Ezra did not put the finishing touches on these narratives, but merely collected them from a variety of sources "sometimes just copying them, and he left them to posterity without having examined or ordered them" (G3 129; C2 206). The remaining books of the Hebrew Bible or Old Testament, the prophetic books and the wisdom literature, are dealt with in a similar fashion, though in far less detail. Here Spinoza's general statement must suffice: "When I pay close attention to these books, I see that the Prophecies in them have been collected from other books and that they aren't always written down in the same order in which the Prophets themselves spoke or wrote them" (G3 142; C2 227).

Finally, the New Testament is treated in an extremely sketchy fashion. The Gospels are completely ignored, and the main point emphasized is that the obvious disagreements between the apostles, whom Spinoza considers as prophets, must not be resolved by any appeal to a mystical exegesis, but should simply be recognized as a perfectly natural consequence of the fact that each of the apostolic authors was a teacher as well as a prophet and, as such, was concerned to communicate the Christian faith *as he understood it*. Thus, basic disagreements, such as that between James and Paul regarding the roles of faith and works in salvation, which generated acrimonious theological disputes, are not to be explained away, but frankly accepted as expressions of different philosophical viewpoints (G3 151–158; C2 240–247).

9.4   Faith and Superstition

Spinoza presents his critique of revelation, the Jewish claim to divine election, and the infallibility of Scripture as part of an endeavor to separate true religion from superstition and to determine the respective spheres of religion, so conceived, and philosophy. Moreover, as we have already seen, one of his avowed reasons for publishing the TTP was his desire to answer the charges of atheism that had been raised against him. Indeed, Spinoza constantly affirms within the work that his arguments relate only to superstition and that they do not undermine true religion or the public peace. Accordingly, to complete our picture of Spinoza's views on religion, the analysis of his critique must be supplemented by some consideration of what he considers to be "true religion" and the function that he here attributes to it.

Actually, Spinoza's position on this point is quite simple, and, in one respect at least, is straightforwardly presented in the TTP. Genuine, or true, religion, the religion taught by all the prophets and the apostles, is morality. This morality, however, is presented in a form in which the multitude can appreciate it. In effect, this means that the Bible presents moral principles by appealing to the imagination, rather than to the intellect, and hence as decrees of God, rather than the eternal truths that they actually are. Since the multitude is led by imagination rather than reason, religion has a necessary social function. Such a view of religion was hardly original with Spinoza. It had already been formulated explicitly by the Arabian philosopher Ibn-Rushd, or Averroës, in the twelfth century,[13] and had found expression in many subsequent politically minded thinkers, most notably Machiavelli.[14] Nevertheless, though not original with Spinoza, it is an integral part of his political thought, since it allows him to both "save religion" and guarantee the autonomy of philosophy.

Here too, Spinoza's strategy requires that he show that this conception of religion and its function is derived from, rather than imposed upon, Scripture. To this end, he emphasizes the fact that, despite vast internal

---

[13] Averroës expressed this view most clearly in his classic work *On the Harmony of Religion and Philosophy*. For a clear statement of the Averroistic position and its influence in the West, see Gilson, *Reason and Revelation in the Middle Ages*, 37–66.

[14] For a discussion of Machiavelli's religious views in relation to those of Spinoza, see Strauss, *Spinoza's Critique of Religion*, 48–49.

disagreement in speculative matters, the Bible in its entirety teaches the same moral doctrine. This doctrine is the demand to love God above all things and one's neighbor as oneself. But since the love of God is manifested only in the love of one's neighbor, Spinoza maintains that the moral teaching of the Bible really reduces to the latter demand. Other moral doctrines found in Scripture, such as those contained in the Ten Commandments, are held to be derived from this principle. This love is, therefore, the genuine kernel of true religion that survives all historical and philosophical criticism. To the extent to which the Bible teaches this love, and to this extent alone, it may be considered the word of God. Moreover, since both the prophets and the apostles addressed their messages to the multitude, this moral teaching is expressed in a simple form, easily comprehensible by everyone. The obvious implication of this is that one should not try to find in the Bible more than is there. It does contain a sound moral teaching, expressed in a popular form, and this enables it to inculcate piety and voluntary obedience (really two expressions for the same thing). But since it does not contain any speculative truths, it should not be treated as an authority on such matters.

On the basis of this conception of the Bible as a virtual textbook of public morality, the function of which is to inspire voluntary obedience, Spinoza develops a doctrine of religious faith and delineates the basic articles of the "true Catholic faith." This faith, we are told, consists in "thinking such things about God that if you had no knowledge of them, obedience to God would be destroyed, whereas if you are obedient to God, you necessarily have those thoughts" (G3175; C2 266). Spinoza's point is that, while a willingness to obey God, or, what for Spinoza amounts to the same thing, a disposition to practice justice and charity toward one's neighbors, entails having certain beliefs, these beliefs need not involve any strong cognitive claims (and certainly not of the kind involved in the second and third forms of cognition); rather, they serve as vehicles for fostering the appropriate disposition. Spinoza lists seven such articles of faith:

  I. *God exists, i.e., there is a supreme being, supremely just and merciful,* or *a model of true life.* Anyone who doesn't know or doesn't believe that God exists cannot obey him or know him as a Judge.

 II. *He is unique.* No one can doubt that this too is absolutely required for supreme devotion, admiration and love toward God. For devotion, admiration and love arise only because the excellence of one surpasses that of the rest.

III. *He is present everywhere, or everything is open to him.* If people believed some things were hidden from him, or did not know that he sees all, they would have doubts about the equity of the Justice by which he directs all things – or at least they would not be aware of it.

IV. *He has the supreme right and dominion over all things, and does nothing because he is compelled by a law, but acts only according to his absolute good pleasure and special grace.* For everyone is absolutely bound to obey him, whereas he is not bound to obey anyone.

V. *The worship of God and obedience to him consist only in Justice and Loving-kindness, or in love toward one's neighbor.*

VI. *Everyone who obeys God by living in this way is saved; the rest, who live under the control of pleasure, are lost.* If men did not firmly believe this, there would be no reason why they should prefer to obey God rather than pleasures.

VII. *Finally, God pardons the sins of those who repent.* No one is without sin. So if we did not maintain this, everyone would despair of his salvation, and there would be no reason why anyone would believe God to be merciful. Moreover, whoever firmly believes that God, out of mercy and the grace by which he directs everything, pardons men's sins, and who for this reason is more inspired by the love of God, that person really knows Christ according to the Spirit, and Christ is in him (G3 177–178; C2 268–269).

The articles of this brief creed are very close to the list of "fundamentals" that were taught by liberal Christians of the time, such as the Latitudinarians in England and the Collegiants and Mennonites in the Netherlands, with whom, as we have seen, Spinoza had a close association. The above-mentioned groups held these fundamentals to be the essential doctrines necessary for salvation. This approach resulted in a simplified, ethically oriented Christianity, with considerable toleration of differences of opinion with regard to the nonessential, or "indifferent," teachings of the various denominations. In reality, however, Spinoza's Averroistic conception of religion is far more radical than these liberal versions of Christianity. For, while these liberal groups desired to simplify doctrine in the interest of both a more sincere faith and a more harmonious society, they adhered in a straightforward way to this simplified faith. Spinoza, on the other hand, distinguishes sharply between the truth of these dogmas and their effectiveness in inculcating obedience. Moreover, unlike the Christian groups, his concern is solely with the latter. "Faith," he writes, "requires not so much true doctrines, as pious doctrines, i.e., those doctrines which move the heart to obedience, even if many of them do not have even the shadow of the truth" (TTP 14 20; C2 267; G3 176).

Nevertheless, we are here far from the intellectual love of God of the *Ethics*, and it is only Spinoza's Averroism that can reconcile such a creed with the basic principles of his metaphysics. The God of religious faith, unlike the God of philosophy, is decked out in human attributes and functions as a lawgiver and judge. Moreover, the religious person views salvation as a reward for virtue, rather than virtue itself, and requires a belief in the mercy and forgiveness of God, without which one would despair of this salvation. The point, however, is that such faith does not contradict but rather operates on an entirely different level from philosophical truth. Its articles are necessary to inculcate piety, or virtue, not in the free individual or philosopher, who lives according to the dictates of reason, but in the multitude, which can never rise above the first level of knowledge. Religion, therefore, appeals to the imagination. It presents moral rules as the commands of a personal God, reinforces these rules with signs and wonders, and connects them with the powerful passions of hope and fear, which are the chief moving forces for the great majority of human beings. In the end, then, true religion differs from superstition not in its truth value, but merely in its usefulness for inculcating obedience and mutual love in the multitude. Superstition, by its very nature, is divisive; it breeds intolerance and social chaos. Genuine, or ethically oriented, religion, on the other hand, is not only a desirable social force, but a necessary ingredient in any society that is not composed entirely of philosophers.

Finally, it is only in light of this conception of religion that we can understand the role that Spinoza assigns to religion in the state and the fact that he grants to the sovereign power supreme right in matters of public worship. This latter point, which seems to contradict his advocacy of freedom of thought, is a logical consequence of the purely social function that Spinoza attributes to religion. This function is to inspire voluntary obedience, and so it is only appropriate that religion be under the control of that power to whom obedience is due, namely the sovereign. Moreover, far from violating liberty of thought, such secular control serves for Spinoza to guarantee it. As the situation in the Netherlands made perfectly clear to him, ecclesiastical control of public affairs was the great enemy of personal liberty. After all, it was the Calvinist clergy who were intolerant and demanded a share of sovereign power. Nor did Spinoza see this demand for political power as a peculiar aberration of Calvinism; rather, he regarded it as a typical attitude on the part of any religious orthodoxy that holds that human beings can be saved only by adherence to its particular creed. Thus, like Hobbes, Spinoza saw in secular control over religion a check on ecclesiastical power and on the fanaticism that the exercise of such power inevitably incites in the multitude. And since sovereign power can control only actions and not thought, its control over religion is limited to observances, or ceremonies. But since these are really indifferent – that is, not intrinsically connected with beliefs – the sovereign's control over such matters serves only to keep the public peace and does not interfere with anyone's freedom of thought. Thus, paradoxical as it may seem, Spinoza, an apostate Jew living in a Christian country, advocates an official state religion, characterized in essentially Christian terms, as the best protection of the freedom of philosophy.

Bibliography

Allison, Henry E. *Kant's Conception of Freedom: A Developmental and Critical Analysis*, Cambridge: Cambridge University Press (2019).

"Kant's Critique of Spinoza," in *Studies in Philosophy and the History of Philosophy: The Philosophy of Baruch Spinoza*, edited by Richard Kennington, Washington, DC: Catholic University of America Press (1980), 99–127.

Kant's Transcendental Deduction: An Analytical and Historical Commentary, Oxford: Oxford University Press (2015).

"The Eternity of Mind: Comments on Matson on Spinoza," in *Spinoza Issues and Directions: The Proceeding of the Chicago Spinoza Conference*, edited by Edwin Curley and Pierre-François Moreau, Leiden; New York: Brill (1990), 96–101.

Aristotle. *Categories: The Works of Aristotle Translated into English*, translated by E. M. Edghill, vol. 1, Oxford: Oxford University Press (1955).

Ariew, Roger and Gabbey, Alan. "The Scholastic Background," in *The Cambridge History of Seventeenth-Century Philosophy*, vol. 2, edited by Daniel Garber and Michael Ayers, Cambridge: Cambridge University Press (1998), 425–453.

Averroës. *On the Harmony of Religion and Philosophy*, translated by George F. Hourani, Oxford: Oxbow Books (2012).

Barker, H. "Notes on the Second Part of Spinoza's Ethics," in *Studies in Spinoza: Critical and Interpretive Essays*, edited by S. Paul Kashap, Berkeley; Los Angeles; London: University of California Press (1972), 101–167.

Spinoza, New York; London: Routledge (2008).

Baxley, Anne Margaret. *Kant's Theory of Virtue: The Value of Autocracy*, Cambridge: Cambridge University Press (2015).

Bayle, Pierre. *Historical and Critical Dictionary*, selections, translated by Richard Popkin, Indianapolis; New York: Bobbs-Merrill (1965).

Boehm, Omri. *Kant's Critique of Spinoza*, New York: Oxford University Press (2014).

Carriero, John. "Conatus," in *Spinoza's Ethics: A Critical Guide*, edited by Yitzhak Y. Melamed, Cambridge: Cambridge University Press (2017), 142–167.

"On the Relation between Mode and Substance in Spinoza's Metaphysics," *Journal of the History of Philosophy* 33 (2) (1995), 245–273.

Cassirer, Ernst. *Das Erkenntnisproblem in der Philosophie und Wissenschaft der neueren Zeit*, vol. 2, Berlin: Bruno Cassirer (1911).

Clarke, Desmond. "Descartes' Philosophy of Science and the Scientific Revolution," in *The Cambridge Companion to Descartes*, edited by John Cottingham, Cambridge: Cambridge University Press (1992), 258–285.

Colerus, John. *The Life of Benedict de Spinoza*, English translation, London (1706), reprinted in Sir Frederick Pollock, *Spinoza: His Life and Philosophy*, 2nd ed., London (1899), 387–418.

Cottingham, John G. "The Intellect, the Will, and the Passions: Spinoza's Critique of Descartes," *Journal of the History of Philosophy* 26 (1988), 39–54.

Curley, Edwin. *Behind the Geometrical Method: A Reading of Spinoza's Ethics*, Princeton, NJ: Princeton University Press (1988).

  "Descartes, Spinoza and the Ethics of Belief," in *Spinoza: Essays in Interpretation*, edited by E. Freeman and M. Mandelbaum, La Salle, IL: Open Court (1975), 159–189.

  "'I Durst Not Write so Boldly,' or How to Read Hobbes' Theological-Political Thesis," in *Hobbes e Spinoza, scienze e politica: atti del Convegno internazionale, Urbino, 14–17 ottobre, 1988*, Urbino: Bibliopolis (1988).

  "Kissinger, Spinoza and Genghis Kahn," in *The Cambridge Companion to Spinoza*, edited by Don Garrett, Cambridge: Cambridge University Press (1996), 315–335.

  "Spinoza's Exchange with Albert Burg," in *Spinoza's Theological-Political Treatise: A Critical Guide*, edited by Yitzhak Y. Melamed and Michael A. Rosenthal, Cambridge: Cambridge University Press (2010), 11–28.

  Spinoza's Metaphysics: An Essay in Interpretation, Cambridge, MA: Harvard University Press (1969).

Curley, Edwin with Walski,Gregory. "Spinoza's Necessitarianism Reconsidered," in *New Essays on the Rationalists*, edited by Rocco J. Genaro and Charles Huenemann, New York: Oxford University Press (1999), 241–262.

Delahunty, R. J. *Spinoza: The Arguments of the Philosophers*, London: Routledge and Kegan Paul (1985).

Deleuze, Gilles. *Spinoza: Practical Philosophy*, San Francisco, CA: City Lights Books (1988).

Della Rocca, Michael. "Egoism and the Imitation of Affects in Spinoza," in *Spinoza by 2000: The Jerusalem Conferences, Ethica IV: Spinoza on Reason and the "Free Man," Ethica IV Spinoza on Reason and the "Free Man,"* Spinoza by 2000 The Jerusalem Conferences, edited by Yirmiyahu Yovel and Gideon Segal, New York: Little Room Press (2004), 123–147.

  Representation and the Mind–Body Problem in Spinoza, New York: Oxford University Press (1996).

  Spinoza, London; New York: Routledge (2008).

Descartes, René. *Descartes' Philosophical Letters*, trans. and edited by Anthony Kenny, Oxford: Clarendon Press (1970).

The Philosophical Writings of Descartes, trans. John Cottingham, Robert Stoothoff, and Dugald Murdoch, Cambridge: Cambridge University Press (1984), 2 vols.

Donagan, Alan. "Essence and the Distinction of Attributes," in *Spinoza: A Collection of Critical Essays*, edited by Marjorie Grene, Notre Dame, IN: University of Notre Dame Press (1979), 164–181.

Spinoza, Chicago, IL: Chicago University Press (1988).

"Spinoza's Proof of Immortality," in *Spinoza: A Collection of Critical Essays*, edited by Marjorie Grene, Notre Dame, IN: University of Notre Dame Press (1979), 241–258.

Förster, Eckart. "Goethe's Spinozism," in *Spinoza and German Idealism*, edited by Eckart Förster and Yitzhak Y. Melamed, Cambridge: Cambridge University Press (2012), 85–99.

Freudenthal, J. *Spinoza Leben und Lehre*, 2nd ed., edited by C. Gebhardt, *Bibliotheca Spinoza curis Societatis Spinozanae*, vol. 5, Heidelberg: Carl Winter (1927).

Garber, Daniel. "Descartes and Spinoza on Persistence and Conatus," in *Studia Spinozana: Spinoza and Descartes*, edited by J. M. Beyssade, W. Klever, and M. Wilson, vol. 10, Würzburg: Königshausen & Neumann (1994), 43–67.

"Descartes' Physics," in *The Cambridge Companion to Descartes*, edited by John Cottingham, Cambridge: Cambridge University Press (1992), 286–334.

"Dr. Fichelson's Dilemma: Spinoza on Freedom and Sociability," in *Spinoza by 2000: The Jerusalem Conferences, Ethica IV: Spinoza on Reason and the "Free Man,"* edited by Yirmiyahu Yovel and Gideon Segal, New York: Little Room Press (2004), 183–207.

"Religion and the Civil State in the TP," in *Spinoza's Political Treatise: A Critical Guide*, edited by Yitzhak Y. Melamed and Hasana Sharp, Cambridge: Cambridge University Press (2018), 128–144.

Garrett, Aaron. *Meaning in Spinoza's Method*, Cambridge: Cambridge University Press (2003).

Garrett, Don. *Nature and Necessity in Spinoza's Philosophy*, New York: Oxford University Press (2018).

"Promising Ideas: Hobbes and Contract in Spinoza's Political Philosophy," in *Spinoza's Theological-Political Treatise: A Critical Guide*, edited by Yitzhak Y. Melamed and Michael Rosenthal, Cambridge: Cambridge University Press (2013), 192–209.

Gatens, Moira. "The Condition of Human Nature Spinoza's Account of the Ground of Human Action in the Tractatus Politicus," in *Spinoza's Political Treatise: A Critical Guide*, edited by Yitzhak Y. Melamed and Michael Rosenthal, Cambridge: Cambridge University Press (2013), 47–60.

Gilson, Etienne. *Reason and Revelation in the Middle Ages*, New York: Scribner (1938).

Gough, J. W. *The Social Contract*, 2nd ed., Oxford: Clarendon Press (1957).

Graetz, H. *Popular History of the Jews*, trans. A. B. Rhine, 5th ed., vol. 5, New York: Jordan Publishing, 1935.

Grotius, Hugo. *The Law of War and Peace*, trans. Francis W. Kelsey, Indianapolis, IN; New York: The Bobbs-Merrill Company, Inc. (1925).

Gueroult, Martial. *Spinoza I, Dieu (Ethique* I), Paris: Aubier (1968).

Spinoza II, L'Ame (Ethique II), Hildesheim: Georg Olms (1970).

Haakonssen, Knud. "Divine/Natural Law Theories in Ethics," in *The Cambridge History of Seventeenth Century Philosophy*, edited by Daniel Garber and Michael Ayers, Cambridge: Cambridge University Press (1998), 1317–1357.

Hallett, H. F. "On a Reputed Equivoque in the Philosophy of Spinoza," in *Studies in Spinoza Critical and Interpretive Essays*, edited by S. Paul Kashap, Berkeley; Los Angeles; London: University of California Press (1972), 168–188.

Hampshire, Stuart. *Freedom of Mind*, Oxford: Oxford University Press (1972).

Spinoza, London: Faber (1954).

Hardin, C. L. "Spinoza on Immortality and Time," in *Spinoza: New Perspectives*, edited by R. W. Shahan and J. Biro, Norman: University of Oklahoma Press (1979), 129–138.

Harris, Errol E. "Spinoza's Theory of Human Immortality," in *Spinoza: Essays in Interpretation*, edited by E. Freeman and M. Mandelbaum, La Salle, Illinois: Open Court (1975), 159–189.

Harvey, Warren Zev. "Politically Mediated Affects Envy in Spinoza's Tractatus Politicus," in *Spinoza's Political Treatise: A Critical Guide*, edited by Yitzhak Y. Melamed and Hasana Sharp, Cambridge: Cambridge University Press (2018), 61–77.

"Spinoza on Ibn Ezra's 'Secret of the Twelve,'" in *Spinoza's Theological-Political Treatise: A Critical Guide*, edited by Yitzhak Y. Melamed and Michael A. Rosenthal, Cambridge: Cambridge University Press (2010), 41–55.

Hobbes, Thomas. *De Cive or The Citizen*, New York: Appleton-Century-Crofts Incorporated (1949).

Leviathan, Oxford: Oxford University Press (1958).

Höffding, Harald. *Spinozas Ethica: Analyse und Charakteristik*, Heidelberg: Curtis Societatis Spinozanae (1924).

Hooker, Michael. "The Deductive Character of Spinoza's Metaphysics," in *Studies in Philosophy and the History of Philosophy: The Philosophy of Baruch Spinoza*, edited by Richard Kennington, Washington, DC: The Catholic University of America Press (1980), 17–34.

Hübner, Karolina. "Spinoza on Being Human and Human Perfection," in *Essays on Spinoza's Ethical Theory*, edited by Matthew J. Kisner and Andrew Youpa, Oxford: Oxford University Press (2014), 124–142.

Hume, David. *An Enquiry Concerning Human Understanding*, edited by Tom L. Beauchamp, Oxford: Oxford University Press (1999).

A Treatise of Human Nature, vol. 1, edited by David Fate Norton and Mary Norton, Oxford: Oxford University Press (2007).

James, Susan. *Passion and Action: The Emotions in Seventeenth-Century Philosophy*, Oxford: Oxford University Press (1997).

"Spinoza, the Body, and the Good Life," in *Essays on Spinoza's Ethical Theory*, edited by Matthew J. Kisner and Andrew Youpa, Oxford: Oxford University Press (2014), 143–159.

Jarrett, Charles. "The Concept of Substance and Mode in Spinoza," *Philosophia* 7 (1977), 83–105.

Joachim, H. H. *A Study of the Ethics of Spinoza*, London, 1901. Reprint. New York: Russell and Russell, 1964.

Spinoza's Tractatus de Intellectus Emendatione, Oxford: Clarendon Press, 1940.

Jonas, Hans. "Spinoza and the Theory of Organism," in *Spinoza: A Collection of Critical Essays*, edited by Marjorie Grene, Notre Dame and Indiana, IN: University of Notre Dame Press (1979), 259–278.

Kant, Immanuel. "An Answer to the Question: What Is Enlightenment," trans. Mary J. Gregor, *The Cambridge Edition of the Works of Immanuel Kant*, Cambridge: Cambridge University Press (1996), 17–22.

Critique of Pure Reason, trans. Paul Guyer and Allen Wood, *The Cambridge Edition of the Works of Immanuel Kant*, Cambridge: Cambridge University Press (1998).

Groundwork for the Metaphysics of Morals, trans. Mary Gregor, *The Cambridge Edition of the Works of Immanuel Kant*, Cambridge: Cambridge University Press (1996), 43–108.

Lectures on the Philosophical Doctrine of Religion, trans. Allen Wood, *The Cambridge Edition of the Works of Immanuel Kant, Religion and Rational Theology*, Cambridge: Cambridge University Press (1996), 335–451.

The Only Possible Basis for a Demonstration of the Existence of God, trans. David Walford, *The Cambridge Edition of the Works of Immanuel Kant*, Cambridge: Cambridge University Press (1992), 111–201.

Kisner, Matthew J. *Spinoza on Human Freedom*, Cambridge: Cambridge University Press (2011).

Klein, Julia R. "Spinoza and Gersonides on Intellectual Eternity," in *Spinoza and Medieval Jewish Philosophy*, edited by Steven Nadler, Cambridge: Cambridge University Press (2014), 177–203.

Klever, W. N. A. "Spinoza's Life and Works," in *The Cambridge Companion to Spinoza*, edited by Don Garrett, Cambridge: Cambridge University Press (1996), 13–60.

Kneale, Martha. "Eternity and Sempiternity," in *Spinoza: A Collection of Critical Essays*, edited by Marjorie Grene, Notre Dame and Indiana, IN: University of Notre Dame Press (1979), 227–240.

Lebuffe, Michael. "The Anatomy of the Passions," in *The Cambridge Companion to Spinoza's Ethics*, edited by Olli Koistinen, Cambridge: Cambridge University Press (2009), 188–222.

Leibniz, Gottfried Wilhelm. "Discourse on Metaphysics," in *Philosophical Papers and Letters*, edited and translated by Leroy E. Loemker, Chicago, IL: The University of Chicago Press (1956), vol. 1, 464–506.

"On the Ethics of Benedict de Spinoza," in *Philosophical Papers and Letters*, edited and translated by Leroy E. Loemker, Chicago, IL: The University of Chicago Press (1956), vol. 1, 300–316.

"The Monadology," in *Philosophical Papers and Letters*, edited and translated by Leroy E. Loemker, Chicago, IL: The University of Chicago Press (1956), vol. 2, 1044–1061.

Machiavelli, Nicolai. *The Discourses*, trans. J. Walker, S.J., London: Penguin Books (1998).

The Prince, trans. Luigi Ricci, New York: Mentor Books (1955).

Mark, Thomas Carson. *Spinoza's Theory of Truth*, New York: Columbia University Press (1972).

Martineau, J. *A Study of Spinoza*, London: Macmillan (1882).

Matheron, Alexandre. *Individu et Communauté chez Spinoza*, Paris: Les Éditions de Minuit (1969).

Matson, Wallace. "Body Essence and Mind Eternity in Spinoza," in *Spinoza Issues and Directions: The Proceeding of the Chicago Spinoza Conference*, edited by Edwin Curley and Pierre-François Moreau, Leiden: Brill (1990), 82–95.

"Spinoza's Theory of Mind," in *Spinoza: Essays in Interpretation*, edited by E. Freeman and M. Mandelbaum, La Salle, IL: Open Court (1975), 49–60.

Melamed, Yitzhak Y. *Spinoza's Metaphysics: Substance and Thought*, Oxford: Oxford University Press (2013).

"The Building Blocks of Spinoza's Metaphysics, Substance, Attributes, and Modes," in *The Oxford Handbook of Spinoza*, edited by Michael Della Rocca, Oxford: Oxford University Press (2018), 84–113.

"When Having Too Much Power Is Harmful: Spinoza on Political Luck," in *Spinoza's Political Treatise: A Critical Guide*, edited by Yitzhak Y. Melamed, Cambridge: Cambridge University Press (2018), 161–174.

McShea, Robert J. *The Political Philosophy of Spinoza*, New York: Columbia University Press (1969).

Nadler, Steven. *A Book Forged in Hell: Spinoza's Scandalous Treatise and the Birth of the Secular Age*, Princeton, NJ: Princeton University Press (2011).

"Doctrines of Explanation in Late Scholasticism and in the Mechanical Philosophy," in *The Cambridge History of Seventeenth Century Philosophy*, edited by Daniel Garber and Michael Ayers, Cambridge: Cambridge University Press (1998), 513–552.

Spinoza: A Life, Cambridge: Cambridge University Press (1999).

Spinoza's Ethics: An Introduction, Cambridge: Cambridge University Press (2006).

Spinoza's Heresy: Immortality and the Jewish Mind, Oxford: Clarendon Press (2001).

"The Lives of Others: Spinoza on Benevolence as a Rational Virtue," in *Essays on Spinoza's Ethical Theory*, edited by Matthew J. Kisner and Andrew Youpa, Oxford: Oxford University Press (2014), 41–56.

"Whatever Is, Is in God: Substance and Things in Spinoza's Metaphysics," in *Interpreting Spinoza: Critical Essays*, edited by Charlie Huenemann, Cambridge: Cambridge University Press (2008), 53–70.

Nietzsche, Friedrich. "Postcard to Overbeck," in *The Portable Nietzsche*, edited and translated by Walter Kaufman, New York: The Viking Press (1954).

Parkinson, G. H. R. *Spinoza's Theory of Knowledge*, Oxford: The Clarendon Press (1954).

Peterman, Alison. "The 'Physical Interlude,'" in *Spinoza's Ethics: A Critical Guide*, edited by Yitzak Y. Melamed, Cambridge: Cambridge University Press (2018), 102–120.

Pollock, F. *Spinoza: His Life and Philosophy*, 2nd ed., London (1899). Reprint. New York: American Scholar Publications (1966).

Popkin, Richard H. "The Historical Significance of Sephardic Judaism in 17th Century Amsterdam," *American Sephardi, Journal of the Sephardic Studies Program of Yeshiva University* 5 (1–2) (1971), 18–27.

Primus, Kristin. "Scientia Intuitiva in the *Ethics*," in *Spinoza's Ethics: A Critical Guide*, edited by Yitzhak Y. Melamed, Cambridge: Cambridge University Press (2017), 169–186.

Radner, Dasie, "Spinoza's Theory of Ideas," *Philosophical Review* 80 (1971), 338–359.

Randall, John Herman, Jr. *Aristotle*, New York: Columbia University Press (1960).

Rorty, Amelie. "Spinoza on the Pathos of Idolatrous Love and the Hilarity of True Love," in *Feminist Interpretations of Benedict Spinoza*, edited by Moira Gatens, State College: Pennsylvania State University Press (2009), 65–86.

Ross, W. D. *Aristotle: A Complete Exposition of His Works and Thought*, Cleveland, OH; New York: Meridian Books (1959).

Roth, Leon. *Spinoza*, London: Allen and Unwin (1954).

Schmaltz, Tad M. "Descartes on the Metaphysics of the Material World," *Philosophical Review* 127 (1) (2018), 1–40.

Shapiro, Lisa. "The Workings of the Human Mind," in *Spinoza's Ethics: A Critical Guide*, edited by Yitzhak Y. Melamed, Cambridge: Cambridge University Press (2017), 205–223.

Sharp, Hasana. "Family Quarrels and Mental Harmony: Spinoza's Oikos Polis Analogy," in *Spinoza's Political Treatise: A Critical Guide*, edited by Yitzhak Y. Melamed and Hasana Sharp, Cambridge: Cambridge University Press (2018), 92–110.

Shein, Noa. "Spinoza's Theory of Attributes," in *Stanford Encyclopedia of Philosophy* (Spring 2018 Edition), edited by Edward N. Zalta, https://plato.stanford.edu/archives/spr2018/entries/spinoza-attributes.

Silverthorne, Michael and Kisner, Matthew J. *Spinoza: Ethics – Proved in Geometrical Order*, Cambridge: Cambridge University Press (2018).

Steinberg, Justin. *Spinoza's Political Psychology: The Taming of Fortune and Fear*, Cambridge: Cambridge University Press (2018).

Stern, Robert. *Hegelian Metaphysics*, Oxford: Oxford University Press (2009).

Stewart, Matthew. *The Courtier and the Heretic: Leibniz, Spinoza, and the Fate of God in the Modern World*, New York; London: W.W. Norton & Company (2006).

Strauss, Leo. *Spinoza's Critique of Religion*, trans. E. M. Sinclair, New York: Schocken Books (1965).

Taylor, A. E. "Some Incoherencies in Spinozism, II," in *Studies in Spinoza Critical and Interpretive Essays*, edited by S. Paul Kashap, Berkeley; Los Angeles; London: University of California Press (1972), 289–309.

Tuck, Richard. *Natural Rights Theories: Their Origin and Development*, Cambridge: Cambridge University Press (1979).

Varden, Helga. "Kant and Lying to the Murderer at the Door," *Journal of Social Philosophy* 41 (2010), 403–421.

Vaughan, C. E. *Studies in the History of Political Philosophy Before and After Rousseau*, vol. 1, Manchester: Manchester University Press (1925).

Walker, Ralph. "Spinoza and the Coherence Theory of Truth," *Mind* 94 (1985), 1–18.

Wernham, A. G. (ed. and trans.). *Spinoza's Political Works*, Oxford: Clarendon Press (1958).

Wilson, Margaret Dauler. "Objects, Ideas and 'Minds': Comments on Spinoza's Theory of Mind," in *The Philosophy of Baruch Spinoza*, edited by Richard Kennington, Washington, DC: The Catholic University of America Press (1980), 103–120.

Wolf, A. "The Life of Spinoza," in *Spinoza's Short Treatise: On God, Man and His Well-Being*, New York: Russell & Russell Inc. (1963), xi–cvi.

Wolfson, H. A. *The Philosophy of Spinoza*, 2 vols., New York: Meridian Books (1958).

Yovel, Yirmiyahu. *Spinoza and Other Heretics*, vol. 1: *The Marrano of Reason*, Princeton, NJ: Princeton University Press (1989).

Spinoza and Other Heretics, vol. 2: *The Adventures of Immanence*, Princeton, NJ: Princeton University Press (1989).

Index

absolute sovereignty, 204, 206, 209, 213, 215,
  220, 223
adequate ideas
  affects and, 125, 147, 156–158, 188
  causation and, 124
  cognition and, 110, 113, 115–116, 173, 199–202
  common notions distinguished from, 112
  conatus and, 133
  definition of, 90
  emotions and, 135
  error and, 103
  eternity and, 199–202
  forms of, 111
  God and, 67, 90, 116, 196
  human body and, 108, 124
  human mind and, 119, 124
  intellect and, 78
  knowledge and, 126
  moral theory and, 160
  overview of, 110
  passions and, 135–146, 184
  truth and, 100, 156
affects. *See also* emotions; passions; *specific affects*
  active affects, 124, 146–148, 157, 174, 184
  adequate ideas and, 125, 147, 156–158, 188
  anti-ascetic approach to, 169
  causation and, 185
  cognition and, 173, 184, 188
  conatus and, 168
  control of, 188
  definition of, 121
  duration of, 185
  egoism and, 172
  emotions' relation to, 121
  evaluation of, 168–175
  excessive forms of, 169, 185
  freedom and, 202
  human body and, 121
  human nature and, 139, 141
  imagination and, 106, 156
  imitation of, 138, 141

law of association of, 137
  law of imitation of, 137
  moral theory and, 121, 124, 151, 156–158,
    168–175
  naturalism and, 120
  order of things and, 120
  passions' relation to, 121
  power and, 188
  prejudice and, 140n23
  reason and, 168–175
  relations between, 137
  relative strength of, 156–158
  self-evaluation and, 171
  setting aside of, 56
  strength of character and, 147
  substance and, 54
  transfer of, 138
  types of, 121, 168
akrasia (weakness of will), 150, 158
ambition, 140–142, 169
amor fati, 34
Amsterdam
  Calvinism in, 2
  commercial trade and, 2
  Jewish community in, 1–4, 6
  Spinoza's life in, 1, 4, 11
  Talmud Torah in, 3
Anselm, St., 61
appetites, 36, 120, 125, 134, 169, 184, 211
Aquinas, Thomas, 23, 25, 149
Aristotle
  action and, 122
  classification and, 112
  creation ex nihilo and, 23
  Descartes and, 44
  final causes and, 24
  knowledge and, 32
  medieval philosophy and, 23
  moral theory and, 32, 149
  naturalism and, 23
  new science and, 23

passion and, 122
predication and, 43
Scripture and, 23
Spinoza's critiques of, 23
substance and, 24, 43, 47, 49
virtue and, 32
Arnauld, Antoine, 29
atheism, Spinoza's thought as a form of, 5, 14, 15,
    48, 234, 239, 251
attributes
    ambiguities and, 51
    cognition and, 53, 79
    conceptual independence of, 53
    definition of, 44, 51–54, 56, 59
    ens realissimum and, 60
    essences and, 53, 57
    eternity and, 68
    explanatory role of, 51
    expression of, 53
    God and, 33, 50, 51–54, 57, 78, 85
    identity of indiscernibles and, 56
    infinite attributes, 33, 50, 54, 56, 59, 60, 66, 79,
        85, 87
    infinity and, 40, 42
    intellect and, 78, 79
    mind–body relationship and, 84, 86
    objectivist interpretation of, 51–54
    order of things and, 87
    perception and, 51
    reality and, 59
    reason and, 52
    relations between, 51
    scholarship on, 199n13
    simplicity and, 53
    subjectivist interpretation of, 51–54
    substance and, 44, 46, 51–54
    thought and, 85
    traditional conception of, 51
autocracy. *See* freedom
Averroës, 251, 253

Bacon, Francis, 10, 247
Bayle, Pierre, 46–49
Bennett, Jonathan, 189, 194, 199n13
Bible. *See* Scripture
blessedness
    achievement of, 33, 41
    cognition and, 41, 100, 115, 197, 198
    definition of, 100, 182
    eternity and, 195, 197–199
    freedom and, 202
    God and, 33, 161
    highest good and, 34, 245
    human mind and, 195, 202
    passions and, 161, 182

peace and, 202
    way to, 188–202
Blijenbergh, Albert, 243n7
body. *See* human body; mind–body relationship
Bouwmeester, John, 13
Boyle, Robert, 12, 19, 23
Bruno, Giordano, 6, 22

Calvinism, 2, 80, 234, 236, 254
Carriero, John, 48, 127
Casearius, Johannes, 11
causation
    active and passive aspects of, 66
    adequate ideas and, 124
    affects and, 185
    cognition and, 39, 49, 90
    definitions and, 38, 67
    determinism and, 75–78, 203
    error and, 103
    essences and, 73, 127
    fatalism and, 75
    free cause, 67, 80
    free will and, 103
    God and, 42, 66–67, 75
    hatred and, 144
    ideas and, 89–90
    infinity and, 66–67
    knowledge and, 71, 187
    love and, 198
    methodology and, 67
    mind–body relationship and, 124
    modes and, 74
    nature and, 40, 42, 66, 75
    necessity and, 66, 75–77, 80, 85
    new science and, 74
    passions and, 124, 137, 146, 184
    reality and, 67
    reason and, 66
    self-causation, 58, 73
    substance and, 49, 58, 91
    transitive causes, 68
    will and, 79
Christianity, 1, 8, 243n7, 243, 253
civil society, 204, 211, 212, 213
cognition. *See also* human mind; intellect;
    thought
    adequate ideas and, 110, 113, 115–116, 173,
        199–202
    affects and, 173, 184, 188
    attributes and, 53, 79
    badness and, 173
    blessedness and, 41, 100, 115, 197, 198
    causation and, 39, 49, 90
    definitions and, 39
    essences and, 113

cognition (cont.)
  eternity and, 193, 202
  forms of, 112
  God and, 41, 52, 65, 100, 116, 161, 182, 188
  human body and, 105
  human mind and, 83, 195
  ideas and, 90
  imagination and, 107
  intellect and, 79, 85
  intuitive cognition, 41, 113–116, 193, 195
  knowledge and, 112, 114
  limits of, 87
  memory and, 114
  moral theory and, 152, 156–158, 173, 174
  nature and, 41, 79, 85
  perception and, 107
  reason and, 113–116
  skepticism and, 102, 109
  true cognition, 158, 174
  truth and, 102
Collegiant community, 8
conatus
  adequate ideas and, 133
  affects and, 168
  appetites and, 134
  argument for, 126, 132–135
  definition of, 126, 134
  desires and, 136
  essences and, 133
  explanatory role of, 126, 128, 133
  final causes and, 132
  historical precedents of, 126, 128
  human body and, 135
  human mind and, 133
  intellect and, 160
  mind–body relationship and, 128
  moral theory and, 149, 158
  overview of, 126
  passions and, 135, 161
  perfection and, 134
  physical interlude and, 126
  power and, 134–135
  reason and, 160
  singular things and, 132
  suicide and, 128, 131
  will and, 134
conscious awareness, 97, 107, 172
Copernicus, Nicolaus, 23
Corpuscular Philosophy, 12
Cottingham, John, 118n33
courage, 32, 123, 147, 186
creation ex nihilo, 23, 69
Critique of Pure Reason (Kant), viii, 63
Cromwell, Oliver, 5
Curley, Edwin, 48–49, 127, 199n13

De Vries, Simon, 8, 11, 37
De Witt brothers, 13, 17, 18, 219
De Witt, John, 12–13
death, 21, 172, 177, 198, 199, 200
deception, 177–181, 210
definitions
  causation and, 38, 67
  cognition and, 39
  explanatory role of, 37–39, 41, 131
  knowledge and, 38
  mathematics and, 38
  methodology and, 37–39, 41, 131
  nature and, 38
  nominal definitions, 37–39, 131
  real definitions, 37–39
  reality and, 67
  reason and, 39
  truth and, 38
Deism, 235
Della Rocca, Michael, 31, 180
democracy
  absolute sovereignty and, 220
  aristocracy and, 230
  broad-based form of, 230
  citizenship in, 218
  definition of, 218, 230
  elitism and, 219
  equality and, 218
  foreign citizens and, 230
  freedom and, 218
  government allowing ideal life in, 218
  human nature and, 219
  intellect and, 219
  justification for, 219
  mob mentality and, 220
  natural rights and, 218
  nature and, 218
  origins of, 212
  overview of, 229
  passions and, 219
  power and, 218
  scholarship on, 219
  servants and, 230
  state of nature and, 212, 218
  states and, 204
  tyranny of the majority and, 221
  unfinished account of, 231
  women and, 230
Der Spyck, Van, 17
Descartes, René
  affects and, 55
  animal spirits and, 123, 184
  Aristotle and, 44
  atheism and, 60
  attributes and, 44, 51

Cartesian circle of, 29, 102
Christianity's compatibility with, 8, 27
cogito and, 27, 29
cognition and, 100
definitions and, 39
doubt and, 30
emotions and, 121
error and, 118–119
extension and, 72
free will and, 27
geometric developments of, 27
God and, 27, 29, 72, 80
human mind and, 97
importance of, 27
influences on, 44
innate ideas and, 110
intellect and, 240
Judaism and, 6
knowledge and, 28
law of inertia in, 128
mathematics and, 27
methodology of, 27, 28, 30, 31, 36, 122
mind–body relationship and, 27, 30, 84,
    123, 124
modes and, 44
moral theory of, 123, 156
naturalism and, 26
new science and, 26, 27
ontological argument and, 61
organism according to, 99
passions and, 121–126, 186
philosophical development of, 27
pineal gland as seat of soul and, 30, 121, 123, 183
predication and, 44
reason and, 27
Scripture and, 247
skepticism and, 28, 102
soul and, 27
Spinoza influenced by, 5, 22, 30
Spinoza's critiques of, 9, 27, 30, 56, 72, 115,
    118–119, 121–126, 183
Stoicism and, 123
substance and, 27, 43–46, 54, 56, 57, 59, 60
voluntary action in, 123
will and, 118–119
Descartes' "principles of Philosophy" (Spinoza), 8,
    11, 20, 29, 37, 97, 102
desires
    ambiguities and, 136
    conatus and, 136
    definition of, 122, 134, 136
    essences and, 134
    freedom and, 125
    goodness and, 158
    human nature and, 134

motivation and, 136
passions and, 122, 136
relative strength of, 125
sexual desire, 169, 185, 231
determinism, 75–78, 203
Discourse on Method (Descartes), 10, 247
Dutch Reformed Church, 236
Dutch Republic, 218, 227, 233

Edwin, Curley, 48–49
egoism
    affects and, 172
    concern for others and, 138
    ethical egoism, 159, 167–168
    freedom and, 177
    moral theory and, 150, 158, 167–168, 177
    naturalism and, 32
    psychological egoism, 149, 158, 172
    self-evaluation and, 172
    state of nature and, 208
Elements (Euclid), 36
elitism, 165, 219
emotions. *See also* affects; passions; *specific
    emotions*
    active emotions, 121, 146–148
    adequate ideas and, 135
    affects' relation to, 121
    control of, 34, 155
    definition of, 120, 135
    freedom and, 34
    imitation of, 140, 164
    moods and, 170
    moral theory and, 155
ens realissimum
    arguments for existence of, 61
    attributes and, 60
    explanatory role of, 64
    God as, viii, 62
    hypostatization and, 63
    necessity and, 62
    reality and, 60
    religion and, 64
    substance and, 60, 62
    transcendental illusion and, 63
error, 102–105, 118
Espinoza, Abraham (grandfather of Spinoza), 3
Espinoza, Michael (father of Spinoza), 3, 5
essences
    abstract universals and, 71
    attributes and, 53, 57
    causation and, 73, 127
    cognition and, 113
    conatus and, 133
    definition of, 127
    desires and, 134

essences (cont.)
  eternity and, 194
  existence, relation to, 58, 73
  God and, 73
  human body and, 192, 193, 195
  human mind and, 192, 194
  modes and, 71
  nominalism and, 162, 175
  objective essence, 39
  passions and, 137
  power and, 81
  true codes and, 71
eternity
  adequate ideas and, 199–202
  attributes and, 68
  blessedness and, 195
  cognition and, 193, 202
  common understanding of, 198
  definition of, 193
  duration and, 193
  epistemic account of human mind's, 188–196,
    199, 202
  essences and, 194
  God and, 68, 194, 196
  human body and, 191, 200
  human mind and, 89, 188–196
  ideas and, 194
  intellect and, 196
  love and, 198
  mind–body and, 200
  modes and, 70
  moral theory and, 174
  perfection and, 201
  personal experience of, 193
  standpoint of, 154, 174
  thought and, 202
  traditional conception of, 193
Ethics (Spinoza)
  aims of, 31, 41, 54, 83, 203
  attributes in, 52
  axioms in, 40
  blessedness in, 41
  causation in, 81
  cognition in, 100, 114
  conservation of motion in, 73
  critical reception of, 37
  definitions in, 37–39, 131
  demonstration in, 40
  difficulty of, 22, 90, 94
  dispassionate tenor of, 144
  doctrine of ideas in, 107
  extension in, 72
  final causes in, 35
  God in, 33, 42, 70, 78
  human mind in, 33

imagination in, 238
intellectual love of God in, 33
intellectualist tradition in, 32
jealousy in, 144
Leibniz's reading of, 20
methodology in, 22, 32, 36–41, 54
modes in, 70, 71
moral theory in, 153–155
nature in, 33, 40
necessity in, 77
posthumous publication of, 16
power in, 81
propositions in, 54
relation to other works of, 16, 153–155
religion in, 239
scholarship on, 37–39, 41, 175, 188–196
social usefulness in, 219
states in, 213
structure of, 36
terminology in, 22
will in, 81
writing of, 11, 13, 16
Euthyphro (Plato), 81
evil, 34, 36, 46, 47, 129, 144, 169, 173, 199, 222

face of the whole universe (mode), 71, 72, 77
fatalism, 75, 78
fear, 123, 137, 164, 170, 172, 177, 189, 198, 200, 235,
    245, 254
final causes
  conatus and, 132
  critiques of, 25, 35, 77
  definition of, 24
  explanatory role of, 25
  free will and, 35
  God and, 25, 35
  goodness and, 35
  human nature and, 35
  imagination and, 25, 35
  mathematics and, 36
  moral theory and, 151, 153
  naturalism and, 24
  new science and, 24, 26
  reason and, 36
  religion and, 35
  traditional conception of, 24
fixed and eternal things, 71–72, 79
free will. *See also* will
  causation and, 103
  error and, 103
  final causes and, 35
  God and, 78, 80
  human mind and, 117
  imagination and, 117, 146
  natural rights and, 209

new science and, 26
rejection of, 31, 103, 117
traditional conception of, 117
freedom
affects and, 202
autocracy and, 155–158, 183–188
blessedness and, 202
death and, 177
deception and, 177–181
definition of, 34, 67, 182, 202
democracy and, 218
desires and, 125
egoism and, 177
emotions and, 34
free person, 21, 165, 175–181, 202
God and, 67, 79–82
human mind and, 83
human nature and, 175
imagination and, 186
moral theory and, 175–181
nature and, 34, 175
necessity and, 34, 203
of speech, 204, 216, 217, 220, 234
of thought, 14, 18, 204, 216, 217, 229, 234, 254
order of things and, 183
passions and, 182, 184
philosophy and, 234
political philosophy and, 19, 203, 234
power and, 216
reason and, 176
religion and, 14, 254
social benefits of, 216
socialization required for, 203
source of, 34
states and, 203, 213, 216, 217
suppression of, 218
will and, 79
Freud, Sigmund, 34

Galileo Galilei, 23, 25–26, 27
Garrett, Don, 132, 180, 200n14
generosity, 147, 165, 166, 168, 186
George, Henry, 224
Gersonides, 4, 22, 189n7
Gnosticism, 69
God. *See also* substance
adequate ideas and, 67, 90, 116, 196
attributes and, 33, 42, 50, 51–54, 56, 78, 85
blessedness and, 33, 161
causation and, 42, 66–67, 75
cognition and, 41, 52, 65, 100, 116, 161, 182, 188
creation and, 65, 79–82
creation ex nihilo and, 69
definition of, 33, 40, 42, 50, 52, 53
ens realissimum and, viii, 62

essences and, 73
eternity and, 68, 194, 196
existence of, 57, 61, 68
explanatory role of, 39, 45, 72
faith and, 252–254
fate and, 81
final causes and, 25, 35
free will and, 78, 80
freedom and, 67, 79–82
grace of, 242
hatred and, 187
human mind and, 83, 100, 115, 116, 191
human nature and, 33
idea of, 70, 85
ideas and, 88, 93, 103, 194
imagination and, 65, 116
immanence of, 48, 68
immutability of, 68
infinity and, 40, 42, 49, 51, 70
intellect and, 33–34, 41, 65, 70, 82, 182, 196–198
intelligibility of, 68, 82
knowledge and, 29, 32–33, 67, 240, 252
law and, 245
love and, 33–34, 41, 65, 182, 186–188, 196–198, 245, 254
methodology and, 39
mind–body relationship and, 85
miracles and, 240
modes and, 49, 50–53, 70, 73, 132
monstrous hypothesis on, 46
moral theory and, 161, 168
natural law and, 207
naturalism and, 23, 26
nature and, 23, 33, 40, 42, 66, 68, 79–82, 240
necessity and, 42, 49, 57, 61, 62, 66, 68, 77, 79–82
new science and, 26, 81
non-anthropomorphic conception of, 78
order of things and, 86
pain and, 187
passions and, 186–188
perfection and, 61
power and, 66, 69, 81, 82
predication and, 49, 52
proofs for existence of, 45, 61–65
reason and, 52
Scripture and, 252–254
simplicity of, 52
Spinoza's conception of, 30, 33, 39, 46, 48–49, 50–53, 67, 116, 186
sufficient reason and, 62
theistic conception of, 42, 48, 50, 65, 78, 79–82, 196
thought and, 85, 86
truth and, 103

God (cont.)
    unification with, 33
    will and, 79–82, 240, 242
good, highest, 23, 34, 164, 245
goodness, 34–36, 152n7, 154, 156, 158, 174
Grotius, Hugo, 5, 206–208, 210

Hague years of Spinoza, 16–21
happiness, 32, 34, 36, 148, 167, 242
hatred
    causation and, 144
    control of, 184
    definition of, 137, 144
    God and, 187
    imagination and, 144
    joy and, 145
    love and, 143, 144, 146, 186
    on behalf of others, 145
    prejudice and, 140n23
    reason and, 170
    returning of, 145
    vengeance and, 145
Hebrew Grammar (Spinoza), 16, 248
Hegel, Georg Wilhelm Friedrich, vii, 72,
    79
highest good, 23, 34, 164
Historical and Critical Dictionary (Bayle),
    46
Hobbes, Thomas
    absolute sovereignty and, 209, 215
    appetites and, 134
    conatus and, 126
    contracts and, 208, 214
    egoism and, 32, 208
    free will and, 117
    mind–body relationship and, 84
    natural law and, 204–209, 214
    natural rights and, 208, 210
    naturalism and, 32
    new science and, 23
    on Spinoza, 233
    perpetual conflict and, 208
    political philosophy and, 204–209
    reason and, 208
    Scripture and, 246, 250
    self-interest and, 32
    self-preservation and, 129
    social contract and, 206
    Spinoza influenced by, 23, 32, 84
    Spinoza's critiques of, 204, 209–213
    state of nature and, 207
    will and, 125
    women and, 231
hope, 136, 170–173
House of Orange, 3, 13, 14, 223

human body. *See also* mind–body relationship
    adequate ideas and, 108, 124
    affects and, 121
    cognition and, 105
    complexity of, 99
    composition of, 99
    conatus and, 135
    error, role in, 104
    essences and, 192, 193, 195
    eternity and, 192, 200
    human mind as idea of, 88, 91–98, 100, 110, 119,
        139, 192
    human mind considered apart from, 188–196,
        200, 201
    ideas and, 111
    imagination and, 106, 108
    knowledge and, 200
    mechanistic conception of, 30, 124
    perception and, 104
    types of body and, 98, 99
human mind. *See also* cognition; intellect;
        mind–body relationship; thought
    adequate ideas and, 119, 124
    blessedness and, 195, 202
    cognition and, 83, 195
    conatus and, 133
    conscious awareness and, 97, 107, 108, 172
    considered apart from human body, 196,
        200, 201
    duration of, 188, 192
    epistemic account of eternality of, 188–196
    essences and, 192, 194
    eternity and, 89, 188–196, 201
    free will and, 117
    freedom and, 83
    God and, 83, 100, 115, 116, 191
    idea of human body and, 88, 91–98, 100, 110,
        119, 139, 166, 192
    ideas and, 88, 194
    imagination and, 191
    immortality and, 191
    indestructible nature of, 190
    intellect and, 83
    knowledge and, 23
    memory and, 191
    nature and, 119
    order of things and, 90, 97, 105, 109
    organic complexity and, 97
    passions and, 104, 137
    peace of mind for, 202
    perception and, 94, 99, 109
    perfection and, 201
    physical interlude on, 98
    power and, 119
    recollection theory of, 196

relation to other minds, 97
scholarship on, 188–196
self-awareness and, 108, 147
substance and, 31
human nature. *See also* nature
  affects and, 139, 141
  democracy and, 219
  desires and, 134
  final causes and, 35
  freedom and, 175
  God and, 33
  human nature and, 26
  imagination and, 35
  imitation and, 140
  model of, 153n8
  moral theory and, 161, 175
  natural law and, 216
  natural rights and, 209
  new science and, 26
  nominalism and, 153n8
  states and, 203, 204
  unity of, 84, 140
Hume, David, 64, 88, 239n5
Huygens, Christian, 7
hylemorphism, 23, 24, 25, 26, 27

Ibn Ezra, 246, 250
idealism, 101
ideas. *See also* adequate ideas
  adventurous ideas, 110
  ambiguities and, 88, 194
  beliefs and, 88, 89, 95
  causation and, 89–90, 110
  cognition and, 90
  common notions as, 110
  definition of, 88, 194
  doctrine of, 107
  error and, 102–105
  eternity and, 194
  formal reality of, 89–90, 91, 194
  God and, 88, 93, 103, 115, 194
  human mind as idea of human body, 88, 110,
    119, 139, 192
  idea of an idea, 107, 109, 133, 156
  imagination and, 108, 112
  impressions and, 88
  innate ideas, 110
  knowledge and, 111
  law of association of, 106
  mathematics and, 110
  methodology and, 92
  mind–body relationship and, 95
  modes and, 91–94
  nonexistent things and, 91–94
  objective reality of, 89–90, 92, 195, 198

order of things and, 89–90, 194
propositions and, 88
scholarship on, 89
singular things and, 93
subjective reality of, 92
substance and, 91
thought and, 88
transcendentals and, 112
truth and, 102, 103
universal ideas, 112, 151
identity of indiscernibles, 55, 56
imagination
  affects and, 106, 156
  cognition and, 107
  conditioning of, 186
  definition of, 106
  error and, 104
  final causes and, 25
  freedom and, 186
  God and, 116
  hatred and, 144
  human body and, 106, 108
  human mind and, 191
  human nature and, 35
  ideas and, 108, 112
  love and, 143
  memory and, 106
  moral theory and, 34
  order of things and, 106
  passions and, 135–146, 186
  religion and, 235, 237, 251
  transcendentals and, 112
immortality, ix, 3, 189, 191, 193, 194
inadequate ideas. *See* adequate ideas
inertia, law of, 98, 128, 132
inertia, psychological law of, 106, 128, 131,
    134
infinity
  causation and, 66–67
  God and, 40, 42, 49, 51, 70
  miracles and, 240
  modes and, 50, 71, 73–74, 92
  nature and, 33, 240
  senses of, 58
  substance and, 49, 58
intellect. *See also* cognition; human mind;
    thought
  activity of, 79
  adequate ideas and, 78
  archetypal intellect, 79
  attributes and, 78, 79
  cognition and, 79, 85
  conatus and, 160
  definition of, 79
  democracy and, 219

intellect (cont.)
  error and, 105
  eternity and, 196
  finite intellects, 79
  God and, 33–34, 41, 65, 70, 82, 182,
    196–198, 240
  human intellect, 31, 54, 71, 78, 90, 115
  human mind and, 83
  infinite intellect, 66, 70, 78–79, 85, 87, 89, 103,
    115, 195
  intellectualism, 156, 162, 164, 167
  love and, 33–34, 65, 196–198
  modes and, 79
  moral theory and, 155, 164, 167
  nature and, 79
  relation between finite and infinite
    intellects, 78
  religion and, 238
  thought and, 85
  will and, 80
intentionality, 87, 129

jealousy, 143–144, 164, 187
Jelles, Jarig, 8, 214
Jesus Christ, 237, 245
joy, 136–137, 138, 141, 145–146, 156,
    169, 172
Judaism and Jewish community
  banning of Spinoza from, 6–7, 234,
    242, 244
  blessedness and, 242
  ceremonies in, 245
  circumcision within, 244
  commercial trade and, 2
  crypto-Jews, 1
  differing experiences of, 244
  divine law in, 245
  exceptionalism of critiqued, 242–246
  forced conversion of, 1
  Inquisition and, 1, 3
  leaders within, 2
  Netherlands communities of, 1
  orthodoxy and, 6
  persecution of, 244
  political conservatism of, 2
  prophecy and, 243
  rationality and, 6
  refugee migration and, 1–2
  Scripture and, 242–246
  shared culture of, 2
  Spanish communities of, 1
  Spinoza's Jewish heritage, 1
  Spinoza's rejection of beliefs and practices
    of, 5
  Spinoza's response to community of, 7

  survival of, 243
  synagogue as seat of power and, 3

Kant, Immanuel
  autocracy and, 155n9
  axioms and, 40
  categorical imperative of, 167–168
  deception and, 180
  ens realissimum and, 63
  existence as perfection and, 63
  God and, 63, 64
  lying and, 181n35
  reason and, 63
  Spinoza critiqued using ideas of, 167–168,
    177–181
  transcendental illusion and, 63
  truthfulness and, 178n31
Kepler, 23
Kisner, Matthew, 163, 168, 181
know thyself, 34
knowledge
  adequate ideas and, 126
  causation and, 71, 187
  cognition and, 112, 114
  deductive systems and, 11
  definitions and, 38
  fixed and eternal things and, 71
  God and, 29, 32–33, 67, 240, 252
  happiness and, 32
  human body and, 200
  human mind and, 23
  ideas and, 111
  limits nature of historical, 249
  mathematics and, 38
  methodology and, 11, 28
  mind–body relationship and, 28
  miracles and, 241
  modes and, 71
  nature and, 27, 38
  problem of, 26
  prophecy and, 237
  religion and, 237
  Scripture and, 249
  skepticism and, 28
KV. *See Short Treatise on God, Man and His
    Well-Being*

La Peyère, Isaac, 247, 250
law. *See also* natural law
  disobedience and, 221
  divine law, 245
  God and, 245
  nature and, vii, 25, 69, 71, 73, 75, 76, 208, 209,
    240–242
  obedience to, 216, 220

public opinion and, 221
reason and, 220, 222
submission to, 222
unjust laws, 220, 222
law of inertia, 98, 128, 132
Leibniz, Gottfried
best of all possible worlds and, 75, 76, 81
determinism and, 76
final causes and, 25
identity of indiscernibles and, 55
innate ideas and, 110
monads and, 53
Spinoza critiqued by, 55–56
substance and, 53
substantial forms and, 24
Leviathan (Hobbes), 210, 233
Louis XIV, 18
love
causation and, 198
definition of, 186
esteem and, 141, 143
eternity and, 198
for like individuals, 142
God and, 33–34, 41, 65, 182, 196–198, 245, 254
hatred and, 143, 144, 146, 186
imagination and, 143
intellect and, 33–34, 65, 182, 196–198
jealousy and, 143–144
knowledge and, 33
motivation and, 143
unrequited love, 187
Ludwig, Karl, 18

Machiavellian, Niccolò, 221, 223, 251
Maimonides, 4, 22, 23, 32, 52, 149, 189n7, 236–237, 240, 244, 248
Marranos, 1–2, 4, 218
mathematics
definitions and, 38
explanatory role of, 25
final causes and, 36
ideas and, 110
knowledge and, 38
naturalism and, 25
new science and, 25
skepticism and, 29
universal mathematics, 27
Medici, Marie de, 4
Medicina Mentis (Tschirnhaus), 20
medieval philosophy, 4, 22–23, 25, 26, 32, 52, 69
Meditations on First Philosophy (Descartes), 28, 29, 36
Melamed, Yitzhak, 49, 53n20, 204n2
memory, 106–107, 114, 191, 193
Menasseh ben Israel, 4–5

Mersenne, Marin, 36
Metaphysical Thoughts (CM) (Spinoza), 11, 76
metaphysics of the remedy, 183
methodology. *See also* philosophical approach of Spinoza
approaches to, 10
axioms and, 40
causation and, 67
definitions and, 37–39, 41, 131
doubt and, 29, 39
first principles in, 41
geometrical method, 36–41
God and, 39
ideas and, 92
importance of, 41
intelligibility and, 31
knowledge and, 11, 28
modern approach to, 10
moral theory and, 31
nature and, 41
new science and, 10, 23
overview of, 36–41
problem of, 10
synthetic method of demonstration, 36
Meyer, Lodewijk, 8, 11, 31
mind. *See* human mind
mind–body relationship
attributes and, 84, 86
Cartesian dualism and, 27, 84, 128
causation and, 124
conatus and, 128
eternity and, 200
God and, 85
human mind as idea of human body, 88, 91–98, 100, 110, 119, 139, 192
human mind's control over human body in, 121–123
ideas and, 95
identity theory of, 84
knowledge and, 28
materialistic theory of, 84
mind apart from human body, 188–196
nature and, 84
necessity and, 84
order of things and, 86, 88
overview of, 83
perception and, 94, 100
problem of, vii, 28, 30
scholarship on, 84n4, 84
substance and, 84, 86
unity of, 84
modes
abstract universals and, 71
causation and, 74
classes and, 71

modes (cont.)
  concrete universals and, 72, 73, 79
  definition of, 70, 71
  dependency of, 70
  essences and, 71
  eternity and, 70
  explanatory role of, 70
  extension and, 72
  face of the whole universe, 71, 72, 77
  finite modes, 49–50, 73–74
  God and, 49, 50–53, 70, 132
  hybrid status of, 92
  immediate and mediate modes, 70
  infinity and, 50, 70–71, 73–74, 92
  intellect and, 79
  knowledge and, 71
  nature and, 42
  order of things and, 91
  relation between finite and infinite modes,
    73–74
  substance and, 44, 49
  traditional conception of, 71
Montaigne, Michel de, 207
Montalto, Elias Rodriguez, 4
moral theory
  adequate ideas and, 160
  affects and, 121, 124, 151, 156–158,
    168–175
  aims of, 149
  altruism and, 161–168
  categorical imperative and, 178
  cognition and, 152, 156–158, 173, 174
  conatus and, 149, 158
  deception and, 177–181
  egoism and, 150, 158, 167–168, 177
  elitism in, 165
  emotions and, 155
  essences and, 175
  eternity and, 174
  final ends and, 151, 153
  freedom and, 155–158, 175–181
  God and, 161, 168
  golden rule in, 150, 167–168
  highest good and, 23, 34, 164
  human bondage and, 155–158
  human nature and, 150–155, 161, 175
  human weakness and, 153, 158
  imagination and, 34
  intellect and, 155, 164, 167
  lesser of two evils in, 173
  meta-ethical foundation of, 150–155, 181
  methodology and, 31
  models required for, 153, 154, 175, 176
  mutuality and, 166
  naturalism and, 149, 151

  norms required for, 151
  obligation and permissibility in, 181n37
  perfection and, 151, 154
  power and, 155–158
  reason and, 158–168, 175
  respect for persons and, 167–168
  scholarship on, 177–181
  Scripture and, 15
  self-control and, 151
  sociality and, 165
  subjectivism and, 152
  temporal considerations in, 174
  tensions in, 166
  traditional approaches to, 149, 161
  true good and, 153–155
  truth and, 157
  universalization in, 178
  virtue ethics and, 32, 34, 149, 153, 154, 155, 158,
    161, 167, 179, 181
  voluntarism rejected in, 156
  wellbeing of others and, 161–168
  will and, 155–158
Mortera, Saul Levi, 4
Mosaic Law, 6
Moses, 248

Nadler, Steven, 164, 189n7
natural law. *See also* law
  absolute sovereignty and, 215
  contracts and, 208, 214
  critiques of, 204–209
  definition of, 205
  God and, 207
  human nature and, 216
  natural rights and, 205
  normativization of, 215
  overview of, 204–209
  political philosophy and, 204
  positive law and, 205
  power and, 215
  reason and, 207
  social contract and, 204–209
  sociality and, 207
  states and, 205
  traditional conception of, 205
natural rights
  democracy and, 218
  free will and, 209
  human nature and, 209
  natural law and, 205
  political philosophy and, 209, 214
  power and, 210, 214, 216
  promises and, 210
  sovereign natural rights, 209
  state of nature and, 210

naturalism
  affects and, 120
  creation ex nihilo and, 23
  final causes and, 24
  God and, 23, 26
  mathematics and, 25
  modern conception of, 23
  moral theory and, 149, 151
  new science and, 23
  political philosophy and, 210
  Scripture and, 26
  traditional conception of, 23
nature. *See also* human nature; state of nature
  active and passive aspects of, 66, 68, 69
  causation and, 40, 42, 66, 75
  cognition and, 41, 79, 85
  creation and, 69
  definition of, 68, 79
  definitions and, 38
  democracy and, 218
  emanation and, 69
  freedom and, 34, 175
  God and, 23, 33, 40, 42, 66, 68, 79–82, 240
  highest good and, 23
  human mind and, 23, 119
  infinity and, 33, 240
  intellect and, 79
  intelligibility and, 68
  knowledge and, 27, 38
  law and, vii, 25, 69, 71, 73, 75, 76, 208, 209,
    240–242
  methodology and, 41
  mind–body relationship and, 84
  modal system of, 69
  modes and, 42
  necessity and, 33, 65, 73, 75, 80
  order of things and, 69, 77, 80
  reason and, 65
  Scripture and, 247
  universal nature, 84
necessity
  causation and, 66, 75–77, 80, 85
  definition of, 76
  ens realissimum and, 62
  freedom and, 34, 203
  God and, 42, 49, 57, 62, 66, 68, 77, 79–82
  logical necessity, 39, 50, 76
  mind–body relationship and, 84
  nature and, 33, 65, 73, 75, 80
  necessitarianism and, 75, 76, 77, 80, 85, 91
  passions and, 186
  susbtance and, 57–58
  will and, 79
Neoplatonism, 69
Nero, 129

new science
  causation and, 74
  Corpuscular Philosophy and, 12
  early modern philosophy and, 26
  extension and, 72
  final causes and, 24, 26
  free will and, 26
  geometric character of, 25
  God and, 26, 81
  human nature and, 26
  hylemorphism and, 26
  Inquisition and, 26
  knowledge and, 26
  mathematics and, 25
  medieval philosophy and, 26
  methodology and, 10, 23
  naturalism and, 23
  philosophical problems resulting from, 26
  primary and secondary properties and, 26
  Scripture and, 26
  skepticism as resulting from, 27
  substance and, 43
Nicholson, Peggy, 108n25
Nietzsche, Friedrich, viii, 34, 150
nominalism, 162, 175
"Notice on the Progress of Optics" (Leibniz),
  20

Oldenburg, Henry, 11–12, 13, 19, 234
omnipotence, 69, 82
"On the Calculation of Chances" (Spinoza),
  16
"On the Rainbow" (Spinoza), 16
ontological argument, viii, 61
Opera Posthuma (Spinoza), 16
order of things
  affects and, 120
  attributes and, 87
  error and, 102–105
  freedom and, 183
  God and, 86
  human mind and, 90, 97, 105, 109
  ideas and, 89–90, 194
  imagination and, 106
  mind–body relationship and, 86, 88
  modes and, 91
  nature and, 69, 77, 80
  parallelism thesis and, 85–88, 90, 104
  passions and, 183, 188
  perception and, 104
  thought and, 86, 101

pain, 95, 121, 136, 169, 184, 187
panpsychism, 96–98
panvitalism, 97

parallelism thesis, 85–88, 90, 104
passions. *See also* affects; emotions; *specific*
     passions
     actions and, 121–126
     adequate ideas and, 135–146, 184
     affects' relation to, 121
     blessedness and, 161, 182
     bondage to, 155–158, 161, 183
     catalogue of, 135–146
     causation and, 124, 137, 146, 184
     civil society and, 212
     conatus and, 135, 161
     conflicts of, 142
     control of, 123, 183–186
     definition of, 124, 135, 146
     democracy and, 219
     desires and, 122, 136
     essences and, 137
     freedom and, 182, 184, 186
     God and, 186–188
     human mind and, 104, 137
     ideas and, 135–146
     imagination and, 135–146, 186
     imitation of, 138, 140
     individuality of, 137
     metaphysics of the remedy and, 183
     necessity and, 186
     order of things and, 183, 188
     patterns of association and, 184
     pleasure and, 186
     political philosophy and, 213
     reason and, 182
     satisfaction and, 141
     social nexus and, 141
     states and, 203
     weakening of, 146
     will and, 186
Passions of the Soul (Descartes), 121
perception
     attributes and, 51
     definition of, 88
     error and, 104
     external bodies and, 105
     human body and, 104
     human mind and, 94, 99, 109
     mind–body relationship and, 94, 100
     order of things and, 104
perfection
     conatus and, 134
     duration and, 155
     eternity and, 201
     existence and, 61, 63, 77
     God and, 61
     human mind and, 201
     moral theory and, 151, 154

singular things and, 154
     will and, 81
philosophical approach of Spinoza. *See also*
     methodology
     aims of, 33, 81
     central themes of, 31–36
     critiques of, 87
     culmination of, 33
     ethics as main thrust of, 31
     happiness and, 34
     ideal of scientific objectivity as life task and, 34
     naturalism of, 23
     new science and, 23
     philosophical alternative to beatific vision
          and, 33
     rationalism and, 33
     religious dimensions of, 32, 34
     terminology in, 22
pity, 138, 140, 165, 170
Plato, 69, 154, 156, 193, 196
pleasure, 135, 169, 184, 186, 197, 253
political philosophy
     absolute sovereignty and, 213
     aims of, 203, 217
     civil wars and, 215
     contracts and, 209
     forms of governance and, 223
     freedom and, 19, 203, 234
     limits of, 220
     natural law and, 204
     natural rights and, 209, 214
     naturalism and, 210
     passions and, 213
     peace and, 217
     power and, 214–222
     social contract and, 204
     states and, 203
     tyranny of the majority and, 221
Political Treatise (TP) (Spinoza)
     audience of, 212
     democracy in, 218, 219, 229, 230
     forms of governance in, 205, 223
     human nature in, 204
     monarchy in, 223–225
     political context of, 17
     political philosophy in, 204
     relation to other works of, 212
     states in, 212
     tyranny of majority and, 221
     unfinished nature of, 16, 204, 229
polytheism, 77
power
     affects and, 188
     conatus and, 134–135
     democracy and, 218

essences and, 81
freedom and, 216
God and, 66, 69, 81, 82
human mind and, 119
limits on, 221, 223–225
moral theory and, 155–158
natural law and, 215
natural rights and, 210, 214, 216
omnipotence and, 69, 82
political philosophy and, 214–222
political power, 214–222
religion and, 255
states and, 203, 214–222, 223
pride, 171–172
principle of sufficient reason, 58, 62, 63, 77
psychological law of inertia, 106, 128, 131, 134
Pufendorf, Samuel, 18

rationalism, 31, 33, 236
reason
    affects and, 168–175
    attributes and, 52
    causation and, 66
    cognition and, 113–116
    conatus and, 160
    definitions and, 39
    final causes and, 36
    freedom and, 176
    God and, 52
    guidance of, 150, 160, 162, 164, 165–167,
        170–171, 173–174, 176–178, 182, 189,
        202
    hatred and, 170
    law and, 220, 222
    moral theory and, 158–168, 175
    natural law and, 207
    natural light of, 27
    nature and, 65
    passions and, 182
    prescriptions of, 158–168
    religion and, 235, 251
    respect for persons and, 168
    Scripture and, 248
    states and, 203, 213, 215
Rebecca (half-sister of Spinoza), 7
Reformation, 3, 13, 14, 233
religion
    articles of faith and, 252–254
    creation and, 57
    critiques of, 235–242
    Deism and, 235
    ens realissimum and, 64
    faith and, 251–255
    final causes and, 35
    freedom and, 14, 254

grace and, 242
imagination and, 237, 251
intellect and, 238
knowledge and, 237
miracles and, 235–242
natural religion, 235
non-literal interpretation of, 238
philosophy and, 239
power and, 255
prophecy and, 235–242
reason and, 235, 251
revelation and, 235–242
Scripture and, 236, 251
social function of, 251, 252–254
Spinoza's critiques of, 35, 42, 57
states and, 228, 236
substance and, 57
superstition and, 235, 239, 251–255
theology and, 234
toleration of, 2, 13
traditional conception of, 197
true religion, 236, 239, 251–255
Rieuwertsz, Jan, 8
Rijnsburg, Spinoza's years in, 8–12
Royal Society, 12

sadness, 135–142, 143–146, 147, 158, 169
Schuller, Georg Hermann, 19–21, 70,
    73
scientific development. *See* new science
Scripture
    alleged infallibility of, 15
    God and, 252–254
    historicity of, 246, 248, 250
    interpretation of, 246–251
    knowledge and, 249
    lacking set teachings or insights, 15
    metaphorical language and, 249
    moral theory and, 15
    naturalism and, 26
    nature and, 247
    new science and, 26
    non-literal interpretation of, 248
    prophecy and, 249, 250
    reason and, 248
    Reformed clergy and, 15
    religion and, 236, 251
    revelation and, 234, 235–242
    Spinoza's views on, 6, 13, 15, 234
    translation of, 249
self-awareness, 108, 147
self-destruction, 127, 129, 155
self-interest, 32, 168, 170, 228
Seneca, 129
sexual desire, 169, 185, 231

Short Treatise on God, Man and His Well-Being
   (KV) (Spinoza)
   Cartesianism critiqued in, 9
   ending of, 9
   Ethics and, 9, 10
   methodology in, 10, 37
   modes in, 70
   moral theory in, 154
   philosophical novelties in, 9
   translation of, 9
   writing of, 9
skepticism, 27, 28, 102, 109, 115, 206, 241
social contract
   explanatory role of, 205
   natural law and, 204–209
   origins of, 205
   political philosophy and, 204
   social contract proper, 205
   state of nature and, 205, 211
   states and, 204, 206
   submission contract and, 205
Socrates, 34
Spinoza, Baruch de
   alleged revolutionary activities of, 6
   banning of, 7, 234, 242, 244
   birthplace of, 1
   correspondence of, 12, 13, 16, 37, 214, 234,
      243n7
   De Witt brothers and, 17
   death of, 7, 16, 20
   early life of, 3
   family of, 1, 3, 7
   followers of, 7, 8, 37
   friends of, 17, 19
   Hague years of, 16–21
   Jewish education of, 3–6, 22
   Jewish heritage of, 1
   Latinization of name of, 7
   lens polishing career of, 7
   philosophical development of, 4, 10, 14, 22
   precursors to, 3
   proposed marriage of, 5
   public perception of, 17, 18
   Rijnsburg years of, 8–12
   secular education of, 5, 22
   teaching efforts of, 11
   threats and attacks against, 18
   Utrecht travels of, 18
   Voorburg years of, 12–16
state of nature
   civil society and, 211
   democracy and, 212, 218
   egoism and, 208
   historical reality of, 211
   natural rights and, 210

   social contract and, 205, 211
   transition from, 211
states
   absolute sovereignty and, 204, 206, 213, 223
   aims of, 203, 213, 217
   aristocracy and, 223, 225–229
   authority of, 216, 221
   constitutions and, 223–225
   democracy and, 204
   forms of governance and, 223
   freedom and, 203, 213, 216, 217
   human nature and, 203, 204
   individual's relation to, 203
   limits of, 221
   mercenaries and, 228
   military defenses and, 225, 228
   monarchy and, 223–225
   passions and, 203
   political philosophy and, 203
   power and, 203, 214–222, 223
   private judgment and, 213
   private property and, 228
   public opinion and, 216
   reason and, 203, 213, 215
   religion and, 228, 236, 254
   republican government, 14
   revolution and, 221, 222
   self-interest and, 228
   social contract and, 204
   society as only possible within, 203
   sovereign and multitude and, 221
   state-owned land and, 224
   surrendering to, 213
   tyranny of, 216
Stoicism, 32, 34, 123, 149, 183, 186, 187
Stuarts (England), 13
substance. *See also* God
   accidents and, 43
   affects and, 54
   attributes and, 44, 46, 51–54
   causation and, 49, 58, 91
   change and, 43
   conceptual independence and, 44
   created substances, 45, 57
   definition of, 44
   demonstrations and, 49
   ens realissimum and, 60
   essence and existence, relation to, 58
   explanatory role of, 43, 45
   extended and thinking distinction in, 57
   human mind and, 31
   hylemorphism and, 23
   ideas and, 91
   identity of indiscernibles and, 56
   indivisibility of, 65

infinity and, 49, 58
mind–body relationship and, 84, 86
modes and, 44, 49
mutability objection and, 47
necessity and, 57–58
new science and, 43
nominalism about, 153n8
ontological independence and, 44
overview of, 43–46
predication and, 43
primary substances, 46, 47, 48
prime matter and, 23
quatenus modifier and, 49
religion and, 57
scholarship on, 55, 60
substance-monism, 45, 47, 55, 57, 58, 60, 65, 86
substance-pluralism, 54, 57
substantial forms, 23
substantivalist framework and, 54
sufficient reason and, 62
thinking substances, 31
thought and, 85
traditional conception of, 43, 47, 49, 54, 57
sufficient reason principle, 58, 62, 63, 76, 77
suicide, 127, 128–131
superstition, 172, 229, 235, 239, 251–255

Talmud Torah (Amsterdam), 3
TdIE. *See Treatise on the Emendation of the Intellect*
Telesio, Bernardino, 22
Theological Political Treatise (TTP) (Spinoza)
absolute sovereignty in, 220
aims of, 204, 233, 239, 242, 251
anonymous publication of, 16
atheism defended against in, 234, 239
attacks at the publication of, 16
critical reception of, 16
defense from banning in, 6
democracy in, 218, 219, 230
Ethics and, 13
freedom in, 15, 217, 220, 234
Jesus in, 245
Judaism in, 2, 242–246
mob mentality and, 220
motivations behind, 13, 234
natural religion in, 235
polemical nature of, 204
political context of, 15
political philosophy in, 204
power in, 216
religious freedom in, 15
reprints of, 16
revolution in, 222
Scripture in, 15, 246, 250

social contract in, 211
social crisis as context of, 14
states in, 212, 216, 217, 228
suppression of, 16
theological portion of, 234
true religion in, 251
writing of, 13, 15
Thomas Aquinas, 23, 25, 149
thought
actions and, 122, 220
attributes and, 85
eternity and, 202
extension, relation to, 85
God and, 85, 86
ideas and, 88
intellect and, 85
intentionality of, 87
logicizing of, 88, 96
order of things and, 86, 101
pansychism, 96–98
reflexivity of, 87
self-containedness of, 85
substance and, 85
TP. *See Political Treatise*
transcendentals, 112
Treatise on the Emendation of the Intellect (TdIE) (Spinoza), 10
aims of, 164
Cartesianism critiqued in, 29
influence of, 20
knowledge and, 11
methodology in, 10
modes in, 71
moral theory in, 153–155, 164
opening of, 10
publication of, 16
skepticism in, 102
true good in, 153–155
truth in, 164
unfinished nature of, 10
truth
adequate ideas and, 100, 156
cognition and, 102
coherence theory of, 101
correspondence theory of, 101
definitions and, 38
falsity and, 156
God and, 103
ideas and, 102, 103
moral theory and, 157
true good, 10, 31, 32, 153–155
Tschirnhaus, Ehrenfried Walter von, 19–20, 67, 87, 100
TTP. *See Short Treatise on God, Man and His Well-Being*

Van Den Ende, Francis, 5
Van Den Ende, Frans, 22
Van Oldenbarnevelt, John, 14
vengeance, 145, 170
virtue ethics, 32, 34, 149, 153, 154, 158, 161, 167,
    179, 181
Voorburg, Spinoza's years in, 12–16

will. *See also* free will
    akrasia and, 150, 158
    causation and, 79
    conatus and, 134

definition of, 80, 134
freedom and, 79
God and, 79–82, 240, 242
intellect and, 80, 118–119
moral theory and, 155–158
necessity and, 79
passions and, 186
perfection and, 81
propositions and, 117
Wilson, Margaret, 108n25
Wolfson, H.A., 137
women, 218, 230–232

For EU product safety concerns, contact us at Calle de José Abascal, 56–1°, 28003 Madrid, Spain or eugpsr@cambridge.org.

www.ingramcontent.com/pod-product-compliance
Ingram Content Group UK Ltd.
Pitfield, Milton Keynes, MK11 3LW, UK
UKHW020356140625
459647UK00020B/2507